La Macarena
Pages 88–95

Seville City Centre

GUADALQUIVIR

LA MACARENA

EL ARENAL

SANTA CRUZ

PARQUE MARÍA LUISA

Santa Cruz
Pages 74–87

El Arenal
Pages 66–73

Parque María Luisa
Pages 96–103

JAÉN

Jaén

GRANADA

Granada

Almería

Málaga

0 km   50
0 miles   50

Granada and Almería
Pages 188–209

Seville
& Andalucía

DK EYEWITNESS TRAVEL

Seville
& Andalucía

Project Editor Anna Streiffert
Art Editor Robert Purnell
Editors Marcus Hardy, Jane Oliver
Designers Malcolm Parchment, Katie Peacock

Picture Research Monica Allende, Naomi Peck
DTP Designers Samantha Borland, Sarah Martin

Main Contributors
David Baird, Martin Symington, Nigel Tisdall

Photographers
Neil Lukas, John Miller, Linda Whitwam

Illustrators
Richard Draper, Isidoro González-Adalid Cabezas (Acanto Arquitectura y Urbanismo S.L.), Steven Gyapay, Claire Littlejohn, Maltings, Chris Orr, John Woodcock

Printed in China

First American edition 1996

17 18 19 20 10 9 8 7 6 5 4 3 2 1

Published in the United States by
DK Publishing, 345 Hudson Street, New York, New York, 10014

Reprinted with revisions 1997, 1998, 1999, 2000, 2001, 2002, 2003, 2004, 2006, 2008, 2010, 2012, 2014, 2016, 2018

Copyright © 1996, 2018 Dorling Kindersley Limited, London
A Penguin Random House Company

A CIP catalog record is available from the Library of Congress.

Published in the UK by Dorling Kindersley Limited.

ISSN 1542-1554

ISBN 978-1-4654-6799-7

Floors are referred to throughout in accordance with European usage; ie the "first floor" is the floor above ground level.

Introducing Seville and Andalucía

Discovering Seville and Andalucía **10**

Putting Seville and Andalucía on the Map **16**

A Portrait of Andalucía **20**

Andalucía Through the Year **38**

The History of Seville and Andalucía **44**

Seville Area by Area

Seville at a Glance **64**

El Arenal **66**

Santa Cruz **74**

La Macarena **88**

Parque María Luisa **96**

Across The River **104**

A Guided Walk **110**

Seville Street Finder **112**

The Patio de la Acequia (Courtyard of the Main Canal) in the Generalife palace, Granada

◀ **Title page** Magnificent domed ceiling of the Museo de Bellas Artes, Seville **Front cover image** Patio de las Doncellas (Courtyard of the Maidens), Real Alcázar, Seville **Back cover image** Cliffslide buildings in the mountain city of Ronda

Contents

Andalucía Area by Area

Andalucía at
a Glance **124**

Huelva and Sevilla **126**

Córdoba and Jaén **138**

Cádiz and Málaga **162**

Granada and Almería **188**

Travellers' Needs

Where to Stay **212**

Where to Eat
and Drink **220**

Shops and Markets **238**

Entertainment
in Andalucía **244**

Outdoor Activities and
Specialist Holidays **248**

Survival Guide

Practical
Information **254**

Travel Information **264**

General Index **274**

Phrase Book **287**

A traditional hand-painted
ceramic plate

The Plaza de España in Parque María Luisa, Seville

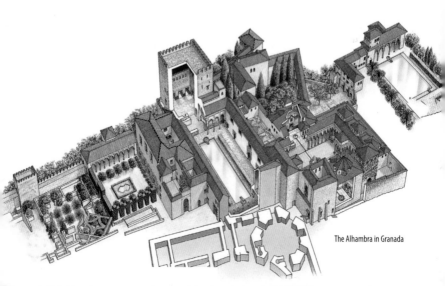

The Alhambra in Granada

HOW TO USE THIS GUIDE

This guide helps you to get the most from your stay in Seville and Andalucía. It provides both expert recommendations and detailed practical information. *Introducing Seville and Andalucía* maps the region and sets it in its historical and cultural context. *Seville Area by Area* and *Andalucía Area by Area*

describe the important sights, with maps, pictures and detailed illustrations. Suggestions on what to eat and drink, accommodation, shopping and entertainment are in *Travellers' Needs*, and the *Survival Guide* has tips on everything from transport to using public telephones.

Seville Area by Area

The centre of Seville has been divided into four sightseeing areas. *Across the River* makes up a fifth area. Each area has its own chapter, which opens with a list of the sights described. All the sights are numbered and plotted on an Area Map. The detailed information for each sight is presented in numerical order, thereby making it easy to locate within the chapter.

A locator map shows where you are in relation to other areas of the city centre.

All pages relating to central Seville have red thumb tabs.

Sights at a Glance lists the chapter's sights by category: Churches, Museums and Galleries, Historic Buildings, Streets and Plazas, etc.

1 Area Map For easy reference, the sights are numbered and located on a map. The sights are also shown on the *Street Finder* on pages 116–21.

2 Street-by-Street Map This gives a bird's-eye view of the heart of each sightseeing area.

A suggested route for a walk covers the more interesting streets in the area.

Stars indicate the sights that no visitor should miss.

3 Detailed information on each Sight All the sights in Seville are described individually. Addresses and practical information are provided. The key to the symbols used in the information block is shown on the back flap.

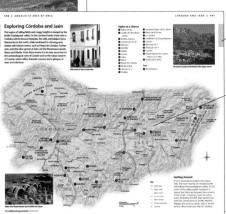

CÓRDOBA AND JAÉN

Córdoba, with its magnificent mosque and pretty Moorish patios, is northern Andalucía's star attraction. Córdoba province encompasses the Montilla and Moriles wine towns and also Baroque treasures such as Priego de Córdoba. Jaén's mountain passes are gateways to the province's beautiful Renaissance towns of Úbeda and Baeza, and to the great wildlife reserves of the northeast.

1 Introduction

The landscape, history and character of each region is described here, showing how the area has developed over the centuries and what it offers the visitor today.

Andalucía Area by Area

In this book, Andalucía has been divided into four distinct regions, each of which has a separate chapter. The most interesting sights to visit have been numbered on a Regional Map.

Each area of Andalucía has colour-coded thumb tabs.

Exploring Córdoba and Jaén

2 Regional Map

This shows the main road network and provides an illustrated overview of the whole region. All entries are numbered and there are also some useful tips on getting around the region by car, bus and train.

3 Detailed information on each entry

All the important towns and other places to visit are dealt with individually. They are listed in order, following the numbering given on the Regional Map. Within each town or city, there is detailed information on important buildings and other sights.

Features give information on topics of particular interest.

The Patios of Córdoba

Córdoba: the Mezquita

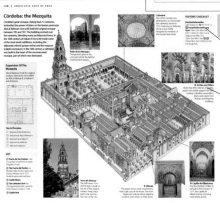

The Visitors' Checklist provides a summary of the practical information you need to plan your visit.

4 Top Sights

These are given two or more full pages. Historic buildings are dissected to reveal their interiors; museums and galleries have colour-coded floorplans to help you locate the most interesting exhibits.

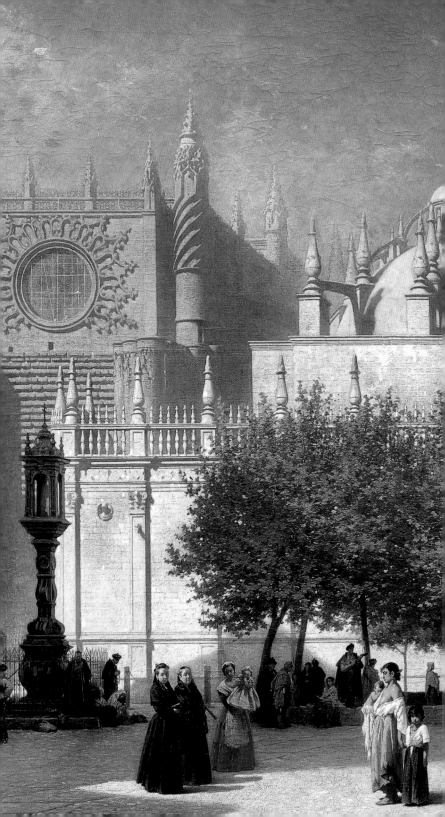

INTRODUCING SEVILLE AND ANDALUCÍA

Discovering Seville
and Andalucía   **10–15**

Putting Seville and
Andalucía on the Map   **16–19**

A Portrait of Andalucía   **20–37**

Andalucía Through the Year   **38–43**

The History of Seville
and Andalucía   **44–61**

DISCOVERING SEVILLE AND ANDALUCÍA

The following tours have been designed to take in as many of Andalucía's highlights as possible, while keeping long-distance travel to a minimum. First comes a two-day tour of Seville, the region's alluring capital, followed by a three-day tour, ideal if you are going to be spending a long weekend in the city. A one-week tour covers some of the highlights of Andalucía and also contains suggestions for expanding it to a ten-day tour if desired. Finally, there is a two-week tour, which rounds up all of the region's most celebrated attractions, including the Mezquita in Córdoba and Granada's magical Alhambra. Pick, combine and follow your favourite tours, or simply dip in and out and be inspired.

La Giralda
Named after its *giraldillo*, the bronze weathervane that depicts Faith, La Giralda is the belltower of Seville's cathedral. Visitors can climb it to enjoy magnificent views over the city.

A Week in Seville and Andalucía

- Be enchanted by the Andalucían capital of **Seville**, crowned by an exquisite minaret-cum-belltower, La Giralda, and a superb royal palace.

- Walk the ancient streets of **Cádiz**, one of the oldest cities in Spain, and relax on its perfect beaches.

- Stroll around the vibrant small city of **Ronda**, draped around a steep gorge and boasting a wealth of fine 18th-century architecture.

- Hang out with the jet set in chic **Marbella**, which combines glamorous yacht-filled marinas with plenty of old-fashioned charm.

- Visit the famous Museo de Picasso in **Málaga**, and enjoy the city's excellent shopping and nightlife.

- Soak up the spirit of Al Andalus in **Córdoba**, its whitewashed old quarter still dominated by the magnificent Mezquita.

Espiel

Cazalla de la Sierra

Aracena

El Pedroso

Nerva

Palma Del Río

Écija

Carmona

Seville

Huelva

Osuna

Utrera

El Rocío

Golfo de Cádiz

Jerez de la Frontera

Arcos de la Frontera

Ronda

Cádiz

Jimena de la Frontera

Gaucín

Marbe

Vejer de la Frontera

Parque Natural de los Alcornocales

Zahara de los Atunes

Tarifa

0 kilometres   50

0 miles   50

◄ *The Cathedral of Seville by Achille Zo*

Two Weeks in Seville and Andalucía

- Explore the region's beautiful capital, **Seville**, famed for its superb art and architecture.
- Listen to flamenco and try some sherry in the delightful little city of **Jerez de la Frontera**.
- Visit the wonderful, whitewashed town of **Vejer de la Frontera** before heading to the picturesque, white-sand beaches nearby.
- Drive through hills carpeted in cork trees and olive groves, admiring a string of **Pueblos Blancos** (white villages).

- Admire the exquisite small Renaissance cities of **Baeza** and **Úbeda**, miraculously unchanged for centuries. Then visit the ancient ruins of what was once the largest city on the peninsula, **Cástulo**.
- Take a night tour around the magical palace of the Alhambra in **Granada**.
- Drive through the mountain villages of **Las Alpujarras**, which preserve their distinct architecture and local traditions.
- Enjoy one of the last stretches of unspoilt coastline on the Mediterranean in the **Parque Natural de Cabo de Gata**.

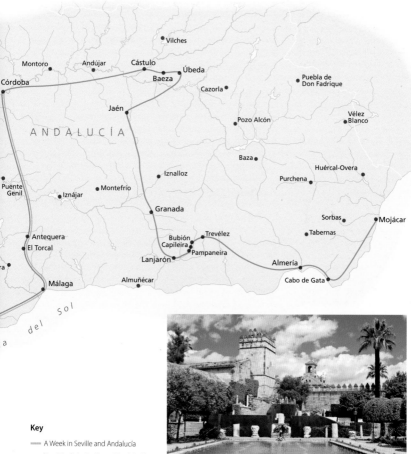

Key

━━ A Week in Seville and Andalucía

━━ Two Weeks in Seville and Andalucía

Alcázar de los Reyes Cristianos, Córdoba
Set in enchanting gardens with water terraces and fountains, the Alcázar de los Reyes Cristianos, a 14th-century palace-fortress of the Catholic Monarchs, offers visitors a tranquil atmosphere and city views.

Two days in Seville

- **Arriving** Arrive at Seville airport, 10 km (6 miles) northeast of the city centre, and linked by a shuttle bus.
- **Transport** This itinerary can be done entirely on foot.
- **Booking ahead** Essential around the time of Semana Santa and Feria de Abril.

Day 1
Morning Begin by visiting the city's most famous landmark, the **cathedral** and its belltower, known as **La Giralda** *(pp82–3)*. Explore the vast interior, which contains Columbus's tomb, and climb the belltower to enjoy views of the city. Next, plunge back into Seville's history at the magnificent **Real Alcázar** *(pp86–7)*, a lavish royal palace.

Afternoon Escape the city heat in the **Parque María Luisa** *(pp102–3)*, an elegantly landscaped 19th-century garden full of charming, colourful tiled benches and fountains. Once you've enjoyed a stroll, peek into the museums, one dedicated to Andalucían folk art and the other to archaeological finds. In the evening, cross the river to have dinner in the traditional **Triana** neighbourhood *(pp106–7)*.

Day 2
Morning Get lost in the white-washed lanes of the enchanting **Santa Cruz** district *(pp76–7)*, full of enticing courtyards and pretty squares. Perhaps drop in to the **Archivo de Indias** *(p84)* or peek into the **Hospital de los Venerables** *(p85)*, before visiting the ravishing **Casa de Pilatos** *(p81)* with its blissful secret garden.

Afternoon Spend a couple of hours at the wonderful **Museo de Bellas Artes** *(pp70–71)*, a fine art collection displayed in a handsomely remodelled 17th-century convent. Then enjoy a spot of shopping along the pedestrianized **Calle Sierpes** *(p78)*, and a delicious tapas supper in one of the many bars

A pretty narrow street in the labyrinthine Santa Cruz district, Seville

around the **Metropol Parasol** *(p95)*. Take in the sunset views from the skywalks.

Three days in Seville

- **Arriving** Arrive at Seville airport, 10 km (6 miles) northeast of the city centre, and linked by a shuttle bus.
- **Transport** This itinerary can be done on foot, but use the city's bus system if you get tired of walking.
- **Booking ahead** Essential around the time of Semana Santa and Feria de Abril.

Day 1
Morning Make your first port of call Seville's beautiful Gothic cathedral and its belltower, **La Giralda** *(pp82–3)*, which is visible from almost anywhere in the

city. After admiring the fantastic, city-wide views from the top of the belltower, look at its 12th-century base from the **Plaza Virgen de los Reyes** *(p84)*, or perhaps drop in to the **Hospital de los Venerables** *(p85)* to view the artworks.

Afternoon While away an enjoyable hour or two in the **Museo de Bellas Artes** *(pp70–71)*, then stroll down to the river to see the **Plaza de Toros de la Maestranza** *(p68)* and the **Torre del Oro** *(p69)*. Enjoy dinner overlooking the river, perhaps at one of the restaurants on **Calle Betis**, many of which have terraces with lovely views.

Day 2
Morning Throw away the map and explore the whitewashed lanes of the magical **Santa Cruz** neighbourhood *(pp76–7)*, its wrought-iron balconies over-flowing with scarlet geraniums. Explore the exquisite noble mansion known as the **Casa de Pilatos** *(p81)*, its salons gleaming with burnished tiles. Relax over a long lunch overlooking one of the pretty squares.

Afternoon Delve into the **Archivo de Indias** *(p84)*, where documents relating to Spain's conquest of the Americas are gathered in a spectacular 16th-century library. Follow it up with a visit to the **Real Alcázar** *(pp86–7)*, richly decorated with stucco and tiles by local artisans. Then take a stroll in the **Jardines de Murillo** *(p85)*.

Exquisite Mudéjar carved arches at Real Alcázar royal palace, Seville

Stunning mountain views over the Sierra de Grazalema nature reserve, Ronda

Day 3

Morning Start your day at the archeological museum in the basement of the **Metropol Parasol** *(p95)*, and enjoy the views from the skywalks. Then go for a stroll in **La Macarena** *(pp90–91)*, one of Seville's most appealing neighbourhoods, named after a much-venerated statue of the Virgin held in the **Basílica de la Macarena** *(p93)*. Visit the **Palacio de Lebrija** *(p78)*, an aristocratic mansion containing a wealth of archaeological treasures, then stop for lunch at one of the arty cafés near the **Alameda de Hércules** *(p92)*.

Afternoon Enjoy a stroll in the elegant **Parque María Luisa** *(pp102–3)*, with its leafy avenues and tiled benches and fountains. Do not miss the imposing **Plaza de España** *(p101)*. The park also contains a pair of fine museums: the **Museo de Artes y Costumbres Populares** *(p103)* and the **Museo Arqueológico** *(p103)*. In the evening, head to the vibrant **Triana** area *(p106–7)* and take a tour of the many traditional tapas bars.

A Week in Seville and Andalucía

- **Arriving** Arrive at Seville airport, 10 km (6 miles) northeast of the city centre, and linked by a shuttle bus.

- **Transport** The Seville section can be done on foot, but a car is essential for the rest of this itinerary.

- **Booking ahead** Essential around time of Semana Santa and Feria de Abril.

Days 1 and 2: Seville

Follow the two-day itinerary on p12.

Day 3: Cádiz

Take the A4/E5 motorway south of Seville and drive to **Cádiz** *(pp168–9)*. Spend the day exploring this enchanting ancient city, which is piled up on a long, narrow isthmus. Amble through the narrow lanes of the **historic quarter** *(pp170–1)*, visiting the atmospheric market and the vast cathedral. Climb the **Torre Tavira** *(p169)*, which contains an enjoyable camera obscura, to take in the splendid views, and then spend an hour or two soaking up the sunshine and atmosphere on one of the city's great beaches.

> **To extend your trip…**
> Head south down the coast towards **Tarifa** *(p173)*. Spend the night there, then head up through the hills of the **Parque Natural de Los Alcornocales** via **Jimena de la Frontera** *(p178)* and **Gaucín** *(p178)* to **Ronda**.

Day 4: Ronda

Drive inland, stopping at the beautiful, whitewashed town of **Arcos de la Frontera** *(p177)*, crowned by a ruined castle. Then cross the northeastern swathe of the **Sierra de Grazalema** nature reserve *(p24)* to **Ronda** *(pp178–9)*. In a dramatic setting, this exquisite little city straddles a deep gorge, spanned by a handsome 18th-century bridge, the **Puente Nuevo** *(p178)*. Explore the elegant streets, flanked by palaces and churches, and visit its historic bullring, considered to be the home of bullfighting.

Day 5: Marbella

An easy 40-minute drive will bring you to **Marbella** *(pp184–5)*, which preserves a picturesque historic quarter and a fine main square shaded by orange trees. Long the resort of choice for aristocrats and celebrities, it remains one of the most chic towns on the Costa del Sol.

Day 6: Málaga

A fast motorway links Marbella with Málaga, about 60 km (37 miles) up the coast. **Málaga** *(pp182–3)* is a vibrant and dynamic city which boasts two exceptional museums – the **Museo de Picasso** and the **Museo Carmen Thyssen** – both are well worth a visit. After spending time at the museums, scramble up to the striking clifftop palace-fortress, the **Alcazaba** *(p183)*, to enjoy the fabulous views and an interesting local history museum.

The Museo de Artes y Costumbres Populares in the Parque María Luisa, Seville

To extend your trip…
In the morning explore **Antequera** (*p183*), then go hiking amid the rugged limestone crags of **El Torcal** (*p183*) or on the Caminito del Rey (*p180*). Spend the night in Antequera.

Day 7: Córdoba

Drive north to **Córdoba** (*pp144–7*), an enticing city still suffused with the spirit of old Al Andalus. The highlight is the astounding **Mezquita** (*pp148–9*), the vast mosque-turned-church which dates back 12 centuries. Explore the twisting lanes of the **Judería** (*p144*), and visit the **Alcázar de los Reyes Cristianos** (*p146*), set in enchanting gardens.

Two Weeks in Seville and Andalucía

- **Arriving** Arrive at Seville airport, 10 km (6 miles) northeast of the city centre, and linked by a shuttle bus.
- **Transport** A car is essential for this tour.
- **Booking ahead** Book Alhambra tickets in advance, particularly if you want to do the night visit. **Tel:** 958 02 79 71, or online at W **alhambra-tickets.es**. More information at W **alhambra-patronato.es**

Garden views of the Palacio del Partal, the oldest palace at the Alhambra, Granada

Resplendent arches and pillars adorning the Mezquita, Córdoba

Day 1: Seville

Pick some highlights from the two-day itinerary on p12.

Day 2: Seville to Cádiz

Potter down to **Jerez de la Frontera** (*p166*), cradle of flamenco and home to some fine, sherry-producing *bodegas* (*p167*). Continue on to the sun-bleached city of **Cádiz** (*pp168–9*), the oldest continually inhabited city in Spain. Explore the dilapidated yet charming historic quarter (*pp170–71*), and tuck into delicious seafood.

Day 3: Tarifa and the Costa de la Luz

Follow the coast south, stopping at hilltop **Vejer de la Frontera** (*p172*) and perhaps enjoy an hour or two on the beaches at **Zahara de los Atunes** (*p172*). **Tarifa** (*p173*), at the tip of Spain, is the country's kite- and wind-surfing capital, with a delightful, whitewashed old quarter and fabulous white-sand beaches.

Day 4: Pueblos Blancos to Ronda

Drive up through the forested hills of the **Parque Natural de Los Alcornocales** (*p173*), visiting some of the area's **Pueblos Blancos** (white villages, *p178*) on the way. **Jimena de la Frontera** and **Gaucín** are two of the prettiest. Spend the night in **Ronda** (*pp178–9*), a town perched over a deep gorge.

Day 5: Ronda to Marbella

After a morning spent strolling the elegant streets of Ronda, drive to **Marbella** (*pp184–5*), one of the most attractive towns on the Costa del Sol. A favourite with the jet set, it boasts glossy marinas and fine beaches, but its historic quarter, with white-washed houses and orange trees, is still its best feature.

Day 6: Marbella to Málaga

Drive up the coast to the vibrant city of **Málaga** (*pp182–3*), which boasts great beaches and nightlife as well as a host of cultural attractions. These are spearheaded by the excellent **Museo de Picasso** and the **Museo Carmen Thyssen** (*pp182–3*). Do not miss a visit to the clifftop **Alcazaba** (*p183*), an ancient fortress that contains an interesting history museum and offers sublime views.

Day 7: Málaga to Córdoba

Drive north to the market town of **Antequera** (*p183*), to pick up picnic supplies before hiking in the surreally beautiful, if arid, landscape of **El Torcal** (*p181*) or on the 3-km (2-mile) long Caminito del Rey walkway perched along the **Garganta del Chorro** (*p180*) (reservations necessary). Then continue north to **Córdoba** (*pp144–9*) to spend the night.

Day 8: Córdoba

Córdoba was once the capital of a rich and powerful caliphate, and, although its influence has long since waned, it remains one of the most beautiful and stirring cities in Spain. The vast, dazzling **Mezquita** (*pp148–9*) continues to dominate the city, as it has for more than 12 centuries. The heart of Córdoba is the **Judería** *(p144)*, a delightful maze of whitewashed lanes and pretty squares which overflow with flowers in spring.

Day 9: Córdoba to Baeza

Drive east from Córdoba to Linares to visit the ancient ruins of **Cástulo** *(p155)*, once the largest city on the peninsula. Stop at Linares Archaeological Museum to see some of the treasures uncovered here. Then head to **Úbeda** *(pp158–9)*, a small Renaissance time capsule, full of splendid palaces and churches. Enjoy lunch on one of the elegant squares, then head south to **Baeza** *(pp156–7)*, another graceful Renaissance town, which, like Úbeda, has been inscribed on UNESCO's list of World Heritage Sites. Spend the night in Baeza.

Day 10: Baeza to Granada

Head south to **Jaén** *(pp152–3)*, a sprawling city surrounded by olive groves. Spend the morning strolling around the upper part of Jaén, visiting the **Castillo de Santa Catalina** *(p152)*, which enjoys impressive views, and the extravagantly decorated **Catedral** *(p152)*. After a lazy lunch, continue driving to Granada where you should spend the night.

Day 11: Granada

Granada *(pp194–202)*, set against the backdrop of the

Holiday-makers sunbathing on a sandy beach, Marbella

Sierra Nevada, is perhaps the city which most deeply evokes Al Andalus. The whitewashed houses of the **Albaícin** *(pp196–7)* cling steeply to one hillside, while the the **Alhambra** *(pp198–9)*, a spellbinding palace set in the perfumed gardens of the **Generalife** *(p202)*, crowns another. Other unmissable sights include the vast **Catèdral** *(p194)* and the **Capilla Real** *(p194)*, which contains the tombs of Ferdinand and Isabella, known as the Catholic Monarchs, who conquered Granada in 1492. Ideally, spend a couple of days in Granada – not least to enjoy the city's famous tapas bars.

Day 12: A drive through Las Alpujarras

Spread along the southern flanks of the Sierra Nevada, **Las Alpujarras** *(pp204–5)* is a

forested region dotted with tiny villages that preserve their distinctive local architecture and traditions. Head south of Granada to **Lanjarón** *(p193)*, famous for its mineral waters, and then follow the narrow mountain roads east. Stop at any of the villages which take your fancy – perhaps **Pampaneira**, **Bubion** and **Capileira** *(see* **Poqueira Valley**, *p203)*, or **Trevélez** *(p204)*, which is famous across the country for its cured hams. Spend the night in the mountains before continuing to **Almería**.

Day 13: Las Alpujarras to Almería

Continue driving through flat and arid countryside to **Almería** *(pp206–7)*, a large port city crowned by a 1000-year-old fortress. Explore the time-worn historic centre, with its flat-roofed houses and palm trees reminiscent of North Africa.

Day 14: Cabo de Gata and Mojácar

Stock up on picnic goodies and head southeast of Almería to explore the **Parque Natural de Cabo de Gata** *(p208)*, an enticing wilderness of rugged hills, secret coves and beaches. There are few towns and villages, and you may need to scramble down cliffs to reach some of the most alluring little bays. Continue along the coast to **Mojácar** *(p209)*, a picturesque town of white, cube-shaped houses arranged around more gorgeous beaches.

The picturesque village of Mojácar with its white, cube-shaped houses

Putting Seville and Andalucía on the Map

Andalucía is Spain's southernmost region, bordered by Extremadura and Castilla-La Mancha to the north and Murcia to the northeast. Its long coastline faces the Atlantic to the west and the Mediterranean to the south and east. One of Spain's largest regions, it covers an area of 87,267 sq km (33,693 sq miles) and has a population of 8.4 million. Seville is the province's capital.

Key

━━ Motorway

━━ Major road

━━ International border

━━ Provincial border

For keys to symbols *see back flap*

Seville City Centre and Greater Seville

Seville city centre is a compact maze of old, narrow streets, with most sights within walking distance. A couple of wide, busy avenues cut through the centre, dividing it into separate areas. This book focuses on these areas, starting with the historic neighbourhoods on each side of Avenida de la Constitución. To the west, along the river, is El Arenal with the Plaza de Toros; and to the east lies the old Jewish quarter of Santa Cruz, dominated by the massive cathedral and the Reales Alcázares. In the north lies La Macarena with its many churches, while the Parque María Luisa stretches out beyond the Universidad, south of the historic centre.

El Arenal: Teatro de la Maestranza and Torre del Oro

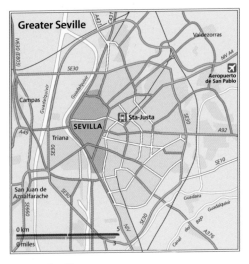

Greater Seville

West of the Guadalquivir river lies the Isla de la Cartuja, former site of Expo '92, and the picturesque Triana quarter. Modern residential areas surround the town centre.

Parque María Luisa: the Plaza de España, built for the 1929 Exposition

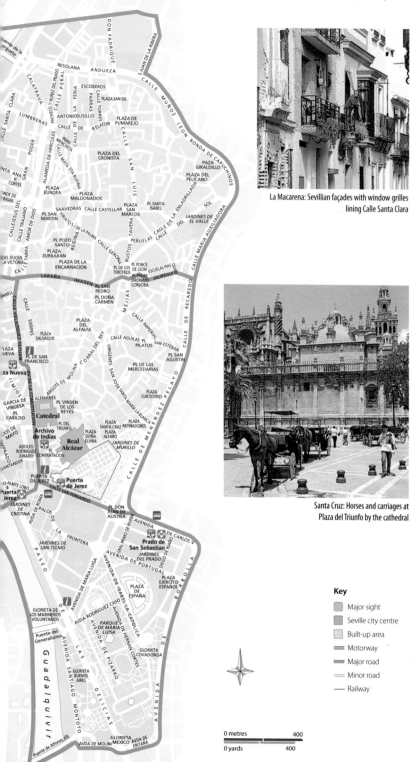

La Macarena: Sevillian façades with window grilles lining Calle Santa Clara

Santa Cruz: Horses and carriages at Plaza del Triunfo by the cathedral

Key

- Major sight
- Seville city centre
- Built-up area
- Motorway
- Major road
- Minor road
- Railway

0 metres   400
0 yards   400

For keys to symbols *see back flap*

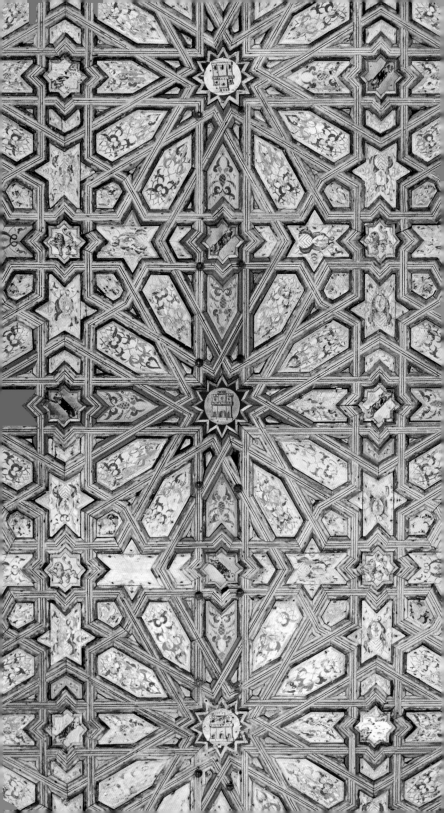

A PORTRAIT OF ANDALUCÍA

Andalucía is where all Spain's stereotypes appear to have come together. Bullfighters, flamenco dancers, white villages and harsh sierras are all here in abundance. But they form only part of an intricate tapestry. Beneath the surface, expect to find many contradictions. Wherever you travel, particularly when you escape from the tourist-engulfed coast, you will come across the unexpected, whether it is a local *fiesta* or a breathtaking view.

Until the 1950s, Andalucía had changed scarcely at all since the middle of the 19th century, when the English traveller, Richard Ford, described it as "a land bottled for antiquarians" – almost a feudal society, with attendant rigid social strata.

Today, Andalucía is a leader in renewable energy and has extensive infrastructure. Young people, whose grandparents may be illiterate, play with digital tablets and plan university careers. Agriculture is still important, but there are also factories making cars and aircraft. The service industries, tourism especially, predominate. In some parts of the region, the proportion of jobs in the tourism sector exceeds 50 per cent of the total jobs there. Yet the 8.4 million citizens retain their characteristic love of talk and folklore, their indifference to time and their abundant hospitality.

The Moorish Legacy

The Andalucían character is complex because it reflects a complicated history. Successive invaders, including the Phoenicians, Romans, Visigoths and Moors, have all left their indelible mark. Although the Christian rulers of Spain ejected both Jews and Moors from their kingdom, they could not remove their influences on the country – let alone on Andalucía. Look at the face of an Andalucían man or woman and you will catch a glimpse of North Africa. Centuries of Moorish occupation *(see pp50–51)* and the inevitable mingling of blood have created a race and culture different from any in Europe.

As you travel around the region, you will find much physical evidence of the Moorish legacy.

Flamenco dancing, a tradition that dates from the 18th century *(see pp32–3)*

◄ Moorish-style wooden ceiling in the Real Alcázar, Seville

The splendour of the Alhambra *(see pp198–9)* and the Mezquita *(see pp148–9)* in Córdoba and ruined fortresses and elaborate tilework all exemplify the Moorish legacy in Andalucía. Workshops across the region still practise crafts handed down from great Moorish kingdoms. Many of the irrigation networks in use today follow those laid out by the Moors, who built *norias* (waterwheels), *aljibes* (tanks for collecting the rain), *albercas* (cisterns), and *acequias* (irrigation channels).

As these words show, the Moors also left a strong linguistic legacy, not only of agricultural terms, but also of words for

Sevillanos enjoying a pre-dinner drink and some tapas *(see pp224–5)*

foods – *naranja* (orange), for example, and *aceituna* (olive). Moorish influence may also account for Andalucíans' love of poetry and fine language. It is no coincidence that Spain's finest poets, including among them Nobel prize winners, come from this region.

People and Culture

Sevillanos work hard to sustain their reputation for flamboyance and hedonism. A 13th-century Moorish commentator noted that they were "the most frivolous and most given to playing the fool". Living up to that image is a full-time occupation, but the visitor should not be deceived by the exuberant façade. One surprising aspect of both Seville and Andalucía is that although the society may appear open and extrovert, it is, in fact, one that also values privacy.

The Andalucían concept of time can also be perplexing. Progressive business types may try to adjust to the rigorous demands of Europe, but in general, northern Europeans' obsession with time is an object of mirth here. The moment is to be enjoyed and tomorrow will look after itself. A concert will often begin well after the advertised time, and lunch can feasibly take place at any time between 1pm and 4:30pm.

Although attitudes to women in Andalucía have been changing and the percentage of women who work outside the home has increased in the 21st century, southern Spain's

Penitents parading a giant float, Semana Santa *(see p42)*

Barren, remote countryside, one of the many faces of Andalucía's varied landscape *(see pp24–5)*

tradition for *machismo* means that there is still some way to go towards changing cultural attitudes.

Paradoxically, the mother is an almost sacred figure in Andalucía, where family ties are written in blood. Although new affluence and a steady movement to the cities is now beginning to erode old values, Andalucía remains a traditional rural society with a distinct emphasis on personal relationships.

Catholicism is very much Spain's dominant religion and there are many religious *fiestas* commemorating saints. The adoration of the Virgin is a striking feature of Andalucía. Apart from a purely religious devotion, the

Sevillian lady in a traditional *mantilla* (headscarf)

Virgin is also subject to a peculiar admiration from the male population. A man who never attends Mass may be ecstatic about the Virgin of his local church; when her statue emerges from the church in procession, he feels fiercely possessive of her. If you try to think of the gorgeously robed figure as a pagan earth mother or fertility goddess, the phenomenon is much easier to understand.

As a society, Andalucía is unafraid of its emotions, which are almost always near the surface. There is no shame in the singing of a *saeta*, the "arrow" of praise launched at the Virgin in Semana Santa (Holy Week), nor is there any ambivalence in the matador's desire to kill his antagonist, the bull. The quintessence of this is flamenco; the pain and passion of its songs reflect not just the sufferings and yearnings of gypsies and the poor, but also Andalucía's soul.

Decorative tilework in the Palacio de Viana *(see p147)*

Nun with convent jams

The Landscape of Andalucía

Each year, several million visitors are drawn to the high-rise resorts along Andalucía's Mediterranean coast. Away from these, however, are empty, windswept Atlantic shores and expansive areas of wetland wilderness. Inland there are rugged mountain ranges clothed with forests of pine, cork and wild olive. Also typical of the landscape are the undulating hills awash with vines, cereals and olive trees. Of Andalucía's total land area, some 17 per cent has been designated national parks or nature reserves in order to protect the region's unique abundance of animal and plant life.

The fertile plains of the Guadalquivir valley are watered by the river and have been the bread basket of Andalucía since Moorish times. Fields of cereals alternate with straight lines of citrus trees.

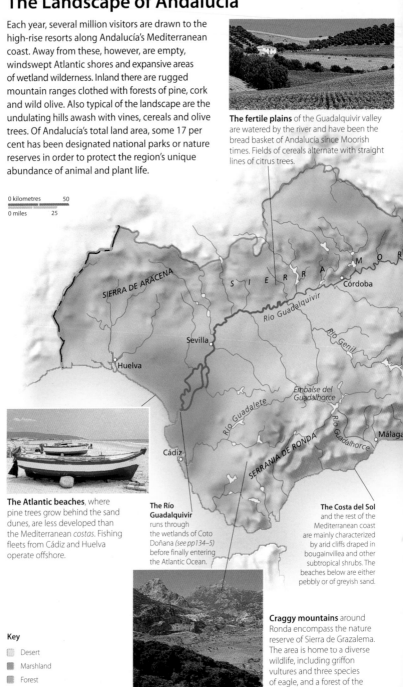

0 kilometres 50

0 miles 25

SIERRA DE ARACENA

SIERRA MOR R

Córdoba

Río Guadalquivir

Río Genil

Sevilla

Huelva

Embalse del Guadalhorce

Río Guadalete

Río Guadalhorce

Málaga

Cádiz

SERRANÍA DE RONDA

The Atlantic beaches, where pine trees grow behind the sand dunes, are less developed than the Mediterranean *costas*. Fishing fleets from Cádiz and Huelva operate offshore.

The Río Guadalquivir runs through the wetlands of Coto Doñana (*see pp134–5*) before finally entering the Atlantic Ocean.

The Costa del Sol and the rest of the Mediterranean coast are mainly characterized by arid cliffs draped in bougainvillea and other subtropical shrubs. The beaches below are either pebbly or of greyish sand.

Craggy mountains around Ronda encompass the nature reserve of Sierra de Grazalema. The area is home to a diverse wildlife, including griffon vultures and three species of eagle, and a forest of the rare Spanish fir.

Key

◻ Desert

◼ Marshland

◼ Forest

◻ Cultivated land

Endless olive groves give the landscape in the provinces of Córdoba and, in particular, Jaén a distinct, crisscrossed pattern. These long-living trees are of great importance to the local economy, for their oil *(see p152)* as well as their beautiful wood.

Vast forests, mainly of Corsican pine, cover the craggy sierras of Cazorla, Segura and Las Villas *(see p160)* in one of Spain's largest nature reserves.

Vegetables and exotic fruits are grown all year round in greenhouses covering many hectares around El Ejido. The soil of Almería is otherwise unproductive.

The Sierra Nevada, Spain's highest mountain range, reaches 3,482 m (11,420 ft) at the peak of Mulhacén. Although only 40 km (25 miles) from the Mediterranean beaches, some areas are snow-capped all year round. The skiing season starts in December and lasts until spring. In summer the area is perfect for hiking and climbing.

Andalucían Wildlife

Southern Spain is blessed with some of the richest and most varied flora and fauna in Europe, including some species which are unique to the area. The best time to appreciate this is in spring when wild flowers bloom and migratory birds stop en route from Africa to northern Europe.

Cork oak grows mainly in the province of Cádiz. Its prized bark is stripped every ten years.

The Cazorla violet, which can only be found in Sierra de Cazorla *(see p161)*, flowers in May.

A mouflon is a nimble and agile wild sheep that was introduced to mountainous areas in the 1970s.

Flamingos gather in great flocks in the wetlands of Coto Doñana and the Río Odiel delta in Huelva.

Moorish Architecture

The first significant period of Moorish architecture arrived with the Cordoban Caliphate. The Mezquita was extended lavishly during this period and possesses all the enduring features of the Moorish style: arches, stucco work and ornamental use of calligraphy. Later, the Almohads imported a purer Islamic style, which can be seen at La Giralda *(see p82)*. The Nasrids built the superbly crafted Alhambra in Granada, while the *mudéjares (see p28)* used their skill to create beautiful Moorish-style buildings such as the Palacio Pedro I, part of Seville's Real Alcázar *(see also pp50–53)*.

Reflections in water combined with an overall play of light were central to Moorish architecture.

Moorish domes were often unadorned on the outside. Inside, however, an intricate lattice of stone ribs supported the dome's weight. Like this one in the Mezquita *(see pp148–9)*, they were inlaid with multicoloured mosaics featuring flower or animal motifs.

Defensive walls

Moorish gardens were often arranged around gently rippling pools and channels.

Development of Moorish Architecture

Pre-Caliphal era 710–929	Caliphal era 929–1031	Almoravid and Almohad era 1091–1248	Nasrid era 1238–1492
	1031–91 Taifa period *(see p50)*		**c.1350** Alhambra palace

700	800	900	1000	1100	1200	1300	1400

785 Mezquita in Córdoba begun	**1184** La Giralda in Seville begun	**c.1350** Palacio Pedro I
	936 Medina Azahara near Córdoba begun	**Mudéjar era,** after c.1215

Azulejos *(see p80)* were used for wall decorations. Patterns became increasingly geometric, as on these tiles in the Palacio Pedro I *(p86)*.

Moorish Arches

The Moorish arch was developed from the horseshoe arch that the Visigoths used in the construction of churches. The Moors modified it and used it as the basis of great architectural endeavours, such as the Mezquita. Subsequent arches show more sophisticated ornamentation and the slow demise of the basic horseshoe shape.

Caliphal arch, Medina Azahara *(see p142)*

Almohad arch, Patio del Yeso *(see p87)*

Mudéjar arch, Salón de Embajadores *(see p87)*

Nasrid arch, the Alhambra *(see p199)*

Moorish Palace

The palaces of the Moors were designed with gracious living, culture and learning in mind. The imagined palace here shows how space, light, water and ornamentation were combined to harmonious effect.

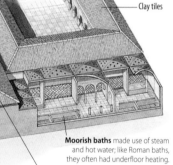

Clay tiles

Moorish baths made use of steam and hot water; like Roman baths, they often had underfloor heating.

Entrance halls were complex to confuse unwanted visitors.

Arcaded galleries provided shade around courtyards.

Water cooled the Moors' elegant courtyards and served a contemplative purpose. Often, as here in the Patio de los Leones *(see p199)*, water had to be pumped from a source far below.

Elaborate stucco work typifies the Nasrid style of architecture. The Sala de los Abencerrajes *(see p199)* in the Alhambra was built using only the simplest materials, but it is nevertheless widely regarded as one of the most outstanding monuments of the period of the Moorish occupation.

Post-Moorish Architecture

The Christian reconquest was followed by the building of new churches and palaces, many by *mudéjares (see p52)*. Later, prejudice against the Moors grew as Christians began to assert their faith. Gothic styles from northern Europe filtered into Andalucía, though Mudéjar influences survived into the 18th century. In the 16th century, Andalucía was the centre of the Spanish Renaissance; and a uniquely Spanish interpretation of the Baroque emerged in the 18th century.

Mudéjar tower, Iglesia de Santa Ana *(see p196)*

The Reconquest (Mid-13th to Late 15th Century)

Moorish craftsmen working on Christian buildings created a hybrid Christian Islamic style known as Mudéjar. Mid-13th-century churches, such as the ones built in Seville and Córdoba, show a varying degree of Moorish influence, but the Palacio Pedro I in the Real Alcázar *(see pp86–7)* is almost exclusively Moorish in style. By the early 15th century, pure Gothic styles, which are best exemplified by Seville Cathedral *(see pp82–3)*, were widespread. After the fall of Granada in 1492 *(see p52)*, a late Gothic style, called Isabelline, developed.

Mudéjar portal, Nuestra Señora de la O *(see p166)*

The Iglesia de San Marcos *(see p94)* is a typical example of a Christian church built at the time of the Reconquest. Mudéjar features include the portal and minaret-like tower.

Bell towers were often added later; this one is a Baroque addition.

Windows are framed by Islamic-style marble columns.

Window openings become progressively narrower towards ground level.

Islamic-style decoration on the main entrance is characteristic of many Mudéjar churches.

Classical arches, a motif of the transitional Isabelline style, look forward to Renaissance architecture.

Gothic window, Seville Cathedral

Heavily worked stone reliefs, as decoration on façades of buildings, have their roots in the Gothic style.

The Palacio Jabalquinto *(see p156)* has a highly ornate façade. Its coats of arms and heraldic symbols, typical of Isabelline buildings, reveal a strong desire to establish a national style.

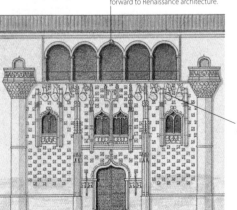

The Renaissance (16th Century)

Early Renaissance architecture was termed Plateresque because its fine detailing resembled ornate silver-work (*platero* means silversmith). The façade of the Ayuntamiento (*see p78*) in Seville is the best example of Plateresque in Andalucía. A High Renaissance style is typified by the Palacio Carlos V. The end of the 16th century saw the rise of the austere Herreran style, named after Juan de Herrera, who drafted the initial plans of the Archivo de Indias (*see p84*).

Plateresque detail on Seville's Ayuntamiento

Courtyard, with Herreran proportions, in the Archivo de Indias

Stone roundels were used as decoration; the central ones would bear the emperor's coat of arms.

Classical pediments adorn the windows.

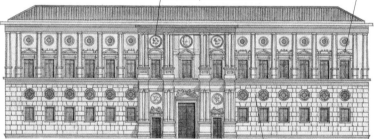

The Palacio Carlos V, begun in 1526, is located in the heart of the Alhambra (*see p199*). Its elegant, grandiose style reflects Carlos V's power as Holy Roman Emperor.

Rusticated stonework gives the lower level a solid appearance.

Baroque (17th and 18th Centuries)

Early Spanish Baroque tended to be austere. The 18th century, however, gave rise to the Churrigueresque, named after the Churriguera family of architects. Although the family's own style was fairly restrained, it had many flamboyant imitations. Priego de Córdoba (*see p154*) is a showcase of the Baroque; La Cartuja (*p195*) in Granada contains a Baroque sacristy.

Flamboyant Baroque sacristy of La Cartuja, Granada

Baroque pinnacles were carved individually from stone.

Palacio del Marqués de la Gomera, Osuna (*p137*)

Repeated string courses define the church's storeys and contribute to the complex decoration of the façade.

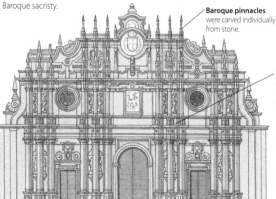

Guadix Cathedral
(*see p204*) comprises a Renaissance building fronted by a Baroque façade. Such a combination of styles is very common in Andalucía.

Bullfighting

Bullfighting *(toreo)* is a sacrificial ritual in which men (and a few women) pit themselves against a bull bred for the ring. In this "authentic religious drama", as poet García Lorca described it, the spectator experiences the fear and exaltation felt by the matador. Opinion is divided on bullfighting, with a growing number of Spaniards opposing the tradition. Catalonia banned bullfighting on grounds of cruelty in 2010. The ban was reversed by Spain's constitutional court in 2016, but Catalonia's regional government continues to ignore this ruling. Many still regard the *toreo* as an essential part of their cultural heritage. Andalucía, the birthplace of bullfighting in Spain, remains steadfast in upholding the tradition.

Maestranza Bullring, Seville
This is regarded, with Las Ventas in Madrid, as one of the top venues for bullfighting in Spain.

The matador wears a *traje de luces* (suit of light), a colourful silk outfit adorned with sequins, beads and embellishments.

Bull Breeding
Well treated at the ranch, the *toro bravo* (fighting bull) is bred specially for aggressiveness and courage. As aficionados of bullfighting point out in its defence, the young bull enjoys a full life while it is being prepared for the ring. Bulls must be at least 4 years old before they fight.

The Bullfight

The *corrida* (bullfight) has three stages, called *tercios*. In the first one, the *tercio de varas*, the matador and *picadores* (horsemen with lances) are aided by *peones* (assistants). In the second stage, *tercio de banderillas*, *banderilleros* stick pairs of darts in the bull's back. In the third stage, *tercio de muleta*, the matador makes a series of passes at the bull with a *muleta* (cape). He then executes the kill, the *estocada*, with a sword.

The matador plays the bull with a *capa* (red cape) in the *tercio de varas* to gauge its intelligence and speed. *Peones* then draw it towards the *picadores*.

Today, horses are heavily padded

Picadores goad the bull with steel-pointed lances, testing its bravery as it charges their horses. The lances weaken the animal's shoulder muscles.

The Bullring

The *corrida* audience sits in the *tendidos* (stalls) or in the *palcos* (balcony), where the *presidencia* (president's box) is. Opposite are the *puerta de cuadrillas*, through which the matador and team arrive, and the *arrastre de toros* (exit for bulls). Before entering the ring, the matadors wait in a corridor *(callejón)* behind the *barreras* and *burladeros* (ringside barriers). Horses are kept in the *patio de caballos* and the bulls wait in the *corrales*.

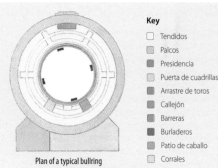

Plan of a typical bullring

Key

☐ Tendidos
☐ Palcos
■ Presidencia
☐ Puerta de cuadrillas
■ Arrastre de toros
■ Callejón
■ Barreras
■ Burladeros
☐ Patio de caballo
☐ Corrales

Manolete

Regarded as one of the greatest matadors ever, Manolete was gored to death by the bull Islero at Linares, Jaén, in 1947.

The passes are made with a *muleta*, a scarlet cape stiffened along one side.

The bull may go free if it shows courage – spectators wave white handkerchiefs, asking the *corrida* president to let it leave the ring alive.

José Tomas is one of Spain's leading matadors. He is famous for his purist approach and for his natural and elegant style with both the *capa* and the *muleta*.

The bull weighs about 500 kg (1,100 lb)

Banderilleros enter to provoke the wounded bull in the *tercio de banderillas*, gauging its reaction by sticking pairs of *banderillas* in its back.

The matador makes passes with the cape in the *tercio de muleta*, then lowers it to make the bull bow its head, and thrusts in the sword for the kill.

The estocada recibiendo is a difficult kill that is rarely seen. The matador awaits the bull's charge rather than moving forwards to meet it.

Flamenco, the Soul of Andalucía

More than just a dance, flamenco is a forceful artistic expression of the sorrows and joys of life. Although it has interpreters all over Spain and even the world, it is a uniquely Andalucían art form, traditionally performed by gypsies (Roma), known as *gitanos* in Spanish. There are many styles of *cante* (song) from different parts of Andalucía, but no strict choreography – dancers improvise from basic movements, following the rhythm of the guitar and their feelings. Flamenco was neglected in the 1960s and '70s, but serious interest has once again returned. Recent years have seen a revival of traditional styles and the development of exciting new forms.

Sevillanas, a folk dance that is strongly influenced by flamenco, is danced by Andalucíans in bars and at social events *(see p244)*.

At a tablao (flamenco club) there will be at least four people on stage, including the hand clapper.

The origins of flamenco are hard to trace. Roma may have been the main creators of the art, mixing their own Indian-influenced culture with existing Moorish and Andalucían folklore, and with Jewish and Christian music. There were Roma in Andalucía by the early Middle Ages, but only in the 18th century did flamenco begin to develop into its present form.

The Spanish Guitar

The guitar has a major role in flamenco, traditionally accompanying the singer. The flamenco guitar developed from the modern classical guitar, which evolved in Spain in the 19th century. Flamenco guitars have a lighter, shallower construction and a thickened plate below the soundhole, used to tap rhythms. Today, flamenco guitarists often perform solo. One of the greatest, Paco de Lucía (1947–2014), began by accompanying singers and dancers, but made his debut as a soloist in 1968. His slick, inventive style, which combined traditional playing with Latin, jazz and rock elements, has influenced many musicians outside the realm of flamenco, such as the group Ketama, who play flamenco-blues.

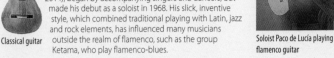

Classical guitar

Soloist Paco de Lucía playing flamenco guitar

Singing is an integral part of flamenco, and the singer often performs solo. Camarón de la Isla (1952–92), a Roma born near Cádiz, is among the most famous contemporary *cantaores* (flamenco singers). He began as a singer of *cante jondo* (literally, "deep songs"), from which he developed his own, rock-influenced style. He has inspired many singers.

Where to Enjoy Flamenco

Flamenco festivals *pp38–43, p244*
Flamenco guitar *pp38–41, p244*
Flamenco in Sacromonte *p197*
Flamenco singing *pp38–41, p244*
Flamenco tablaos *p244*
Flamenco dress *p239*

Eva Yerbabuena is a *bailaora* (female dancer) renowned for her amazing footwork and intensity. Sara Baras is another dancer famous for her personal style. Both lead their own acclaimed flamenco companies. Other international flamenco stars include Juana Amaya.

The proud yet graceful posture of the *bailaora* seems to suggest a restrained passion.

A harsh, vibrating voice is typical of the singer.

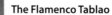

Traditional polka-dot dress

The bailaor (male dancer) plays a less important role than the *bailaora*. However, many have achieved fame, including Antonio Canales. He has introduced a new beat through his original foot movements.

The Flamenco Tablao

These days it is rare to come across spontaneous dancing at a tablao, but if dancers and singers are inspired, an impressive show usually results. Artists performing with duende *("magic spirit") will hear appreciative* olés *from the audience.*

Flamenco Rhythm

The unmistakable rhythm of flamenco is created by the guitar. Just as important, however, is the beat created by hand-clapping and by the dancer's feet in high-heeled shoes. The *bailaoras* may also beat a rhythm with castanets; Lucero Tena (born in 1938) became famous for her solos on castanets. Graceful hand movements are used to express the dancer's feelings of the moment – whether pain, sorrow or happiness. Hand and body movements are choreographed, but styles vary from person to person.

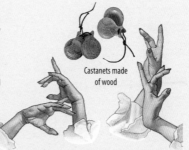

Castanets made of wood

Flamenco hand movements, intricate and complex

The Land of Sherry

The Phoenicians introduced the vine to the Jerez region 3,000 years ago. Later, Greeks, then Romans, exported wine from these gentle hills bordering the Atlantic. However, the foundations of the modern sherry trade were laid by British merchants who settled here after the Reconquest *(see pp52–3)*. They discovered that the chalky soil, climate and local grapes produced fine wines, particularly if fortified with grape spirit. The connection persists today with companies such as John Harvey still under British ownership.

Preparing soil to catch the winter rain

Grapes thriving in the chalky soil near Jerez

Sanlúcar de Barrameda

Jerez de la Frontera

Rota

El Puerto de Santa María

Cádiz

Puerto Real

San Fernando

Chiclana de la Frontera

Rio Guadalete

Sherry Regions

Sherry is produced at bodegas, or wineries, in the towns of Jerez de la Frontera, Sanlúcar de Barrameda and El Puerto de Santa María. It is also produced in smaller centres such as Rota and Chiclana de la Frontera.

Key

Sanlúcar de Barrameda

Jerez de la Frontera

El Puerto de Santa María

— Delimited sherry-producing region

0 km   10

0 miles   5

Different Types of Sherry

Three months after pressing, and before the fortification process, all sherry is classified as one of five principal types.

Fino is by far the favoured style in Andalucía. Dry, fresh, light and crisp, it is excellent as an apéritif or with tapas. It should always be served chilled.

Manzanilla is similar to *fino*, but comes exclusively from Sanlúcar. Light, dry and delicate, it has a highly distinctive, salty tang.

Amontillado is *fino* aged in the barrel. The "dying" flor (yeast) imparts a strong, earthy taste. Some brands are dry, others slightly sweetened.

Oloroso (which in Spanish means fragrant) is a full, ruddy-coloured sherry, with a rich, nutty aroma. It is sometimes sweetened.

Cream sherry is a full, dark, rich blend of *oloroso* with Pedro Ximénez grapes. As the sweetest type, it is often drunk as a dessert wine.

How Sherry is Made

Sherry is mixed from two principal grape varieties: Palomino, which produces a drier, more delicate sherry; and Pedro Ximénez, which is made into a fuller, sweeter sherry type.

Grape-drying is only required for Pedro Ximénez grapes. They are laid on *esparto* mats to shrivel in the sun, concentrating the sugar before they are pressed.

Crusher and de-stemmer

Grape-pressing and de-stalking, in cylindrical stainless steel vats, is usually done at night to avoid the searing Andalucían heat.

Grape-picking takes place during the first three weeks in September. Palomino grapes are taken as quickly as possible to the presses to ensure freshness.

Fermentation vat in steel

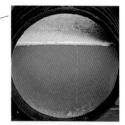

Flor, a yeast, may form on the exposed surface of young wine in the fermentation vat, preventing oxidization and adding a delicate taste. If *flor* develops, the wine is a *fino*.

Fortification is the addition of pure grape spirit, raising the level of alcohol from around 11 per cent by volume to around 18 per cent for *olorosos*, and 15.5 per cent for *finos*.

The solera system

The youngest solera contains new wine.

Sherry for bottling is taken from the oldest solera at the bottom row.

The finished product

The solera system assures that the qualities of a sherry remain constant. The wine from the youngest solera is mixed with the older below, taking on its character. The oldest solera contains a tiny proportion of very old wine.

Beach Life and Leisure in Andalucía

Thanks to its subtropical climate with an average of 300 days' sunshine a year, the coastline of Andalucía – in particular the Costa del Sol – has become one of the most favoured playgrounds for those looking for fun and relaxation. In the 1950s, there was nothing more than a handful of fishing villages (see p185). Now the area attracts several million tourists a year who are well catered for by the vast array of hotels and apartments along the coast. The varied coastline lends itself perfectly to the whole gamut of water sports (see p246), while just inland golf courses have become a major feature of the landscape (see p246). Some of the most popular golf courses are shown on this map, together with a selection of the beaches most worth a visit.

Sunbathing on one of Marbella's beaches, Costa del Sol

Huelva

Sevilla •

•
Real Club de Golf Sevilla

Costa

• **Montecastillo Golf**

See inset

Cádiz
•

Marbella
•

Costa Natura ④

Club de Golf Valderrama •

Golf La Alcaidesa •

Costa

①
Caños de Meca

②
Bolonia ③

Tarifa

de la Luz

Costa de la Luz in western Andalucía is a stretch of largely unspoiled beaches, refreshingly free from crowds and tower blocks. Atlantic winds make it a wind- and kitesurfer's paradise.

Costa Tropical is punctuated by pretty coves, ideal for scuba diving. The water is warmer and clearer than on Costa de la Luz, while the sand is coarse and stony.

0 kilometres   50

0 miles   25

Andalucía's Best Beaches

① Caños de Meca
Charming white, sandy beach sheltered by cliffs and sand dunes.

② Bolonia
Picturesque beach with Roman ruins close by.

③ Tarifa
Sweeping white sands, and winds and waves perfect for skilled windsurfers.

④ Costa Natura
Popular nudist beach just outside Estepona.

⑤ Babaloo Beach
Trendy spot just off Puerto Banús. Gym and jetskiing.

⑥ Victor's Beach
A classic Marbella beach for stylish barbecue parties.

⑦ Don Carlos
Perhaps Marbella's best beach, shared by the exclusive Don Carlos beach club.

⑧ Cabopino/Las Dunas
Nudist beach and sand dunes beside modern marina. Not too crowded.

⑨ Rincón de la Victoria
Nice unspoiled family beach area just east of Málaga.

⑩ La Herradura
A stony but picturesque bay west of Almuñécar.

⑪ Playa de los Genoveses
One of the unspoilt beaches between Cabo de Gata and the village of San José.

⑫ Playa Agua Amarga
Excellent sand beach in secluded fishing hamlet turned exclusive resort.

Costa de Almería is famous for its picturesque fishing villages and rocky landscapes, which come to life in the breathtaking sunsets. Beaches tend to have escaped overdevelopment, in particular those in the nature reserve of Cabo de Gata, such as San José, here.

Agua Amarga ⑫

Playa de los Genoveses ⑪

Almería •

La Herradura ⑩

Málaga ⑨

Rincón de la Victoria

Costa Tropical

Costa de Almería

del Sol

Costa del Sol

Apart from the crowds of holiday-makers, half a million foreign residents have chosen to live on the Costa del Sol. Complementing the luxury and high life of Marbella are a number of popular beaches and more than 30 of Europe's finest golf courses, including the prestigious Club de Golf Valderrama, host of the 1997 Ryder Cup tournament.

Málaga •

Club de Campo de Málaga •

Torremolinos •

Golf •

• Torrequebrado

Club Milas Golf •
La Cala Golf •

Golf Rio Real
• Marbella Golf

Club de Golf Las Brisas •

Club Dama de Noche •

Marbella ⑥

Guadalmina Golf •

Monte Mayor Golf •

Babaloo Beach ⑤

Victor's Beach

Don Carlos ⑦

Cabopino and Las Dunas ⑧

Player on the green at the high-profile Marbella Golf

ANDALUCÍA THROUGH THE YEAR

Festivals and cultural events fill Andalucía's calendar. Every town and village has an annual *feria* (fair) with stalls, dancing, drinking, fireworks and bullfights. These are held from April to October throughout Andalucía. There are also many *fiestas*, all exuberant occasions when religious devotion mixes with *joie de vivre*. Spring is an ideal time to visit; the countryside is at its most beautiful, the climate is mild and *ferias* and *fiestas* celebrate the ending of winter. Summer brings heat to the interior and crowds to the *costas*. Autumn is greeted with more *fiestas* and heralds the opening of music and theatre seasons. In winter, jazz, pop and classical concerts can be enjoyed in the cities. The first snow on the Sierra Nevada marks the start of the skiing season. Note that dates for all events, especially *fiestas*, may change from year to year; check with the tourist board (see p257).

Almond trees in blossom on the lush hillsides of Andalucía

Spring

Few parts of the world can match the beauty of spring in Andalucía. After winter rains, the hills and plains are green and lush, and water cascades along riverbeds and irrigation channels. Country roads are a riot of wild flowers; almond blossom covers the hillsides and strawberries are harvested. Popular festivals abound, many of them religious, though often linked with pagan ceremonies marking the end of winter.

March
Cristo de la Expiración *(Friday, nine days before Palm Sunday)*, Orgiva *(see p204)*. One of Andalucía's most ear-splitting *fiestas*; shotguns are fired and rockets, gunpowder and fire-crackers are set off.
Semana Santa *(Palm Sunday– Good Friday)*. Seville celebrates this event spectacularly *(see p42)*, and there are processions in every town and village. On Holy Wednesday in Málaga *(see pp182– 3)*, a prisoner is freed from jail and in gratitude joins in one of the processions. This tradition began two centuries ago, when prisoners, braving a plague, carried a holy image through the city's streets. In Baena *(see p151)*, the streets vibrate to the sound of thousands of drums.

April
Fiesta de San Marcos *(25 Apr)*, Ohanes, Sierra Nevada. Accompanying the image of San Marcos through the streets are young men leading eight bulls. The bulls are persuaded to kneel before the saint.
Feria de Abril *(two weeks after Easter)*, Seville *(see p42)*.
Romería de Nuestra Señora de la Cabeza *(last Sunday in Apr)*, Andújar *(see p43)*. Major pilgrimage.

May
Día de la Cruz *(first week of May)*, Granada *(see pp194–202)* and Córdoba *(see p42)*.
Feria del Caballo *(first week of May)*, Jerez de la Frontera *(see p166)*. Horse fair.
Festival Internacional de Teatro y Danza *(throughout May)*, Seville. World-class companies perform in Teatro de la Maestranza *(see pp72–3)*.
Festival de los Patios *(second week in May)*, Córdoba *(see p42)*. Patios are on display.
Romería de San Isidro *(15 May)*. *Romerías* are held in many towns, including Nerja *(see p182)*, for San Isidro.
Concurso Nacional de Flamenco *(second week in May; every third year: 2019, 2022)*, Córdoba. National flamenco competition.
Feria de Mayo *(last week of May)*, Córdoba *(see p42)*.
Romería del Rocío *(late May or early Jun)*, El Rocío *(see p42)*.

Feria del Caballo, held in Jerez de la Frontera in May

Average Daily Hours of Sunshine

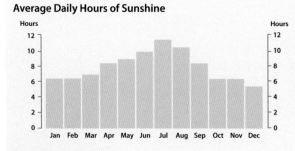

Hours

| 12 | 10 | 8 | 6 | 4 | 2 | 0 |

Jan Feb Mar Apr May Jun Jul Aug Sep Oct Nov Dec

Hours

12 / 10 / 8 / 6 / 4 / 2 / 0

Sunshine Chart
Even in winter, few days in Andalucía are entirely without sunshine. From the spring, the sunshine starts to build up progressively, and by midsummer it can be dangerous to go out even for a short time without adequate skin protection.

Bullrunning during the Lunes de Toro *fiesta* in Grazalema

Summer

During the hot summer months, the *siesta* (afternoon nap) comes into its own. Many people finish work at lunch time and most of the entertainment takes place in the cool of evening. Foreign tourists flocking to the coasts are joined by thousands of Spaniards. Large pop concerts are held in coastal towns.

June

Corpus Christi (*late May or early Jun*) is commemorated in Granada (*see p43*). In Seville, the *seises*, young boys dressed in doublet and hose, dance before the cathedral altar. At Zahara (*see p176*), near Ronda, houses are decked out with greenery.
Noche de San Juan (*23, 24 Jun*). The evening of 23 June sees dancing, drinking and singing around bonfires on beaches across Andalucía in honour of St John the Baptist. Lanjarón (*see p193*) celebrates with a

water battle in its streets in the early hours of 24 June.
Romería de los Gitanos (*third Sun in Jun*), Cabra (*see p151*). A procession made up of thousands of Roma (gypsies) heads for a hilltop shrine.
Festival Internacional de Música y Danza (*mid-Jun–early Jul*), Granada (*see pp194–202*). Performers come to Granada from all over the world. Many events are held in the Alhambra's Generalife (*p202*).

July

Festival de la Guitarra (*first two weeks of Jul*), Córdoba (*see pp144–50*). Guitar festival presenting all musical styles, from classical to flamenco.
Blues Festival (*mid-Jul*), Cazorla (*see p160*). The largest blues festival in the country.
Fiesta de la Virgen del Carmen (*around 15 Jul*). Many coastal communities honour this Virgin by regattas and other sporting events. In the evening, the Virgin's image is put aboard a

fishing boat, which parades across the sea amid fireworks.
Lunes de Toro (*around 17 Jul*), Grazalema (*see p176*). Bullrunning daily for a week.

August

Fiestas Colombinas (*around 3 Aug*), Huelva (*see p131*). A Latin American dance and music festival in celebration of Columbus's voyage. It is dedicated to a different Latin American country every year.
Fiestas Patronales de Santa María de la Palma (*15 Aug*), Algeciras. A saint's image is rescued from the sea. It is cleaned, then carried in a procession of boats to a beach. Later it is returned to the sea.
Feria de Málaga (*two weeks in mid-Aug, see p43*).
Fiestas de la Exaltación del Río Guadalquivir (*third week in Aug*), Sanlúcar de Barrameda (*see p166*). Horse races are held on the beach.
Feria de Almería (*last week in Aug, see p43*).

The Costa del Sol – popular with tourists and with the Spanish

Average Monthly Rainfall

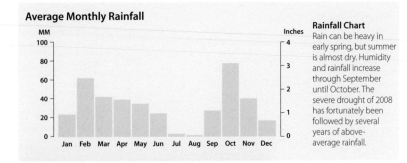

Rainfall Chart
Rain can be heavy in early spring, but summer is almost dry. Humidity and rainfall increase through September until October. The severe drought of 2008 has fortunately been followed by several years of above-average rainfall.

Chirimoya harvest on the subtropical coast at Almuñécar *(see p193)*

Autumn

This is a most pleasant time to visit Andalucía. The weather is settled, but without the searing summer heat, and the holiday crowds are easing. Grape harvests are in full swing and being celebrated in towns and villages. The theatres start to open for drama and concerts. Along the subtropical coast of the Mediterranean, sweet potatoes and *chirimoyas* (custard apples) are harvested. Inland, mushrooms, freshly picked, feature on menus.

September

Feria de Pedro Romero *(first two weeks in Sep)*, Ronda *(see pp178–9)*. This *fiesta* celebrates the founder of modern bullfighting *(see p179)*. All participants in the Corrida Goyesca wear costumes reflecting the era of Goya, a great bullfighting fan.

Fiesta de Cascamorras *(6 Sep)*, Baza *(see p204)*. A bizarre *fiesta* in which a figure known as Cascamorras comes from neighbouring Guadix to try to steal a statue of the Virgin (Virgen de la Piedad). Youths covered with oil taunt him and chase him out of town. He is sent back to Guadix empty-handed, where he receives further punishment for his failure.

Moros y Cristianos *(15 Sep)*, Válor *(see p205)*. Re-creation of the Reconquest battles.

Fiesta de la Vendimia *(second or third week of Sep)*, La Palma del Condado *(see p133)*. A lively *fiesta* to bless the first grape juice.

Romería de San Miguel *(last Sunday of Sep)*, Torremolinos *(see p184)*. One of the largest *romerías* in Andalucía.

Bienal de Arte Flamenco *(last two weeks of Sep, even-numbered years)*, Seville.

Moros y Cristianos fiesta, Válor

A fabulous opportunity for enthusiasts to see world-class flamenco artists, such as Cristina Hoyos.

Sevilla en Otoño *(Sep–Nov)*, Seville. A variety of cultural events, including dance, theatre and exhibitions, and, in addition, sports.

October

Fiesta del Vino *(5–9 Oct)*, Cádiar *(see p205)*. A feature of this *fiesta* in the mountains of the Alpujarras is the construction of a fountain, which gushes forth wine.

Festival Iberoamericano de Teatro *(last two weeks of Oct)*, Cádiz *(see pp168–9)*. Latin American theatre festival.

November

Festival Internacional de Jazz *(early Nov)*, Granada *(see pp194–202)* and Seville.

Festival de Cine Iberoamericano *(last two weeks of Nov)*, Huelva *(see p131)*. Latin American film festival.

People covered in oil during the Cascamorras festivities in Baza

Average Monthly Temperature

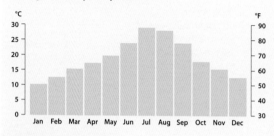

Temperature Chart
Andalucía enjoys a warm Mediterranean climate throughout the year, although it can become cold at night. Temperatures rise from January to the summer months when, in some cities inland, they can far exceed the average for the region.

Medieval music at the Fiesta de los Verdiales in Málaga

Winter

At this time of year the ripe olives are harvested in abundance. The restaurants serve venison, wild boar and partridge dishes as this is the hunting season. Skiers flock to the Sierra Nevada. Though winter is the rainy season and it is cold at night, many days have sunshine. By February, almond blossom and strawberries begin to appear again.

December

La Inmaculada Concepción *(8 Dec)*, Seville. The *tuna*, groups of wandering minstrels, take to the streets around the Plaza del Triunfo and Santa Cruz *(see pp76–7)*.
Fiesta de los Verdiales *(28 Dec)*, Málaga *(see pp182–3)*. On Spain's equivalent of April Fool's Day, *El Día de los Santos Inocentes*, thousands of town and country folk gather at the Venta del Túnel, on the outskirts of Málaga. They come to hear *pandas* (bands) compete in performing

verdiales, wild, primitive music from Moorish times, played on medieval instruments.

January

Día de la Toma *(2 Jan)*, Granada *(see pp194–202)*. This *fiesta* recalls the ousting of the Moors in 1492 *(see p52)*. Queen Isabel's crown and King Fernando's sword are paraded through the streets, and the royal standard flies from the balcony of the Ayuntamiento.
Día de Reyes *(6 Jan)*. On the evening before this public holiday, the Three Kings arrive, splendidly dressed, to parade through town centres across Andalucía. They ride in small carriages that are drawn either by tractors or horses and, during processions, throw sweets to the excited children. The next day is Epiphany when children receive gifts.
Certamen Internacional de Guitarra Clásica Andrés Segovia *(first week of Jan)*, Almuñécar *(see p193)*. Classical guitar competition in homage to the master.

February

Los Carnavales *(second or third week in Feb)*. Carnival is widely celebrated, most spectacularly in Cádiz *(see p43)* and Isla Cristina *(see p130)*.
Festival de Música Antigua *(Feb and Mar)*, Seville. Early music is performed on historic instruments.
Jerez Annual Flamenco Festival *(end Feb/early Mar)*, Jerez *(see p166)*. Flamenco performances and workshops.

Public Holidays

New Year's Day (1 Jan)
Epiphany (6 Jan)
Día de Andalucía (28 Feb)
Easter Thursday and Good Friday (variable)
Labour Day (1 May)
Assumption (15 Aug)
National Day (12 Oct)
All Saints' Day (1 Nov)
Constitution Day (6 Dec)
Immaculate Conception (8 Dec)
Christmas Day (25 Dec)

Ski station on the snow-covered slopes of the Sierra Nevada *(see p203)*

Fiestas in Andalucía

There is nothing quite like a Spanish *fiesta* or *feria*, and those of Andalucía are among the most colourful. *Fiestas* may commemorate an historic event or a change of season. More often they mark a religious occasion; Semana Santa (Holy Week), for example, is celebrated all over Andalucía. Feasting, dancing, singing, drinking – often right around the clock – are all integral to a *fiesta*. At a *feria* there will often be a decorated fairground, revellers dressed in traditional flamenco attire, and processions of horses and carriages. Throughout Andalucía you will also come across *romerías*, in which processions carry holy effigies through the countryside to a shrine.

Dancers in their finery at Seville's Feria de Abril

a flamenco accent (out of a thousand *casetas*, about a quarter are open to the public). There are bullfights in the Maestranza bullring *(see p72)*.

Huelva and Sevilla

One of Spain's most popular *fiestas*, the Romería del Rocío, is held during Pentecost. More than 70 brotherhoods trek to the shrine of El Rocío *(see p133)* amid Las Marismas, the marshlands at the mouth of the Guadalquivir. They are joined by pilgrims travelling on horseback, on foot or by car. All pay homage to the Virgen del Rocío, also called the White Dove or the Queen of the Marshes. There is drinking and dancing for several days and nights, until the early hours of Monday morning when the Virgin is brought out of the shrine. Young men from the nearby town of Almonte carry her through the crowds for up to 12 hours, fighting off anybody who tries to get near.

Córdoba and Jaén

May is a nonstop *fiesta* in Córdoba *(see pp144–50)*. The Día de la Cruz – the Day of the Cross – is held on the first three days of the month. Religious brotherhoods and neighbourhoods compete with each other to create the most colourful, flower-decorated crosses, which are set up in squares and at street corners.

Following this is the Festival de los Patios (around 5–15 May), when the

Seville

Semana Santa, or Holy Week (Palm Sunday–Good Friday) is celebrated in flamboyant style in Seville. More than 100 *pasos* (floats bearing religious effigies) are carried through the streets of the city. They are accompanied by *nazarenos*, members of some 50 brotherhoods dating back to the 13th century, wearing long robes and tall pointed hoods. As the processions sway through the streets, appointed singers burst into *saetas*, shafts of song in praise of the Virgin. Emotion reaches fever-pitch in the early hours of Good Friday, when the Virgen de La Macarena is paraded, accompanied by 2,500 *nazarenos (see p93)*.

During their Feria de Abril, the spring fair held around two weeks after Easter, the *sevillanos* go on a spree for a week. Daily, from about 1pm, elegant

horsemen and women wearing brightly coloured flamenco dresses show off their finery in a parade known as the *Paseo de Caballos*. At night, *casetas* (temporary marquees) throb to *sevillanas*, a popular dance that has

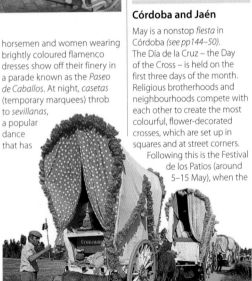

Pilgrims taking part in the Romería del Rocío in Huelva province

patios of the city's old quarter are thrown open for visitors to come and admire. Crowds go from patio to patio, at each one launching into flamenco dance or song.

During the last week of May, Córdoba holds its lively *feria*. It is as colourful as the Feria de Abril in Seville, but more accessible to strangers. This festival, with roots in Roman times, welcomes the spring.

The Romería de Nuestra Señora de la Cabeza takes place on the last Sunday in April at the Santuario de la Virgen de la Cabeza (*see p155*), a remote shrine in the Sierra Morena. Over 250,000 people attend, some making the pilgrimage on foot or on horseback. At the site, flames shoot up day and night from a torch fed by candles lit by the faithful. Then the Virgin, known as La Morenita, is borne through the crowd to cries of ¡*Guapa, guapa!* (beautiful, beautiful!).

Penitents at the Romería de Nuestra Señora de la Cabeza in April

Cádiz and Málaga

For two weeks in February, Los Carnavales (Carnival) is celebrated with more flair and abandon in Cádiz (*see p168*) than anywhere else in Andalucía. Some say it rivals the carnival in Río de Janeiro. Groups of singers practise for months in advance, composing outrageous satirical ditties that poke fun at anything from the current fashions to celebrities, especially politicians. Often sumptuously costumed, they perform their songs in the Falla Theatre in a competition lasting for several days. Then they

Costumed revellers at the February Carnival (Los Carnavales) in Cádiz

take part in a parade. The whole city puts on fancy dress and crowds of revellers throng the narrow streets of the city's old quarter, shouting, singing, dancing and drinking.

The Feria de Málaga in the middle of August each year, celebrates the capture of the city from the Moors by the Catholic Monarchs (*see p52*). Eager to outdo Seville, Málaga (*see pp182–3*) puts on a fine show. The residents, famous for their ability to organize a good party, put on traditional costume and parade, along with decorated carriages and elegant horsefolk, through the fairground. The entertainment goes on for a week nonstop, and top bullfighters perform at the city's bullring in La Malagueta.

Granada and Almería

Corpus Christi, held in late May or early June, is one of the major events in Granada (*see pp194–202*). On the day before Corpus a procession of bigheads (costumed caricatures with outsized heads) and giants parades through the city, led by the *tarasca*, a woman on a huge dragon. The next day, the *custodia*, or monstrance, is carried from the cathedral all through the streets. For a week afterwards there is bullfighting, flamenco and general revelry.

The *feria* in Almería (*see pp206–7*), which is held at the end of August, is in honour of the Virgen del Mar. There are funfairs, processions, sporting events and bullfights. The city's Virgin dates back to 1502, when a coastguard on the lookout for Berber pirates found an image of the Virgin washed up on a beach.

Feria de Málaga, celebrating the capture of the city from the Moors

THE HISTORY OF SEVILLE AND ANDALUCÍA

Andalucía's early history is an extraordinary tale of ancient cities – Cádiz *(see pp168–9)*, founded in 1100 BC, is the oldest city in Europe – and waves of settlers, each one contributing new ideas and customs.

Hominids first inhabited the region about one million years ago. *Homo sapiens* had arrived by 25,000 BC, and by the Iron Age a strong Iberian culture had emerged. Later, trade and cultural links developed first with the Phoenicians, then with the Greeks and Carthaginians. These ties and the abundance of natural raw materials, such as iron, gold and copper ore, made this part of Iberia one of the wealthiest areas of the Mediterranean.

Attracted by its riches, the Romans made their first forays into southern Spain in 206 BC. They ruled for almost 700 years. Their place was eventually taken by the Visigoths as the Western Roman Empire crumbled in the 5th century AD. The Moors, who followed, flourished first in Córdoba, then in Seville, and, towards the end of their almost 800-year rule, in the Nasrid kingdom of Granada. After the fall of Granada to the Christians in 1492, Spain entered an era of expansion and prosperity. The conquest of the New World made Seville one of the most affluent cities in Europe, but much of this wealth was squandered on wars by the Habsburg kings. By the 18th century, Spain had fallen into economic decline; in the 19th and early 20th centuries poverty led to political conflict and, ultimately, the Civil War.

The years after the Civil War saw continuing poverty, though tourism in the 1960s and 1970s did much to ease this. With Franco's death and Spain's entry into the EU, the Spanish began to enjoy prosperity and democratic freedoms. Andalucía still lagged behind, however. The Expo '92 fostered economic growth in the region. Since then, there have also been advances in wind and solar farms. One of Europe's largest solar farms is in Sanlúcar la Mayor, near Seville.

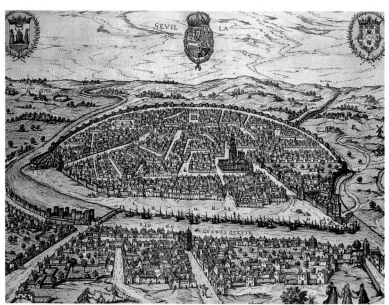

The 16th-century port of Seville, where ships brought wealth from the Americas to the Holy Roman Empire

◀ 18th-century lithograph of the Puerta de la Justicia in the Alhambra *(see pp198–9)*

Early Andalucía

Neanderthals inhabited Gibraltar around 50,000 BC. *Homo sapiens* arrived 25,000 years later and Neolithic tribespeople from Africa settled in Spain from about 7000 BC. By the time the Phoenicians arrived to trade in precious metals, they were met by a sophisticated Iberian culture. They later established trading links with the semi-mythical Iberian kingdom of Tartessus. The Greeks, already settled in northeastern Spain, started to colonize the south from about 600 BC. Meanwhile, Celts from the north had mixed with Iberians. This culture, influenced by the Greeks, created beautiful works of art. The Carthaginians arrived in about 500 BC and, according to legend, destroyed Tartessus.

Areas of influence

▨ Greek ☐ Phoenician

This figure's arms are outstretched in an attitude of prayer.

Burial Sight at Los Millares
Los Millares *(see p207)* was the site of an early metal-working civilization in about 2300 BC. Up to 100 corpses were buried on a single site; the huge burial chambers were covered with earth to make a gently sloping mound.

Cave Paintings
From approximately 25,000 BC, people painted caves in Andalucía. They portrayed birds, fish, land animals, people, weapons and other subjects with a skilful naturalism.

Iberian Bronze Figures
These bronze figurines from the 5th–4th centuries BC are votive offerings to the gods. They were discovered in a burial ground near Despeñaperros in the province of Jaén. The Romans regarded the Iberians who crafted them as exceptionally noble.

1,000,000–750,000 BC Stones worked by hominids at Puerto de Santa María, Cádiz	25,000–18,000 BC *Homo sapiens* make cave paintings and rock engravings	4000 BC Burials at Cueva de los Murciélagos in Granada leave Neolithic remains; esparto sandals, religious offerings and other items
Stone tool		**4500 BC** Farmers begin to grow crops and breed cattle

1,000,000 BC	50,000 BC	10,000 BC	8000 BC	6000 BC	4000 BC

50,000 BC Neanderthals inhabit Gibraltar	**7000 BC** Neolithic colonists arrive, perhaps from North Africa. Farming begins on Iberian Peninsula	*Neolithic ochre pot*

Goddess Astarte
The Phoenicians founded Cádiz in about 1100 BC. They brought their own goddess, Astarte, who became popular across Andalucía as the region absorbed eastern influences.

The headdress shows this is a votaress, devoted to her god.

The hand of this priestess is raised in benediction.

Greek Urn
The ancient Greeks imported many artifacts from home; their style of decoration had a strong influence on Iberian art.

Where to See Early Andalucía

Cave paintings can be seen in the Cueva de la Pileta near Ronda la Vieja (p177). At Antequera (p181) there are Bronze Age dolmens dating from 2500 BC; at Los Millares (p207) there are burial chambers dating from the Copper Age. Replicas of the famous Tartessian Carambolo Treasure are in the Museo Arqueológico in Seville (p101) and Iberian stone carvings from Porcuna are exhibited in Jaén (p153). The Museo Arqueológico de Linares has relics dating from the Iberian period (see p155).

León de la Puerta Norte discovered at Cástulo can be seen in the Museo Arqueológico de Linares.

Dama de Baza
This female figure, dating from around 500–400 BC, may represent an Iberian goddess. It is one of several such figures found in southern Spain.

Carambolo Treasure
Phoenician in style, this treasure is from Tartessus. Although many artifacts have been uncovered, the site of this kingdom has yet to be found.

2300 BC Beginning of the Bronze Age; dolmen-style burials take place at Los Millares (see p207)

800–700 BC Kingdom of Tartessus at its height, influenced by the Phoenicians

Tartessian buckle

219 BC Carthaginians take Sagunto, eastern Spain

241 BC First Punic War between Carthage and Rome

2000 BC	1000 BC	800 BC	600 BC	400 BC

1100 BC Foundation of Cádiz by the Phoenicians

800 BC Celts from northern Europe move southwards

600 BC Greek colonists settle on the coasts of Andalucía

500 BC Carthage colonizes southern Spain

213 BC Carthagenians crush the Romans in the city of Cástulo

Romans and Visigoths

The Romans came to Spain during a war against Carthage in 206 BC. Attracted by the wealth of the peninsula, they stayed for 700 years; in 200 years they conquered Spain (Hispania) and split it into provinces. Baetica, with Corduba (Córdoba) as its capital, corresponded roughly to what is now Andalucía. Cities were built, while feudal lords created vast estates, exporting olive oil and wheat to Rome. Baetica became one of the wealthiest of Rome's provinces with a rich, Ibero-Roman culture. The Visigoths who followed continued to assert Roman values until the Moors arrived in AD 711.

Roman Territory AD 100

   Roman Baetica
   Other provinces

Hadrian
Emperors Hadrian and Trajan were born in Baetica. A great many politicians, writers and philosophers from the province also moved to Rome, some enjoying great fortune.

Private villas   Paved streets   Temple

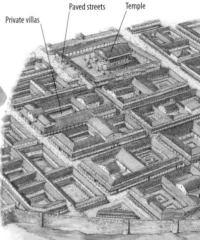

Roman Mosaics in Andalucía
Private houses, temples and public buildings all had mosaic floors. Many themes, from the gods to hunting, were represented.

Italica Reconstructed

Scipio Africanus founded Itálica (see p136) in 206 BC after his defeat of the Carthaginians. The city reached its height in the 2nd and 3rd centuries AD and was the birthplace of the emperors Hadrian and Trajan. Unlike Córdoba, it was not built over in post-Roman times and today Itálica is a superbly preserved example of a Roman city.

---

206 BC Scipio Africanus gains victory against the Carthaginians at Alcalá del Río; Itálica is founded

55 BC Birth of Seneca the Elder in Córdoba

AD 27 Andalucía is named Baetica

Suicide of Seneca

65 Suicide of Seneca the Younger after his plotting against Nero

117 Hadrian is crowned Emperor

200 BC	100 BC	AD 1	100	200

200 BC Romans conquer more of southern Spain and reach Cádiz

61 BC Julius Caesar is governor of Hispania Ulterior (Spain)

Julius Caesar

98–117 Trajan, from Itálica, is emperor. Local senators enjoy influence in Rome

69–79 Emperor Vespasian grants Roman status to all towns in Hispania

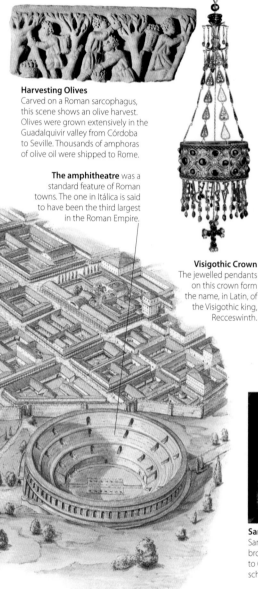

Harvesting Olives
Carved on a Roman sarcophagus, this scene shows an olive harvest. Olives were grown extensively in the Guadalquivir valley from Córdoba to Seville. Thousands of amphoras of olive oil were shipped to Rome.

The amphitheatre was a standard feature of Roman towns. The one in Itálica is said to have been the third largest in the Roman Empire.

Visigothic Crown
The jewelled pendants on this crown form the name, in Latin, of the Visigothic king, Recceswinth.

Where to See Roman and Visigothic Andalucía

Roman remains can be seen at the sights of Itálica (*see p136*), Carmona (*p136*) and Ronda la Vieja (*p177*); in Málaga there is a partially excavated Roman amphitheatre, and Roman columns can be seen at the Alameda de Hércules in Seville (*p92*). The Museo Arqueológico in Seville (*p101*), Córdoba (*p147*) and Cádiz (*p168*) all have Roman artifacts on display. Visigothic pillars and capitals can be viewed in the Mezquita in Córdoba (*pp148–9*). Roman mosaics dating from around the 2nd century AD can be seen at the ruins of Cástulo, just outside Linares.

The Roman ruins at Itálica (*see p136*) are situated 9 km (5.5 miles) north of Seville.

San Isidoro and San Leandro
San Isidoro (560–635) of Seville, like his brother, San Leandro, converted Visigoths to Christianity; he also wrote a great scholastic work, *Etymologies*.

---

415 Visigoths arrive in Spain from northern Europe

446 Tarraconensis in north still Roman; Rome attempts to win back rest of Spain

632 Death of Prophet Muhammad

| 300 | 400 | 500 | 600 |

409 Vandals sack Tarraconensis (Tarragona)

Theodosius, born in Hispania

476 Visigoths control whole of Spain

589 Third Council of Toledo in central Spain. Visigothic King Reccared converted from Arianism to Catholicism

635 Death of San Isidoro of Seville

The Moorish Conquest

Called in to resolve a quarrel among the Visigoths, the Moors first arrived in 710. They returned in 711 to conquer Spain; within 10 years, the north alone remained under Christian control. The Moors named their newly conquered territories Al Andalus and in 929 they established an independent caliphate. Córdoba, its capital, was the greatest city in Europe, a centre for art, science and literature. In the 11th century the caliphate collapsed into 30 feuding *taifas* (party states). Almoravids, tribesmen from North Africa, invaded the region in 1086, and in the 12th century Almohads from Morocco ousted the Almoravids and designated Seville their capital.

Moorish Domain AD 800
☐ Al Andalus

Abd al Rahman III receives the Byzantine envoy.

Apocalypse
An 11th-century account of an 8th-century text, *Commentaries on the Apocalypse* by Beato de Liébana, this illustration shows Christians going to war.

Bronze Stag
This 10th-century caliphal-style bronze is from Medina Azahara.

The Court of Abd al Rahman III

Abd al Rahman III began his palace of Medina Azahara (see p142) in 936. This 19th-century painting by Dionisio Baixeres shows a Byzantine envoy presenting the caliph with the works of the Greek scientist Dioscorides. The Moors of Córdoba possessed much knowledge of the ancient world, which was later transmitted to Europe. The Medina was sacked by Berber mercenaries in 1010.

Visigothic king and Moorish chief

756 Abd al Rahman I reaches Spain and asserts himself as ruler, declaring an independent emirate based around Córdoba

936 Construction of Medina Azahara begins

929 Abd al Rahman III proclaims caliphate in Córdoba

700 ___ **800** ___ **900**

711 Invasion under Tariq ben Ziyad

710 First Moorish intervention in Spain

785 Construction of the Mezquita begins at Córdoba

822–52 Rule of Abd al Rahman II

Coin from the reign of Abd al Rahman III

912–61 Rule of Abd al Rahman III

961–76 Al Hakam II builds great library at Medina Azahara; expands Mezquita

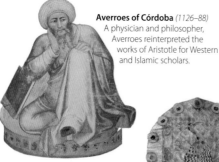

Averroes of Córdoba *(1126–88)*
A physician and philosopher, Averroes reinterpreted the works of Aristotle for Western and Islamic scholars.

Horseshoe arches were a major feature here, as in the Mezquita *(see pp148–9)* at Córdoba.

Mozarabic Bible
Moorish society integrated Jews and Mozarabs (Christians living an Islamic lifestyle). Illustrations like this one, from a 10th-century Bible, are in a Moorish decorative style.

Clerics prepare the manuscript to be given to Abd al Rahman III.

Cufic Script
Islamic artists, forbidden to use representations of the human figure, made ample use of calligraphy for decoration.

Where to See Moorish Andalucía

The Mezquita in Córdoba *(see pp148–9)* and the ruins of the palace at Medina Azahara *(p142)* are the most complete remnants of Spain's Moorish caliphate. Artifacts found at Medina Azahara can be seen in the Museo Arqueológico in Córdoba *(see p147)*. The Alcazaba at Almería *(see p206)* dates from the 10th century, when this city was still part of the caliphate, while the Alcazaba at Málaga *(see p183)* was built during the ensuing Taifa period. The Torre del Oro *(see p73)* and La Giralda *(see p82)* in Seville are both Almohad structures.

The Alcazaba in Almería *(p206)*, dating from the 10th century, overlooks the old town.

Irrigation in Al Andalus
The water wheel was vital to irrigation, which the Moors used to grow newly imported crops such as rice and oranges.

Al Mansur

976–1002 Al Mansur, military dictator, comes to power

1010 Medina Azahara sacked by Berbers

1012 *Taifas* emerge as splinter Moorish states

1031 Caliphate ends

1085 Fall of Toledo in north to Christians decisively loosens Moorish control over central Spain

1000

1086 Almoravids invade

1100

1120 Almoravid power starts to wane

1126 Birth of Averroes, Arab philosopher

1135 Maimónides, Jewish philosopher, born in Córdoba

Maimónides

1147 Almohads arrive in Seville; build Giralda and Torre del Oro

1175–1200 Height of Almohad power. Previously lost territory won back from Christians

1200

The Reconquest

The war between Moors and Christians, which started in northern Spain, arrived in Andalucía with a landmark Christian victory at Las Navas de Tolosa in 1212; Seville and Córdoba fell soon afterwards. By the late 13th century only the Nasrid kingdom of Granada remained under Moorish control. Meanwhile, Christian monarchs such as Alfonso X and Pedro I employed Mudéjar *(see p28)* craftsmen to build churches and palaces in the reconquered territories – Mudéjar literally means "those permitted to stay". Granada eventually fell in 1492 to Fernando and Isabel of Aragón and Castilla, otherwise known as the Catholic Monarchs.

Moorish Domain in 1350
☐ Nasrid kingdom

The Catholic Monarchs enter Granada; Fernando and Isabel were awarded this title for their services to Christendom.

Boabdil

Cantigas of Alfonso X
Alfonso X, who won back much of Andalucía from the Moors, was an enlightened Christian monarch. His illuminated *Cantigas* are a vivid account of life in Reconquest Spain.

The Fall of Granada

This relief by Felipe de Vigarney (1480 – c.1542), in Granada's Capilla Real (see p194), shows Boabdil, the last Moorish ruler, surrendering the city in 1492. Trying to establish a Christian realm, the Catholic Monarchs converted the Moors by force and expelled the Jews. The same year, Columbus got funds for his voyage to America (see p131).

Almohad Banner
This richly woven tapestry is widely believed to be the banner captured from the Moors by the Christians at the battle of Las Navas de Tolosa.

1226
Fernando III takes Baeza

1236
Fernando III conquers Córdoba

1252–84 Alfonso X reconquers much of Andalucía. Toledo Translators' School in the north continues to translate important works of Moorish literature

Pedro I of Castilla

1333 Moors add tower to the 8th-century Keep (see p174) on Gibraltar

1220　　　　**1260**　　　　**1300**　　　　**1340**

1212 Almohad *(see p50)* power broken by Christian victory at Las Navas de Tolosa

1248 Fernando III takes Seville

1238 Nasrid dynasty established in Granada. Alhambra *(see p198)* is begun

1350–69 Reign of Pedro I of Castilla, who rebuilds Seville Alcázar in Mudéjar style. His lack of Spanish patriotism provokes civil war against Henry II of Trastámara

Alfonso X

Fernando and Isabel
The unification of Spain can be traced back to Isabel of Castilla and Fernando of Aragón, dubbed "The Catholic Monarchs".

Where to See Reconquest Andalucía

Many of the Reconquest buildings in Andalucía are Mudéjar in style *(see p28)*. The most notable are the Palacio Pedro I in the Real Alcázar *(p87)* and parts of the Casa de Pilatos *(p81)*, both in Seville. Christian churches built in Andalucía during the 13th, 14th and 15th centuries are also either completely Mudéjar in style or have Mudéjar features such as a minaret-like bell tower or portal; as, for example, the Iglesia de San Marcos *(p94)* in Seville. During this period the Nasrids of Granada built the most outstanding example of Moorish architecture in Spain, the Alhambra and Generalife *(pp198–202)*. Seville Cathedral *(pp82–3)* was constructed in the 15th century as a high Gothic assertion of the Catholic faith.

Nasrid warriors

Crown
This Mudéjar-style crown, bearing the coats of arms of Castilla and León, is made of silver, ivory and coral.

Astrolabe
As this 15th-century navigation tool shows, the Moors had great technical expertise.

The Palacio Pedro I *(see p86)* in Seville is considered to be the most complete example of Mudéjar architecture in Spain.

Boabdil's Demise
Legend has it that Boabdil wept as he left Granada. He moved to Laujar de Andarax until 1493, then later to Africa.

1369 Henry II of Trastámara personally kills Pedro I; lays seeds of monolithic Castilian regime

La Pinta, one of Columbus's ships

1492 Columbus sails to America

1492 Fall of Granada to the Catholic Monarchs

1380	1420	1460

1469 Marriage of Fernando of Aragón to Isabel of Castilla

1474 Isabel proclaimed queen in Segovia

1479 Fernando becomes king of Aragón; Castilla and Aragón united

Forced baptism of the Moors

Seville's Golden Age

The 16th century saw the rise of a monolithic Spanish state, led by the Catholic Monarchs. Heretics were persecuted and the remaining Moors treated so unjustly that they often rebelled. In 1503 Seville was granted a monopoly on trade with the New World and Spain entrusted with "converting" the Indians by the pope. In 1516 the Habsburg Carlos I came to the throne, later to be elected Holy Roman Emperor; Spain became the most powerful nation in Europe. Constant war, however, consumed the wealth that its main port, Seville, generated. By the 1680s the Guadalquivir had silted up, trade had passed to Cádiz and Seville declined.

Spanish Empire in 1700

Spanish territories

La Giralda *(see p82)*, once an Almohad minaret, is now the belfry of Seville's cathedral.

Carlos I (1516–56)
Carlos I of Spain was made Holy Roman Emperor Carlos V in 1521. His election enabled the Holy Roman Empire to gain access to the immense wealth that Spain, Seville in particular, generated at this time.

Map of Central America
Within 30 years of Columbus's first voyage, the distant lands and seas of Central America had become familiar territory to Spanish navigators profiting in gold and the slave trade.

Seville in the 16th Century

This painting by Francisco Pacheco (1564–1654) shows Seville at its height. With the return of treasure fleets from the New World, astonishing wealth poured into the city and it became one of the richest ports in Europe. The population grew, religious buildings proliferated and artistic life found new vigour. Despite the prosperity of the city, poverty, crime and sickness were endemic.

1502 Moors rebel in Las Alpujarras *(see pp204–5)*; they are baptized or expelled by the Inquisition

1516 Death of Fernando

Seville Inquisition banner

1519 Hernán Cortés conquers Mexico

1588 Spanish Armada fails in attack on England

1559 Inquisition persecutes Protestants in Seville

1587 Cádiz raided by Francis Drake

1580 Seville becomes largest city in Spain

1500　**1525**　**1550**　**1575**

1506 Death of Isabel

1516–56 Reign of Carlos I, later Holy Roman Emperor

1532 Pizarro conquers Peru

1519 Magellan sails from Sanlúcar de Barrameda on first circumnavigation of the world

1556–98 Reign of Felipe II

1558 Second Moorish rebellion in Las Alpujarras

Ferdinand Magellan (1480–1521)

Inquisition
Fears of heresy laid the ground for the Spanish Inquisition to be set up in the 15th century. In the 16th century autos-da-fé (trials of faith) were held in Seville in the Plaza de San Francisco (see p78).

Unloading and loading took place virtually in the heart of the city.

Velázquez
Born in Seville in 1599, Diego Velázquez painted his earliest works in the city, but later became a court painter in Madrid. This crucifix is a detail of a painting he made at the behest of Felipe IV.

Ships from other parts of Europe brought goods to the city; this merchandise would be traded later in the New World.

The Last Moors
The last Moors were expelled in 1609; this destroyed southern Spain's agriculture, which had taken over 700 years to develop.

Where to See the Golden Age in Andalucía

The Isabelline style (see p28), lasting testament to nationalistic fervour of the early 16th century, can be seen in the Capilla Real (p194) in Granada and the Palacio de Jabalquinto in Baeza (pp156–7). Baeza and Úbeda (pp158–9) both prospered during the Renaissance in Spain and contain some of the best architecture of this period in Andalucía. The Plateresque (p29) façade of the Ayuntamiento (pp78–9) in Seville is a good example of the style, while the Palacio Carlos V (p195) in Granada is the best example of Classical Renaissance architecture in Spain. The Archivo de Indias (pp84–5) was built according to the principles of Herreran style (p29). The Hospital de la Caridad (p73) is a fine 17th-century Baroque building.

The Capilla Real (see p194) in Granada was built to house the bodies of the Catholic Monarchs, Fernando and Isabel.

1598–1621 Reign of Felipe III

1608 Cervantes, active in Madrid and Seville, publishes *Don Quixote*

Original edition of Don Quixote

1609 Expulsion of Moors by Felipe III

1649 Plague in Seville kills one in three

| 1600 | 1625 | 1650 | 1675 |

1599 Velázquez born in Seville

1596 Sack of Cádiz by the English fleet

1617 Murillo born in Seville

1630 Madrid becomes Spain's largest city. Zurbarán moves to Seville

1665–1700 Carlos II, last of the Spanish Habsburgs

Young beggar by Murillo (1617–82)

Bourbon Kings

The 13-year War of the Spanish Succession saw Bourbons on the throne in place of the Habsburgs and, under the Treaty of Utrecht, the loss of Gibraltar to the British *(see p174)*. Later, ties with France dragged Spain into the Napoleonic Wars: following the Battle of Trafalgar, the Spanish king Carlos IV abdicated and Napoleon Bonaparte placed his brother Joseph on the Spanish throne. The Peninsular War ensued and, with British help, the French were driven out of Spain. After the Bourbon restoration, Spain, weakened by further strife, began to lose her colonies. Andalucía became one of Spain's poorest regions.

Spain in Europe (1812)
- Napoleonic dependencies
- Napoleonic rule

Romantic Andalucía
Andalucía's Moorish legacy helped to establish it as a land of beauty and myth, making it popular with travellers of the Romantic era.

The Constitution is proclaimed to the people of Cádiz.

Carlos III
A Bourbon monarch of the Enlightenment and an innovator in matters of society and science, Carlos III tried to establish colonies of farm workers in the sparsely populated Sierra Morena.

The 1812 Constitution

During the Peninsular War, Spain's Parliament met in Cádiz, and in 1812 produced an advanced liberal constitution. However, after the Bourbon restoration in 1814, Fernando VII banned all liberal activity. Ironically, during the First Carlist War, Fernando's daughter, Isabel II, contesting her right to the throne against her uncle Don Carlos, turned to the liberals for support.

1701 Felipe V of Bourbon begins his reign

1717 American trade moves to Cádiz

1726 Spain tries to retake Gibraltar

1779–83 Great Siege of Gibraltar

1700 **1725** **1750** **1775**

1701–13 War of the Spanish Succession

1724 Felipe V abdicates but is reinstated

1713 Treaty of Utrecht; Gibraltar ceded to Britain

1746–59 Reign of Fernando VI

1759–88 Carlos III

1771 Royal Tobacco Factory in Seville is completed

1788–1808 Reign of Carlos IV

Battle of Bailén
In 1808, at Bailén, a Spanish army comprising local militias beat Napoleon's experienced French army, taking 22,000 prisoners.

Battle of Trafalgar
In 1805, the Spanish, allied at the time to Napoleon, lost their fleet to the British admiral, Nelson.

Where to See Bourbon Andalucía

Eighteenth-century Baroque architecture can be seen all over Andalucía. The prime examples in Seville are the former Royal Tobacco Factory, now the city's Universidad (*see pp100–101*), and the Plaza de Toros de la Maestranza (*p72*). Osuna (*p137*), Écija (*p137*) and Priego de Córdoba (*p154*) all have fine examples of the style. The lower levels of Cádiz Cathedral (*p168*) are the most complete example of a Baroque church found in Spain. The Puente Isabel II (*p107*) is a fine showcase of 19th-century *arquitectura de hierro* (iron architecture).

The Puente Isabel II is an example of the architecture of Andalucía's "industrial" age.

Support
for the constitution came from a wide section of society, including women.

Washington Irving
In *Tales of the Alhambra (1832)* the American diplomat Washington Irving perpetuated a highly romanticized view of Andalucía.

Seville's Tobacco Factory
Carmen (1845), by Prosper Mérimée (*see p100*), was inspired by the women – more than 3,000 of them – who worked in the tobacco factory.

1808 Joseph Bonaparte made king of Spain. Battle of Bailén	**1812** Liberal constitution drawn up in Cádiz	*Isabel II*	**1870–73** Reign of King Amadeo of Savoy	**1873–4** First Republic, proclaimed after Amadeo abdicates
	1814–33 (Bourbon restoration) Reign of Fernando VII		**1868** Isabel II loses her throne in "glorious" revolution	
1800	**1825**	**1850**		**1875**
1805 Battle of Trafalgar	**1814** South American colonies begin struggle for independence	**1843** Isabel II accedes to throne	**1846–9** Second Carlist War	**1872–6** Third Carlist War
	1808–14 Peninsular War; Seville occupied by the French 1810–12	**1833** First Carlist War	**1874** Second Bourbon restoration: Alfonso XII made king	*Alfonso XII*

The Seeds of Civil War

Andalucía continued to decline, remaining so deeply feudal that by the early 20th century social protest was rife. The 1920s brought dictator General Primo de Rivera and relative, but short-lived, social order. In 1931, a Republican government, initially comprising liberals and moderate socialists, came to power. A rigid social order made real reforms slow to arrive, however, and 1931–36 saw growing conflict between extreme left and right wing (including the Falange) elements. Finally, in 1936, the Nationalist General Franco, leading a Moroccan-based garrison, invaded Spain, declaring war on the Republic.

Andalucía in 1936

▨ Nationalist territory
☐ Republican territory

Moorish Revival
By the late 19th century, regionalism, *andalucismo*, led to a revival of Moorish-style architecture. An example is Seville's Estación de Córdoba.

Women fought alongside men against the Nationalist army.

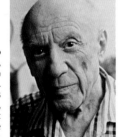

Picasso
Pablo Picasso, was born in Málaga in 1881. His most famous work, *Guernica*, depicts the tragic effects of the Civil War.

The Republican Army
In Andalucía, Franco attacked the Republican army at the very start of the war. Cádiz and Seville fell to Nationalists, but other Andalucían towns held out longer. Franco seized Málaga in 1937, executing thousands of Republicans.

1876 Composer Manuel de Falla born in Cádiz

1882–1912 Growing militancy of farm workers

1885–1902 Regency of María Cristina

1895–8 Cuban War

Fighting during Cuban War, 1898

1880

1890

1900

1881 Pablo Picasso born

1885 Anarchist group *Mano Negra* active in Andalucía

1893 Guitarist Andrés Segovia born near Jaén

1898 Cuba gains independence with US aid; Cádiz and Málaga begin to decline

1902–31 Reign of Alfonso XIII

Casas Viejas
In 1933, peasants were massacred after an uprising by anarchists at Casas Viejas in the province of Cádiz. The incident further served to undermine the Republican government.

Where to See Early 20th-Century Architecture in Andalucía

This period is characterized by architectural revivals. The regionalist style can be seen at the Plaza de España (see p102), the Museo Arqueológico (p103), and the Museo de Artes y Costumbres Populares (p103), all in the Parque María Luisa. The Teatro Lope Vega (p101) is in a Neo-Baroque style.

The Pabellón Real (see p103) in the Parque María Luisa is a pastiche of the late Gothic, Isabelline style (see p28).

EXPOSICION GENERAL ESPAÑOLA
SEVILLA 1929 BARCELONA

1929 Exposition
This trade fair was intended to boost Andalucía's economy. Unfortunately, it coincided with the Wall Street Crash.

Arms were supplied to the Republican army by the then Soviet Union.

Federico García Lorca
The outspoken poet and playwright was murdered by local Falangists in his home town, Granada, in 1936.

General Queipo de Llano
Queipo de Llano broadcast radio propaganda to Seville as part of the Nationalists' strategy to take the city.

1923–30 Dictatorship of General Primo de Rivera

1929 Ibero-American Exposition, Seville

1933 Massacre at Casas Viejas

Republican poster

1936 Civil War starts

1910 **1920** **1930** **1940**

1917–20 Bolshevik Triennium; communists lead protests in Andalucía

José Antonio Primo de Rivera

1931–39 Second Republic

1933 Falange founded by José Antonio Primo de Rivera; later supports Franco

1936 Franco becomes head of state

1939 Civil War ends; over 500,000 dead

Modern Andalucía

By 1945 Spain remained the only Nationalist state in Europe. When Franco died in 1975 and Juan Carlos I came to the throne, the regions clamoured for devolution from Franco's centralized government. In 1982, the Sevillian Felipe González came to power and, in the same year, Andalucía became an autonomous region. Spain joined the European Union in 1986 and, benefitting from European investors in agriculture, the 1990s saw economic growth. Seville evolved into a modern city, hosting the Expo '92 world fair, and its economy continues to improve steadily.

Autonomous regions
Present-day Andalucía

The Hungry Years
After the Civil War, Spain was isolated from Europe and after World War II, received no aid; amid widespread poverty and rationing, many Andalucíans left to work abroad.

A public balcony consisting of skywalks on the top level provides panoramic views of Seville's old quarter.

Feria
Despite the repressive regime that Franco established, the spirit of the Andalucían people remained evident in events such as the *feria* in Seville.

Metropol Parasol
Designed by German architect Jürgen Mayer and completed in 2011, the striking Metropol Parasol, one of the largest timber structures ever built, soars above the Plaza Encarnación in Seville. This ultra-modern construction in the historic centre features wooden mushroom-like canopies with walkways providing panoramic views. The basement houses an archaeological museum whose glass floors reveal fascinating ancient Roman ruins below.

1940 Franco refuses to allow Hitler to attack Gibraltar from Spanish territory

1953 Spain is granted economic aid in return for allowing US bases on Spanish soil

1966 Palomares incident: two US aircraft collide and four nuclear bombs fall to earth, one in the sea, but do not explode. The Duchess of Medina Sidonia, "the red duchess", leads protest march on Madrid

1976 Adolfo Suárez appointed prime minister and forms centre-right government

| 1940 | 1950 | 1960 | 1970 | 19 |

1940–53 The Hungry Years
Franco meets American President Eisenhower (1953)

1962 Development of Costa del Sol begins

1969 Spain closes its border with Gibraltar

1975 Franco dies. Third Bourbon restoration; Juan Carlos I accedes to the throne

Torre Sevilla
Designed by Argentinian architect César Pelli, the Torre Sevilla is the tallest skyscraper in Andalucía. It houses a luxury hotel on the top 12 floors *(see p216)* and offices.

PS10 Solar Power Plant
Opened in 2007 near Seville, this is Europe's first commercially operating power station.

Where to See Modern Andalucía

Some of the most striking buildings of modern Andalucía were built in the 1990s. Expo '92 left Seville with five new bridges over the Guadalquivir river, while at Cartuja '93 *(see p108)* Expo's core pavilions still stand and now serve as offices while other buildings are used for events. The Teatro de la Maestranza *(pp72–3)*, in El Arenal, was also built during this period.

Pabellón de Navegación at La Cartuja has a museum about the history of maritime navigation and hosts temporary exhibitions

An elevated plaza frequently hosts cultural events under the shade of the canopy.

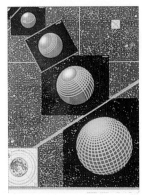

Expo '92
Hosted by Seville, Expo '92 placed Andalucía at the centre of a world stage. Some 41 million people visited over the 6 months it was open.

Felipe González
In 1982, the year after an attempted coup by the Civil Guard colonel Antonio Tejero, Felipe González, leader of the socialist PSOE, claimed a huge electoral victory.

2004 Spanish Socialist Workers' Party wins the general elections

1982 Andalucía becomes an autonomous region

1985 Spain-Gibraltar border opens

1996 In the general election González loses to a coalition led by Aznar

2006 Seville FC are the UEFA Cup champions

2010 Spain wins the FIFA World Cup

2013 Spanish unemployment reaches a record high; youth unemployment stands at 50 per cent

1990	2000	2010	2020

1981 Colonel Tejero attempts coup and holds Spanish parliament hostage; Juan Carlos intervenes

Colonel Tejero

2006 In March, the Basque terrorist organization ETA announces a permanent ceasefire

2007 Madrid to Málaga high-speed AVE train line opens

2014 King Juan Carlos abdicates the throne to his son, Felipe VI

2011 Mariano Rajoy is elected Prime Minister of Spain

2009 Andalucía's first subway system opens in Seville

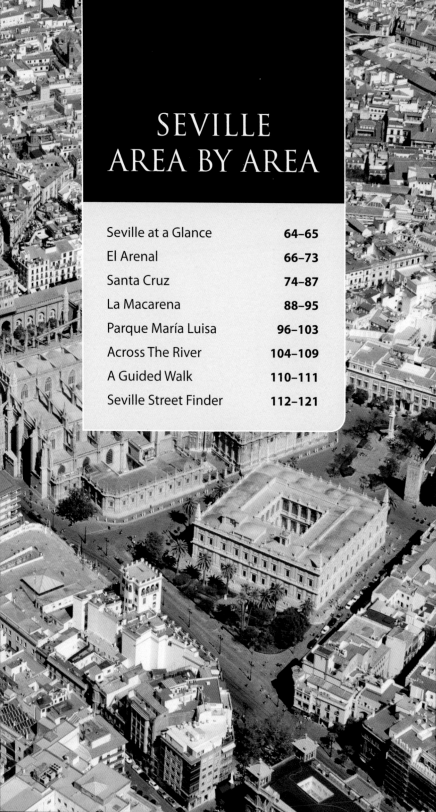

SEVILLE
AREA BY AREA

Seville at a Glance	**64–65**
El Arenal	**66–73**
Santa Cruz	**74–87**
La Macarena	**88–95**
Parque María Luisa	**96–103**
Across The River	**104–109**
A Guided Walk	**110–111**
Seville Street Finder	**112–121**

Seville at a Glance

The capital of Andalucía is a compact and relaxing city with a rich cultural heritage. Conveniently, many of its principal sights can be found within or very near the city centre, which is set on the east bank of the Río Guadalquivir. Most visitors head straight for the cathedral and La Giralda, Real Alcázar and Museo de Bellas Artes. Among other highly popular monuments are the exquisite Renaissance palace of Casa de Pilatos and Seville's bullring, the Plaza de Toros de la Maestranza. There are, however, many other churches, monuments and neighbourhoods to discover in the four central areas described in this section, and more, further afield, across the river.

The splendid ceiling of Museo de Bellas Artes *(see pp70–71)*

El Arenal
Pages 66–73

La Giralda rising above the massive Gothic cathedral *(see pp82–3)*

Plaza de Toros de la Maestranza seen from the river *(see p72)*

The Moorish Torre del Oro, built to defend Seville *(see p73)*

◀ Aerial view of Santa Cruz area, with La Giralda, Real Alcázar and Archivo de Indias in foreground

One of many elaborate floats in the Basílica de la Macarena, during Easter Week in Seville *(see p93)*

La Macarena
Pages 88–95

The impressive wooden structure of the Metropol Parasol, located in Plaza de la Encarnación, acts as a grand gateway to La Macarena *(see p89)*

Santa Cruz
Pages 74–87

Roman relief of Leda and the Swan, Casa de Pilatos *(see p81)*

Sumptuous Mudéjar arches and decor in Salón de Embajadores, Real Alcázar *(see pp86–7)*

Parque María Luisa
Pages 96–103

Plaza de España in the green oasis of Parque María Luisa *(see pp102–3)*

Patio of Real Fábrica de Tabacos, today the Universidad *(see p100)*

EL ARENAL

Bounded by the Río Guadalquivir and guarded by the mighty 13th-century Torre del Oro, El Arenal used to be a district of munitions stores and shipyards. Today, this quarter is dominated by the dazzling white bullring, the Plaza de Toros de la Maestranza, where the Sevillians have been staging *corridas* for more than two centuries. The many classic bars and wine cellars in the neighbouring streets are especially busy during the summer bullfighting season.

Once central to the city's life, the influence of the Guadalquivir declined as it silted up during the 17th century. By then, El Arenal had become a notorious underworld haunt clinging to the city walls. After being converted into a canal in the early 20th century, the river was restored to its former navigable

glory just in time for Expo '92. The east riverfront was transformed into a tree-lined, shady promenade with excellent views of Triana and La Cartuja across the river *(see pp106–9)*. Boat trips and sightseeing tours depart from the Torre del Oro. Close by is the smart Teatro de la Maestranza, where opera, classical music and dance take place before discerning audiences.

The Hospital de la Caridad testifies to the city's continuing love affair with the Baroque. Its church is filled with famous paintings by Murillo, and the story of the Seville School is told with pride in the immaculately restored Museo de Bellas Artes further north. The city's stunning collection of great works by Zurbarán, Murillo and Valdés Leal is reason enough to visit Seville.

Sights at a Glance

Historic Buildings

❸ Plaza de Toros
   de la Maestranza

❺ Hospital de la
   Caridad

❻ Torre del Oro

Museums

❶ *Museo de Bellas Artes*
   pp70–71

Churches

❷ Iglesia de la Magdalena

Theatres

❹ Teatro de la Maestranza

☐ **Restaurants** *p228*

1 El Aguador de Velazquez
2 Bodeguita Casablanca
3 La Brunilda Tapas
4 El Burladero
5 Enrique Becerra
6 Petit Comité
7 Taberna del Alabardero

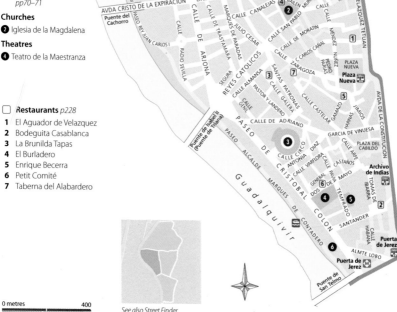

0 metres   400
0 yards   400

See also Street Finder maps 1, 3, 5

◀ The striking Baroque domed ceiling of the Museo de Bellas Artes

For keys to symbols *see back flap*

Street-by-Street: El Arenal

Once home to the port of Seville from where ships sailed to the New World in the 16th century, El Arenal also housed the artillery headquarters and ammunition works. These days it is a well-heeled area and a popular desination for bars and restaurants. It is home to Seville's bullring, the Plaza de Toros de la Maestranza and the modern Maestranza theatre. The riverfront is dominated by one of Seville's best-known monuments, the Moorish Torre del Oro, while the long, tree-lined promenade beside Paseo de Cristóbal Colón is the perfect setting for a romantic walk along the Guadalquivir.

❸ ★ Plaza de Toros de la Maestranza
Seville's 18th-century bullring, one of Spain's oldest, has a Baroque façade in white and ochre.

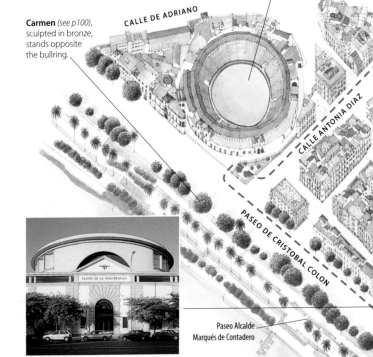

Carmen (see p100), sculpted in bronze, stands opposite the bullring.

CALLE DE ADRIANO

CALLE ANTONIA DIAZ

PASEO DE CRISTOBAL COLON

Paseo Alcalde
Marqués de Contadero

❹ Teatro de la Maestranza
This showpiece theatre and opera house opened in 1991. Home of the Orquesta Sinfónica de Sevilla, it also hosts international opera and dance companies.

0 metres   75
0 yards   75

The Guadalquivir
The river used to cause catastrophic inundations. After floods in 1947, a barrage was constructed. Today, peaceful boat trips start from the Torre del Oro.

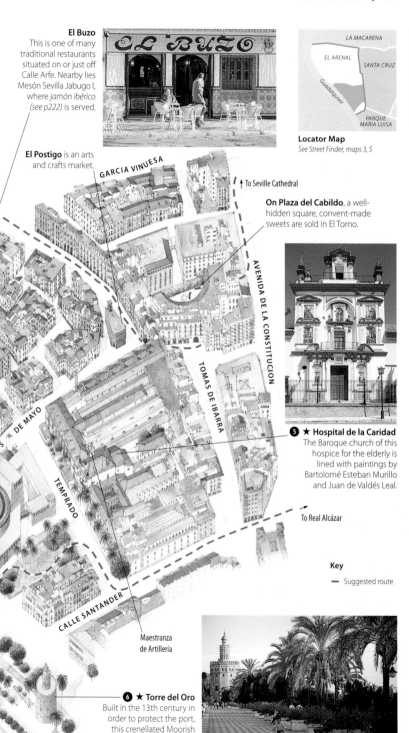

El Buzo
This is one of many traditional restaurants situated on or just off Calle Arfe. Nearby lies Mesón Sevilla Jabugo I, where *jamón ibérico* (see p222) is served.

Locator Map
See Street Finder, maps 3, 5

El Postigo is an arts and crafts market.

GARCIA VINUESA

↑ To Seville Cathedral

On Plaza del Cabildo, a well-hidden square, convent-made sweets are sold in El Torno.

AVENIDA DE LA CONSTITUCION

TOMAS DE IBARRA

5 ★ Hospital de la Caridad
The Baroque church of this hospice for the elderly is lined with paintings by Bartolomé Esteban Murillo and Juan de Valdés Leal.

S DE MAYO

TEMPRADO

→ To Real Alcázar

Key
— Suggested route

CALLE SANTANDER

Maestranza de Artillería

6 ★ Torre del Oro
Built in the 13th century in order to protect the port, this crenellated Moorish tower now houses a small maritime museum.

❶ Museo de Bellas Artes

The former Convento de la Merced Calzada has been restored to create one of the finest art museums in Spain. The convent, which was completed in 1612 by Juan de Oviedo, is built around three patios, which today are adorned with flowers, trees and *azulejos (see p80)*. The museum's impressive collection of Spanish art and sculpture extends from the medieval to the modern, focusing on the work of Seville School artists such as Bartolomé Esteban Murillo, Juan de Valdés Leal and Francisco de Zurbarán.

for disabled

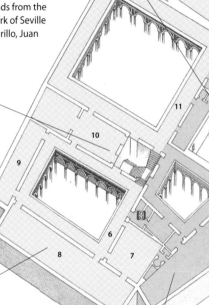

First floor

The Claustro de los Bojes is enclosed by Tuscan-style arches.

★ San Hugo en el Refectorio (1655)
One of several works by Zurbarán for the monastery at La Cartuja *(see p109)*, this scene depicts the Carthusian Order of monks first renouncing the eating of meat.

Gallery Guide

Signs provide a self-guided chronological tour through the museum's 14 galleries, starting by the Claustro del Aljibe. Works downstairs progress from the 14th century through to Baroque; those upstairs from the Baroque to the early 20th century.

La Inmaculada
This stirring *Inmaculada* (1672), by Valdés Leal (1622–90) is in Sala 8, a gallery devoted to the artist's forceful religious paintings.

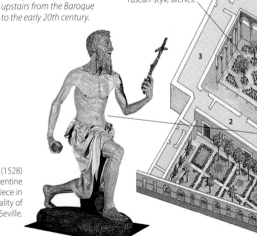

★ San Jerónimo (1528)
Sculpted by the Florentine Torrigiano, this masterpiece in terracotta brought the vitality of the Italian Renaissance to Seville.

★ La Virgen de la Servilleta
This Virgin and Child (1665–8), painted on a napkin (*servilleta*), is one of Murillo's most popular works.

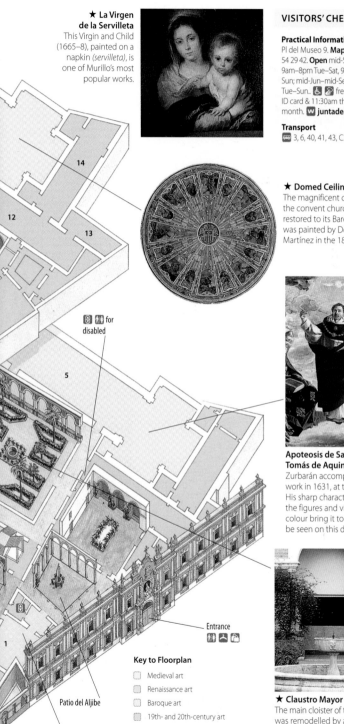

VISITORS' CHECKLIST

Practical Information
Pl del Museo 9. **Map** 5 B2. **Tel** 955 54 29 42. **Open** mid-Sep–mid-Jun: 9am–8pm Tue–Sat, 9am–3pm Sun; mid-Jun–mid-Sep: 9am–3pm Tue–Sun.. free with EU ID card & 11:30am third Wed of month. **juntadeandalucia.es**

Transport
3, 6, 40, 41, 43, C3, C4, C5.

★ Domed Ceiling
The magnificent ceiling of the convent church, now restored to its Baroque glory, was painted by Domingo Martínez in the 18th century.

for disabled

5

Apoteosis de Santo Tomás de Aquino
Zurbarán accomplished this work in 1631, at the age of 33. His sharp characterization of the figures and vivid use of colour bring it to life, as can be seen on this detail.

Entrance

1

Patio del Aljibe

Ground floor

Key to Floorplan
- ☐ Medieval art
- ☐ Renaissance art
- ☐ Baroque art
- ☐ 19th- and 20th-century art
- ☐ Non-exhibition space

★ Claustro Mayor
The main cloister of the monastery was remodelled by architect Leonardo de Figueroa in 1724.

For hotels and restaurants in this area see p216 and p228

Madonna and Child in the Baroque
Iglesia de la Magdalena

❷ Iglesia de la Magdalena

Calle San Pablo 10. **Map** 3 B1 (5 B3). 🚇
Plaza Nueva. 🚌 40, 41, 43, C5. **Tel** 954
22 96 03. **Open** 7:45am–11am Mon &
Fri, 7:45am–1:30pm Tue–Thu & Sat,
8:45am–2pm Sun; winter: 6:30pm–
9pm Mon–Fri; summer: 7:30pm–
9:45pm Sun. 🕍 8am, 9am, 10am,
10:30am, 8:15pm Mon–Sat; 9am,
10:30am, noon, 8:15pm Sun.
🅦 rpmagdalena.org

This immense Baroque church
by Leonardo de Figueroa,
completed in 1709, has been
restored to its former glory. In its
southwest corner is the Capilla
de la Quinta Angustia, a Mudéjar
chapel with three cupolas,
which survived from an earlier
church where the great Spanish
painter Bartolomé Murillo *(see
pp70–71)* was baptized in 1618.
The font used for his baptism
stands in the baptistry. The west

front is surmounted by a belfry
painted in vivid colours.

Among the religious works
in the church are a painting by
Francisco de Zurbarán,
St Dominic in Soria, in the Capilla
Sacramental (to the right of the
south door), and frescoes by
Lucas Valdés above the sanctuary
depicting *The Allegory of the
Triumph of Faith*. On the wall of
the north transept is a cautionary
fresco, which depicts a medieval
auto-da-fé (trial of faith).

❸ Plaza de Toros de la Maestranza

Paseo de Colón 12. **Map** 3 B2 (5 B4).
🚇 Puerta de Jerez. 🚇 Archivo de
Indias. 🚌 3, 21, 40, 41, C3, C4, C5.
Tel 954 21 03 15. **Open** 9:30am–7pm
daily (to 9pm Apr–Oct); 9:30am–3pm
on bullfight days. 🎫 🅴
🅦 realmaestranza.com

Seville's famous bullring is
arguably the finest in the whole
of Spain and hosts *corridas*,
or bullfights *(see pp30–31)*.
Although the art of the matador
(bullfighter) is a controversial
subject for many, the sunlit
stage, with its whitewashed
walls, red fences and merciless
circle of sand, remains important
to the city's psyche. Even if you
dislike the idea of bullfighting,
this arcaded arena, dating from
1761 to 1881, is an aesthetic
marvel and worth a visit.

Guided tours start from the
main entrance on Paseo de
Colón. On the west side is the
Puerta del Príncipe (Prince's
Gate), through which the very
best of the matadors are carried

triumphant on the shoulders
of admirers from the crowd.
Passing the *enfermería* (emergency hospital), visitors reach
a museum which details the
history of the bullfight in Seville.
Among its large collection of
costumes, portraits and posters
are scenes showing early
contests held in the Plaza de San
Francisco. The tour continues to
the chapel where matadors pray
for success, and then on to the
stables where the horses of the
picadores (lance-carrying
horsemen) are kept.

Bullfighting season starts on
Easter Sunday and continues
intermittently until October.
Most *corridas* are held on
Sunday evenings. The bullring
accommodates as many as
12,500 spectators.

Entrance with 19th-century ironwork,
Teatro de la Maestranza

❹ Teatro de la Maestranza

Paseo de Colón 22. **Map** 3 B2 (5 C5).
🚇 Puerta de Jerez. 🚇 Puerta de
Jerez. 🚌 3, 21, 40, 41, C4, C5.
Tel 954 22 33 44 (information).
Open for performances. 🎫 🅴
🅦 teatrodelamaestranza.es

Close to the Plaza de Toros, and
with echoes of its circular bulk,
is Seville's 1,800-seat opera
house and theatre. It opened
in 1991 and many international
opera companies perform here
(see p245). Like many of the
edifices built in the run-up to
Expo '92 *(see pp60–61)*, it was
designed in a rather austere

Arcaded arena of the Plaza de Toros de la Maestranza, begun in 1761

Finis Gloriae Mundi by Juan de Valdés Leal in the Hospital de la Caridad

style by architects Luis Marín de Terán and Aurelio del Pozo. Ironwork remnants of the 19th-century ammunition works that first occupied the site decorate the river façade. Tickets are sold from the box office in the adjacent Jardín de la Caridad.

❺ Hospital de la Caridad

Calle Temprado 3. **Map** 3 B2 (5 C5).
🚇 Puerta de Jerez. 🚌 Puerta de Jerez. 🚌 3, 21, 40, 41, C4, C5. **Tel** 954 22 32 32. **Open** 9am–1:30pm, 3:30–7:30pm daily. 🎟

Founded in 1674, this charity hospital is still used today as a sanctuary for the elderly and the infirm. In the gardens opposite the entrance stands a statue of its benefactor, Miguel de Mañara. The complex was designed by Pedro Sánchez Falconete. The façade of the hospital church, with its whitewashed walls, terracotta stonework and framed *azulejos* (see p80) provides a glorious example of Sevillian Baroque.

Inside are two square patios adorned with plants, 18th-century Dutch *azulejos* and fountains with Italian statues depicting Charity and Mercy. At their northern end a passage to the right leads to another patio, where a 13th-century arch from the city's shipyards survives. A bust of Mañara stands amid rose bushes. Inside the church there are many original canvases by some of

the leading artists of the 17th century, despite the fact that some of its greatest artworks were looted by Marshal Soult at the time of the Napoleonic occupation of 1810 (see p57). Immediately above the entrance is the ghoulish *Finis Gloriae Mundi* (The End of the World's Glories) by Juan de Valdés Leal, while opposite hangs his morbid *In Ictu Oculi* (In the Blink of an Eye). Many of the other works are by Murillo, including *St John of God Carrying a Sick Man*, portraits of the Child Jesus, *St John the Baptist as a Boy* and *St Isabel of Hungary Curing the Lepers*. Looking south from the hospital's entrance you can

see the octagonal Torre de Plata (Tower of Silver) rising above Calle Santander. Like the Torre del Oro nearby, it dates from Moorish times and was built as part of the city defences.

❻ Torre del Oro

Paseo de Colón s/n. **Map** 3 B2 (5 C5).
🚇 Puerta de Jerez. 🚌 Puerta de Jerez. 🚌 3, 6, 21, 40, 41, C3, C4, C5. **Tel** 954 22 24 19. **Open** 9:30am–1:30pm Tue–Fri, 10:30am–6:45pm Sat & Sun. **Closed** Aug. 🎟 (free Tue).

In Moorish times the Tower of Gold formed part of the walled defences, linking up with the Real Alcázar (see pp86–7) and the rest of the city walls. It was built as a defensive lookout in 1220, when Seville was under the rule of the Almohads (see pp50–51), and had a companion tower on the opposite river bank. A mighty chain would be stretched between the two to prevent ships from sailing upriver. In 1760 the turret was added. The gold in the tower's name may refer to gilded *azulejos* that once clad its walls, or to New World treasures unloaded here. The tower has had many uses, but is now the Museo Marítimo, exhibiting maritime maps and antiques.

The Torre del Oro, built by the Almohads

Don Juan of Seville

Miguel de Mañara (1626–79), founder and subsequent benefactor of the Hospital de la Caridad, is frequently linked with Don Juan Tenorio. The amorous conquests of the legendary Sevillian seducer were first documented in 1630 in a play by Tirso de Molina. They have since inspired works by Mozart, Molière, Byron and Shaw. Mañara is thought to have led an equally dissolute life prior to his conversion to philanthropy – apparently this was prompted by a premonition of his own funeral which he experienced one drunken night.

The legendary Don Juan with two of his conquests

SANTA CRUZ

The Barrio de Santa Cruz, Seville's old Jewish quarter, is a warren of white alleys and patios that has long been the most picturesque corner of the city. Many of the best-known sights are grouped here: the cavernous Gothic cathedral with its landmark Giralda; the splendid Real Alcázar with the royal palaces and lush Jardines del Alcázar; and the Archivo de Indias, whose documents tell of Spain's exploration and conquest of the New World.

Spreading northeast from these great monuments is an enchanting maze of whitewashed streets. The artist Bartolomé Esteban Murillo lived here in the 17th century while his contemporary, Juan de Valdés Leal, decorated the Hospital de los Venerables with fine Baroque frescoes.

Further north, busy Calle Sierpes is one of Seville's favourite shopping streets. Its adjacent market squares, such as the charming Plaza del Salvador, provided backdrops for Cervantes' stories. Nearby, the ornate façades and interiors of the Ayuntamiento and the Casa de Pilatos, a gem of Andalucían architecture, testify to the great wealth and artistry that flowed into the city in the 16th century.

Sights at a Glance

Streets, Squares and Gardens

2 Calle Sierpes
8 Plaza Virgen de los Reyes
9 Plaza del Triunfo
13 Jardines de Murillo

Churches

4 Iglesia del Salvador
7 Seville Cathedral and La Giralda pp82–3

Historic Buildings

1 Palacio de Lebrija
3 Ayuntamiento
5 Museo del Baile Flamenco
6 Casa de Pilatos
10 Archivo de Indias
11 Real Alcázar pp86–7
12 Hospital de los Venerables

Restaurants pp228–9

1 Albarama
2 Becerrita
3 Casa Plácido
4 Casa Robles
5 Corral del Agua
6 Doña Elvira
7 Donaire Azabache
8 Hard Rock Café
9 Mama Bistro
10 El Modesto
11 Oriza
12 La Quinta Braseria
13 San Marco
14 El Traga
15 Vineria San Telmo

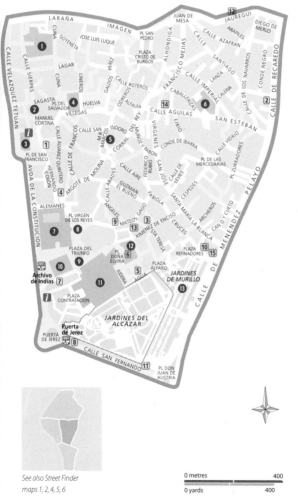

See also Street Finder maps 1, 2, 4, 5, 6

0 metres 400
0 yards 400

◀ Mudéjar tiles in the Patio de las Doncellas (Courtyard of the Maidens) at Real Alcázar

For keys to symbols *see back flap*

Street-by-Street: Santa Cruz

The maze of narrow streets to the east of Seville cathedral and the Real Alcázar represents Seville at its most romantic and compact. As well as the expected souvenir shops, tapas bars and strolling guitarists, there are plenty of picturesque alleys, hidden plazas and flower-decked patios to reward the casual wanderer. Once a Jewish ghetto, its restored buildings, with characteristic window grilles, are now a harmonious mix of up-market residences and tourist accommodation. Good bars and restaurants make the area well worth a visit.

❽ Plaza Virgen de los Reyes
Horse carriages line this plaza which has an early 20th-century fountain by José Lafita.

Palacio Arzobispal, the 18th-century Archbishop's Palace, is still used by Seville's clergy.

Convento de la Encarnación (see p84)

❼ ★ Seville Cathedral and La Giralda
This huge Gothic cathedral and its Moorish bell tower are Seville's most popular sights.

❿ Archivo de Indias
Built in the 16th century as a merchants' exchange, the Archive of the Indies now houses documents relating to the Spanish colonization of the Americas.

❾ Plaza del Triunfo
A Baroque column celebrates the city's survival of the great earthquake of 1755. Opposite is a modern statue of the Immaculate Conception.

For hotels and restaurants in this area see p216 and pp228–9

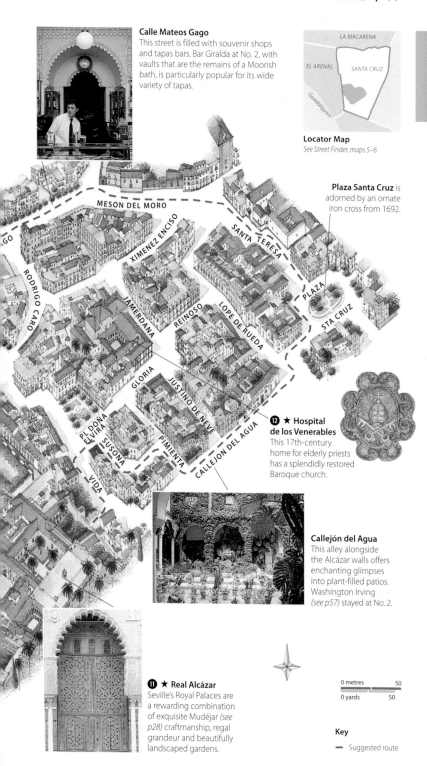

Calle Mateos Gago
This street is filled with souvenir shops and tapas bars. Bar Giralda at No. 2, with vaults that are the remains of a Moorish bath, is particularly popular for its wide variety of tapas.

Locator Map
See Street Finder, maps 5–6

LA MACARENA

EL ARENAL   SANTA CRUZ

Guadalquivir

Plaza Santa Cruz is adorned by an ornate iron cross from 1692.

MESON DEL MORO

XIMENEZ ENCISO

SANTA TERESA

RODRIGO CARO

JAMERDANA

REINOSO

LOPE DE RUEDA

PLAZA

STA CRUZ

GLORIA

JUSTINO DE NEVE

PL DOÑA ELVIRA

PIMIENTA

CALLEJÓN DEL AGUA

SUSONA

VIDA

⑫ ★ Hospital de los Venerables
This 17th-century home for elderly priests has a splendidly restored Baroque church.

Callejón del Agua
This alley alongside the Alcázar walls offers enchanting glimpses into plant-filled patios. Washington Irving *(see p57)* stayed at No. 2.

⑪ ★ Real Alcázar
Seville's Royal Palaces are a rewarding combination of exquisite Mudéjar *(see p28)* craftmanship, regal grandeur and beautifully landscaped gardens.

0 metres   50
0 yards   50

Key
— Suggested route

Roman mosaic, from Itálica,
in the Palacio de Lebrija

❶ Palacio de Lebrija

Calle Cuna 8. **Map** 3 C1 (6 D2). 🚌 27,
32. **Tel** 954 22 78 02. **Open** 10:30am–
7:30pm Mon–Fri, 10am–2pm &
4–6pm Sat, 10am–2pm Sun. 🖼 🎫
🌐 palaciodelebrija.com

The home of the family of the
Countess Lebrija since 1901,
this mansion illustrates palatial
life in Seville. The ground floor
houses Roman and medieval
exhibits. A guided tour of the
first floor features a library
and art, such as the Moorish
inspired *azulejos (see p80).*
    The house itself dates from
the 15th century and has some
Mudéjar *(see p28)* features,
including the arches around
the main patio. Many of its
Roman treasures were taken
from the ruins at Itálica *(see
p136)*, including the mosaic
floor in the main patio. The
artesonado ceiling above
the staircase came from the
palace of the Dukes of Arcos
in Marchena, near Seville.
Ancient roman glass ware,
coins and later examples

of marble from Medina Azahara
(see p142) are displayed in
rooms off the main patio.

❷ Calle Sierpes

Map 3 C1 (5 C3).

The street of the snakes,
running north from Plaza
de San Francisco, is Seville's
main pedestrianized shopping
promenade. Long-established
stores selling the Sevillian
essentials – hats, fans and
the traditional *mantillas* (lace
headdresses) – stand alongside
clothes boutiques, souvenir
shops, bargain basements
and lottery kiosks. The best
time to stroll along it is when
the *sevillanos* themselves do –
during the early evening *paseo.*
    The parallel streets of Cuna
and Tetuán on either side also
offer some enjoyable window-
shopping. Look out for the
splendid 1924 tiled advert for
Studebaker automobiles
(see p80) at Calle Tetuán 9.
    At the southern end of Calle
Sierpes, on the wall of the
Banco Central Hispano, a plaque
marks the site of the Cárcel Real
(Royal Prison), where the
famous Spanish writer Miguel
de Cervantes (1547–1616)
(see p55) was incarcerated.
Walking north from here, Calle
Jovellanos to the left leads
to the Capillita de San José.
This small, rather atmospheric
chapel, built in the 17th century,
contrasts sharply with its
commercial surroundings.
Further on, at the junction
with Calle Pedro Caravaca,
you can take a look back into

the anachronistic, upholstered
world of the Real Círculo de
Labradores, a private men's
club founded in 1856. Right at
the end of the street, take the
opportunity to peruse Seville's
best-known *pastelería* (cake
shop), La Campana.

Plateresque doorway, part of the façade
of Seville's Ayuntamiento

❸ Ayuntamiento

Plaza Nueva 1. **Map** 3 C1 (5 C3).
🚊 Plaza Nueva. **Tel** 955 47 12 32.
🎫 **Open** for tours only, 5 & 7:30pm
Mon–Thu.

Seville's city hall stands between
the historic Plaza de San
Francisco and the modern
expanse of Plaza Nueva.
    In the 15th–18th centuries,
Plaza de San Francisco was the
venue for autos-da-fé, public
trials of heretics held by the
Inquisition *(see p55)*. Those found
guilty would be taken to the
Quemadero and burnt alive.
(This site is now the Prado de
San Sebastián, north of Parque
María Luisa, *see pp102–3.*) These
days, Plaza de San Francisco is
the focus of activities in Semana
Santa and Corpus Christi
(see pp38–9).
    Plaza Nueva was once the
site of the Convento de San
Francisco. In its centre is an
equestrian statue of Fernando III,
who liberated Seville from the
Moors *(see p52)* and was
eventually canonized in 1671.
    The Ayuntamiento, begun in
1527, was finished in 1534. The
east side, looking on to Plaza de
San Francisco, is a fine example

Tables outside La Campana, Seville's most famous *pastelería*

of the ornate Plateresque style *(see p29)* favoured by the architect Diego de Riaño. The west front is part of a Neo-Classical extension built in 1891. It virtually envelops the original building, but richly sculpted ceilings survive in the vestibule and in the lower Casa Consistorial (Council Meeting Room). This room contains Velázquez's *Imposition of the Chasuble on St Ildefonso*, one of many artworks in the building. The upper Casa Consistorial has a dazzling gold coffered ceiling and paintings by Zurbarán and Valdés Leal.

❹ Iglesia del Salvador

Pl del Salvador. **Map** 3 C1 (6 D3). **Tel** 954 21 16 79. **Open** Sep–Jun: 11am–6pm Mon–Sat, 3–7:30pm Sun; Jul & Aug: 10am–5:30pm Mon–Sat, 3–7:30pm Sun. 🅰

This church has been completely restored. Its cathedral-like proportions result in part from the desire of Seville's Christian conquerors to outdo the Moors' architectural splendours. A mosque first occupied the site; part of the Moorish patio survives beside Calle Córdoba, boxed in by arcades incorporating columns embellished with Roman and Visigothic capitals.

By the 1670s the mosque, long since consecrated for Christian worship, had fallen into disrepair. Work started on a new Baroque structure, designed by Esteban García. The church was completed in 1712 by Leonardo de

Baroque façade of the Iglesia del Salvador on the Plaza del Salvador

Figueroa. Inside, the nave is by José Granados, architect of Granada cathedral *(see p194)*. In the Capilla Sacramental there is a fine statue, *Jesus of the Passion*, made in 1619 by Juan Martínez Montañés (1568–1649). In the northwest corner, a door leads to the ornate Capilla de los Desamparados and a Moorish patio. Over the exit on Calle Córdoba, the bell tower rests on part of the original minaret.

Adjacent to the church is the Plaza del Salvador, a meeting place for locals of all ages. The bronze statue commemorates the sculptor Montañés. On the east side of the church, the Plaza Jesús de la Pasión is given over to shops catering to weddings – the Iglesia del Salvador is a favourite among *sevillanos* for getting married.

❺ Museo del Baile Flamenco

Calle Manuel Rojas Marcos 3. **Map** 3 C1 (6 D3). **Tel** 954 34 03 11. **Open** 10am–7pm daily. 🅰 🅰 ⓦ **museoflamenco.com**

Although flamenco was supposedly born across the river, in Triana, the Barrio de Santa Cruz has become its de facto home in Seville. This museum of flamenco dance, occupying a restored 18th-century house on a small street between the Plaza del Alfalfa and the cathedral, is intended as an introduction of the art form to the visitor. As much as a space for exhibits in the traditional sense, it is also a venue for live performances of flamenco and a school offering regular classes in flamenco music and dance.

The Sign of Seville

The curious abbreviation "no8do" is emblazoned everywhere from the venerable walls of the Ayuntamiento to the sides of the municipal buses. It is traditionally said to stand for *"No me ha dejado"* ("She has not deserted me"). These words were reputedly uttered by Alfonso the Wise, after the city remained loyal to him in the course of a dispute with his son Sancho during the Reconquest *(see pp52–3)*. The double-loop symbol in the middle represents a skein of wool, the Spanish word for which is *madeja*, thus *no (madeja) do*.

The traditional emblem of Seville, here in stone on the Ayuntamiento

The Art of Azulejos

Cool in summer, durable and colourful, glazed ceramic tiles have been a striking feature of Andalucían façades and interiors for centuries. The techniques for making them were first introduced by the Moors – the word *azulejo* derives from the Arabic *az-zulayj* or "little stone". Moorish *azulejos* are elaborate mosaics made of unicoloured stones. In Seville the craft flourished and evolved in the potteries of Triana *(see pp106–7)*. A later process, developed in 16th-century Italy, allowed tiles to be painted in new designs and colours. The onset of the Industrial Revolution enabled *azulejos* to be mass-produced in ceramics factories including, until 1980, the famous "Pickman y Cia" at the monastery of La Cartuja *(see p109)*.

Mudéjar-Style Azulejos

The Moors created fantastic mosaics of tiles in sophisticated geometric patterns as decoration for their palace walls. The colours used were blue, green, black, white and ochre.

16th-century Mudéjar tiles, Casa de Pilatos

Interlacing motifs, Patio de las Doncellas

Mudéjar tiles in the Patio de las Doncellas, Real Alcázar

Sign for the Royal Tobacco Factory (now part of the Universidad, *see pp100–101*) made in painted glazed tiles in the 18th century

Azulejos for Commercial Use

As techniques for making and colouring *azulejos* improved, their use was extended from interior decor to decorative signs and shop façades. Even billboards were produced in multicoloured tiles. The eye-catching results can still be seen all over Andalucía.

Contemporary glazed ceramic beer tap

Azulejo billboard advertising the latest model of Studebaker Motor Cars (1924), situated on Calle Tetuán, off Calle Sierpes *(see p78)*

Genoan fountain and Gothic balustrades in the Mudéjar Patio Principal of the Casa de Pilatos

❻ Casa de Pilatos

Plaza de Pilatos 1. **Map** 4 D1 (6 E3).
Tel 954 22 52 98. **Open** 9am–6pm
daily (to 7pm Jul & Aug). 🎨 🎫 1st
floor. ♿ ground floor. 🌐 **fundacion
medinaceli.org**

In 1518 the first Marquess of
Tarifa departed on a Grand Tour
of Europe and the Holy Land.
He returned two years
later, enraptured by the
architectural and decorative
wonders of High Renais-
sance Italy. He spent the
rest of his life creating a
new aesthetic, which
was very influential. His
palace in Seville, called
the House of Pilate
because it was thought
to resemble Pontius
Pilate's home in
Jerusalem, became a
luxurious showcase
for the new style.

Over the centuries, subsequent
owners added their own embellishments. The Casa de Pilatos is
now the residence of the Dukes
of Medinaceli and is still one of
the finest palaces in Seville.

Visitors enter it through a
marble portal, commissioned
by the Marquess in 1529 from
Genoan craftsmen. Across the
arcaded Apeadero (carriage
yard) is the Patio Principal. This
courtyard is essentially Mudéjar
(see p28) in style with *azulejos*
and intricate plasterwork. It is

Lantern in the
entrance portal

surrounded by irregularly
spaced arches capped with
delicate Gothic balustrades. In
its corners stand three Roman
statues, Minerva, a dancing
muse and Ceres, and a Greek
fourth statue, a 5th-century BC
original of the goddess Athena.
In its centre is a fountain
imported from Genoa. To
the right, through the Salón
del Pretorio with its coffered
ceiling and marquetry, is the
Corredor de Zaquizamí.
Among the antiquities
in adjacent rooms are
a bas-relief of *Leda and
the Swan* and two
Roman reliefs com-
memorating the Battle
of Actium in BC 31.
Further along, in the
Jardín Chico there is
a pool with a bronze
of Bacchus.
Coming back to the Patio
Principal, you turn right into the
Salón de Descanso de los Jueces.
Beyond this is a rib-vaulted
chapel, which has a sculpture
dating from the 1st century AD,
Christ and the Good Shepherd.
Left through the Gabinete de
Pilatos, with its small central
fountain, is the Jardín Grande.
The Italian architect, Benvenuto
Tortello, created the loggias in
the 1560s.
Returning once more to the
main patio, behind the statue of
Ceres, a tiled staircase leads to

the apartments on the upper
floor. It is roofed with a
wonderful *media naranja* (half
orange) cupola built in 1537.
There are Mudéjar ceilings in
some rooms, which are filled
with family portraits, antiques
and furniture. Plasterwork by
Juan de Oviedo and frescoes
by Francisco de Pacheco still
survive in rooms, which bear
these artists' names.

West of the Casa de Pilatos,
the Plaza de San Ildefonso is
bounded by the Convento de
San Leandro, famous for the
yemas (sweets made from egg
yolks) sold from a *torno* (drum).
Opposite the convent is the
Neo-Classical Iglesia de San
Ildefonso, which has statues
of San Hermenegildo and San
Fernando by Pedro Roldán.

Escutcheons in the coffered
ceiling of the Salón del Pretorio

❼ Seville Cathedral and La Giralda

Seville's cathedral occupies the site of a great mosque built by the Almohads (*see pp50–51*) in the late 12th century. La Giralda, its bell tower, and the Patio de los Naranjos are a legacy of this Moorish structure. Work on the Christian cathedral, the largest in Europe, began in 1401 and took just over a century to complete. As well as enjoying its Gothic immensity and the works of art in its chapels and Treasury, visitors can climb La Giralda for superb views over the city, or enjoy views of the city from the cathedral rooftop (reservations necessary).

★ La Giralda
The bell tower is crowned by a bronze weathervane (*giraldillo*) depicting Faith, from which it takes its name. A replica has replaced the original vane.

The Rise of La Giralda

The minaret was finished in 1198. In the 14th century the original Muslim bronze spheres at its top were replaced by Christian symbols. In 1568 Hernán Ruiz added the Renaissance belfry, which blends perfectly with the Moorish base.

| 1198 | 1400 | 1557 (plan) | 1568 |

Group entrance

KEY

① **Roman pillars** brought from Itálica (*see p136*) surround the cathedral steps.

② **Puerta del Perdón**

③ **The Sacristía Mayor** houses many works of art, including paintings by Murillo.

④ **The Tomb of Columbus** dates from the 1890s. His coffin is carried by bearers representing the kingdoms of Castile, León, Aragón and Navarra.

⑤ **Puerta del Bautismo**

⑥ **Iglesia del Sagrario**, a large 17th-century chapel, is now used as a parish church.

★ Patio de los Naranjos
In Moorish times worshippers would wash hands and feet in the fountain under the orange trees before praying.

Retablo Mayor
Santa María de la Sede, the cathedral's patron saint, sits at the high altar below a waterfall of gold. The 44 gilded relief panels of the *retablo* were carved by Spanish and Flemish sculptors between 1482 and 1564.

VISITORS' CHECKLIST

Practical Information
Avenida de la Constitucion s/n.
Map 3 C2 (5 C4). **Tel** 954 56 57 43. **Open** Cathedral & La Giralda: 11am–3:30pm Mon, 11am–5pm Tue–Sat, 2:30–6pm Sun. 🎫 🎧 free audioguide Mon pm. ♿ 🛈 Cathedral: 8–10:30am (8–9am in summer); Capilla Real: 8am–2pm, 4–7pm. **W** **catedraldesevilla.es**

Transport
🚇 Archivo de Indias.
Ⓜ Puerta de Jerez.

Main entrance

Puerta de la Asunción
Though Gothic in style, this portal was not completed until 1833. A stone relief of the Assumption of the Virgin decorates the tympanum.

★ **Capilla Mayor**
The overwhelming, golden Retablo Mayor in the main chapel is enclosed by monumental iron grilles forged in 1518–32.

Baroque façade of the Palacio Arzobispal

❽ Plaza Virgen de los Reyes

Map 3 C2 (6 D4). Palacio Arzobispal:
Closed to the public. Convento de la
Encarnación: **Closed** to the public.

The perfect place to pause for
a while and admire the Giralda
(see p82), this historic plaza
presents an archetypal Sevillian
tableau: horse-drawn carriages,
orange trees, flower-sellers and
imposing religious buildings. At
its centre is an early 20th-century
monumental lamppost and
fountain by José Lafita, with
grotesque heads copied from
Roman originals in the Casa de
Pilatos *(see p81)*.

At the north of the square
is the Palacio Arzobispal or
the Archbishop's Palace, begun
in the 16th century, finished in
the 18th, and commandeered
by Marshal Soult, the commander
of the French troops, during the
Napoleonic occupation of 1810
(see pp56–7). A fine Baroque
palace, it has a jasper staircase
and paintings by Zurbarán
and Murillo.

On the opposite side of the
square is the whitewashed
Convento de la Encarnación,
which was founded in 1591.
The convent stands on grounds
that have also been the site of
a mosque and of a hospital.

The Plaza Virgen de los Reyes
was once home to the Corral
de los Olmos (Courtyard of the
Elms), a rogues' inn which
features in the writings of
Spain's greatest literary figure
Miguel de Cervantes *(see p55)* –
on one of the convent walls a
plaque bears an inscription
testifying to this.

❾ Plaza del Triunfo

Map 3 C2 (6 D4).

The beautiful Plaza del Triunfo
was built to celebrate the
triumph of the city over an
earthquake in 1755. It lies at the
centre of a group of UNESCO
World Heritage buildings – the
Seville Cathedral *(see pp82–3)*,
the Archivo de Indias and the
Real Alcázar *(see pp86–7)*. The
earthquake devastated the
city of Lisbon, over the border
in Portugal, but caused
comparatively little damage in
Seville – a salvation attributed
to the city's great devotion to
the Virgin Mary. She is honoured
by an impressive Baroque
column beside the Archivo de
Indias. In the centre of the Plaza
del Triunfo a monument
commemorates Seville's belief
in the Immaculate Conception.

In Calle Santo Tomás, off
the southeastern corner of the
Plaza del Triunfo, lies a building
used by the Archivo de Indias.
Formerly the Museo de Arte
Contemporáneo – now in the
Monasterio de Santa Mariá
de las Cuevas *(see p109)* – the
building is no longer open to
the public. Dating from 1770,
it was once a barn where tithes
collected by the Church were
stored. Parts of the Moorish city
walls were uncovered during
the renovation of the building.

❿ Archivo de Indias

Avda de la Constitución s/n.
Map 3 C2 (6 D5). 🖼 Archivo de
Indias. 🚇 Puerta de Jerez. **Tel** 954
50 05 28. **Open** 9:30am–5pm Mon–
Sat, 10am–2pm Sun.

The archive of the Indies
illustrates Seville's pre-eminent
role in the colonization and
exploitation of the New World.
Built between 1584 and 1598
to designs by Juan de Herrera,
co-architect of El Escorial near
Madrid, it was originally a *lonja*
(exchange), where merchants
traded. In 1785, Carlos III had
all Spanish documents relating
to the "Indies" collected under
one roof, creating a fascinating
archive. It contains letters from
Columbus, Cortés, Cervantes,
and George Washington, the

Façade of the Archivo de Indias by
Juan de Herrera

first American president, and the correspondence of Felipe II. The vast collection amounts to some 86 million handwritten pages and 8,000 maps and drawings. An extensive programme of document digitization is ongoing.

Visitors to the Archivo de Indias climb marble stairs to library rooms where drawings and maps are exhibited in a reverential atmosphere. Displays change on a regular basis; one might include a watercolour map from the days when the city of Acapulco was little more than a castle, drawings recording a royal *corrida* (bullfight) held in Panama City in 1748 or designs and plans for a town hall in Guatemala.

⓫ Real Alcázar

See pp86–7.

⓬ Hospital de los Venerables

Plaza de los Venerables 8. **Map** 3 C2 (6 D4). 🚇 Archivo de Indias. **Tel** 954 56 26 96. **Open** 10am–6pm daily. 🎟 except 2–6pm Tue & first Thu of each month. ♿ 📷

Located in the heart of the Barrio de Santa Cruz, the Hospital of the Venerables was founded as a home for elderly priests. It was begun in 1675 and completed around 20 years later by Leonardo de Figueroa. FOCUS (Fundación Fondo de Cultura) has restored it as a cultural centre.

It is built around a central, sunken patio. The upper floors, along with the infirmary and the cellar, are used as galleries for exhibitions. A separate guided tour visits the hospital church, a showcase of Baroque splendours, with frescoes by Juan de Valdés Leal and his son Lucas Valdés.

Other highlights include the sculptures of St Peter and St Ferdinand by Pedro Roldán, flanking the east door; and *The Apotheosis of St Ferdinand* by Lucas Valdés, top centre in the *retablo* of the main altar. Its frieze (inscribed in Greek) advises visitors to "Fear God and Honour the Priest". In the sacristy, the ceiling has an effective *trompe l'oeil* depicting *The Triumph of the Cross* by Juan de Valdés Leal.

⓭ Jardines de Murillo

Map 4 D2 (6 E5).

These formal gardens at the southern end of the Barrio de Santa Cruz once used to be orchards and vegetable plots in the grounds of the Real Alcázar. They were donated to the city in 1911. Their name commemorates Seville's best-known painter, Bartolomé Murillo (1617–82), who lived in nearby Calle Santa Teresa. A long promenade, Paseo de Catalina de Ribera, pays tribute to the founder of the Hospital de las Cinco Llagas, which is now the seat of the Parlamento de Andalucía *(see p93)*. Rising

Monument to Columbus in the Jardines de Murillo

above the garden's palm trees is a monument to Columbus, incorporating a bronze of the *Santa María*, the caravel that bore him to the New World in the year of 1492 *(see p131)*.

Fresco by Juan de Valdés Leal in the Hospital de los Venerables

⑪ Real Alcázar

In 1364 Pedro I *(see p52)* ordered the construction of a royal residence within the palaces built by the city's Almohad rulers *(see pp50–51)*. Within two years, craftsmen from Granada and Toledo had created a jewel box of Mudéjar patios and halls, the Palacio Pedro I, which now forms the heart of Seville's Real Alcázar. Later monarchs added their own distinguishing marks – Isabel I *(see p52)* despatched navigators to explore the New World from her Casa de la Contratación, while Carlos V *(see p54)* had grandiose, richly decorated apartments built.

Gardens of the Alcázar
Laid out with terraces, fountains and pavilions, these gardens provide a delightful refuge from the heat and bustle of Seville.

★ **Salones de Carlos V**
Vast tapestries and lively 16th-century *azulejos* decorate the vaulted halls of the apartments and chapel of Carlos V.

KEY

① **Patio del Crucero** lies above the old baths.

② **Jardín de Troya**

③ **Casa de la Contratación**

④ **The façade** of the Palacio Pedro I is a unique example of Mudéjar style.

⑤ **The Patio de la Montería** was where the court met before hunting expeditions.

★ **Patio de las Doncellas**
The Patio of the Maidens boasts plasterwork by the top craftsmen of Granada.

★ **Salón de Embajadores**
Built in 1427, the dazzling
dome of the Ambassadors'
Hall is made up of carved and
gilded interlaced wood.

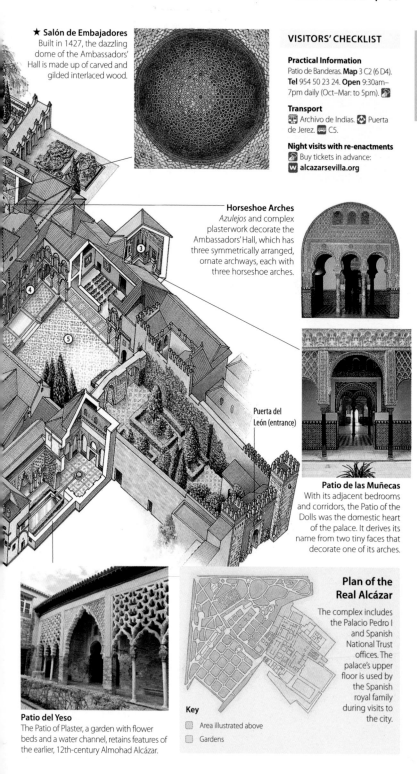

Horseshoe Arches
Azulejos and complex
plasterwork decorate the
Ambassadors' Hall, which has
three symmetrically arranged,
ornate archways, each with
three horseshoe arches.

**Puerta del
León (entrance)**

Patio de las Muñecas
With its adjacent bedrooms
and corridors, the Patio of the
Dolls was the domestic heart
of the palace. It derives its
name from two tiny faces that
decorate one of its arches.

Patio del Yeso
The Patio of Plaster, a garden with flower
beds and a water channel, retains features of
the earlier, 12th-century Almohad Alcázar.

Key
- Area illustrated above
- Gardens

Plan of the
Real Alcázar

The complex includes
the Palacio Pedro I
and Spanish
National Trust
offices. The
palace's upper
floor is used by
the Spanish
royal family
during visits to
the city.

LA MACARENA

The north of Seville, often overlooked by visitors, presents a characterful mix of Baroque and Mudéjar churches, old-style neighbourhood tapas bars and washing-filled back streets. Its name is thought to derive from the Roman goddess, Macaria, the daughter of the hero Hercules. La Macarena is a traditional district and the power of church and family is still strong there.

The futuristic Metropol Parasol, a buzzing urban space opened in 2011, makes for a surprising gateway into the area, otherwise best defined by the Basílica de la Macarena, an important shrine to Seville's venerated Virgen de la Esperanza Macarena. Beside this modern church stands a restored entrance gate and remnants of defensive walls, which enclosed the city during the Moorish era.

Among many churches and convents in this quarter, the Monasterio de San Clemente and Iglesia de San Pedro retain the spirit of historic Seville, while the Convento de Santa Paula offers a rare opportunity to peep behind the walls of a closed religious community. The 13th-century Torre de Don Fadrique in Convento de Santa Clara is a notable sight in the western part of the area. Further north is the former Hospital de las Cinco Llagas, now restored as the seat of Andalucía's Parliament.

Sights at a Glance

Churches and Convents
1 Monasterio de San Clemente
2 Torre de Don Fadrique
4 Basílica de la Macarena
9 Iglesia de San Marcos
10 Convento de Santa Paula
11 Iglesia de San Pedro
12 Iglesia de Santa Catalina

Boulevards
3 Alameda de Hércules

Historic Buildings
5 Cámara Oscura
6 Parlamento de Andalucía
8 Palacio de las Dueñas

Monuments
7 Murallas

Modern Architecture
13 Metropol Parasol

☐ **Restaurants** *p229*
1 Contenedor
2 Eslava

See also Street Finder maps 1, 2, 5, 6

◄ Revered weeping statue of the Virgen de la Esperanza Macarena, Basílica de la Macarena

Street-by-Street: La Macarena

A stroll in this area provides a glimpse of everyday life in a part of Seville that has so far avoided developing the rather tourist-oriented atmosphere that is a feature of Santa Cruz. Calle de la Feria, the main street for shopping and browsing, is best visited in the morning when there is plenty of activity and its market stalls are filled with fresh fish and vegetables. Early evening, meanwhile, is a good time to discover the district's large number of fine churches, which are open for Mass. It is also the time when local people visit the bars for a drink and tapas.

❽ Palacio de las Dueñas
Boxed in by the surrounding houses, this 15th-century Mudéjar palace has an elegant patio. It was the private residence of the Dukes of Alba, whose tiled coat of arms can be seen above the palace entrance.

Calle de la Feria
On Thursday mornings, El Jueves, Seville's oldest market, takes place on this street full of shops.

Iglesia San Juan de la Palma is a small Mudéjar church. Its brickwork belfry was added in 1788.

CALLE CASTELLAR

ESPIRITU SANTO

FERIA

DUEÑAS

CALLE GERONA

DOÑA MARIA CORONEL

JERONIMO HERNANDEZ

SOR ANGELA DE

CALLE REGINA

LA CRUZ

⓫ ★ Iglesia de San Pedro
The church where Velázquez was baptized is a mix of styles, from Mudéjar to these modern tiles decorating its front.

In Convento de Santa Inés the nuns make and sell cakes.

Key

— Suggested route

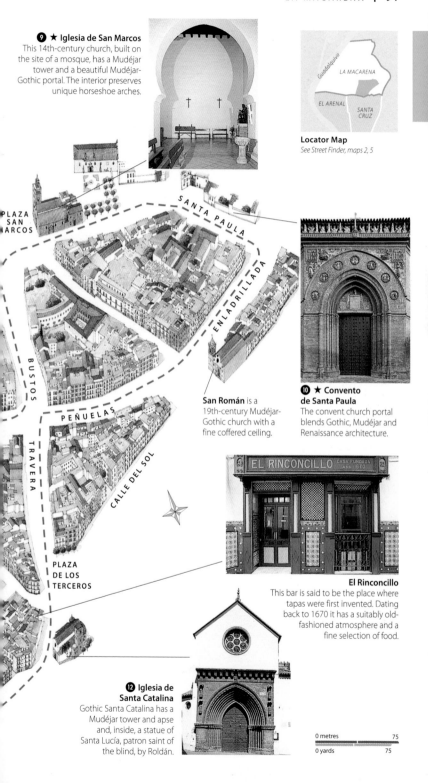

❾ ★ Iglesia de San Marcos
This 14th-century church, built on the site of a mosque, has a Mudéjar tower and a beautiful Mudéjar-Gothic portal. The interior preserves unique horseshoe arches.

Locator Map
See Street Finder, maps 2, 5

San Román is a 19th-century Mudéjar-Gothic church with a fine coffered ceiling.

❿ ★ Convento de Santa Paula
The convent church portal blends Gothic, Mudéjar and Renaissance architecture.

El Rinconcillo
This bar is said to be the place where tapas were first invented. Dating back to 1670 it has a suitably old-fashioned atmosphere and a fine selection of food.

⓬ Iglesia de Santa Catalina
Gothic Santa Catalina has a Mudéjar tower and apse and, inside, a statue of Santa Lucía, patron saint of the blind, by Roldán.

| 0 metres | 75 |
| 0 yards | 75 |

❶ Monasterio de San Clemente

Calle Reposo 9. **Map** 1 C3. 🚇 C3, C4.
Tel 954 37 80 40. Church **Open** for Mass
only: 7:55am, 8:30am, 6:15pm Mon–Sat
(6pm Thu); 7:30am, 10am, 6pm Sun &
public hols. 🔡 **sanclementesevilla.es**

Behind the ancient walls of the
Monasterio de San Clemente is
a tranquil cloister and an arcade
with a side entrance to the
monastery's church.

This atmospheric church can
also be entered through an arch
in Calle Reposo. Its features range
from the 13th to 18th centuries,
and include a fine Mudéjar
artesonado ceiling, *azulejos (see
p80)* dating from 1588, a Baroque
main *retablo* by Felipe de Rivas
and early 18th-century frescoes
by Lucas Valdés.

❷ Torre de Don Fadrique

Espacio de Santa Clara, Calle Becas s/n.
Map 1 C4. **Tel** 955 47 13 02. **Open**
9am–2pm, 5–9pm Tue–Sat; 11am–
3pm Sun. **Closed** first week of Sep.

One of the best-preserved
historical surprises in Seville,
this 13th-century tower stands
like a chess-piece castle in the

Torre de Don Fadrique in the patio of
Convento de Santa Clara

Marble columns at the southern end of Alameda de Hércules

Convento de Santa Clara. It
overlooks a tree-lined courtyard,
whose Gothic entrance was
built during the 16th century
as part of Seville's first university
and transplanted here in the
19th century.

Constructed in 1252, the tower
formed part of the defences for
the palace of the Infante Don
Fadrique. On the façade
Romanesque windows sit
below Gothic ones. More
than 80 steps lead to the
upper floor, from which
there are views across
the city towards La
Giralda and Puente
de la Barqueta.

The convent of
Santa Clara was
founded in 1260,
though the present
buildings date from the
15th century. The Mannerist
entrance portico is by Juan
de Oviedo. Inside, the nave
has a Mudéjar coffered ceiling
and a superb main *retablo*
sculpted by Juan Martínez
Montañés in 1623. The convent
has now been converted into a
cultural centre, which hosts
classical music concerts as well
as flamenco performances.

Gargoyle on the Torre
de Don Fadrique

❸ Alameda de Hércules

Map 2 D4.

This tree-lined boulevard was
originally laid out in 1574. The
former marshy area was thus
turned into a fashionable
promenade for use by *sevillanos*
of the Golden Age *(see pp54–5)*.
After the relocation of the
Sunday morning flea
market to Charco de la
Pava *(see p108)*, the
the Alamada was
redeveloped in
2006–8 and is now
a trendy, clean
promenade with a
bohemian charm.

At the southern end
stand two marble
columns brought here from a
Roman temple dedicated to
Hercules in what is now Calle
Mármoles (Marbles Street),
where three other columns
remain. Time-worn statues of
Hercules and Julius Caesar cap
the Alameda's columns.

One of the main centres of
night life in Seville, the Alameda
de Hércules has an eclectic mix
of bars, restaurants and cafés.

For hotels and restaurants in this area see p216 and p229

❹ Basílica de la Macarena

Calle Bécquer 1. **Map** 2 D3. 🚌 C1, C2, C3, C4. **Tel** 954 90 18 00. **Open** 9am–2pm, 5–9pm daily (from 9:30am Sun). Treasury: **Open** same times as the basílica. **Closed** Easter hols. 🅿

The Basílica de la Macarena was built in 1949 in the Neo-Baroque style by Gómez Millán as a new home for the much-loved Virgen de la Esperanza Macarena. It butts on the 13th-century Iglesia de San Gil, where the Virgin was housed until a fire in 1936.

The image of the Virgin stands above the main altar amid waterfalls of gold and silver. It has been attributed to Luisa Roldán (1656–1703). The wall-paintings by Rafael Rodríguez Hernández have themes focusing on the Virgin.

In the museum housed in the Treasury there are magnificent processional garments as well as gowns made from *trajes de luces* (suits of lights), donated no doubt by grateful bullfighters. The floats used in Semana Santa (see p42), among them La Macarena's elaborate silver platform, can also be admired.

❺ Cámara Oscura

C/ Resolana s/n. **Map** 2 D3. **Open** noon–5pm Tue–Sun (but closed when raining). **Tel** 679 09 10 73.

The camera obscura at the Tower of Perdigones has fantastic

Virgen de la Macarena

Devotions to the Virgen de la Macarena reach their peak during Semana Santa (see p42), when her statue is borne through the streets on a canopied float decorated with swathes of white flowers, candles and ornate silverwork. Accompanied by hooded penitents and cries of ¡guapa! (beautiful!) from her followers, the virgin travels along a route from the Basílica de la Macarena to the cathedral (see pp82–3) in the early hours of Good Friday.

Float of the Virgen de la Macarena in Semana Santa processions

views of the 1992 World Expo fairground, Cartuja Island and the Guadalquivir river. It projects real time images, with movement, by using mirrors and magnifying glasses over a periscope.

❻ Parlamento de Andalucía

C/ Parlamento de Andalucía s/n. **Map** 2 E3. **Open** By written application or call the protocol office. **Tel** 954 59 21 00. ♿ 📷 🅦 **parlamentodeandalucia.es**

The Parliament of Andalucía has its seat in an impressive Renaissance building, the Hospital de las Cinco Llagas (five wounds). The hospital, founded in 1500 by Catalina de Ribera, was originally sited near Casa de

Pilatos. In 1540 work began on the new site, on what was to become Europe's largest hospital. Designed by a succession of architects, its south front has a Baroque central portal by Asensio de Maeda.

The hospital was completed in 1613, and admitted patients until the 1960s. In 1992 it was restored for the Parliament.

At the heart of the complex, the Mannerist church, built by Hernán Ruiz the Younger in 1560, makes up the debating chamber.

❼ Murallas

Map 2 E3.

A section of the defensive walls that once enclosed Seville survives along calles Andueza and Muñoz León. It runs from the rebuilt Puerta de la Macarena at the Basílica de la Macarena (see p93) to the Puerta de Córdoba some 400 m (1,300 ft) further east.

Dating from the 12th century, it was constructed as a curtain wall with a patrol path in the middle. The original walls had over 100 towers; the Torre Blanca is one of seven that can be seen here. At the eastern end stands the 17th-century Iglesia de San Hermenegildo, named after the Visigothic king who was allegedly martyred on the site. On the southern corner of this church, remains of Moorish arches can be seen.

Renaissance façade and Baroque portal of Parlamento de Andalucía

The Gothic-Mudéjar patio of the 15th-century Palacio de las Dueñas

❽ Palacio de las Dueñas

Calle Dueñas 5. **Map** 2 D5 (6 E1).
Tel 954 21 48 28. **Open** Apr–Sep:
10am–7:15pm; Oct–Mar: 10am–
5:15pm. 🎨 except Mon after 4pm.

Built in Renaissance style with
Mudéjar and Gothic influences,
this pretty, late 15th-century
palace is the official residence
of the Dukes of Alba. After the
death of the Duchess of Alba in
2014, the ground floor of the
palace was opened to the public.
Considered one of the most
beautiful palaces in Seville, the
Palacio de las Dueñas has lovely
courtyards and gardens. Famous
Spanish poet Antonio Machado
(1875–1939) was born here, and
many of his verses highlight the
beauty and grandeur of this
extraordinary estate.
The palace is a treasure trove
of antiques and grand rooms
with elegant period furniture.
There are also displays of family
photos and personal letters. A
room is dedicated to the history
of the Feria de Abril (Seville
spring fair) *(see p42)*.

❾ Iglesia de San Marcos

Plaza de San Marcos. **Map** 2 E5 (6 E1).
Tel 954 50 26 16. **Open** 7–8:30pm (to
8pm in winter) Mon–Sat, 12:30pm Sun.
Mass: 8pm (winter), 8:30pm (summer)
Mon–Sun (also 12:30pm Sun).

This 14th-century church
retains several Mudéjar
features, notably its Giralda-
like tower (based on the
minaret of an earlier
mosque) and the
decoration on the Gothic
portal on Plaza de San
Marcos. The restoration
of the interior has
highlighted unique
horseshoe arches in the
nave. A statue of St Mark
with book and quill pen,
attributed to Juan de
Mesa, is in the far left corner. In
the plaza is the Convento de
Santa Isabel, founded in 1490. It
became a women's prison in the
19th century. The church dates
from 1609. Its Baroque portal,
facing onto Plaza de Santa
Isabel, has a bas-relief of *The
Visitation* by Andrés de Ocampo.

St John the Baptist by
Montañés in the Convento
de Santa Paula

❿ Convento de Santa Paula

C/ Santa Paula 11. **Map** 2 E5 (6 F1).
Tel 954 53 63 30. **Open** 10am–1pm
Tue–Sun. 🎨 🎨

Seville has many enclosed
religious complexes, but few are
accessible. This is one of them,
a convent set up in 1475 and
currently home to 27 nuns from
four continents. The public is
welcome to enter through two
different doors in the Calle Santa
Paula. Knock on the brown one,
marked No. 11, to have a look at
the convent museum. Steps
lead to two galleries crammed
with religious paintings and
artifacts. The windows of the
second door look onto the
nuns' cloister, which echoes
with laughter in the
afternoon recreation
hour. The nuns make
a phenomenal range
of marmalades and
jams, which visitors
may purchase in a
room near the exit.
Ring the bell by a
brick doorway nearby
to visit the convent
church, reached
by crossing a
meditative garden.
Its portal vividly
combines Gothic
arches, Mudéjar brickwork,
Renaissance medallions, and
ceramics by the Italian artist,
Nicola Pisano. Inside, the nave
has an elaborate wooden roof
carved in 1623. Among its
statues are St John the Evangelist
and St John the Baptist, carved
by Juan Martínez Montañés.

Sevillian Bell Towers

Bell towers rise above the rooftops of
Seville like bookmarks flagging the
passing centuries. The influence of La
Giralda *(see p82)* is seen in the Moorish
arches and tracery adorning the
14th-century tower of San Marcos, and
the Mudéjar brickwork which forms the
base for San Pedro's belfry. The churches
of Santa Paula and La Magdalena reflect
the ornate confidence of the Baroque
period, while the towers of San
Ildefonso illustrate the Neo-Classical
tastes of the 19th century.

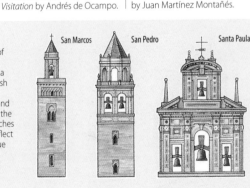

San Marcos   San Pedro   Santa Paula

For hotels and restaurants in this area see p216 and p229

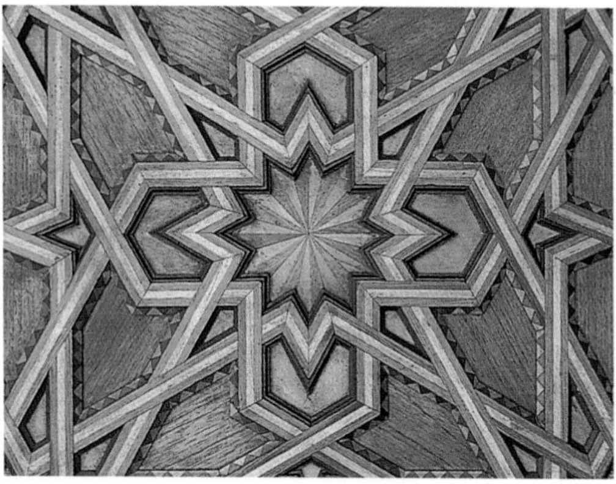

Intricate pattern on a chapel door in the Iglesia de San Pedro

⓫ Iglesia de San Pedro

Plaza San Pedro. **Map** 2 D5 (6 E2). **Tel** 954 21 68 58. **Open** 9am, 11am, 8pm Mon–Sat, 10am, 11am, noon, 1pm & 8pm Sun. ♿

The church where the painter Diego Velázquez was baptized in 1599 presents a typically Sevillian mix of architectural styles. Mudéjar elements survive in the lobed brickwork of its tower, which is surmounted by a Baroque belfry. The principal portal, facing Plaza de San Pedro, is another Baroque adornment added by Diego de Quesada in 1613. A statue of St Peter looks disdainfully down at the heathen traffic below.

The poorly lit interior has a Mudéjar wooden ceiling and west door. The vault of one of its chapels is decorated with exquisite geometric patterns formed of interlacing bricks. Behind the church, in Calle Doña María Coronel, cakes and biscuits are sold from a revolving drum in the wall of the Convento de Santa Inés. An arcaded patio fronts its restored church, with frescoes by Francisco de Herrera and a nun's choir separated from the public by a screen. The preserved body of Doña María Coronel, the convent's 14th-century founder, is honoured in the choir every 2 December.

⓬ Iglesia de Santa Catalina

Plaza Ponce de Léon. **Map** 2 D5 (6 E2). **Tel** 954 21 74 41. **Closed** for restoration; end date not known.

Built on the former site of a mosque, this 14th-century church has a Mudéjar tower modelled on La Giralda *(see p82)*, best viewed from Plaza Ponce de Léon, which has been spared the customary Baroque hat. On the west side, by Calle Alhóndiga, the Gothic portal is originally from the Iglesia de Santa Lucía, which was knocked down in 1930. Within its entrance is a horseshoe arch. At the far left end of the nave, the Capilla Sacramental is by Leonardo de Figueroa. On the right, the Capilla de la Exaltación has a decorative ceiling, circa 1400, and a figure of Christ by Pedro Roldán.

⓭ Metropol Parasol

Plaza de la Encarnación. **Map** 2 D5 (6 D2). **Tel** 95 547 15 80 (Museum), 954 56 15 12 (Observation decks & skywalks). **Open** Observation decks & skywalks: 10am–11pm Sun–Thu, 10am–11:30pm Fri & Sat. Antiquarium: 10am–7:30pm Tue–Sat, 10am–1:30pm Sun & public hols. **W** **setasdesevilla.com**

This ultra-modern structure, commonly referred to as "Las Setas" (The Mushrooms), is a striking contrast of modern architecture and astounding archeaological finds: the Observation Deck provides a soaring view of the city, with skywalks circling around the core of gastrobars, while the first floor has an open-air plaza, which hosts cultural events. The market buzzes with life on the ground floor, and the Antiquarium museum, housed in the basement, showcases the archeaological remains that were found when this project began in 1973, with extensive Roman ruins from the Tiberius era (c 14 AD–37 AD), and a Moorish house from the 12th and 13th centuries.

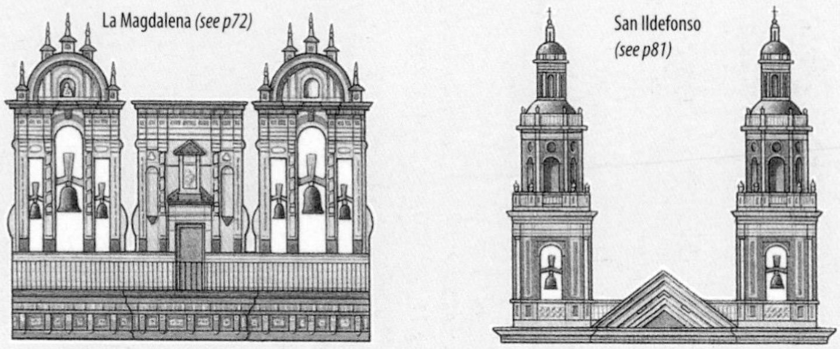
La Magdalena *(see p72)*
San Ildefonso *(see p81)*

PARQUE MARÍA LUISA

The area south of the city centre is dominated by the extensive, leafy Parque María Luisa, Seville's principal green area. A large part of it originally formed the grounds of the Baroque Palacio de San Telmo, dating from 1682. Today the park is devoted to recreation; with its fountains, flower gardens and mature trees it provides a welcome place to relax during the long, hot summer months. Just north of the park lies Prado de San Sebastián, the former site of the *quemadero*, the platform where many victims of the Inquisition *(see p55)* were burnt to death. The last execution took place here in 1781.

Many of the historic buildings situated within the park were erected for the Ibero-American Exposition of 1929. This international jamboree sought to reinstate Spain and Andalucía on the world map. Exhibitions from Spain, Portugal and Latin America were displayed in attractive, purpose-built pavilions that are today used as museums, embassies, military headquarters and also cultural and educational institutions. The grand historic five-star Hotel Alfonso XIII and the crescent-shaped Plaza de España are the most striking legacies from this surge of Andalucían pride.

Nearby is the Royal Tobacco Factory, forever associated with the fictional gypsy heroine, Carmen, who toiled in its halls. Today it is part of the Universidad, Seville's university.

Sights at a Glance

Museums
- ❼ Museo de Artes y Costumbres Populares
- ❽ Museo Arqueológico

Theatres
- ❹ Teatro Lope de Vega

Gardens
- ❺ *Parque María Luisa pp102–3*

Historic Buildings
- ❶ Hotel Alfonso XIII
- ❷ Palacio de San Telmo
- ❸ Universidad
- ❻ Plaza de España

☐ **Restaurants** *p229*
1 San Fernando

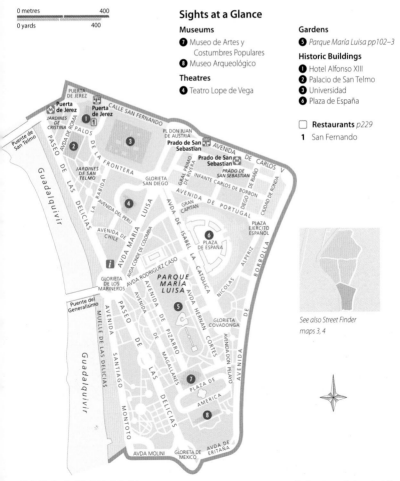

See also Street Finder maps 3, 4

◀ Striking façade of the Palacio de San Telmo

For keys to symbols *see back flap*

Street-by-Street: Around the Universidad

South of the Puerta de Jerez, a cluster of stately buildings stands between the river and Parque María Luisa. The oldest ones owe their existence to the Guadalquivir itself – the 17th-century Palacio de San Telmo was built as a training school for mariners, while the arrival of tobacco from the New World prompted the construction of the monumental Royal Tobacco Factory, today the Universidad de Sevilla. The 1929 Ibero-American Exposition added pavilions in various national and historic styles and also the opulent Hotel Alfonso XIII, creating an area of proud and pleasing architecture that will entertain visitors as they walk towards the Parque María Luisa.

Paseo de las Delicias
This riverside walk flanks the Jardines de San Telmo. Its name means the "walk of delights".

Pabellón de Chile is now the Escuela de Artes Aplicadas (School of Applied Arts).

Pabellón de Perú
Modelled on the Archbishop's Palace in Lima, this pavilion has a vividly carved façade. It is typical of the nationalistic designs used for the Exposition buildings.

Pabellón de Uruguay

To Triana

LAS DELICIAS

LA RABID

PASEO DE

GUADALQUIVIR

Costurero de la Reina
Today it serves as the municipal tourist office, but the "Queen's sewing box" used to be a garden lodge.

0 metres 75
0 yards 75

Key

— Suggested route

AVENIDA DE MARÍA LUISA

Monument to El Cano, who completed the first world circumnavigation in 1522 after Magellan was killed on route.

For hotels and restaurants in this area see p216 and p229

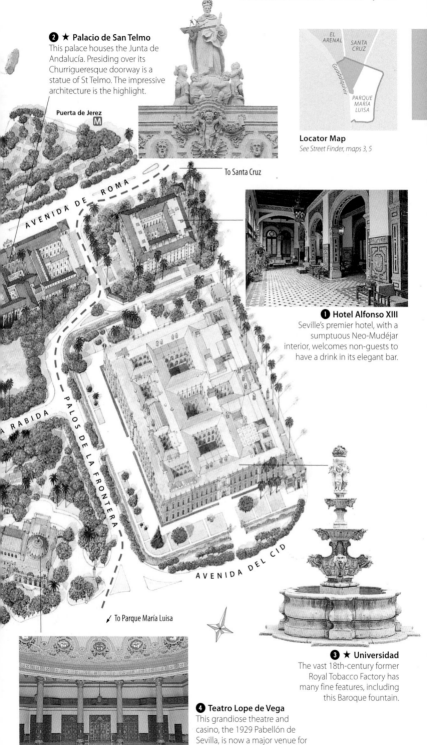

2 ★ **Palacio de San Telmo**
This palace houses the Junta de Andalucía. Presiding over its Churrigueresque doorway is a statue of St Telmo. The impressive architecture is the highlight.

Puerta de Jerez Ⓜ

Locator Map
See Street Finder, maps 3, 5

EL ARENAL
SANTA CRUZ
Guadalquivir
PARQUE MARÍA LUISA

To Santa Cruz

AVENIDA DE ROMA

A RABIDA

PALOS DE LA FRONTERA

AVENIDA DEL CID

To Parque María Luisa

1 **Hotel Alfonso XIII**
Seville's premier hotel, with a sumptuous Neo-Mudéjar interior, welcomes non-guests to have a drink in its elegant bar.

3 ★ **Universidad**
The vast 18th-century former Royal Tobacco Factory has many fine features, including this Baroque fountain.

4 **Teatro Lope de Vega**
This grandiose theatre and casino, the 1929 Pabellón de Sevilla, is now a major venue for staging concerts and shows.

❶ Hotel Alfonso XIII

Calle San Fernando 2. **Map** 3 C3 (6 D5).
🚇 Puerta Jerez. 🚌 Puerta Jerez.
🚌 C5. **Tel** 954 91 70 00. 🚻
🌐 hotel-alfonsoxiii-sevilla.com

At the southeast corner of
Puerta de Jerez is Seville's
best-known luxury hotel,
named after King Alfonso XIII
who reigned 1902–31, when
Spain became a republic. It
was built between 1916 and
1928 for visitors to the 1929
Ibero-American Exposition (see
p59). The building is in Regio-
nalista style, decorated with
azulejos (see p80), wrought iron
and ornate brickwork. Its centrepiece is a grand colonnaded
patio with a fountain and
orange trees. Non-residents
are welcome to visit one of
the hotel's bars or restaurants.

Central patio with fountain in the elegant Hotel Alfonso XIII

Churrigueresque adornments of the portal
of Palacio de San Telmo

❷ Palacio de San Telmo

Avenida de Roma s/n. **Map** 3 C3.
🚇 Puerta Jerez. 🚌 Puerta de Jerez.
🚌 3, 5, 21, 37, 41, C3, C4, C5. **Tel** 955
00 10 10. **Open** Thu, Sat & Sun by
appointment only. 🖂 🚻 🎦
🌐 juntadeandalucia.es

This imposing palace was built
in 1682 to serve as a marine
university, training navigators
and high-ranking officers. It is
named after St Telmo, patron
saint of navigators. In 1849 the
palace became the residence
of the Dukes of Montpensier –
until 1893 its vast grounds
included what is now Seville's

glorious Parque María Luisa
(pp102–3). The palace became
a seminary in 1901, and today it
is the presidential headquarters
of the Junta de Andalucía (the
regional government).

Overlooking Avenida de
Roma is the palace's star feature,
the exuberant Churrigueresque
portal designed by architect
Antonio Matías de Figueroa, and
completed in 1734. Surrounding
the Ionic columns are allegorical
figures of the Arts and Sciences.
St Telmo can be seen holding
a ship and charts, flanked by
the sword-bearing St Ferdinand
and St Hermenegildo with
a cross.

The north façade, which
is on Avenida de Palos de la
Frontera, is crowned by a row of
sculptures of Sevillian celebrities.
These sculptures were added
in 1895 by Susillo. Among them
are representations of several
notable artists such as Murillo,
Montañés and Velázquez.

❸ Universidad

Calle San Fernando 4. **Map** 3 C3.
🚇 Puerta Jerez. 🚌 Puerta de Jerez.
🚌 5, 21, 34, C1, C2, C3, C4. **Tel** 954 55
11 23. **Open** 8am–8:30pm Mon–Sat.
🎦 11am Mon–Thu except in Aug
(free); 9:30am–12:30pm & 4–6pm Fri &
9:30am–12:30pm Sat (by appt).
🌐 us.es

The former Real Fábrica de
Tabacos (Royal Tobacco Factory)
is now part of Seville University.
It was a popular attraction for
19th-century travellers in search
of Romantic Spain. Three-quarters
of Europe's cigars were then
manufactured here, rolled on the
thighs of over 3,000 cigarreras
(female cigar-makers), who were
said "to be more impertinent
than chaste", as the writer Richard
Ford observed in his 1845
Handbook for Spain. The factory
complex is the largest building
in Spain after El Escorial in Madrid
and was built between 1728–
71. The moat and watchtowers

Carmen

The hot blooded cigarreras
working in Seville's Royal Tobacco
Factory inspired the French author,
Prosper Mérimée, to create his
famous gypsy heroine, Carmen.
The short story he wrote in 1845
tells the tragic tale of a sensual
and wild woman who turns her
affections from a soldier to a
bullfighter and is then murdered
by her spurned lover. Bizet based
his famous opera of 1875 on this
impassioned drama, which
established Carmen as an
incarnation of Spanish romance.

Carmen and Don José

show the importance given to protecting the king's lucrative tobacco monopoly. To the right of the main entrance is the former prison where workers caught smuggling tobacco were kept. To the left is the chapel, now used by university students.

The discovery of tobacco in the New World is celebrated in the principal portal, which has busts of Columbus *(see p131)* and Cortés. This part of the factory was once used as residential quarters – to either side of the vestibule lie patios with plants and ironwork. Ahead, the Clock Patio and Fountain Patio lead to the former working areas. The tobacco leaves were first dried on the roof, then shredded by donkey-powered mills below. Production now takes place in a factory on the other side of the river, by the Puente del Generalísimo.

Dome of the Neo-Baroque Teatro Lope de Vega, opened in 1929

❹ Teatro Lope de Vega

Avenida María Luisa s/n. **Map** 3 C3. 🚇 & 🚌 Prado de San Sebastian. 🚌 5, 21, 34, C1, C2, C3, C4. **Tel** 955 47 28 28 (ticket office). **Open** for performances only. 🚹
🌐 teatrolopedevega.org.

Lope de Vega (1562–1635), often called "the Spanish Shakespeare", wrote more than 1,500 plays. This Neo-Baroque theatre which honours him was opened in 1929 as a casino and theatre for the Ibero-American Exposition *(see p59)*. Its colonnaded and domed buildings are still used to stage performances and plays *(see pp244–5)*. Visitors to the Café del Casino can relax and enjoy a coffee amid its faded opulence.

❺ Parque María Luisa

See pp102–3.

❻ Plaza de España

Parque María Luisa. **Map** 4 D3 & D4

This impressive semicircular plaza was designed by architect Aníbal González as the centrepiece for the 1929 Ibero-American Exposition. A series of alcoves decorated with stunning tiles each represent a Spanish province and depict the history of Spain. The imposing Renaissance–Neo-Moorish building fronting the plaza, with its North and South towers, is a major city landmark. A canal follows the curve of the building's façade and is crossed by colourful footbridges.

❼ Museo de Artes y Costumbres Populares

Pabellón Mudéjar, Parque María Luisa. **Map** 4 D5. 🚌 1, 3, 6, 30, 31, 34, 37. **Tel** 955 54 29 51. **Open** 9am–7:30pm Tue–Sat, 9am–2:30pm Sun (Jun–mid-Sep: 9am–2:30pm Tue–Sun). 🚹 🚹

Housed in the Mudéjar Pavilion of the 1929 Ibero-American Exposition *(see p59)*, this museum is devoted to the popular arts and traditions of Andalucía. Exhibits in the basement include workshop scenes detailing crafts such as leatherwork, ceramics

and cooperage. There is also an informative account of the history of the *azulejo*. Upstairs is a display of 19th-century costumes, furniture, musical instruments and rural machinery. Romantic images of flamenco, bullfighting, and the Semana Santa and Feria de Abril *(see p42)* are a compendium of the Sevillian cliché.

❽ Museo Arqueológico

Plaza de América, Parque María Luisa. **Map** 4 D5. 🚌 1, 3, 6, 30, 31, 34, 37. **Tel** 955 12 06 32. **Open** 9am–7:30pm Tue–Sat, 9am–2:30pm Sun (Jun–mid-Sep: 9am–2:30pm Tue–Sun). 🚹 🚹

The Renaissance pavilion of the 1929 Ibero-American Exposition is now Andalucía's museum of archaeology. The basement houses Paleolithic to early-Roman exhibits, such as copies of the remarkable Tartessian Carambolo treasures *(see p47)*. This hoard of 6th-century BC gold jewellery was discovered near Seville in 1958.

Upstairs, the main galleries are devoted to the Roman era, with statues and fragments rescued from Itálica *(see p136)*. Highlights include a 3rd-century BC mosaic from Écija *(see p137)*, a statue of the Venus of Itálica and sculptures of local-born emperors Trajan and Hadrian. The rooms continue to Moorish Spain via Palaeo-Christian sarcophagi, Visigothic relics and artifacts from Medina Azahara *(see p142)*.

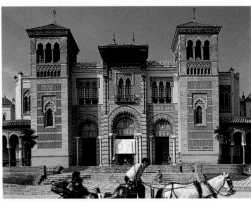

Museo de Artes y Costumbres Populares, the former Mudéjar Pavilion

5 Parque María Luisa

This vast park takes its name from Princess María Luisa de Orléans, who donated part of the grounds from the Palacio de San Telmo *(see p100)* to the city in 1893. The area was landscaped by Jean-Claude Forestier, director of the Bois de Boulogne in Paris, who created a leafy setting for the pastiche pavilions of the 1929 Ibero-American Exposition *(see p59)*. The most dazzling souvenirs from this extravaganza are the Plaza de España and Plaza de América, both the work of Anibal González, which set the park's theatrical mood. Sprinkling fountains, flowers and cool, tree-shaded avenues all go to make this park a refreshing retreat from the heat and dust of the city.

6 ★ Plaza de España
Tiled benches line this semicircular plaza, centrepiece of the 1929 Exposition.

KEY

① **Glorieta de la Infanta** has a bronze statue honouring the park's benefactress, the Princess María Luisa de Orléans.

② **Glorieta de Bécquer**, is a tribute to the Romantic Sevillian poet, Gustavo Adolfo Bécquer (1836–70). Allegorical figures, depicting the phases of love, add charm to this monument. It was sculpted by Lorenzo Coullaut Valera in 1911.

③ **Starting point for horse and carriage rides**

④ **Pabellón Real** (the Royal Pavilion)

⑤ **The Monte Gurugú** is a mini-mountain with a tumbling waterfall.

Isleta de los Patos
In the centre of the park is a lake graced by ducks and swans. A gazebo situated on an island provides a peaceful resting place.

Fuente de los Leones
Ceramic lions guard this octagonal fountain, which is surrounded by myrtle hedges. Its design was inspired by the fountain in the Patio de los Leones at the Alhambra *(see p199)*.

❽ ★ Museo Arqueológico
The Neo-Renaissance Pabellón de las Bellas Artes today houses a regional archaeological museum. Many finds from nearby Roman Itálica *(see p136)* are among the exhibits.

❼ ★ Museo de Artes y Costumbres Populares
The pavilions of Plaza de América evoke the triumph of the Mudéjar, Gothic and Renaissance styles. The Pabellón Mudéjar houses a museum of Andalucían folk arts.

Ceramics
Brightly painted Sevillian ceramics from Triana decorate the park in the form of floral urns, tiled benches and playful frogs and ducks placed around the fountains.

ACROSS THE RIVER

On the west bank of the Guadalquivir, old Seville meets the new. Since Roman times, pottery has been made in Triana, an area named after the emperor Trajan. It has traditionally been a working-class district, famous for the bullfighters and flamenco artistes that came from its predominantly Roma (gypsy) community. With cobbled streets and shops selling ceramics, it still has an authentic, lived-in feel. Iglesia de Santa Ana is a fine Mudéjar-Gothic church. From the riverside restaurants and bars along Calle Betis there are views of Seville's towers and belfries.

In the 15th century, a Carthusian monastery was built in what was then a quiet area north of Triana – hence the name that the district acquired: Isla de la Cartuja. Later Columbus resided here, planning his future exploits. Mainly due to this connection, La Cartuja was the site for Expo '92 *(see pp108–9)*. The monastery buildings were restored and several pavilions of strikingly modern design built. The majority of the pavilions now house offices; a branch of the University of Seville is also here. The Expo site has been redeveloped to include the Isla Mágica theme park *(see p108)*.

Sights at a Glance

Theme Parks
1 Isla Mágica
2 Cartuja '93

Markets
3 Charco de la Pava Flea Market

Traditional Areas
6 *Triana pp106–7*

Churches and Monasteries
4 Monasterio de Santa María de las Cuevas
7 Iglesia de Nuestra Señora de la O
8 Iglesia de Santa Ana

Modern Architecture
5 Torre Sevilla

Key
▢ Seville city centre
▢ Greater Seville
▬ Motorway
▬ Major road
▭ Minor road

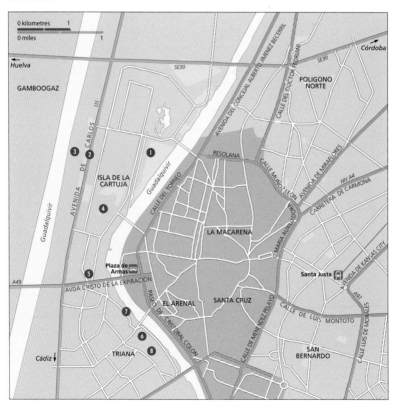

⬅ Looking towards Triana district and the bell tower of Iglesia de Santa Ann at sunset

For keys to symbols *see back flap*

❺ Triana

Named after the Roman emperor Trajan, this quarter has, since early times, been famous for its potteries. Plenty of workshops still produce and sell tiles and ceramics. Once Seville's gypsy quarter, this *barrio* also has a reputation for producing great bullfighters, sailors and flamenco artists. It remains a traditional working-class district, with compact, flower-filled streets and a tangibly independent atmosphere. Visitors to Triana can buy tiles and wander through its narrow streets during the day, and enjoy the lively bars and romantic views across the Río Guadalquivir at night.

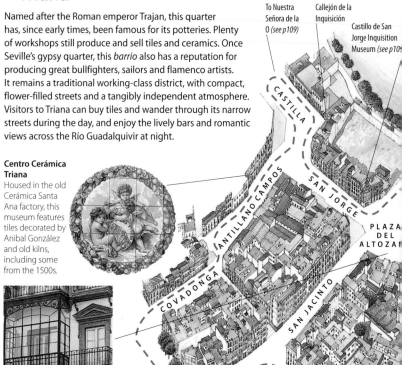

To Nuestra Señora de la O *(see p109)*

Callejón de la Inquisición

Castillo de San Jorge Inquisition Museum *(see p10)*

CASTILLA

SAN JORGE

PLAZA DEL ALTOZA

ANTILLANO CAMPOS

COVADONGA

SAN JACINTO

RODRIGO DE TRIANA

Centro Cerámica Triana
Housed in the old Cerámica Santa Ana factory, this museum features tiles decorated by Aníbal González and old kilns, including some from the 1500s.

Plaza del Altozano
At the west end of Puente de Isabel II, this plaza features glass-fronted, wrought-iron balconies called *miradores*.

Santa Justa and Santa Rufina as represented by Murillo (c.1665)

Santa Justa and Santa Rufina

Two Christians working in the Triana potteries in the 3rd century have become Seville's patron saints. The city's Roman rulers are said to have thrown the young women to the lions after they refused to join a procession venerating Venus. This martyrdom has inspired many works by Sevillian artists, including Murillo and Zurbarán *(see pp70–71)*. The saints are often shown with the Giralda, which, apparently, they protected from an earthquake in 1755.

Calle Rodrigo de Triana
This street in white and ochre is named after the Andalucían sailor who first caught sight of the New World on Columbus's epic voyage of 1492 *(see p131)*.

Puente de Isabel II, also known as Puente de Triana, leads to El Arenal.

Capillita del Carmen
A chapel, built by Aníbal González in 1926, stands at the west end of Puente de Isabel II, an iron bridge designed by Gustavo Steinacher and Fernando Bernadet in 1845.

Locator Map
See Street Finder, map 3

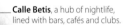

Calle Betis, a hub of nightlife, lined with bars, cafés and clubs.

Capilla de los Marineros, a sailors' chapel, was built between 1759 and 1815.

Calle Pelay Correa
Hung with flowers and often washing, these narrow streets evoke the close-knit flavour of old Triana.

Abades Triana, with its terrace overlooking the river, is renowned for its creative cuisine *(see p229)*.

❽ Iglesia de Santa Ana
Founded in the 13th century by Alfonso X, this is the oldest parish church in Seville. Triana's most popular place of worship, it has been splendidly restored.

Key

— Suggested route

0 metres 75
0 yards 75

❶ Isla Mágica

Pabellón de España, Isla de la Cartuja.
Map 1 B3. **Tel** 902 16 17 16. **Open**
times vary – see website for opening
hours (which change throughout the
year) as well as package deals (hotel
and park entry). 🅿 🆆 islamagica.es

Opened in 1997, the popular
Isla Mágica theme park
occupies part of the Isla de
la Cartuja site redeveloped
for Expo '92 (see pp60–61).
    The park recreates the exploits
of the explorers who set out
from Seville in the 16th century
on voyages of discovery to the
New World. The first of the seven
zones which visitors experience
is Seville, Port of the Indies,
followed by the Gateway to the
Americas, the World of the Maya,
the Pirate's Lair, El Dorado and
Agua Mágica. The Jaguar is the
most thrilling ride for visitors –
a rollercoaster hurtling at 85 km/h
(53 mph) along its looping
course, but head also for The
Anaconda, a flume ride, and The
Orinoco Rapids on which small
boats are buffeted in swirling
water. The Fountain of Youth is
designed for children, with
carousels and fighting pirates.
    For an additional fee, Agua
Mágica offers four zones of
water-based fun. Playa Quetzal
has a large swimming pool with
simulated waves and a beach;
Isla de Tobagones is a maze of
waterslides; Rio Lento features
a slow-moving river that visitors
can float down; and Mini Paraiso
has a pool and smaller slides

aimed at younger children.
Shows in the park include
street performances and dance
shows as well as IMAX cinema
screenings. Check the Isla Magica
website for up-to-date information on shows and times.

The Pabellón de Europa, built on Isla de
la Cartuja for Expo '92

❷ Cartuja '93

Paseo del Oeste (renamed Calle
Leonardo da Vinci). **Map** 1 A3.

This science and technology
park occupies the western side
of the Expo '92 site. Visitors can
walk along Calle Leonardo da
Vinci and the service roads for
close-up views of some of Expo
'92's most spectacular pavilions.
These buildings, however, now
part of the Andalucían World
Trade Centre, belong to public

and private companies and are
closed to visitors. Groups of
buildings south and east of the
Parque Alamillo are part of Seville
University, which has links with
Cartuja '93. To its south lie the
gardens surrounding the ancient
Monasterio de Santa María de las
Cuevas, now housing a contem-
porary art museum (see p109).

❸ Charco de la Pava Flea Market

Open Sun am.

Situated beyond the Olympic
Stadium, along the River
Guadalquivir, is the Charco de
La Pava flea market. The market
occupies a large open space on
the far side of the Cartuja and is
held on Sunday mornings. It is a
popular spot among locals and
tourists who come here for a
leisurely browse through the
bric-a-brac. Stretched out along
the ground are all manner of
goods for sale, from rusty farming
tools to brass ornaments,
paintings and old photographs.
The market was, for many years,
held at Alameda de Hércules
(see p92) in the Macarena area
in Northern Seville.
    Stop for lunch in the Torre
Sevilla, where there are
restaurants and bars, or enjoy a
relaxed meal while listening to
jazz at the Centro Andaluz de
Arte Contemporáneo cafeteria.

❹ Monasterio de Santa María de las Cuevas

Calle Americo Vespucio 2, Isla de la
Cartuja. **Map** 1 A4. **Tel** 955 03 70 70.
Monastery & Centro Andaluz de Arte
Contemporaneo: **Open** 11am–9pm
Tue–Sat, 11am–3:30pm Sun & public
hols. 🅿 (free Tue–Fri 7–9pm &
11am–9pm Sat). 🅴 🆉
🆆 museosdeandalucia.es

This huge complex, which was
built by the Carthusian monks
in the 15th century, is closely
tied to Seville's history. Columbus
stayed and worked here, and
even lay buried in the crypt of
the church, Capilla Santa

Reconstructed wooden ship at the Isla Mágica theme park

Main entrance of the Carthusian Monasterio de Santa María de las Cuevas, founded in 1400

Ana, from 1507 to 1542. The Carthusians lived here until 1836 and commissioned some of the finest works of the Seville School, including masterpieces by Zurbarán and Montañés – these are now housed in the Museo de Bellas Artes (see pp70–71).

In 1841 Charles Pickman, a British industrialist, built a ceramics factory on the site. After decades of successful business, production ceased in 1980 and the monastery was restored as a central exhibit for Expo '92. Also of interest are the Capilla de Afuera by the main gate, and the Casa Prioral, which has an exhibition of the restoration. There is a Mudéjar cloister, made of of marble and brick. The chapter house has a number of tombstones of rich patrons of the monastery.

The Centro Andaluz de Arte Contemporáneo features contemporary art exhibitions, as part of the Museo de Arte Contemporaneo. The centre's permanent collection is mostly by 20th-century Andalucían artists while its temporary exhibitions include paintings, photographs, installations and performance art by international artists. Past exhibitions have featured everything from sculpture to digital art.

❺ Torre Sevilla

C/ Gonzalo Jiménez de Quesada 2. 🚌 C1, C2, 6 & 43. 🅦 torre-sevilla.com

Located on the southern edge of La Cartuja, the Torre Sevilla presides over the Guadalquivir river and offers commanding panoramic views. Designed by Argentinian architect César Pelli, the 180-m- (590-ft-) tall tower opened in 2017 with 40 floors. The Eurostars Torre Sevilla five-star hotel occupies the top 12 storeys (see p216). The remaining floors are used as commercial office and retail space. Next to the complex is the CaixaForum Seville cultural and arts centre, and a shopping mall with more than 80 shops.

❻ Triana

See pp106–7.

The colourful belfry of Nuestra Señora de la O in Triana

❼ Iglesia de Nuestra Señora de la O

C/ Castilla. **Map** 3 A1. **Tel** 954 33 75 39. **Open** daily. Castillo de San Jorge Inquisition Museum: **Tel** 954 33 22 40. **Open** 9am–1:30pm Mon–Fri, 10am–2pm Sat, Sun & hols.

The Church of Our Lady of O, built in the late 17th century, has a belfry decorated with locally made azulejos. Inside, Baroque sculptures include a Virgin and Child with silver haloes, attributed to Duque Cornejo, in the far chapel to the left as you enter. On the other side of the high altar is a fine group by Pedro Roldán depicting St Anne, St Joachim and Mary, the Virgin; a Jesus of Nazareth bearing his cross in the main chapel is by the same sculptor. The church is in Calle de Castilla, whose name comes from the notorious castle in Triana where the Inquisition had its head-quarters from the 16th century. The castle houses a museum dedicated to the Inquisition.

❽ Iglesia de Santa Ana

Entrance at Calle Vázquez de Leca 1. **Map** 3 B2. **Tel** 954 27 08 85. **Open** 10:30am–1:30pm Mon, 11am–1:30pm Thu.

One of the first churches built in Seville after the Reconquest (see pp52–3), Santa Ana was founded in 1276 but has been much remodelled over the centuries. Today it is a focal point for the residents and cofradías (the religious brotherhoods) of Triana.

The vaulting of the nave is similar to Burgos cathedral's vaulting, suggesting that the same architect worked on the two churches. The west end of the nave has a 16th-century retablo, richly carved by Alejo Fernández. The sacramental chapel in the north wall has a Plateresque entrance.

In the baptistery is the Pila de los Gitanos, or Gypsy Font, which is believed to pass on the gift of flamenco song to the children of the faithful.

A 90-Minute Walk in Seville

This walk begins in one of the city's most elegant parks and explores one of its oldest *barrios* (neighbourhoods): the medieval Jewish quarter of Santa Cruz. The tiny alleys and squares of Santa Cruz conceal a museum to one of the city's great painters, Murillo, as well as a host of churches and many crafts galleries and restaurants. The walk then takes you through Seville's grandest square before heading for the Guadalquivir River, a historic bridge and the Triana area, famous for its ceramics district and the birthplace of Seville's flamenco culture.

A sun-drenched alley in the neighbourhood of Santa Cruz

Key

••• Walk route

Plaza Santa Cruz to the Rio Guadalquivir

The small Santa Cruz square, with its birdcage and garden, sits close to both the Jardines de Murillo ①, where there is a monument to Columbus, and the walls of the Real Alcázar. Take Calle Santa Teresa past the museum and birthplace of painter Bartolomé Esteban Murillo (1618–82) ②; the pieces held here are minor compared to those kept in the Museo des Bellas Artes *(see pp70–71)*.

Patio of a house in the Santa Cruz quarter

For keys to symbols *see back flap*

Opposite is the 16th-century Convento San José del Carmen, also known as Convento de las Teresas, an order of the Carmelites. Turning right near the top of Calle de Mateos Gago, you pass the 17th-century Iglesia de Santa Cruz ③ with its triple carillon. Turn left into Calle Guzman El Bueno ("Guzman the Good"), named after the defender of Tarifa during the Moorish invasion. Calle Guzman features some classic town mansions built around spacious interior patios. Cross into the Argote de Molina and walk behind the Palacio Arcobispal ④ down to the gates of the cathedral courtyard, the chief remaining Moorish section of this building; worshippers would wash here before entering the original mosque.

Take a sharp right into Calle Hernando Colon, where odd little shops selling collectables jostle with souvenir stores. Colon leads into Plaza de San Francisco and the Ayuntamiento ⑤ (town hall), begun in 1527 by architect Diego de Riaño. It is one of the best examples of Renaissance architecture in Spain. Cross the square to Calle Sierpes, one of Seville's oldest shopping streets. Sierpes is the place to buy fans, mantilla shawls and hats, not least at Maquedano (No. 40) ⑥ which always has an impressive window display. Where Sierpes meets tiny Plaza La Campana, turn left

(7) Iglesia de la Magdalena, completed in 1709

Tips for Walkers

Starting point: Plaza Santa Cruz.
Length: 3.5 km (2 miles).
Getting there: Plaza Santa Cruz is a short walk from Calle de Menéndez Pelayo, close to the Real Alcázar and Cathedral.
Stopping-off points: María Trifulca, on Puente de Isabel II, has tables overlooking the river and a rooftop terrace. It's a great place to stop for a drink or a seafood meal.

Puente de Isabel II to Puente de San Telmo

The bridge enters the *barrio* of Triana, forever associated with flamenco, bullfighting and

María Trifulca restaurant on Puente de Isabel II (Puente Triana)

on Calle Martin Villa to Plaza del Duque de la Victoria and its statue of Velazquez. Turn right into Calle San Eloy; at its end is the Iglesia de la Magdalena (7), a church built in 1709 on the remains of an earlier Moorish mosque. Its interior features works by Zurbarán and Valdés, and its exquisite representation of the Virgen del Amparo (protection) is a star of the Easter Semana Santa processions. It is claimed she intervened on behalf of petitioners during the aftershocks of the 1755 earthquake and in the 19th century the church served as a refuge for homeless children. Circle to the front of the church and right into Calle San Pablo, which becomes Reyes Catolicos, leading straight to Puente de Isabel II (8). Built in 1852 on the foundations of a long-lost 12th-century Arab bridge, it is also known as Puente de Triana.

Azulejos of Santa Ana church in Triana

ceramics (*azulejos*). For workshops and shops, bear right into Calles San Jorge and then left into Antillano (9) and Alfareria. This runs into Calle Rodrigo de Triana. Turn left into Calle Victoria and right into Pelay Correa to reach Seville's oldest church, the 13th-century Iglesia Santa Ana (10). Its interior features major works by 16th-century sculptors such as Jurate and Ocampo. Behind the church, take a right on Triana's bar-lined riverfront, Calle Betis (11), with views across to the Plaza de Toros, the Torre del Oro and, to the left, sculptor Eduardo Chillida's modernist peace monument, *La Tolerancia* (Tolerance). Betis runs to the 1931 Puente de San Telmo, which leads to the Jardines de Cristina (12), a major bus hub, and to Calle San Fernando (13), which passes the Universidad and continues to the Jardines de Murillo.

(8) Puente de Isabel II, stretching over the Guadalquivir river

STREET FINDER

Key

- Major sight
- Place of interest
- Other building
- 🚆 Railway station
- 🚌 Bus terminus
- 🚢 River boat boarding point
- 🅿 Parking
- 𝑖 Tourist information
- ✚ Hospital
- 🚓 Police station
- ✝ Church
- ⛪ Convent and Monastery
- ═ Railway line
- Pedestrianized street
- Ⓜ Metro station
- Metro-Centro tram stop

Scale of Maps 1–2 & 3–4

0 metres 250
0 yards 250
1 : 13,000

Scale of Maps 5–6

0 metres 150
0 yards 150
1 : 8,250

Key to abbreviations used in the Street Finder

Avda	Avenida	**d**	de, del, de la,	**Pl**	Plaza	**Sra**	Señora
C	Calle		de las, de los	**Po**	Paseo	**Sta**	Santa

A

Abad Gordillo, C d	2 C5 (5 B2)
Abades, C de los	3 C1 (6 D4)
Abogado R Medina, C	2 E2
Abril, Calle	2 F2
Abuyacub, Calle	2 F3
Acetres, Calle	3 C1 (6 D2)
Adelantado, Calle	2 D3
Adolfo R Jurado, C	5 C5
Adriano, Calle de	3 B2 (5 B4)
Agata, Calle	2 E1
Aguamarina, Calle	2 E2
Aguiar, Calle	1 B5 (5 A2)
Aguilas, Calle	4 D1 (6 E3)
Aire, Calle del	3 C1 (6 D4)
Alameda de Hércules	2 D4
Alamillo, Viaducto del	1 A1
Alamillo, Puente del	2 D1
Albacara, Calle	2 E3
Albaida, Calle de la	2 F3
Albareda, Calle de	3 B1 (5 C3)
Alberto Lista, C d	6 D1
Albuera, Calle	3 A1 (5 A3)
Alcaicería d Loza, C	3 C1 (6 D3)
Alcalde Isacio Contreras, C	4 D2 (6 F4)
Alcalde Marqués d Contadero, Po	3 B2 (5 B4)
Alcázares, C de	2 D5 (6 D2)
Alcores, Pasaje los	4 D1 (6 E4)
Alcoy, Calle de	1 C4

Alejo Fernández	4 D2 (6 F4)
Alemanes, Calle	3 C2 (6 D4)
Alerce, Calle	4 E1
Alfalfa, Calle	3 C1 (6 D3)
Alfalfa, Plaza del	3 C1 (6 D3)
Alfaqueque, Calle	1 B5 (5 B1)
Alfarería, Calle de	3 A1
Alfaro, Plaza	4 D2 (6 E5)
Alfonso de Cossio, C	4 E4
Alfonso de Orleans y Borbón, C de	3 A5
Alfonso XII, C de	1 B5 (5 B2)
Alfonso XIII, Puente de	3 C5
Algamitas, Calle	2 F3
Alheli, Calle	2 F3
Alhóndiga, C d	2 D5 (6 E2)
Almadén d Plata, C	2 F4
Almansa, Calle	3 B1 (5 B4)
Almensilla, Calle	2 F3
Almirante Lobo, C	3 B2 (5 C5)
Almirante Tenorio, Calle	2 E5 (6 F2)
Almirante Topete, C	4 F5
Almirante Ulloa, C d	5 B2
Almonacid, Calle	4 E3
Alonso Tello, Calle	4 E2
Altozano, Pl del	3 A2 (5 A4)
Alvarez Quintero, C	3 C1 (6 D3)
Alvaro Alonso Barba, Avda	1 C2
Amadeo Jannone, Pl	3 A3
Amador de los Ríos, Calle	4 E1 (6 F2)
Amante Laffon, C	2 F3

Amapola, Calle	2 D4 (6 E1)
Amargura, Calle	2 D4
Amatista, Calle	2 E2
América, Plaza de	1 B2
América, Plaza de	4 D5
Amistad, Calle	4 D1 (6 E3)
Amor de Dios, C d	1 C5 (5 C1)
Amores, Pasaje de	2 D4
Amparo, Calle del	6 D1
Andreu, Pasaje	6 D4
Andueza, Calle de	2 D3
Angel María Camacho, C	3 C1 (6 D3)
Angeles, Calle	3 C2 (6 D4)
Aniceto Saenz, C d	2 E4
Animas, Calle	3 A4
Antilla, Playa de la	2 E2
Antillano, Calle	3 A2
Antolínez, Calle	1 C5 (5 B1)
Antonia Díaz, C d	3 B2 (5 B4)
Antonia Saenz, C d	2 E4
Antonio Bienvenida, C	3 B5
Antonio Martelo, Plaza	2 F5
Antonio M Montaner, C	4 E5
Antonio Pantión, C	2 E3
Antonio Salado, C	1 B5 (5 B2)
Antonio Susillo, C	2 D4
Aponte	1 C5 (5 C2)
Aposentadores, C	2 D5 (6 D1)
Arapiles, Calle	2 E5 (6 F2)
Archeros, Calle	4 D2 (6 E4)
Arcos, Calle	3 B3

Ardilla, C de la	3 A3
Arenal, Calle	3 B1 (5 B4)
Arenal, Calle	4 F5
Arfe, Calle	3 B2 (5 C4)
Argote de Molina, C	3 C1 (6 D4)
Arguijo, Calle	2 D5 (6 D2)
Arjona, Calle de	3 A1 (5 A3)
Armas, Plaza de	1 B5 (5 A2)
Armenta, Calle	6 E3
Arqueros, Calle	3 A4
Arrayán, Calle	2 D4
Arroyo, Calle de	2 F5
Arte de la Seda, C	1 C3
Artemisa, Calle	2 E5 (6 F1)
Asunción, C d	3 B3
Atanasio Barrón, C	4 D1 (6 F4)
Ateneo, Pasaje	3 C1 (5 C3)
Atienza, Calle	2 D5 (6 D1)
Augusto Peyre, C	4 D5
A Plasencia, C	3 C1 (6 D3)
Aurora, Calle	3 B2 (5 C4)
Autonomía, Plaza	2 F3
Ave María, Calle	6 E2
Avellana, Calle	2 E3
Averroes, Calle	4 E1
Azafrán, Calle del	2 E5 (6 E2)
Aznalcazar, Calle	4 F3
Aznalcollar, Calle	4 F3
Aznalfarache, Calle	2 E3
Azofaifo, Calle	5 C2

B

Badajoz 3 B1 (5 C3)
Bailén, Calle de 1 B5 (5 B2)
Bajeles, Calle 1 B5 (5 A1)
Bamberg, Calle 3 C1 (6 D3)
Baños, Calle de 1 B5 (5 B1)
Barcelona, Calle 3 B1 (5 C3)
Barco, Calle 2 D4
Barqueta, Puente de la 1 E3
Barrau, Calle 4 E3
Barzola, Avenida de la 2 F2
Basílica, Calle 2 D3
Bécquer, Calle de 2 D3
Begonia, Calle 2 F3
Béjar, Calle 3 A3
Benidorm, Calle 3 A1 (5 A3)
Bernal Vidal 3 A2 (5 A5)
Bernardo de Toro, C 2 F2
Bernardo Guerra, Calle 3 B2 (5 B5)
Betis, Calle 3 A2 (5 A5)
Bilbao, Calle 3 B1 (5 C3)
Blanca Paloma, C 2 F2
Blanco de los Ríos, C 6 D3
Blasco de Garay, Plaza 1 B5 (5 A1)
Blasco Ibáñez, C 2 F1
Bobby Deglané, Calle 5 B3
Bogotá, Calle de 4 D5
Borbolla, Avenida de 4 D5
Bordador Rodríguez
    Ojeda, Calle 2 E4
Bosque, Calle 4 E1
Boteros, Calle 3 C1 (6 D3)
Brasil, Calle 4 D4
Brenes, Calle 2 F2
Brillante, Calle 2 E2
Buen Suceso, Plaza 6 D2
Buiza y Mensaque, Calle 3 C1
    (6 D2)
Bustos Tavera, C 2 D5 (6 E2)
Butrón, Calle de 2 E5 (6 F1)

C

Caballerizas, Calle 4 D1 (6 E3)
Cabeza del Rey
    Don Pedro, Calle 6 E3
Cabildo, Plaza 3 C2 (5 C4)
Cabo Noval, Calle 3 C1
Cachorro, Puente d 3 A1
Cádiz, Avenida de 4 D2 (6 E5)
Calafate, Calle 3 A3
Calatrava, Calle 1 C3
Caleria, Calle 4 D1 (6 E3)
California, Calle 4 E4
Callao, Plaza 3 A2 (5 A4)
Callejón de Pazos 4 D2
Camino de Almez 2 E1
Camino de los
    Descubrimientos 1 B4
Campamento, Calle 4 E3
Campo de los Mártires, C 4 E1
Campos, Calle 3 A2
Canalejas, Calle 3 B1 (5 B3)
Canarios, Calle 4 D2 (6 E4)
Cancionera, Calle 4 F5
Cano y Cueto, Calle 4 D2 (6 E4)
Cantabria, C d 1 C5 (5 C1)
Capitán Vigueras, C 4 D2 (6 F5)
Cardenal
    Cervantes, Calle 4 D1 (6 E2)
Cardenal Spínola, C 1 C5 (5 C1)
Carlos Alonso, C 6 E4
Carlos Arniches, Calle 2 F1
Carlos Brujes, Calle 4 F5
Carlos Cañal, Calle 3 B1 (5 B3)
Carlos Haya, Calle 3 A5
Carlos V, Avda de 4 D3
Carmen Benítez, Pl 4 E1 (6 F3)
Carmen Díaz, Calle 2 F1
Carmona, Carretera de 2 F4
Carranza, Calle 2 D3
Carreta, Calle el 2 D3
Carretas, C de las 2 F2
Cartuja, Pasarela d 1 A4 (5 A1)
Castelar, Calle 3 B1 (5 B4)
Castellar, Calle 2 D5 (6 D1)
Castilla, Calle de 3 A1
Cazalla de la Sierra, C 2 F1
Cedaceros, Calle 6 D2
Cefiro, Calle 4 F1

Celinda, Calle 6 E3
Cenicero, Calle 6 F2
Cepeda, Calle 1 B5 (5 B2)
Cerrajería, Calle 5 C2
Cerro Murlano, Calle 4 F5
Cervantes, Calle 6 D1
Céspedes, C d 4 D1 (6 E4)
Cetina, Calle 2 E4
Chapina, Puente del 3 A1
Chavez Nogales 4 E2
Chicuelo, Calle de 3 A5
Chile, Avenida de 3 C3
Chipiona, Playa de 2 E2
Cidro, Calle de 2 E1
Circo, Calle 3 B2 (5 B4)
Ciriaco Esteban 3 B1 (5 B3)
Cisne, Calle 3 A2 (5 A5)
Cisneros, Calle 5 B1
Ciudad de Ronda, Calle 4 D3
Clavijo, Calle del 1 C4
Cofia, Calle 4 E2 (6 F5)
Colombia, Calle 4 D5
Compañía, Calle de 6 D2
Compás del Porvenil, C 4 D4
Concepción, Calle 6 F3
Concha Espina, Calle 3 A3
Concordia, Plaza de la 5 C1
Conde de Barajas,
    Calle de 1 C4 (5 C1)
Conde de Cifuentes, C 4 D2 (6 E5)
Conde de Colombia, Avda 3 C4
Conde d Halcón, Avda d 2 F3
Conde d Ibarra, C 4 D1 (6 E3)
Conde de Torrejón,
    Calle 2 D4 (6 D1)
Conde Negro, C 4 D1 (6 F3)
Conil, Playa de 4 F1
Constancia, Calle 3 A3
Constantina, Calle 2 F2
Constitución,
    Avenida de la 3 C1 (5 C4)
Contratación, Pl d 3 C2 (6 D5)
Coral, Calle 2 E2
Córdoba, Calle 6 D3
Corinto Aceituno, C 2 E4
Corral del Rey, C 3 C1 (6 D3)
Correa de Arauxo, C 2 E3
Corta, Puente de la 1 A1
Cortes, Calle las 1 C5 (5 C1)
Costa de la Luz, C 4 F3
Costa Rica, Calle 4 E4
Costillares, Calle 3 A5
Coullaut Valera, Calle 4 E5
Covadonga, Calle 3 A2
Crédito, Calle 1 C4
Crisantemo, Calle 2 F3
Cristo de Burgos, Plaza 6 E2
Cristo de la Expiración,
    Avenida del 3 A1 (5 A3)
Cristo del Calvario, C 5 B3
Cristóbal Colón,
    Paseo de 3 B2 (5 B4)
Cronista, Pl del 2 D4
Cruces, Calle 4 D2 (6 E4)
Crucis, Via 4 F1
Cruz Roja, Avda de la 2 E4
Cruz, Calle 4 E4
Cruzadas, Calle las 4 D4
Cuarzo, Calle 2 E2
Cuba, Plaza de la 3 B3
Cueva de la Mora, C 2 E1
Cuna, Calle 3 C1 (6 D2)
Curro Romero, C 3B5
Curtidores, Plaza 4 D2 (6 F4)
Curtidurías, C de 1 B4

D

Dársena, Calle 1 B5 (5 A1)
Dean López Cepero, C 4 D1
Delgado, Calle 5 C1
Delicias, Po de las 3 C3
Demetrio d Ríos, C 4 D2 (6 F4)
Descalzos, Calle 6 E2
Diamante, Calle 2 E2
Diamela, Calle 6 E3
Diego de Almagro, C 2 E1
Diego de la Barrera, C 4 E4
Diego de Merlo, C 2 E5 (6 F2)
Diego de Riaño, C 4 D3

Diego M Barrios, C 4 F5
Diego Puerta, Calle 2 F2
Dionisio A Galiano, C 2 E3
Divina Pastora, Calle 2 D4
Dobe Levadizo, Puente de 3C5
Doctor Antonio Cortés
    Lladó, Calle 4 E4
Doctor Arruga, Calle 2 F5
Doctor Barraquer, Pl del 2 D2
Doctor Delgado Roig, C 2 F5
Doctor Domínguez Rodiño 2 E2
Doctor Fedriani, C 2 E2
Doctor Félix Rodríguez
    de la Fuente, Calle 3 A3
Doctor Gabriel Sánchez
    de la Cuesta, Calle 4 E4
Doctor Herrera Carmona, Calle 2 E2
Doctor Jaime Marcos, C 2 E2
Doctor Jiménez Díaz, C 2 F3
Doctor Leal Castaño, C 2 E2
Doctor Letamendi,
    Calle del 2 D4 (6 D1)
Doctor Lupiañez, C 2 F3
Doctor Marañón, Calle 2 E2
Doctor Morote Calafat, C 2E2
Doctor Muñoz Peralta, C 2 E2
Doctor Pedro Castro, C 4 D3
Doctor Relimpio, Calle 2 E5
Doctor Royo, Calle 2 E2
Doctor Seras, Calle 2 E2
Dolores Fernández, Pl 2 E3
Don Alonso El Sabio, C 6 D2
Don Fadrique, Calle 2 D3
Don Juan de Austria, Pl 4 D3
Don Pedro Niño,
    Calle de 2 D5 (6 D1)
Don Pelayo, Avda 4 D4
Doña Carmen, Pl 2 D5 (6 E2)
Doña Clarines, C 4 F5
Doña Elvira, Pl de 3 C2 (6 D5)
Doña María
    Coronel, C 2 D5 (6 D2)
Dos de Mayo, C 3 B2 (5 C5)
Dos Hermanas, C 4 D2 (6 E4)
Drs. Glez Meneses, C 2 E2
Duarte, Calle 3 B2 (5 B5)
Dueñas, Calle 2 D5 (6 E1)
Duende, Calle 3 B1 (5 C4)
Duque Cornejo, C 2 E4
Duque de la
    Victoria, Pl del 1 C5 (5 C2)
Duque d Montemar, C 2 D4
Duque d Veragua, C 5 B1

E

Eduardo Cano, Calle 1 B4
Eduardo Dato, Avda d 4 E2
Eduardo Rivas, Calle 4 F2
Ejército Español, Pl 4 D3
Elvira, Calle 4 E2
Encarnación, Pl d 2 D5 (6 D2)
Enladrillada, C d 2 E5 (6 F1)
Enramadilla, C d 4 E3
Enrique Mensaque, C 3 A3
Enrique Morillo, Pl 2 F1
Ensenada, Calle 4 D1 (6 E3)
Eritaña, Avda de 4 D5
Escarpín, Calle 2 D5 (6 D2)
Escoberos, Calle 2 D3
Escudero y Peroso, C 4 F5
Escuelas Pías, C 2 E5 (6 E2)
Eslava, Calle 1 C4
Esmeralda, Calle 2 E2
España, Plaza de 4 D3
Esperanza, Calle 2 D3
Espinosa y Carcel, C 4 F3
Espíritu Santo, C 2 D5 (6 E1)
Estella, Calle 4 D1 (6 F4)
Estepa, Calle 4 F5
Estepona, Calle 2 E2
Estrellita Castro, Calle 1 C3
Eucalipto, Calle 2 E2
Europa, Plaza 2 D4 (6 D1)
Evangelista, Calle 3 A3 (5 A5)
Expo, Plaza 1 A4
Exposición, Calle 4 E4

F

F. A. Toledo, Calle 2 E3
Fabie, Calle 3 A2 (5 A5)
Fabiola, Calle 4 D1 (6 E4)
Fancelli, Calle 2 D3
Farnesio, Calle 6 E4
Faustino Alvarez, Calle 2 D3
Febo, Calle 3 A3
Federico Rubio, C de 6 E3
Federico Sánchez
    Bedolla, C 3 B2 (5 C4)
Felipe II, Calle de 4 D5
Feria, Calle de la 2 D4
Fernán Caballero, C d 5 B2
Fernán Sánchez Tovar, C 2 E3
Fernández de Ribera, C 4 F3
Fernández Ardavin, C 2 F1
Fernández de Guadalupe, C 2 F4
Fernández y
    Gonzáles, C 3 C1 (5 C4)
Fernando de Mata, C 2 F2
Fernando Tirado, C 4 F2
Fernando IV, Calle de 3 A4
Fernando Villalón, Calle 4 E4
Filipinas, Calle 4 E4
Flecha, Calle 2 D3
Florencia, Calle 2 F5
Florencio Quintero, C 2 E4
Florida, Calle d 4 D1 (6 F4)
Flota, Calle 3 A2 (5 A5)
Fortaleza, Calle 3 B3
Francisco Carrión Mejias, Calle 6 E2
Francisco de Ariño, C 2 F4
Francisco Moraga, C 2 F4
Francos, C d 3 C1 (6 D3)
Fray Alonso, C 4 D1 (6 F3)
Fray Ceferino
    González, C 3 C2 (6 D4)
Fray de Deza, Calle 5 A2
Fray Diego de Cádiz, C 2 E4
Fray Isidoro de Sevilla, C 2 E3
Fray Luis de Granada, C 2 E3
Fray Pedro de Zúñiga, C 4 F2
Fray Serafín Madrid, C 2 F1
Fresno, Calle 2 E1
Froilán de la Serna, C 2 E3
Fuente, Plaza de la 2 F3
Fuenteovejuna, Calle 4 E2

G

G. Azcarate, Calle 2 F3
G. Moscardo, Calle 5 C2
Galena, Calle 2 E2
Galera, Calle 3 B1 (5 B3)
Galindo, Calle 6 D3
Gallinato, Calle 4 E2 (6 F5)
Gallos, Calle de 2 E5 (6 F1)
Gamazo, Calle 3 B1 (5 C4)
Gandesa, Calle 6 D3
Garci-Pérez, Calle 6 E3
Garci Fernández, Calle 2 F4
García de Vinuesa, C d 3 B2 (5 C4)
García Morato, Avda d 3 A5
García Ramos, C d 1 B5 (5 B2)
Gardenia, Calle 2 F3
Gaspar Alonso, Calle 4 D4
Gaspar de Alvear, C 2 E1
Gavidia, Pl d 1 C5 (5 C1)
General Castaños, C 3 B2 (5 C5)
General García de la
    Herranz, Calle 4 F4
General Marva, Calle 2 F4
General Merry, Calle 4 E5
General Polavieja, Calle 3 C1 (5 C3)
General Primo de
    Rivera, Calle 4 D3
General Ríos, C 4 D2 (6 F5)
Generalísimo, Puente del 3 C4
Genil, Calle 3 B1 (5 B4)
Génova, Calle 3 B3
Geranio, Calle 2 F3
Gerona, Calle 2 D5 (6 E1)
Giraldillo, Plaza 2 E4
Girasol, Calle 2 F3
Gitanillo de Triana, C 3 A5
Gladiolo, Calle del 2 F3
Gloria, Calle 6 D5
Glorieta Buenos Aires 3 C4
Glorieta Covadonga 4 D4

Glorieta de los
  Marineros Voluntarios **3 C4**
Glorieta del Alferez Provisional **3 B4**
Glorieta México **4 D5**
Glorieta San Diego **3 C3**
Goles, Calle de **1 B5 (5 B1)**
Golfo, Calle **6 D3**
Gomara, Avenida **4 D5**
González Cuadrado, C **2 D4**
González de León, Calle **6 F4**
González Quijano, Pasaje **2 D4**
Gonzalo Bilbao, C **2 E5 (6 F2)**
Gonzalo Díaz, Calle **4 E5**
Gonzalo Núñez de
  Sepúlveda, Calle **2 F3**
Gonzalo Segovia, Calle **3 B3**
Gota de Rocío, C **2 E1**
Goyeneta, C d **2 D5 (6 D2)**
Gran Capitán, C **4 D3**
Granada, Calle **5 C3**
Granate, Calle **2 E2**
Gravina, Calle de **1 B5 (5 B2)**
Guadalhorce, Avda d **3 C5**
Guadalquivir, C d **1 C4**
Guadalupe, Calle **4 D1 (6 F3)**
Guadarrama, Calle **4 F4**
Guadiana, Calle **2 D4**
Guinés, Calle **3 C2 (5 C5)**
Guzmán El Bueno,
  Calle de **3 C1 (6 D4)**

H

Habana, Calle **3 C2 (5 C5)**
Harinas, Calle d **3 B2 (5 C4)**
Herbolarios, Calle **3 C1 (6 D4)**
Hermanas d Cruz, C **2 F2**
Hermandades, Calle **2 F2**
Hermano Pablo, Calle **2 F1**
Hernán Cortés, Avda de **4 D4**
Hernán Cortés, Calle **1 C4**
Hernándo Colón, Calle **3 C1 (6 D4)**
Herrera El Viejo, C **1 C5 (5 B2)**
Hiniesta, Calle **2 E4 (6 E1)**
Hiniesta, Calle la **2 E4**
Hombre de Piedra, C d **1 C4**
Honderos, Calle **2 E3**
Horacio Hermoso Araujo, C **4 F5**
Huelva, Calle de **3 C1 (6 D3)**
Huestes, Calle **4 E3**

I

Igueldo, Calle **4 F4**
Imaginero Castillo
  Lastrucci, Calle **1 B4 (5 B1)**
Imperial, Calle **4 D1 (6 E3)**
Infanta Luisa
  de Orleans, Calle **4 D3**
Infante Carlos
  de Borbón, Calle **4 D3**
Infantes, Calle **2 D4 (6 E1)**
Inocentes, Calle **2 D4**
Iris, Calle **3 B2 (5 B4)**
Irún, Calle **4 D1 (6 F4)**
Isabel II, Puente d **3 A5 (5 A4)**
Isabel La Católica, Avda d **4 D3**
Isabela, Calle **4 E4**

J

Jabugo, Calle **2 F4**
Jacinta Martos, C **3 A2**
Jauregui, Calle de **2 E5 (6 F2)**
Javier, Calle **5 C2**
Jerónimo Hernández,
  C **2 D5 (6 D1)**
Jesús del Gran
  Poder, C d **1 C5 (5 C2)**
Jesús Cautivo, Avda **4 F5**
Jesús de la Redención, Pl **6 E2**
Jesús de la Vera Cruz, C **1 C5 (5 B2)**
Jiménez Aranda, C **4 E4**
Jimios, Calle **3 B1 (5 C4)**
Joaquín Costa, C **2 D4**
Joaquín Guichot, C **3 C1 (5 C4)**
Joaquín Hazaña, C **3 C2 (5 C5)**
Jorge de Montemayor, C **2 E3**
José Bermejo, Calle **2 F1**
José Cruz Conde, Calle **4 D3**

José de la Camara, C **4 E2**
José de Velilla, C d **3 B1 (5C2)**
José Gestoso, C **2 D5 (6 D2)**
José Laguillo, C **2 F5**
José Luis Luque, C **2 D5 (6 D2)**
José Maluquer, C **2 F3**
José María Izquierdo, C **2 F4**
José María Martínez
  Sánchez Arjona, C **3 A3**
José María Moreno
  Galván, C **4 D2 (6 F5)**
José María Osborne, C **4 D3**
Joselito el Gallo, C **3 A5**
Jovellanos, Calle **3 C1 (5 C3)**
Juan A Cavestany, C **4 E1**
Juan Belmonte, Calle de **3 A5**
Juan Castillo, Calle **6 F4**
Juan de Astorga, C **2 D3**
Juan de Aviñón, C **4 D2 (6 E5)**
Juan de la Cosa, C **4 E5**
Juan de Matacarriazo **4 D2 (6 F5)**
Juan de Mesa, C **2 D5 (6 E2)**
Juan de Roble, C **2 D3**
Juan de Vera, C **4 E1 (6 F3)**
Juan de Zoyas, C **4 F2**
Juan Manuel Rodríguez
  Correa, Calle **2 E3**
Juan Núñez, Calle **2 F3**
Juan Pablos, Calle **4 D5**
Juan Pérez Montalbán, C **2 D4**
Juan Rabadán, Calle de **1 B4**
Juan R Jiménez, C **3 B4**
Juan Romero, C **3 A2 (5 A5)**
Juan S Elcano, C **3 B3**
Judería, Calle **3 C2 (6 D5)**
Julio César, C de **3 B1 (5 B3)**
Júpiter, Calle de **4 E1 (6 F2)**
Justino de Neve, C **6 E5**
Justino Matute, Calle **3 A2**
Juzgado, Calle **2 E4**

K

Kansas City, Avenida de **4 F1**

L

Laboriosa, C de la **4 E1**
Lagar, Calle del **3 C1 (6 D2)**
Lamarque de Novoa, C **2 F4**
Lanza, Calle de **4 D1 (6 E3)**
Laraña Imagen, C d **2 D5 (6 D2)**
Laurel, Calle **6 D1**
Lealtad, Calle de **3 A3**
Legión, Pl d **3 A1 (5 A2)**
Leiria, Calle **3 A2**
Leon XIII, Calle de **2 E4**
Leoncillos, Calle **6 F2**
Lepanto, Calle **2 D5 (6 D1)**
Lerena, Calle **2 D5 (6 D1)**
Levíes, Calle de **4 D1 (6 E4)**
Lictores, Calle **4 E1**
Liñán, Calle **1 B5 (5 A2)**
Lineros, Calle de **3 C1 (6 D3)**
Lira, Calle **2 E4**
Lirio, Calle **4 D1 (6 E3)**
Llerena, Calle de **2 F3**
Llop **3 C1 (6 D2)**
Lope de Rueda, C **6 E4**
Lope de Vega, C **4 E1 (5 C2)**
López de Gomara, C **3 A3**
López Pintado, C **4 D1 (6 E2)**
Lora del Río, Calle **4 F5**
Luca de Tena, C **3 A2 (5 A5)**
Lucero, Calle **2 D4**
Luchana, Calle **3 C1 (6 D3)**
Lucía de Jesús, C **3 A3**
Luis Cadarso, Calle **4 E1**
Luis de Belmonte, C **4 F2**
Luis de Morales, C d **4F2**
Luis de Vargas, C **3 A1 (5 A3)**
Luis Montoto, C d **4 E1 (6 F3)**
Lumbreras, Calle **1 C4**
Luz Arriero, Calle **3 A3**

M

Macarena, Calle **2 E4**
Macasta, Calle **2E4**
Madre de Dios, Calle **6 E4**

Madre Dolores Márquez, C **2 E4**
Madre Rafols, Calle **3 A4**
Madre San Marcelo, C **2 F3**
Madreselva, Calle **2 F3**
Madrid, Calle de **3 B1 (5 C3)**
Maese Farfán, C **4 F2**
Maestre Amete, Calle **2 F4**
Maestre Angulo, Calle **2 F4**
Maestro Quiroga, C **2 E4**
Magallanes, Avda d **3 C4**
Málaga, Avda d **4 D2 (6 E5)**
Malaquita, Calle **2 E2**
Maldonados, Pl **2 D4 (6 D1)**
Mallen, Calle **4 F1**
Mallol, Pasaje **2 E4 (6 F1)**
Malvaloca, Calle **4 F5**
Manuel Bermudo
  Barrera, Calle **4 D3**
Manuel Carretero, Calle **2 F3**
Manuel Casana, Calle **4 F3**
Manuel Cortina, Calle **3 C1**
Manuel Mateos, Calle de **2 E3**
Manuel Pacheco, Calle **4 D4**
Manuel Ródenas, Calle **2 F3**
Manuel Rodríguez
  Alonso, Calle **3 A3**
Manuel Rojas
  Marcos, C **3 C1 (6 D3)**
Manuel Siurot, Avda de **4 D5**
Manuel Villalobos, C **2 F3**
Manzana, Calle **2 E3**
Mar Caspio, Calle **2 F2**
Mar Negro, Calle **2 F2**
Mar Rojo, Calle de **2 F2**
Maracaibo, Calle **2 F1**
Maravillas, Calle **2 D4 (6 E1)**
Marbella, Playa **2 E2**
Marcelino Champagnat, C **3 A3**
Marchena, Calle **4 F5**
Marco Sancho, Calle **2 D4**
Marcos d Cabrera, C **2 D3**
María Auxiliadora, C **2 E5 (6 F2)**
María Luisa, Avda d **3 C4**
María, Calle la **2 F4**
Mariana de Pineda, C **6 D5**
Marianillo, Calle **3 A3**
Mariscal, Calle **4 D2 (6 E4)**
Mármoles, Calle **3 C1 (6 D3)**
Marqués d Lozoya, C **2 D3**
Marqués de Estella, C **4 E3**
Marqués de la Mina, C d **1 C4**
Marqués de
  Paradas, Calle **1 B5 (5 A1)**
Marqués del Duero,
  Calle **A 1 (4 A3)**
Marteles, Calle **2 E4 (6 F1)**
Martín Villa, Calle **5 C2**
Martínez de Medina, C **4 F2**
Martínez Montañéz,
  Calle de **1 C5 (5 C1)**
Marzo, Calle **2 F2**
Matahacas, Calle **2 E5 (6 F1)**
Mateo Alemán, C **3 B1 (5 B3)**
Mateos Gago, C d **3 C2 (6 D4)**
Matienzo, Calle **3 B2 (5 C5)**
Mazagón, Playa de **2 E2**
Medalla Milagrosa, C **2 E3**
Medina y Galnares, C **2 E1**
Medina, Calle **1 C4**
Meléndez Valdés, C **2 F1**
Membrillo, Calle **2 E1**
Méndez Núñez, C **3 B1 (5 C3)**
Mendigorría, Calle **1 C4**
Mendoza Ríos, C d **1 B5 (5 B2)**
Menéndez Pelayo,
  Calle de **4 D2 (6 E5)**
Menéndez Pidal, C **2 F2**
Menjíbar, Calle **6 D1**
Mercedarias, Pl d **4 D1 (6 E3)**
Mercedes de Velilla **6 D2**
Mesón del Moro, C **6 E4**
Miguel Cid,
  Calle de **1 C5 (5 B1)**
Miguel Mañara, C **6 D5**
Miño, Calle del **3 A3**
Miraflores, Avenida de **2 F4**
Misericordia, Calle **6 D2**
Moguer, Calle **2 F1**
Molini, Avenida de **3 C5**
Molino, Calle **2 D4**
Molviedro, Plaza **3 B1 (5 B3)**

Moncayo, Calle **4 F4**
Monederos, Calle **2 D3**
Monsalves, Calle **1 C5 (5 B2)**
Monte Carmelo, C d **3 B3**
Montevideo, Calle **4 D4**
Moratín, Calle de **3 B1 (5 B3)**
Morera, Calle **2 E4**
Morería **6 D2**
Morgado, Calle de **6 D1**
Morón, Calle **4 F5**
Muelle de las Delicias **3 C4**
Mulhacén, Calle **4 F4**
Muñoz León, C **2 E3**
Muñoz Olive, C d **3 B1 (5 C3)**
Muñoz y Pavón, C **6 E3**
Murillo, Calle **3 B1 (5 B3)**

N

Naoc, Calle de **3 A3**
Naranco, Calle **4 F4**
Naranjo, Calle **2 E1**
Narciso Bonaplata, C **1 C4**
Nardo, Calle **6 F4**
Navarros, C d **4 D1 (6 F3)**
Nebli, Calle **4 E2**
Nicolás Alperiz, C **4 D4**
Niebla, Calle de la **3 A4**
Niña de la Alfalfa, C **2 F2**
Niña, Calle **2 F4**
Niño Ricardo, Calle **6 E2**
Nuestra Sra de la O, Po **3 A1**
Nuestra Sra de la Paz, C **4 E4**
Nuestra Sra de los
  Angeles, Calle **3 A3**
Nueva Torneo **2 D2**
Nueva, Plaza **3 B1 (5 C3)**
Núñez de Balboa, C **3 B2 (5C5)**

O

O'Donnell, Calle **3 B1 (5 C2)**
Odreros, Calle **3 C1 (6 D3)**
Oeste, Paseo **1 A3**
Opalo, Calle **2 E2**
Orden de Malta, C **2 D3**
Orotava, Calle **2 F1**
Orquídea, Calle **2 F2**
Ortiz de Zúñiga, C **6 D2**
Osario, Calle **2 E5 (6 F2)**
Oscar Carvallo, C **4 F2**
Otoño, Calle **2 E2**
Otumba, Calle de **3 B1 (5 C3)**

P

Pacheco y Núñez del
  Prado, Calle **2 D4**
Padre Campelo, Calle **4 F3**
Padre Cañete, Calle **5 C1**
Padre Damián, C d **3 B4**
Padre Jerónimo
  Córdoba, Plaza **2 E5 (6 E2)**
Padre Manjón, C **2 E4**
Padre Marchena, C **3 B1 (5 C3)**
Padre Méndez
  Casariego, C **4 E1**
Padre Tarín, C **1 C5 (5 C1)**
Pages del Corro, C **3 A2 (5 A5)**
Pajaritos, Calle **6 D3**
Palacio Malaver, Calle **2 D4**
Palma del Río, Calle **2 F3**
Palmera, Avda de la **4 D5**
Palos de la Frontera, C d **3 C3**
Paraíso, Calle **3 A3**
Parras, Calle **2 D3**
Particular, Calle **3 A4**
Pascual de Gayangos,
  Calle de **1 B4 (5 B1)**
Pascual Márquez, C d **3 A5**
Pastor y Landero,
  Calle de **3 B1 (5 B3)**
Patricio Sáenz, C **2 E4**
Pavia, Calle **3 B2 (5 C4)**
Paz, Avenida de la **4 F5**
Pedro Caravaca, Calle **5 C2**
Pedro del Toro, Calle **5 A2**
Pedro Gual Villalbí, Avda **2 F1**
Pedro Miguel, Calle de **2 D4**
Pedro Parias, C **3 B1 (5 C3)**

Pedro P Fernández, C 3 A4
Pedro Roldán, C 4 D2 (6 F4)
Pedro Tafur, Calle 2 E3
Pelay Correa, C d 3 A2 (5 A5)
Pelicano, Plaza del 2 E4
Peñalara, Calle 4 F4
Pensamiento, C 2 F3
Peñuelas, Calle 2 E5 (6 E1)
Pepe Hillo, Calle 3 B5
Pepe Luis Vázquez, C 3 B5
Perafán de Ribera, C 2 D3
Peral, Calle del 2 D4
Pérez Galdós, C 3 C1 (6 D3)
Pérez Hervás, C 2 F5
Peris Mencheta, C 2 D4
Perú, Avenida del 3 C3
Pilar de Gracia, C 3 A2 (5 A5)
Pilatos, Plaza de 4 D1 (6 E3)
Pimienta, Calle 3 C2 (6 D5)
Pinta, Calle 2 F4
Pinto, Calle 2 E5 (6 F2)
Pinzón, Avda de 4 D4
Pinzones, Calle 2 F4
Pío XII, Plaza de 2 F3
Pirineos, Calle de los 4 E2
Pizarro, Avenida de 3 C4
Pizarro, Calle 1 C4
Placentines, C 3 C1 (6 D4)
Plácido F Viagas 4 E4
Poeta Fernando de
  los Ríos, Calle 2 F1
Polancos, Calle de 2 F1
Ponce de León, Pl 2 E5 (6 E2)
Portaceli, Calle 4 E2
Portugal, Avda de 4 D3
Potro, Calle del 1 C5 (5 C1)
Pozo Santo, Pl 2 D5 (6 D1)
Pozo, Calle del 2 D4
Prada, Calle 2 D4
Prado de San Sebastian 6 D3
Presidente Carrero
  Blanco, Avda de 3 B5
Previsión, Calle 2 F3
Primavera, Calle 2 F2
Progreso, Calle del 4 D4
Prosperidad, Calle 3 A3
Puebla de las Mujeres, C 4 F5
Puente y Pellón 6 D2
Puerta de Carmona 4 D1 (6 F3)
Puerta de Jerez, Pl 3 C2 (6 D5)
Puerta Real 1 B5 (5 A2)
Puerto Rico, C 2 F2
Pumarejo, Plaza de 2 D4
Puñonrostro, C 6 F2
Pureza, C de la 3 A2 (5 A5)
Purgatorio, Calle 2 E3

Q

Quevedo, C d 2 D5 (6 D1)
Quinita Flores, C 4 F5

R

Rábida, Calle la 3 C3
Rafael González
  Abreu, C 3 B1 (5 B4)
Rafael María de Labra, C 4 E5
Rafael Ortega, Plaza 3 B5
Ramírez de Bustamante, C 4 E5
Ramón de Carranza, Avda 3 A5
Ramón y Cajal, Avda de 4 F4
Rastro, Calle 4 D2 (6 F5)
Raza, Avda de la 3 C5
Recaredo, C d 2 E5 (6 E1)
Redes, Calle de 1 B5 (5 B2)
Refinadores, Pl 4 D2 (6 E4)
Regina, Calle 2 D5 (6 D1)
Relator, Calle de 2 D4
Reposo, Calle 1 C3
República Argentina,
  Avenida de la 3 A4
República Dominicana, Pl 3 A4
Requena, Calle 3 A2
Resolana, C d 2 D3
Reyes Católicos, C 3 A1 (5 A4)
Ricardo de Checa, C 5 B2
Ricardo Torres Bombita, C 3 A5
Río de Janeiro, Calle 2 F1
Río de la Plata, C 4 E1

Rioja, Calle 3 B1 (5 C3)
Rivero, Calle 5 C2
Rocío, Calle 3 A2 (5 A5)
Rodó, Calle 3 B2 (5 C4)
Rodrigo d Triana, C 3 A2 (5 A5)
Rodríguez Caso, Avda 3 C4
Rodríguez Marín, C 4 D1 (6 E3)
Roelas, Calle 1 C4
Roma, Avenida de 3 C3
Romanticismo, Avda del 2 E1
Romeros, Calle de 2 F2
Ronda de Capuchinos, C 2 E4
Ronda de Pío XII, Calle 2 F2
Ronda Urbana Norte 2 E1
Rosaleda, Calle la 2 F4
Rosario Vega, C 3 B3
Rosario, C d 3 B1 (6 D3)
Rositas, Calle 3 B1 (5 B3)
Rubens, Calle 1 C5 (5 C1)
Rubí, Calle 2 E1
Ruiseñor, Calle 3 A2
Ruiz de Alda, Plaza de 4 E3

S

Saavedras, Calle 2 D5 (6 D1)
Sacrificio, Pl del 4 F1
Sagasta, Calle 3 C1 (5 C3)
Sagunto, Calle 2 D3
Salado, Calle de 3 A3
Sales y Ferre, Calle 6 D3
Salesianos, Calle 2 E5
Salvador, Plaza 3 C1 (6 D3)
San Agustín, Pl de 4 D1 (6 F3)
San Benito, C 4 E1
San Bernardo, C d 4 E3 (6 F5)
San Blas, Calle de 2 D4
San Clemente 6 E4
San Diego, Calle d 3 B2 (5 C4)
San Eloy, Calle d 1 C5 (5 B2)
San Esteban, C d 4 D1 (6 F3)
San Fernando, C 3 C2 (6 D5)
San Florencio, C 4 F2
San Francisco de
  Paula, C de 1 C5 (5 C1)
San Francisco Javier, Avda 4 F4
San Francisco, Pl d 3 C1 (5 C3)
San Gil Contreras, Pl 2 D3
San Gregorio, C d 3 C2 (6 D5)
San Hermenegildo, C d 2 E4
San Ignacio, C d 4 F2
San Isidoro, C 3 C1 (6 D3)
San Jacinto, C d 3 A2 (5 A5)
San Joaquín, C d 2 F5
San Jorge, Calle 3 A2 (5 A4)
San José, Calle d 4 D1 (6 E4)
San Juan Bosco, C de 2 F4
San Juan de Avila, C de 5 C2
San Juan de la
  Palma, C 2 D5 (6 D1)
San Juan de la Ribera, C 2 E3
San Juan, Calle de 6 D3
San Julián, Calle de 2 E4
San Lázaro, Avda de 2 E2
San Luis, Calle de 2 D4
San Marcos, Plaza 2 E5 (6 E1)
San Martín, Plaza 2 D5 (6 D1)
San Miguel, Calle 1 C5 (5 C1)
San Pablo, Calle d 3 B1 (5 B4)
San Pedro Mártir, C 3 B1 (5 B2)
San Pedro, Plaza 2 D5 (6 D2)
San Román, Plaza 6 E1
San Roque, C de 3 B1 (5 B2)
San Salvador, C 4 D3
San Sebastián, Pl de 4 D3
San Telmo, Puente de 3 B3
San Vicente, C d 1 C5 (5 B2)
Sánchez Barcárizetgui, C 5 A3
Sánchez d Castro, C 2 E5 (6 F1)
Sánchez Perrier, C d 2 E3
Sánchez Pizjuan, Avda 2 D2
Sancho Dávila, Avda d 3 C3
Sanjurjo, Avenida 4 F5
Sanlúcar La Mayor 4 F5
Santa Ana, Calle de 1 C4
Santa Bárbara, C 5 C1
Santa Clara, C d 1 C4
Santa Cruz, Pl d 4 D2 (6 E4)
Santa Fé, Calle 3 A4
Santa Isabel, Pl 2 E5 (6 E1)

Santa Justa, Calle 2 F5
Santa María
  La Blanca, C 4 D2 (6 E4)
Santa María, C 2 F4
Santa Marina, C 2 E4
Santa Paula, C d 2 E5 (6 F1)
Santa Rosa, Calle 4 D4
Santa Rufina, C d 2 D4
Santa Teresa, C d 4 D2 (6 E4)
Santa Vicenta María, C 1 C5 (5 B2)
Santander, C 3 B2 (5 C5)
Santas Patronas, C d 3 B1 (5 B3)
Santiago Montoto, Avda 3 C4
Santiago, Calle 2 E5 (6 E2)
Santo Angel, C 3 A4
Santo Domingo de la
  Calzada, Calle 4 F2
Santo Rey, Calle 4 E3 (6 F5)
Sargento Provisional, Pl 3 A4
Saturno, Calle 2 E5 (6 F2)
Sauceda, Calle 5 C2
Segura, Calle 3 A1 (5 A3)
Seises, Pasaje 3 B2 (5 C4)
Sierpes, Calle 3 C1 (5 C2)
Sierra de Gata, C 4 F5
Sierra del Castañe, C 4 F5
Siete Revueltas, C d 6 D3
Simpecado, C 2 E2
Socorro, Calle 2 E5 (6 E1)
Sol, Calle del 2 E5 (6 F1)
Sollo, C 2 E4
Sor Angela de la Cruz, C de 2 D5
Sor Francisca Dorotea, C 2 F2
Sorda, Calle 2 E4

T

Tabladilla, Calle 4 D5
Tadeo Soler, Calle 3 A3
Taf, Calle el 2 D3
Talgo, Calle el 2 D3
Tamboril, Calle 2 F2
Tarifa, Calle de 1 C5 (5 B2)
Teatinos, Avda de los 4 F5
Teide, Calle 2 D4
Tello de Guzmán, C 4 E5
Temprado, Calle 3 B2 (5 C5)
Teniente Borges, C 1 C5 (5 C2)
Teniente C Seguí, C 5 C3
Teniente Vargas
  Zúñiga, C 3 B1 (5 B3)
Tenor Manuel García, C 4 E5
Tentudia, Calle 4 E3
Teodosio, C de 1 C5 (5 B1)
Ter, Calle el 2 D2
Terceros, Pl de los 2 D5 (6 E2)
Tibidabo, Calle 4 F4
Tintes, Calle 4 D1 (6 F3)
Tirso de Molina, C 3 B1 (5 B3)
Tolosa Latour, C 4 F5
Tomás de Ibarra, C 3 C2 (5 C4)
Toneleros, C 5 C4
Topacio, Calle 2 E2
Torcuato Pérez, C 2 E3
Torneo, Calle del 1 B5 (5 A1)
Torreblanca, C 2 D4
Torremolinos, C 3 A1 (5 A3)
Torres, Calle 2 D3
Torrigiano, Calle 2 D3
Torrijos, Calle 3 A2 (5 A5)
Trabajo, C d 3 A3
Trajano, Calle 1 C5 (5 C1)
Trastámara, C d 3 A1 (5 A3)
Triana, Puente de 3 A2 (5 A4)
Trinidad, Calle 2 E4
Triunfo, Pl del 3 C2 (6 D4)
Trovador, Calle de 4 E2
Troya, Calle de 3 B3
Trujillo, Calle 2 F2
Turia, Calle del 3 A4
Turmalina, Calle 2 E2

U

Úbeda, Calle 4 E1 (6 F3)
Ulia, Calle de 4 F4
Unidad, Calle de la 4 E2
Urquiza, Calle 2 F5

V

Valdelagrana, Playa de 2 E2
Valdés Leal, Calle 3 B1 (5 B4)
Valladares, Calle 3 A2 (5 A4)
Valle, Calle del 2 E5 (6 F2)
Valme, Calle 4 E3
Valparaíso, C d 4 D5
Vara del Rey, C 2 E5 (6 F2)
Varflora, Calle 3 B2 (5 B4)
Vargas Campos, C 5 C2
Vázquez d Leca, C 3 B2 (5B5)
Velarde, Calle 3 B2 (5B4)
Velázquez Tetuán, C 3 C1 (5 C2)
Venecia, Calle 2 F5
Venta de los Gatos, C 2 D1
Verano, Calle 2 F2
Verde, Calle 2 D4 (4 D1)
Verde, Calle 4 D1 (6 E4)
Verónica, C d 2 E5 (6 F1)
Veruela, Calle de 2 E1
Vib-Arragel, C 1 C3
Victoria, Calle 3 A2 (5 A5)
Vida, Calle 3 C2 (6 D5)
Vidrio, Calle del 4 F1
Villa Jamerdana, Pasaje 6 D4
Villegas, Calle 3 C1 (6 D3)
Virgen de África, C 3 A4
Virgen de Aguas Santas, C 3 A4
Virgen de Araceli, C 3 B4
Virgen de Begoña, C 3 B3
Virgen de Belén, C 3 A3
Virgen de Consolación, Pje 3 B3
Virgen de Escardiel, C 2 F1
Virgen de Fátima, C 3 A3
Virgen de Gracia y
  Esperanza, C 2 E5 (6 F2)
Virgen de Guaditoca, C 3 B4
Virgen de Alegría, C 4 D1 (6 E4)
Virgen de la Antigua, C 3 A4
Virgen de la Cinta, C 3 A4
Virgen de la Estrella, C 3 A4
Virgen de la Luz, C 6 F3
Virgen de la Oliva, C 3 A4
Virgen de la Sierra, C 4 D3
Virgen de las Huertas, C 3 B3
Virgen d Montañas, C 3 A4
Virgen de Loreto, Calle 3 A4
Virgen d Libros, C 5 B1
Virgen de Montserrat, C 3 A4
Virgen de Luján, C 3 A4
Virgen de Regla, C 3 B3
Virgen de Robledo, C 3 B4
Virgen de Setefilla, C 3 B3
Virgen de Valvanera, C 4 F2
Virgen del Aguila, C 3 A4
Virgen del Buen Aire, C 3 A3
Virgen del Monte, C 3 A4
Virgen del Pepetuo
  Socorro, C 3 A3
Virgen del Refugio, C 3 A4
Virgen d Subterrránio, C 2 D4
Virgen del Valle, C 3 B3
Virgen Milagrosa, Pl 3 B3
Vírgenes 4 D1 (6 E3)
Viriato, Calle del 2 D5 (6 D1)
Virtud, Calle 3 A3
Vista Florida, Plaza 2 E3
Vista Hermosa, Calle 2 E3
Voluntad, Calle 3 A3
Vulcano, Calle 2 D4

X

Ximénez de Enciso, C 4 D2 (6 E4)

Y

Yuste, Calle de 1 C3

Z

Zafiro, Calle 2 E2
Zamora, Pasaje 4 D1 (6 F4)
Zamudio, Calle 6 E3
Zaragoza, Calle 3 B3 (5 C3)
Zaruen 1 B4 (5 B1)
Zurbarán, Plaza 2 D5 (6 D2)
Zurradores, Plaza 4 D1 (6 F4)

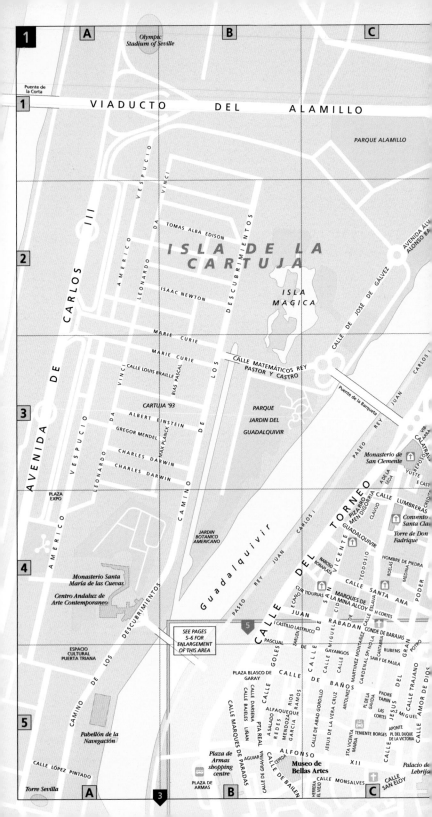

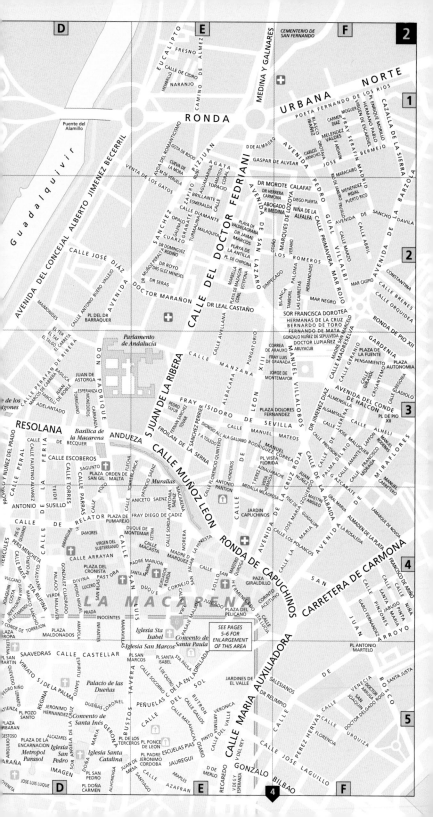

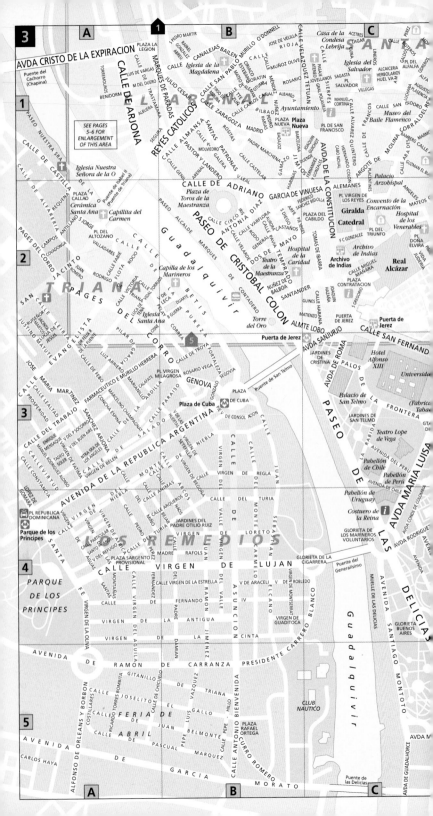

ANDALUCÍA AREA BY AREA

Andalucía at a Glance	**124–125**
Huelva and Sevilla	**126–137**
Córdoba and Jaén	**138–161**
Cádiz and Málaga	**162–187**
Granada and Almería	**188–209**

Andalucía at a Glance

Andalucía is a region of contrasts where snowcapped mountains rise above deserts and Mediterranean beaches, and Moorish palaces can be found standing next to Christian cathedrals. Its eight provinces, which in this guide are divided into four areas, offer busy towns such as Granada and Córdoba with their astonishing architectural treasures, as well as sleepy villages, endless olive groves and nature reserves of great beauty.

Roof of the Mihrab in the Mezquita, Córdoba's top sight *(see pp148–9)*

The amphitheatre in the Roman city of Itálica *(see p48 and p136)*, just outside Seville

Golden chalice from the rich treasury of Cádiz cathedral *(see p168)*

CÓRDO

Jabugo

HUELVA

SEVILLA

Cór

Seville

Huelva

MÁLA

Cádiz

CÁDIZ

Los Barrios

Arcos de la Frontera, one of the pretty *pueblos blancos* (white villages, *see pp176–7*) so typical of Andalucía

◄ The magnificent Alhambra in Granada

Baroque west front of the elegant cathedral in Jaén *(see p152)*

The imposing Moorish castle of Baños de la Encina *(see p155)* in the province of Jaén

0 kilometres   50

0 miles   25

JAÉN

Jaén

ALMERÍA

Archidona

Granada

GRANADA

Almería

Málaga

Gardens of the Alhambra in Granada *(see pp194–202)*

Cabo de Gata, a nature reserve with excellent beaches *(see p208)*

HUELVA
AND SEVILLA

Andalucía's western extremities and the plains surrounding
Seville are rarely explored by travellers in southern Spain.
There are isolated beaches along Huelva province's Atlantic coast
and good walking country in the northern sierras. The Parque Nacional
de Doñana on the Guadalquivir delta is Europe's largest nature reserve;
inland, orange groves straddle the river's valley.

As Roman legions under Scipio Africanus
crossed southern Spain on their westward
trek in the 3rd century BC, they founded
a formidable metropolis, Itálica. Its well-
preserved ruins remain north of Seville.
Later, the Moors held the region as part of
the Emirate of Al Andalus. They peppered
it with their whitewashed, fortified towns,
of which Carmona, in Sevilla province, is a
fine example. After the Christian Reconquest
(see pp52–3), Moorish traditions persisted
through Mudéjar architecture *(see pp28–9)*,
blending with Baroque and Renaissance
in cities such as Osuna, which flourished
in the 16th century.

Huelva province is inextricably bound
up with another chapter in the history of
world conquest – in 1492 Columbus set
out on his epic voyage from Palos de la

Frontera, which at the time was an important
port. He stayed nearby, at the Franciscan
Monasterio de la Rábida, built earlier that
century. Running along Huelva's northern
border is a ridge of mountains, of which
the forested Sierra de Aracena forms part.
This ridge continues into Sevilla province
as the Sierra Norte de Sevilla. Here, goats
forage, birds of prey fly overhead and
streams gush through deep chasms. The
landscape erupts in a riot of wild flowers
in spring, turning brown as the searing
summer sets in.

The Parque Nacional de Doñana
preserves the dunes and marshlands
near the mouth of the Guadalquivir to
the south. Here, teeming birdlife and
wetland fauna thrive on the mudflats
and shallow, saline waters.

Iglesia de Nuestra Señora del Rocío, El Rocío, where many pilgrims converge each Pentecost Sunday

◀ Whitewashed buildings in a village in the Sierra de Aracena

Exploring Huelva and Sevilla

Cosmopolitan Seville is the natural base from which to explore the far-flung corners of Huelva and Sevilla provinces, such as the little-visited and extraordinarily beautiful Sierra de Aracena and the rugged Sierra Norte. The Atlantic coast offers a virtually unbroken stretch of beaches and the Parque Nacional de Doñana features a fascinating marsh landscape abundant in wildlife. Between the coast and the mountains are rolling agricultural plains, interrupted by vineyards in fertile El Condado. Among the region's historic towns are Écija and Osuna, with fine Baroque features, while the history of Columbus can be traced in the towns around Huelva.

The mines of Riotinto, Sierra de Aracena

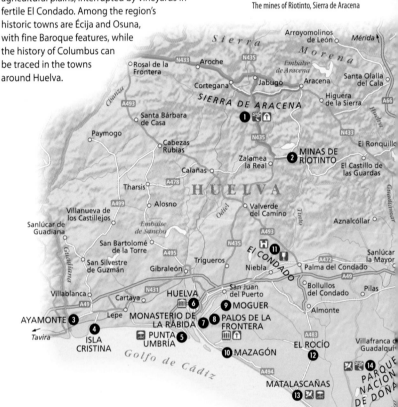

Fishing boats in the harbour of Punta Umbría

For additional map symbols *see back flap*

Key

▭▭ Motorway

┈┈┈ Motorway under construction

── Major road

┄┄┄ Minor road

── Scenic route

─•─ Main railway

── Minor railway

▬▬▬ International border

▬▬▬ Provincial border

Getting Around

The busy A4, linking Córdoba with Seville, slices through the eastern half of the region, bypassing Écija and Carmona, then streaks on down to Jerez de la Frontera and Cádiz as the AP4. Another motorway, the A92, brings traffic from Málaga and Granada. All join a ring-road at Seville, with the A49 continuing to Huelva and Portugal. These cities are also connected by rail. A complex and inexpensive bus network run by many different companies links most towns. To explore the more remote parts of the region, particularly mountain roads, it is essential to have private transport.

A well-known *bodega* advertisement in the rolling hills of the Sierra de Aracena

Sights at a Glance

1. Sierra de Aracena
2. Minas de Ríotinto
3. Ayamonte
4. Isla Cristina
5. Punta Umbría
6. Huelva
7. Monasterio de la Rábida
8. Palos de la Frontera
9. Moguer
10. Mazagón
11. El Condado
12. El Rocío
13. Matalascañas
14. *Parque Nacional de Doñana pp134–5*
15. Lebrija
16. Itálica
17. Sierra Norte
18. Carmona
19. Écija
20. Osuna
21. Estepa

A ham shop in Jabugo, Sierra de Aracena

❶ Sierra de Aracena

Huelva. **Road map** A2. 🚃 El Repilado.
🚃 Aracena. *i* Calle Pozo de la Nieve,
s/n, in reception area of La Gruta de
las Maravillas, (663 93 78 77). 🚌 Sat.
W aracena.es

This wild mountain range in
northern Huelva province is one
of the most remote and least
visited corners of Andalucía. Its
slopes, covered with cork, oak,
chestnut and wild olive, are cut
by rushing streams and many
tortuous mountain roads.

The main town of the region,
Aracena, squats at the foot of
a ruined Moorish fortress on a
hillside pitted with caverns.
One of these, the **Gruta de las
Maravillas**, can be entered to
see its underground lake in a
chamber hung with stalactites.
Near the fortress, the **Iglesia del
Castillo**, which was built in the
13th century by the Knights
Templar, has a Mudéjar tower.

The village of **Jabugo** also
nestles amid these mountains.
It is famed across Spain for its
tasty cured ham, *jamón ibérico*,
or *pata negra (see p222)*.

Gruta de las Maravillas
Pozo de la Nieve. **Tel** 663 93 78 76.
Open 10am–1:30pm, 3–6pm. 🅿️ 📷

❷ Minas de Riotinto

Huelva. **Road map** A2. 🚃 Riotinto.
Tel 959 59 00 25. Minas de Riotinto
& Museo Minero: **Open** 10:30am–3pm,
4–7pm daily (mid-Jul–Sep: to 8pm).
Closed 1 & 6 Jan, 25 Dec 🅿️ 🔶 📷
W parquemineroderiotinto.es

A fascinating detour off the
N435 between Huelva city and
the Sierra de Aracena leads to
the opencast mines at Riotinto.
These have been excavated
since Phoenician times; the
Greeks, Romans and Visigoths
exploited their reserves of iron,
copper, silver and mineral ores.

The lip of the crater overlooks
walls of rock streaked with green
and red fissures. Below, the trucks
at work in the mines appear toy-
sized. The **Museo Minero** in the
village explains the history of
the mines and of the Riotinto
Company. At weekends and on
public holidays there is a train
tour in restored 1900 carriages.

❸ Ayamonte

Huelva. **Road map** A3. 🚹 18,000. 🚃
i Calle Huelva 37 (959 32 07 37).
🚌 Sat morning.

Before the road bridge over the
lower Guadiana river was completed in 1992, anyone who
was crossing between southern
Andalucía and the Algarve coast
of Portugal had to pass through
Ayamonte. The small, flat-
bottomed car ferry across the
jellyfish-infested mouth of the
Guadiana river still operates and
is an alternative for those who
are making the journey between
the two countries. Visitors can
watch the ferry from the tower
of Ayamonte's **Iglesia San
Francisco**, which has a fine
Mudéjar ceiling. The more
adventurous can head northwest
to the small town of **Sanlúcar
de Guadiana**, from where it
is possible take a zip-line to
cross the border into Portugal
(www.limitzero.com).

❹ Isla Cristina

Huelva. **Road map** A3. 🚹 18,000. 🚃
i Calle San Francisco 12 (959 33 26
94). 🚌 Thu. **W** islacristina.org

Once a distinct island, Isla
Cristina is now surrounded by
marshes. Situated near the
mouth of the Guadiana river, it
is an important fishing port, home
to a fleet of tuna and sardine
trawlers. With a fine sandy
beach, Isla Cristina is now a
popular summer resort. Situated
on the main seafront is an
excellent choice of restaurants,
which serve delicious, freshly
landed fish and seafood.

Tuna and sardine trawlers moored for the night in the port of Isla Cristina

Frescoes depicting the life of Columbus at Monasterio de la Rábida

Museo Provincial
Alameda Sundheim 13.
Tel 959 65 04 24. **Open** 9am–
7:30pm Tue–Sat, 9am–3:30pm
Sun & public hols (mid-Jun–mid-
Sep: 9am–3:30pm Tue–Sun &
public hols).

❼ Monasterio de la Rábida

Huelva. **Road map** A3. from Huelva.
Tel 959 35 04 11. **Open** 10am–1pm,
4–6:15pm Tue–Sat, 10:45am–1pm,
4–6:15pm Sun (to 7pm Jul & Aug).
monasteriodelarabida.com

In 1491, a dejected Genoese explorer found refuge in the Franciscan friary at La Rábida, which is across the Odiel estuary from Huelva. King Fernando and Queen Isabel had refused to back his plan to sail west to the East Indies. The prior, Juan Pérez, who as the confessor of the queen had great influence, eventually succeeded in getting this decision reversed. The following year, this sailor, by the name of Columbus, became the first European to reach the Americas since the Vikings.

La Rábida friary, which was built on Moorish ruins in the 15th century, is now a shrine to Columbus. Frescoes painted by Daniel Vásquez Díaz in 1930 glorify Columbus's life. The Sala de las Banderas contains a small casket of soil from every Latin American country. Worth seeing are the Mudéjar cloisters, the lush gardens and the beamed chapterhouse.

❺ Punta Umbría

Huelva. **Road map** A3. 14,000.
i Avenida Ciudad de Huelva s/n (959
49 51 60). Mon. **punta
umbria.es**

Punta Umbría is one of the main beach resorts in Huelva province. It sits at the end of a long promontory, with the Marismas del Odiel wetlands to one side and a sandy beach bordering the Gulf of Cádiz to the other. The Riotinto Company first developed the resort in the late 19th century for its British employees. These days, however, it is mainly Spanish holiday-makers who stay in the beachside villas.

A long bridge crosses the marshes, giving road access from Huelva. It is more fun to follow a trail blazed by Riotinto expatriates seeking the sun and take the ferry across the bird-rich wetlands.

over the commercial world. That Columbus set sail from Palos de la Frontera, across the estuary, is Huelva's main claim to international renown. This fact is celebrated in the excellent **Museo Provincial**, which also has several exhibitions charting the history of the mines at Riotinto. Some archaeological finds from the very early days of mining are cleverly presented.

To the east of the centre, the Barrio Reina Victoria is a bizarre example of English suburbia in the very heart of Andalucía. It is a district of bungalows in mock-Tudor style, built by the Riotinto Company for its staff in the early 20th century.

South of the town, at Punta del Sebo, the Monumento a Colón, a 1929 bleak statue of Columbus by Gertrude Vanderbuilt Whitney, dominates the Odiel estuary.

Bronze jug, Museo Provincial, Huelva

❻ Huelva

Huelva. **Road map** A3. 130,000.
i Calle Jesús Nazareno 21 (959 65
02 00). Fri. **turismohuelva.org**

Founded as Onuba by the Phoenicians, the town had its grandest days as a Roman port. It prospered again in the early days of trade with the Americas, but Seville soon took over. Its decline culminated in 1755, when Huelva was almost wiped out by the great Lisbon earthquake. Today, industrial suburbs sprawl around the Odiel quayside, from which the Riotinto Company once exported its products all

Columbus in Andalucía

Cristóbal Colón – Christopher Columbus to the English-speaking world – was born in Genoa in Italy, trained as a navigator in Portugal and conceived the idea of reaching the Indies by sailing westwards. In 1492 he sailed from Palos de la Frontera and later the same year landed on Watling Island in the Bahamas, believing that he had fulfilled his ambition.

Columbus made three further voyages from bases in Andalucía, reaching mainland South America and other islands in what are still termed the West Indies in deference to his mistake. He died at Valladolid in 1506.

Columbus takes his leave before setting sail

Historic map at the Casa Museo de Martín Alonso Pinzón in Palos de la Frontera

❽ Palos de la Frontera

Huelva. **Road map** A3. 🏔 12,000. 🚌
ℹ️ Parque Botánico José Celestino Mutis, Paraje de la Rábida (959 49 46 64). 🛒 Sat.

Palos is an unprepossessing agricultural town on the eastern side of the Río Odiel's marshy delta. Yet it is a major attraction on the Columbus heritage trail.

On 3 August 1492, Columbus put out to sea from Palos in his ship, the *Santa María*, with the caravels the *Pinta* and the *Niña*, whose captains were Martín and Vicente Pinzón, brothers from Palos. A statue of Martín Pinzón stands in the town's main square, and his former home has been turned into a small museum of exploration, named the **Casa Museo de Martín Alonso Pinzón**.

The Gothic-Mudéjar **Iglesia San Jorge** dates from the 15th century. It has a fine portal, through which Columbus left after hearing Mass before his famous voyage. Afterwards, he boarded the *Santa María* at a pier, which is now forlornly silted up.

These days, Palos's prosperity comes from the thousands of hectares of strawberry beds in the surrounding fields, which soak up the sun.

🏛 **Casa Museo de Martín Alonso Pinzón**
Calle Colón 24. **Tel** 959 10 00 41. **Open** 10am–2pm Mon–Fri. 🚫

❾ Moguer

Huelva. **Road map** A3. 🏔 15,000. 🚌
ℹ️ Calle Andalucía 17, Teatro Felipe Godínez (959 37 18 98). 🛒 Thu.
🌐 andalucia.org

A beautiful, whitewashed town, Moguer is a network of shaded courtyards and narrow streets lined with flower boxes. It is a delight to stroll around, exploring treasures such as the 16th-century hermitage of **Nuestra Señora de Montemayor** and the Neo-Classical **Ayuntamiento**. Moguer is also the birthplace of the poet and 1956 Nobel laureate, Juan Ramón Jiménez. The **Museo de Zenobia y Juan Ramón Jiménez**

charts the poet's life and work, and is located in his restored former home.

The walls of the 14th-century **Monasterio de Santa Clara** enclose some splendid, stone-carved Mudéjar cloisters. The nuns' dormitory, kitchen and refectory capture some of the atmosphere of their life inside the enclosure.

The **Monasterio de San Francisco** is worth seeing for its church, with a superb white tower and Baroque portals.

🏛 **Museo de Zenobia y Juan Ramón Jiménez**
Calle Juan Ramón Jiménez 10. **Tel** 959 37 21 48. **Open** Tue–Sun. **Closed** Sun pm & public hols. 🚫 🎦

🏛 **Monasterio de Santa Clara**
Plaza de las Monjas. **Tel** 959 37 01 07. **Open** Tue–Sun. **Closed** often closed on Sat for events; public hols. 🚫

Mazagón's sandy beach on the Costa de la Luz

❿ Mazagón

Huelva. **Road map** A3. 🏔 3,500. 🚌
ℹ️ Edificio Mancomunidad, Avda de los Conquistadores s/n (959 37 60 44). 🛒 Fri evening.

One of the more remote beach resorts of the Costa de la Luz, Mazagón shelters among pine woods 23 km (14 miles) southeast of Huelva. Virtually deserted in winter, it comes to life in summer when mainly Spanish holiday-makers arrive to fish, sail and enjoy the huge, and often windswept, beach. Visitors to the resort may still take pleasure in the solitude, however, while taking long walks along the endless Atlantic shoreline and among the sand dunes.

The 16th-century Nuestra Señora de Montemayor in Moguer

Moorish walls surrounding Niebla in El Condado

⓫ El Condado

Huelva. **Road map** B2. 🚉 🚌 Palma del Condado. 🛈 Plaza de España 14, Palma del Condado (959 40 24 09).

The rolling, fecund hills to the east of Huelva produce several of Andalucía's finest wines. El Condado, defined roughly by Niebla, Palma del Condado, Bollullos del Condado and Rociana del Condado, is the heart of this wine-growing district.

Niebla is of ancient origin. Its bridge is Roman, but its solid walls are Moorish, as is the now ruined, 12th-century **Castillo de Niebla**, also known as Castillo de los Guzmanes.

Around Niebla, vineyards spread out over the landscape, which is dotted with villages close to the main *bodegas*. These include Bollullos del Condado, which has the largest cooperative winery in Andalucía and also the **Centro del Vino Condado de Huelva**. Here you can learn about wine-growing techniques and taste their wines before making your purchase.

Bollullos and Palma del Condado are good examples of the popular young white wines produced in the region.

Palma del Condado is best visited in September when the inhabitants celebrate the year's *vendimia* (grape harvest).

🏛 Castillo de Niebla
C/ Campo Castillo s/n. **Tel** 959 36 22 70.
Open 10am–2pm, 5–9pm Mon–Sun.

🏛 Centro del Vino Condado de Huelva
Calle San José 2. **Tel** 959 41 38 75.
Open 10am–2pm, 4–7pm Tue–Sat.

⓬ El Rocío

Huelva. **Road map** B3. 🏔 2,500.
🚌 🛈 Centro Doñana, Avda de la Canaliega s/n (959 44 38 08). 🗓 Tue.

Bordering the wetlands of the Doñana region *(see pp134–5)*, the village of El Rocío is for most of the year a tranquil, rural backwater, which attracts few visitors.

At the Romería del Rocío *(see pp42–3)* in May, however, nearly a million people converge on the village. Many are pilgrims who travel from all over Spain by bus, car, horse, or even on gaudily decorated ox-carts or on foot. They come to **Ermita de Nuestra Señora del Rocío** that has a statue reputed to have been behind miraculous apparitions since 1280. Pilgrims are joined by revellers, who are enticed by the promise of plentiful wine, music and a great party.

⓭ Matalascañas

Huelva. **Road map** A3. 🏔 1,200. 🚌
🛈 Parque Dunar, s/n (959 43 00 86).
🗓 Thu.

Matalascañas is the largest Andalucían beach resort west of the Guadalquivir river. Thousands holiday here, lying in the sun, riding, sailing or water-skiing by day and dancing to the latest disco beat at night. At Romería del Rocío, the resort overflows with pilgrims and revellers.

Matalascañas is totally self-contained. To one side there are dunes and forests stretching as far as Mazagón, to the other the wild peace of the Doñana *(see pp134–5)*.

Iglesia de Nuestra Señora del Rocío in the village of El Rocío

⓮ Parque Nacional de Doñana

The National Park of Doñana is ranked among Europe's greatest wetlands. Together with its adjoining protected areas (Parque Natural de Doñana), the park covers over 50,000 hectares (185,000 acres) of marshes and sand dunes. The area used to be hunting grounds (*coto*) belonging to the Dukes of Medina Sidonia and was never suitable for human settlers. The wildlife flourished and, in 1969, the area became officially protected. In addition to a wealth of endemic species, thousands of migratory birds come to stay here in winter when the marshes flood again, after months of drought.

Shrub Vegetation
Backing the sand dunes is a thick carpet of lavender, rock rose and other low shrubs.

Prickly Juniper
This species of juniper (*Juniperus oxycedrus*) thrives in the wide dune belt, rooting deep into the sand. The trees sometimes get buried beneath the dunes.

Palacio del Acebrón

El Rocío

La Rocina

H612

El Acebuche

Matalascañas

Palacio de Doñana

Laguna de Santa Olaya

Key

- ▢ Marshes
- ▨ Dunes
- ••• Parque Nacional de Doñana
- ••• Parque Natural de Doñana
- ▬ Road
- ☼ Viewpoint

Coastal Dunes
Softly rounded, white dunes, up to 30 m (99 ft) high, fringe the park's coastal edge. The dunes, ribbed by prevailing winds off the Atlantic, shift constantly.

KEY

① **Monte de Doñana**, the wooded area behind the sand dunes, provide shelter for lynx, deer and boar.

② **Wild cattle** use the marshes as water holes.

Official Tour
Numbers of visitors are controlled very strictly. On official day tours along rough tracks, the knowledgeable guides point out elusive animals while ensuring minimal environmental impact.

For additional map symbols *see back flap*

Deer
Fallow deer *(Dama dama)* and larger Red deer *(Cervus elaphus)* roam the park. Stags engage in fierce contests in late summer as they prepare for breeding.

Imperial Eagle
The very rare Imperial eagle *(Aquila adalberti)* preys on small mammals.

VISITORS' CHECKLIST

Practical Information
Road map B3.
Marginal areas: **Open** daily.
Closed 1 Jan, 6 Jan, Pentecost, 25 Dec. 🛈 La Rocina: **Tel** 959 43 95 69; 🛈 Palacio del Acebrón: exhibition "Man and the Doñana". **Open** summer: 10am–3pm, 4–8pm; winter: 9am–7pm. **Tel** 959 50 61 22. 🛈 El Acebuche: reception, exhibition, café, shop. **Open** 8am–9pm (to 7pm in winter). **Tel** 959 43 96 29. Self-guided footpaths: La Rocina and Charco de la Boca; El Acebrón from Palacio del Acebrón; Laguna del Acebuche from Acebuche.
Inner park areas: **Open** summer: Mon–Sat; winter: Tue–Sun. Guided tour only. Jeeps leave El Acebuche 8:30am & 3pm (8:30am & 5pm in summer). Booking compulsory. **Tel** 959 43 04 32. 🅿
📱 donanareservas.com

Greater Flamingo
During the winter months, the salty lakes and marshes provide the beautiful, pink Greater flamingo *(Phoenicopterus ruber)* with crustaceans, its main diet.

The Lynx's Last Refuge
The lynx is one of Europe's rarest mammals. In Doñana about 50 individuals of Spanish lynx *(Lynx pardinus)* have found a refuge. They have yellow-brown fur with dark brown spots and pointed ears with black tufts. A research programme is under way to study this shy animal, which tends to stay hidden in scrub. It feeds mainly on rabbits and ducks, and sometimes on deer fawn.

The elusive lynx, only spotted with patience

Río Guadiamar

José Antonio Valverde

Marisma de Iznalcázar

Marisma Gallega

②

Río Guadalquivir

Sanlúcar de Barrameda

Fábrica de Hielo

0 kilometres 5
0 miles 5

Scenic view over the rooftops of Lebrija with their distinctive red tiles

⑮ Lebrija

Sevilla. **Road map** B3. 🏔 24,000. 🚌
🚆 ℹ Casa de Cultura, Calle Tetuán
15 (955 97 40 68). 🔺 Tue.

The pretty, walled town of
Lebrija enjoys panoramic views
over the neighbouring sherry-
growing vineyards of the Jerez
region (see p34).

Narrow cobbled streets lead
to **Iglesia de Santa María de la
Oliva**. This is a 12th-century
Almohad mosque with many
original Islamic features, which
was consecrated as a church by
Alfonso X (see p52).

⑯ Itálica

Sevilla. **Road map** B2. 🚌 from Plaza de
Armas, Seville. **Tel** 955 12 38 47. **Open**
Apr–mid-Jun: 9am–7:30pm Tue–Sat,
9am–2:30pm Sun & public hols; mid-
Jun–mid-Sep: 9am–2:30pm Tue–Sun;
mid-Sep–Mar: 9am–5:30pm Tue–Sat,
9am–2:30pm Sun & public hols.

Scipio Africanus established
Itálica in 206 BC, as one of
the first cities founded by the
Romans in Hispania. Later, it
burgeoned, both as a military
headquarters and as a cultural
centre, supporting a population
of several
thousand.
Emperors
Trajan and
Hadrian were both
born in Itálica. The
latter bestowed imperial
largesse on the city
during his reign in the
2nd century AD, adding
marble temples and other
fine buildings.

Roman mosaic
from Itálica

Archaeologists have speculated
that the changing course of the
Guadalquivir may have led to
the demise of Itálica. Certainly,
the city declined steadily after
the fall of the Roman Empire,
unlike Seville, which flourished.

At the heart of the site you
may explore the crumbling
remains of a vast amphitheatre,
which once seated 25,000. Next
to it is a display of finds from
the site, although many of the
treasures are displayed in the
Museo Arqueológico in Seville
(see p101). Visitors can wander
among the traces of streets
and villas. Little remains of the
city's temples or baths, as
most stone and marble was
plundered by builders over
the subsequent centuries.

The village of **Santiponce**
lies just outside the site. Here,
some better-preserved Roman
remains, including baths and a
theatre, have been unearthed.

⑰ Sierra Norte

Sevilla. **Road map** B2. 🚆 Estación de
Cazalla y Constantina. 🚌 Constantina;
Cazalla. ℹ Calle Paseo del Moro 2,
Cazalla de la Sierra (954 88 35 62).

An austere mountain range
flanks the northern border
of Sevilla province.
Known as the Sierra
Norte de Sevilla,
it is a part of the
greater Sierra
Morena, which
forms a natural frontier
between Andalucía and
the plains of La Mancha and
Extremadura. The region is

sparsely populated and, as it
is relatively cool in summer,
it can offer an escape from
the relentless heat of Seville.
In winter, you may meet the
occasional huntsman carrying
a partridge or hare.

Cazalla de la Sierra, the
main town of the area, seems
surprisingly cosmopolitan and
is popular with young sevillanos
at weekends. It has made a unique
contribution to the world of
drink, namely Liquor de Guindas.
This is a concoction of cherry
liqueur and aniseed, whose
taste is acquired slowly, if at all.

Constantina, to the east, is
more peaceful and has superb
views across the countryside.
A romantic aura surrounds the
ruined castle, which is situated
high above the town.

Grazing cow in the empty expanses of the
Sierra Norte de Sevilla

⑱ Carmona

Sevilla. **Road map** B2. 🏔 25,000. 🚌
ℹ Alcázar de la Puerta de Sevilla s/n
(954 19 09 55). 🔺 Mon & Thu.
🌐 turismo.carmona.org

Travelling east from Seville
on the NIV A4, Carmona is
the first major town you come
to. It rises above expansive
agricultural plains. Sprawling
suburbs spill out beyond the
Moorish city walls, which can
be entered through the old
Puerta de Sevilla. Inside, there
is a dense concentration of
mansions, Mudéjar churches,
squares and cobbled streets.

The grandeur of Plaza de San
Fernando is characterized by
the strict Renaissance façade
of the old **Ayuntamiento**. The
present town hall, located just
off the square, dates from the

Tomb of Servilia, Necrópolis Romana, Carmona

18th century; in its courtyard are some fine Roman mosaics. Close by lies **Iglesia de Santa María la Mayor**. Built in the 15th century over a mosque, whose patio still survives, this is the finest of the churches. Dominating the town, however, are the imposing ruins of the **Alcázar del Rey Pedro**, once a palace of Pedro I, also known as Pedro el Cruel (the Cruel) *(see p52)*. Parts of it now form a parador *(see p217)*.

Just outside Carmona is the **Necrópolis Romana**, the extensive remains of a Roman burial ground. A site museum displays some of the worldly goods buried with the bodies. These include statues, glass and jewellery, as well as urns.

🏛 **Ayuntamiento**
Calle Salvador 2. **Tel** 954 14 00 11. **Open** 8am–3pm Mon–Fri. **Closed** public hols.

🏛 **Necrópolis Romana**
Avenida Jorge Bonsor 9. **Tel** 600 14 36 32. **Open** Tue–Sat. **Closed** Mon & public hols.

⑲ Écija

Sevilla. **Road map** C2. 🏛 40,000. 🚌 ℹ Calle Elvira 1A, Palacio de Benamejí (955 90 29 33). 🛍 Thu. 🌐 turismoecija.com

Ecija is nicknamed "the frying pan of Andalucía" owing to its famously torrid climate. In the searing heat, the palm trees which stand on the Plaza de España provide some blissful shade. This is an ideal place to sit and observe daily life. It is also the focus of evening strolls and coffee-drinking.

Écija has eleven Baroque church steeples. A good number are adorned with gleaming *azulejos* *(see p80)* and together they make an impressive sight. The most florid of these is the **Iglesia de Santa María,** over-looking Plaza de España. **Iglesia de San Juan**, adorned with an exquisite bell tower, is a very close rival.

The **Palacio de Peñaflor** is also in Baroque style. Its pink marble doorway is topped by twisted columns, while a pretty wrought-iron balcony runs along the front façade.

🏛 **Palacio de Peñaflor**
C/Caballeros 32. **Tel** 954 83 02 73. **Closed** for major renovation work.

⑳ Osuna

Sevilla. **Road map** C3. 🏛 17,500. 🚌 🚌 ℹ Calle Sevilla 37 (954 81 57 32). 🛍 Mon.

Osuna was once a key Roman garrison town before being eclipsed during the Moorish era. The Dukes of Osuna, who wielded immense power, restored the town to prominence in the 16th century. During the 1530s they founded the grand collegiate church, **Colegiata de Santa María**. Inside is a Baroque *retablo*, and paintings by José de Ribera. The dukes were also the founders of the town's **Universidad**, a rather severe building with a beautiful patio.

Some fine mansions, among them the Baroque **Palacio del Marqués de la Gomera**, are also a testament to the former glory of this town.

㉑ Estepa

Sevilla. **Road map** C3. 🏛 12,000. 🚌 ℹ Calle Aguilar y Cano s/n (955 91 27 17). 🛍 Mon, Wed & Fri. 🌐 estepa.es

Legend has it that when the invading Roman army closed on Estepa in 207 BC, the townsfolk committed mass suicide rather than surrender. These days, life in this small town in the far southeast of Sevilla province is far less dramatic. Its fame today derives from the production of its renowned biscuits – *mantecados* and *polvorones*. Wander among the narrow streets of iron-grilled mansions, and sit on the main square to admire the beautiful black and white façade of the Baroque church, **Iglesia del Carmen**.

Wall painting on the ornate Baroque façade of Palacio de Peñaflor, Écija

CÓRDOBA AND JAÉN

Córdoba, with its magnificent mosque and pretty Moorish patios, is northern Andalucía's star attraction. Córdoba province encompasses the Montilla and Moriles wine towns, as well as Baroque treasures such as Priego de Córdoba. Jaén's mountain passes are gateways to the province's beautiful Renaissance towns of Úbeda and Baeza, and to the great wildlife reserves of the mountain ranges.

Córdoba, on Andalucía's mighty river, the Guadalquivir, was a Roman provincial capital over 2,000 years ago, but its golden age came with the Moors. In the 10th century it was the western capital of the Islamic empire, rivalling Baghdad in wealth, power and sophistication. Today it is an atmospheric city, its ancient quarters and buildings reflecting a long and glorious history.

Córdoba's surrounding countryside is dotted with monuments to its Moorish past, such as the Caliph's palace of Medina Azahara. To the south lies the Campiña, an undulating landscape covered in endless olives and vines, and green and gold expanses of sunflowers and corn. Here and there are whitewashed villages and hilltop castles with crumbling walls.

Running across the north of Córdoba and Jaén provinces is the Sierra Morena. Deer and boar shelter in the forest and scrub of this broad mountain range. The sierras dominate Jaén province. The great Río Guadalquivir springs to life as a sparkling trout stream in the Sierra de Cazorla, the craggy wilderness along its eastern border. Through the ages, mule trains, traders, highwaymen and armies have used the cleft in Sierra Morena, known as Desfiladero de Despeñaperros, to cross from La Mancha and Castilla to Andalucía.

Ancient castles perched on heights, once strategic outposts on the Moorish/Christian frontier, now overlook the peaceful olive groves punctuated by historic towns preserving gems of post-Reconquest architecture.

The city of Jaén with its spectacular cathedral against a backdrop of the Sierra Mágina mountains

◀ Rows of granite and marble pillars and Moorish striped arches inside Córdoba's Mezquita mosque-cathedral

Exploring Córdoba and Jaén

This region of rolling fields and craggy heights is divided by the fertile Guadalquivir valley. On the northern banks of the river is Córdoba with its famous Mezquita. The wild, uninhabited Sierra Morena lies to the north, while southward is a farming area dotted with historic towns, such as Priego de Córdoba. Further east, amid the olive groves of Jaén, are the Renaissance jewels, Baeza and Úbeda. From these towns it is an easy excursion to the archaeological ruins of Cástulo and to the nature reserve of Cazorla, which offers dramatic scenery and a glimpse of deer and wild boar.

Main street of Cabra at siesta time

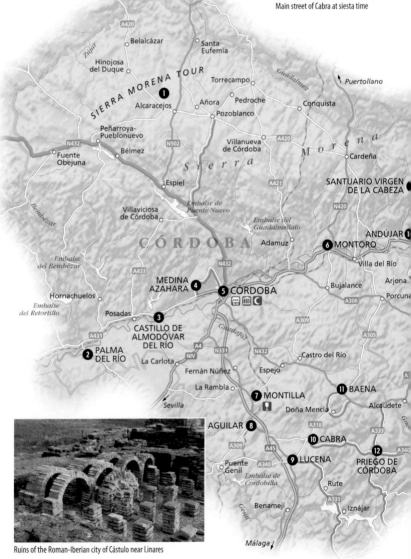

Ruins of the Roman-Iberian city of Cástulo near Linares

For additional map symbols *see back flap*

Sights at a Glance

- ❷ Palma del Río
- ❸ Castillo de Almodóvar del Río
- ❹ Medina Azahara
- ❺ *Córdoba pp144–50*
- ❻ Montoro
- ❼ Montilla
- ❽ Aguilar
- ❾ Lucena
- ❿ Cabra
- ⓫ Baena
- ⓬ Priego de Córdoba
- ⓭ Alcalá la Real
- ⓮ *Jaén pp152–3*
- ⓯ Andújar

- ⓰ Santuario Virgen de la Cabeza
- ⓱ Baños de la Encina
- ⓲ La Carolina
- ⓳ Desfiladero de Despeñaperros
- ⓴ Cástulo
- ㉑ *Baeza pp156–7*
- ㉒ *Úbeda pp158–9*
- ㉓ Cazorla
- ㉔ Parque Natural de Cazorla, Segura y Las Villas
- ㉕ Segura de la Sierra

Tour

- ❶ Sierra Morena

The town of Cazorla on the border of the nature reserve

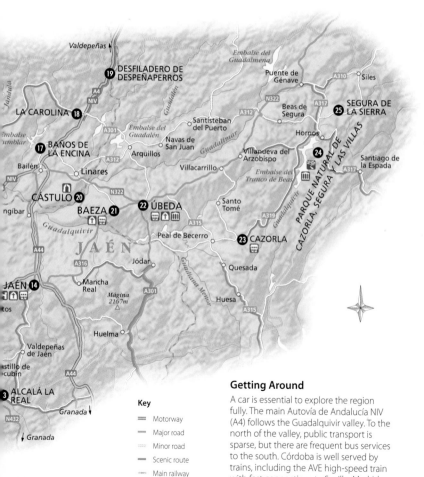

Getting Around

A car is essential to explore the region fully. The main Autovía de Andalucía NIV (A4) follows the Guadalquivir valley. To the north of the valley, public transport is sparse, but there are frequent bus services to the south. Córdoba is well served by trains, including the AVE high-speed train with fast connections to Seville, Madrid, Málaga and as far as Lleida. Jaén is served by four direct trains per day to Córdoba.

Key

- ═══ Motorway
- ━━━ Major road
- ┅┅┅ Minor road
- ━━━ Scenic route
- ┅┅┅ Main railway
- ┅┅┅ Provincial border
- △ Summit

❷ Palma del Río

Córdoba. **Road map** C2. 🏛 19,500.
🚉 🚌 ℹ️ Plaza Mayor de Andalucía
s/n (957 64 43 70). 🗓 Tue.
🌐 **palmadelrio.es**

Remains of the walls built by
the Almohads in the 1100s
are a reminder of the frontier
days of this farming town.
The Romans established a
settlement here, on the main
route from Córdoba
to Itálica (see p136),
almost 2,000 years ago.
The Baroque **Iglesia
de la Asunción** dates
from the 18th century.
The monastery of
San Francisco is now
a delightful hotel
(see p218), and
guests dine in
the 15th-century
refectory of the
Franciscan monks.
Palma is the home
town of the late

Bell tower, La
Asunción

El Cordobés, one of Spain's most
famous matadors. As a youth he
would creep out into the fields
around the town to practise with
the bulls. His biography, *Or I'll
Dress You in Mourning*, gives a
vivid view of Palma and of the
hardship that followed the end
of the Civil War.

❸ Castillo de Almodóvar del Río

Córdoba. **Road map** C2. **Tel** 957 63
40 55. **Open** 11am–2:30pm, 4–7pm
Mon–Fri (to 8pm Apr–Sep), 11am–
7pm Sat, Sun & public hols (to 8pm
Apr–Sep). 🌐 **castillode
almodovar.com**

One of Andalucía's most
dramatic silhouettes breaks
the skyline as the traveller
approaches Almodóvar del Río.
The Moorish castle, with parts
dating back to the 8th century,
overlooks the white-washed
town and surrounding fields.

Detail of wood carving in the main hall of
Medina Azahara

❹ Medina Azahara

Ctra Palma del Rio, km 5.5, Córdoba.
Road map C2. **Tel** 957 10 49 33.
Open Apr–mid-Jun: 9am–8pm Tue–
Sat, 9am–3pm Sun & public hols; mid-
Jun–mid-Sep: 9am–3pm Tue–Sun;
mid-Sep–Mar: 9am–6pm Tue–Sat,
9am–3pm Sun & public hols. 🎟 (free
for EU citizens).

To the northwest of Córdoba lies
the remains of a Moorish palace

❶ Sierra Morena Tour

The austere Sierra Morena runs across northern
Andalucía. This route through Córdoba province
takes in a region of oak- and pine-clad hills, where
hunters stalk deer and boar. It also includes the
open plain of Valle de los Pedroches, where storks
make their nests on church towers. The area,
little visited by tourists, is sparsely populated. Its
individual character is more sober than the usual
image of Andalucía and it makes a delightful
excursion on a day out from Córdoba.

④ **Hinojosa del Duque**
"Catedral de la Sierra", the vast, 15th-century
pile of the Gothic-Renaissance Iglesia
San Juan Bautista, dominates the town.
It has a Churrigueresque *retablo*.

Rising at Fuente Obejuna

On 23 April 1476, townsfolk
stormed the palace of the hated
lord, Don Fernando Gómez
de Guzmán. He was hurled
from a palace window, then
hacked to pieces in the main
plaza. When questioned by
a judge who committed
the crime, the men and
women replied as one,
"Fuente Obejuna, señor!"
Nobody was punished,
at least according
to Lope de Vega's best-known play,
named after the village.

Lope de Vega
(1562–1635)

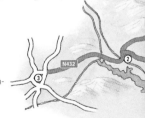

② **Peñarroya-
Pueblonuevo**
This was once
an important
copper- and iron-
mining centre.

③ **Fuente Obejuna**
The Plaza Lope de Vega is
often the venue for Lope
de Vega's famous play. The
parish church, Nuestra
Señora del Castillo, was
built in the 15th century.

① **Bélmez**
Remains of a
13th-century castle
crown a hill, from which
there are fine views.

built in the 10th century for Caliph Abd al Rahman III, who named it after his wife. More than 10,000 workers and 15,000 mules ferried building materials from as far as North Africa.

The palace is built on three levels and includes a mosque, the caliph's residence and fine gardens. Alabaster, ebony, jasper and marble decoration adorned its many halls.

Unfortunately, the glory was short-lived. The palace was sacked by Berber invaders in 1010. Then, over centuries, it was ransacked for its building materials. Now, the ruins give only glimpses of its former splendour – a Moorish main hall, for instance, with marble carvings and a fine wooden ceiling. The palace is being restored, but progress is slow.

❺ Córdoba

See pp144–50.

❻ Montoro

Córdoba. **Road map** D2. 🏔 9,600. 🚌
ℹ️ Calle Corredera 25 (957 16 00 89).
🗓️ Tue. 🌐 **montoro.es**

Spread over five hills that span a bend in the River Guadalquivir, Montoro dates from the times of the Greeks and Phoenicians. Today the economy of this rather lethargic town depends on its olive groves. The solid bridge, which was designed by Enrique de Egas, was started in the time of the Catholic Monarchs *(see pp52–3)* and took

more than 50 years to finish. The townswomen sold their jewellery to raise funds for the bridge, hence its name: **Puente de las Donadas** (Bridge of the Donors).

Steep streets give the town charm. In Plaza de España are the **Ayuntamiento**, former seat of the ducal rulers, with a Plateresque façade, and the Gothic-Mudéjar **Iglesia de San Bartolomé**.

Leather bags and embossed saddlery are among several enduring crafts that are still produced in Montoro.

The 16th-century bridge spanning the Guadalquivir at Montoro

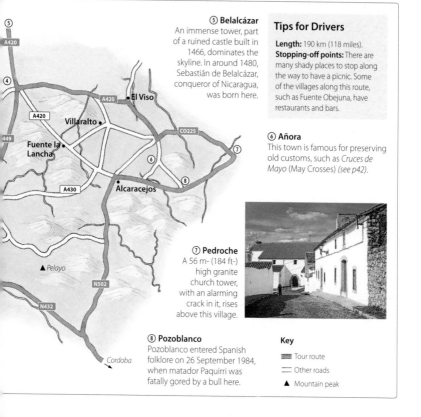

❺ ④ A420 ④ A420 Villaralto 449 **Fuente la Lancha** A430 **Alcaracejos** A420 **El Viso** CO225 ⑥ ⑦ ⑧ ▲ *Pelayo* N502 N432 *Cordoba*

⑤ Belalcázar
An immense tower, part of a ruined castle built in 1466, dominates the skyline. In around 1480, Sebastián de Belalcázar, conqueror of Nicaragua, was born here.

⑥ Añora
This town is famous for preserving old customs, such as *Cruces de Mayo* (May Crosses) *(see p42).*

⑦ Pedroche
A 56 m- (184 ft-) high granite church tower, with an alarming crack in it, rises above this village.

⑧ Pozoblanco
Pozoblanco entered Spanish folklore on 26 September 1984, when matador Paquirri was fatally gored by a bull here.

Tips for Drivers

Length: 190 km (118 miles).
Stopping-off points: There are many shady places to stop along the way to have a picnic. Some of the villages along this route, such as Fuente Obejuna, have restaurants and bars.

Key

▬▬ Tour route
━━ Other roads
▲ Mountain peak

⑤ Street-by-Street: Córdoba

The heart of Córdoba is the old Jewish quarter near the Mezquita, known as the Judería. A walk around this area gives the visitor the sensation that little has changed since this was one of the greatest cities in the Western world. Narrow, cobbled streets where cars cannot penetrate, secluded niches, wrought-iron gates, tiny workshops where silversmiths create fine jewellery – all appears very much as it was 1,000 years ago. Traffic roars along the riverfront, past the replica of a Moorish water wheel and the towering walls of the Great Mosque. Most of the sights are in this area, while modern city life takes place some blocks north, around the Plaza de las Tendillas.

Sinagoga
Hebrew script covers the interior walls of this medieval synagogue, the only one remaining in Andalucía.

Baños del Alcázar Califales
These 10th-century Arab baths now house a museum recreating the history and uses of the baths.

Capilla de San Bartolomé, in Mudéjar style, contains elaborate plasterwork.

To Barrio de San Basilio

★ **Alcázar de los Reyes Cristianos**
Water terraces and fountains add to the tranquil atmosphere of the gardens belonging to the palace-fortress of the Catholic Monarchs, constructed in the 14th century.

0 metres 75
0 yards 75

Key

— Suggested route

For hotels and restaurants in this region see pp217–18 and pp231–2

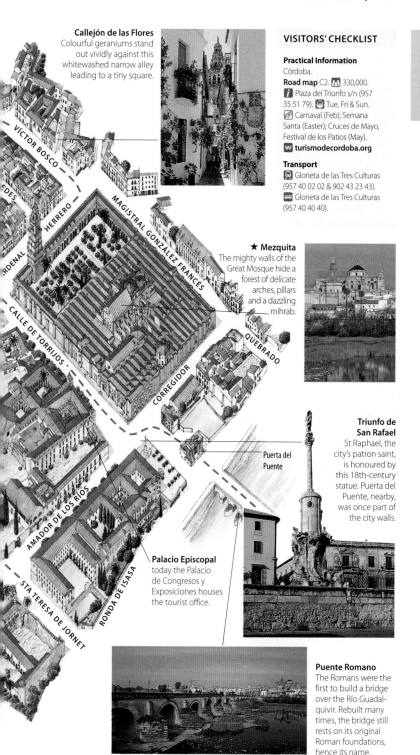

Callejón de las Flores
Colourful geraniums stand out vividly against this whitewashed narrow alley leading to a tiny square.

VISITORS' CHECKLIST

Practical Information
Córdoba.
Road map C2. ⚡ 330,000.
ℹ️ Plaza del Triunfo s/n (957 35 51 79). 🏛️ Tue, Fri & Sun.
🎭 Carnaval (Feb); Semana Santa (Easter); Cruces de Mayo, Festival de los Patios (May).
🌐 **turismodecordoba.org**

Transport
🚌 Glorieta de las Tres Culturas (957 40 02 02 & 902 43 23 43).
🚍 Glorieta de las Tres Culturas (957 40 40 40).

★ Mezquita
The mighty walls of the Great Mosque hide a forest of delicate arches, pillars and a dazzling mihrab.

Puerta del Puente

Triunfo de San Rafael
St Raphael, the city's patron saint, is honoured by this 18th-century statue. Puerta del Puente, nearby, was once part of the city walls.

Palacio Episcopal
today the Palacio de Congresos y Exposiciones houses the tourist office.

Puente Romano
The Romans were the first to build a bridge over the Río Guadalquivir. Rebuilt many times, the bridge still rests on its original Roman foundations, hence its name.

Exploring Córdoba

Córdoba's core is the old city around the Mezquita on the banks of the Guadalquivir. Its origins are probably Carthaginian; the name may be derived from Kartuba, Phoenician for "rich and precious city". Under the Romans it was a provincial capital and birthplace of philosopher Seneca. However, Córdoba's golden age was in the 10th century when Abd al Rahman III created an independent caliphate with Córdoba as its capital. Its influence spread to North Africa and the Balearic Islands. Córdoba was a centre of trade, industry and learning, where Jews and Christians lived alongside Muslims. Civil war (see pp50–51) ended the caliphate and the city was pillaged. It declined after falling to Fernando III in 1236, although a number of fine buildings have since been erected.

Naranjas y Limones (Oranges and Lemons) in Museo Julio Romero de Torres

✡ Sinagoga

Calle Judíos 20. **Tel** 957 74 90 15. **Open** mid-Jun–mid-Sep: 9am–3:30pm Tue–Sun; mid-Sep–mid-Jun: 9am–8:30pm Tue–Sat, 9am–to 3:30pm Sun & hols.

Constructed around 1315, the Mudéjar-style synagogue is one of three in Spain preserved from that era. The other two are in Toledo. The women's gallery and decorative plasterwork, with Hebrew script, are of particular interest. The synagogue lies in the Judería, the Jewish quarter, which has hardly changed since Moorish times. In a plaza nearby is a bronze statue of Maimónides, a 12th-century Jewish sage.

⬚ Museo Taurino

Plaza de Maimónides 1. **Tel** 957 20 10 56. **Open** mid-Jun–mid-Sep: 8:30am–3pm Mon–Sat, 8:30am–to 2:30pm Sun; mid-Sep–mid-Jun: 8:30am–8:45pm Tue–Fri, 8:30am–to 4:30pm Sat, 8:30am–2:30pm Sun. 🅰
Ⓦ **museotaurinodecordoba.es**
Housed in a 16th-century mansion, this museum features memorabilia from some of Córdoba's most popular bullfighters, including paintings, sculptures, posters and costumes, or *trajes de luces*.

⬚ Baños del Alcázar Califales

Campo Santo de los Mártires. **Tel** 608 15 88 93. **Open** mid-Jun–mid-Sep: 8:30am–2:30pm Tue–Sat, 9:30am–2:30pm Sun & hols; mid-Sep–mid-Jun: 8:30am–8:45pm Tue–Fri; 8:30am–4:30pm Sat; 9:30am–2:30pm Sun & hols. 🅰 (free 8:30–10:30am Mon–Fri). ♿

Built in the Umayyad Palace under orders from Al-Hakam II

in the 10th century, these well-preserved Arab baths reflect the classical order of Roman baths: cold rooms, warm rooms and hot rooms. A museum recreates the social and religious history and uses of the baths.

⬚ Alcázar de los Reyes Cristianos

C/Caballerizas Reales s/n. **Tel** 957 42 01 51. **Open** mid-Jun–mid-Sep: 8:30am–2:30pm Tue–Sat, 9:30am–2:30pm Sun; mid-Sep–mid-Jun: 8:30am–8:45pm Tue–Fri, 8:30am–4:30pm Sat, 8:30am–3pm Sun. 🅰

This palace-fortress was built in 1328 for Alfonso XI. Fernando II and Isabel stayed here during their campaign to conquer Granada from the Moors (see p52). Later it was used by the Inquisition (see p55), and then as a prison. The gardens, with ponds and fountains, are open in the evenings in July and August. Behind the palace's walls are Roman mosaics.

⬚ Puente Romano

This arched bridge has Roman foundations, but was rebuilt by the Moors. Nearby, south of the Mezquita is the 1571 Puerta del Puente, designed by Hernán Ruiz.

⬚ Torre de la Calahorra

Tel 957 29 39 29. **Open** daily. Oct–Apr: 10am–6pm; May–Sep: 10am–2pm, 4:30–8:30pm. 🅰
At the end of the Puente Romano, this 14th-century tower houses a museum about the life, culture and philosophy of 10th-century Córdoba.

⬚ Mezquita

See pp148–9.

⬚ Museo Arqueológico

Plaza Jerónimo Páez 7. **Tel** 957 35 55 17. **Open** mid-Jun–mid-Sep: 9am–3pm Tue–Sun & public hols; mid-Sep–mid-Jun: 10am–8pm Tue–Sat, 10am–3pm Sun & public hols. 🅰

Located in a Renaissance mansion, this excellent archaeological museum features remains of a Roman theatre found beneath the building, including mosaics and pottery, as well as impressive finds from the Moorish era. Highlights in the museum include Moorish items such as a 10th-century bronze stag found at Medina Azahara (see p142). Also on display is a marble sculpted head of the Emperor Augustus, dating to the 1st century AD, which was found in the area.

Moorish bronze of a stag from Medina Azahara in the Museo Arqueológico

⃞ Museo Julio Romero de Torres

Plaza del Potro 1. **Tel** 957 47 03 56.
Open mid-Jun–mid-Sep: 8:30am–2:30pm Tue–Sat, 9:30am–2:30pm Sun & hols; mid-Sep–mid-Jun: 8:30am–8:45pm Tue–Fri, 8:30am–4:30pm Sat; 8:30am–2:30pm Sun & public hols. 🗟

Julio Romero de Torres (1874–1930), who was born in this house, captured the soul of Córdoba in his paintings. Many depict nudes in stilted poses. His style varied from the macabre *Cante Hondo* (1930) to the humorous *Naranjas y Limones* (1928).

⃞ Museo de Bellas Artes

Plaza del Potro 1. **Tel** 957 10 36 43.
Open mid-Jun–mid-Sep: 9am–3:30pm Tue–Sun & public hols; mid-Sep–mid-Jun: 9am–8:30pm Tue–Sat, 9am–3:30pm Sun & public hols.

Located in a former charity hospital, this museum exhibits sculptures by local artist Mateo Inurria and Seville School paintings by Zurbarán (*see p70*).

Daily market in the arcaded Plaza de la Corredera

⃞ Plaza de la Corredera

Built in the 17th century in Castilian style, this arcaded square has been the scene of bullfights and other public events. The buildings have been restored, but the cafés under the arches retain an air of the past. A market is held here daily.

⃞ Palacio de Viana

Plaza Don Gome 2. **Tel** 957 49 67 41.
Open Jul & Aug: 9am–3pm Tue–Sun (also 9–11pm Fri & Sat); Sep–Jun: 10am–7pm Tue–Sat; 10am–3pm Sun. 🗟

Tapestries, furniture, porcelain and paintings are displayed in this 17th-century mansion. Purchased by a savings bank in 1981, the former home of the Viana family is kept much as they left it. There are 14 beautiful patios and a delightful garden.

Central fountain in the garden of the 17th-century Palacio de Viana

Sights at a Glance

① Sinagoga
② Museo Taurino
③ Baños del Alcázar Califales
④ Alcázar de los Reyes Cristianos
⑤ Puente Romano
⑥ Torre de la Calahorra
⑦ Mezquita

⑧ Museo Arqueológico
⑨ Museo Julio Romero de Torres & Museo de Bellas Artes
⑩ Plaza de la Corredera

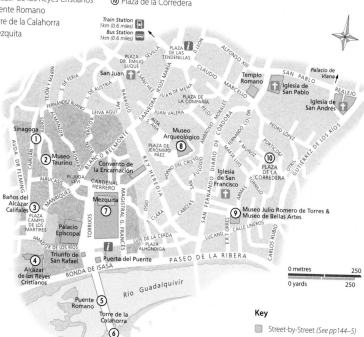

Key

⬛ Street-by-Street (*See pp144–5*)

For keys to symbols *see back flap*

Córdoba: the Mezquita

Córdoba's great mosque, dating back 12 centuries, embodied the power of Islam on the Iberian peninsula. Abd al Rahman I *(see p50)* built the original mosque between 785 and 787. The building evolved over the centuries, blending many architectural forms. In the 10th century al Hakam II *(see p50)* made some lavish additions, including the elaborate *mihrab* (prayer niche) and the *maqsura* (caliph's enclosure). In the 16th century a cathedral was built in the heart of the reconsecrated mosque, part of which was destroyed.

Patio de los Naranjos
Orange trees grow in the courtyard where the faithful washed before prayer.

Expansion of the Mezquita

Abd al Rahman I built the original mosque. Extensions were added by Abd al Rahman II, al Hakam II and al Mansur.

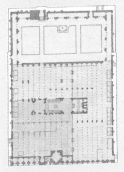

Key to Floorplan

- ☐ Mosque of Abd al Rahman I
- ☐ Extension by Abd al Rahman II
- ☐ Extension by al Hakam II
- ☐ Extension by al Mansur
- ☐ Patio de los Naranjos

KEY

① **Puerta de San Esteban** is set in a section of wall from an earlier Visigothic church.

② **The Puerta del Perdón** is a Mudéjar-style entrance gate, built during Christian rule in 1377. Penitents were pardoned here.

③ **Capilla Mayor**

④ **The cathedral choir** has Churrigueresque stalls, carved by Pedro Duque Cornejo in 1758.

⑤ **Capilla Real**

Torre del Alminar
This bell tower, 93 m (305 ft) high, is built on the site of the original minaret. Steep steps lead to the top for a fine view of the city.

Cathedral
Part of the mosque was destroyed to accommodate the cathedral, started in 1523. Featuring an Italianate dome, it was chiefly designed by members of the Hernán Ruiz family.

VISITORS' CHECKLIST

Practical Information
Calle Torrijos s/n. **Tel** 957 47 05 12.
Open 10am–7pm Mon–Sat, 8:30–11:30am & 3–7pm Sun & religious hols (Nov–Feb: 10am–6pm Mon–Sat & 3–6pm Sun & religious hols).
9:30am Mon–Sat; 10:30am & 1pm Sun & public hols.
w mezquitadecordoba.org

★ Arches and Pillars
More than 850 columns of granite, jasper and marble support the roof, creating a dazzling visual effect. Many of them were taken from Roman and Visigothic buildings.

★ Mihrab
This prayer niche, richly ornamented, held a gilt copy of the Koran. The worn flagstones indicate where pilgrims circled it seven times on their knees.

★ Capilla de Villaviciosa
The first Christian chapel to be built in the mosque, in 1371, the Capilla de Villaviciosa has stunning multi-lobed arches.

The Patios of Córdoba

Since early times, family and social life in Andalucía have revolved around the courtyard or patio, which is at the heart of the classic Mediterranean house. The sleeping accommodation and living rooms were built round this space, which introduces air and light into the house. Brick arches, colourful tiles, ironwork, orange and lemon trees, and pots full of flowers add to the charm of these cool and tranquil retreats. Córdoba takes pride in all its patio gardens, be they palatial spaces in the grandest residences or tiny courtyards in humble homes, shared by many. There are traditional patios in the San Lorenzo and Judería quarters and in Barrio San Basilio, west of the Mezquita.

Whitewashed walls

Tiled portrait of saint

Orange trees

Festival de los Patios, when scores of patios are thrown open to the public, takes place in early May *(see pp42–3)*. The most beautifully decorated patio wins a prestigious prize.

Andalucían Patio

This scene, painted by García Rodríguez (1863–1925), evokes a style of patio that is still common in Andalucía. The patio walls are usually immaculately whitewashed, contrasting with the colourful display of geraniums and carnations in terracotta pots. Fragrant blooms of jasmine add to the atmosphere.

Moorish-style lamps, which now have electric bulbs, light the patio in the late evening.

Azulejos, a reminder of the region's Moorish past, decorate many patios, adding to their colourful display.

Cancelas are attractively designed iron gates which screen the private patio from the street outside.

A central fountain or well traditionally provided water and remains a feature of many patios today.

● Montilla

Córdoba. **Road map** C2. ⛰ 23,000.
🚌 🚆 ℹ️ Calle Capitan Alonso de
Vargas 3 (957 65 24 62). 🛒 Fri.

Montilla is the centre of an
important wine-making region,
but one that finds it difficult to
emerge from the shadow of a
more famous rival. The excellent
white wine is made in the same
way as sherry (see pp34–5) and
tastes rather like it but, unlike
sherry, does not need fortifying
with alcohol. Some *bodegas*,
including **Alvear** and **Pérez
Barquero**, are happy to
welcome visitors.

The Mudéjar **Convento de
Santa Clara** dates from 1512
and the **castle** from the 18th
century. The town library is in
the **Casa del Inca**, so named
because Garcilaso de la Vega,
who wrote about the Incas,
lived there in the 16th century.

🏠 **Bodega Alvear**
Avenida María Auxiliadora 1. **Tel** 957 65
01 00. **Open** daily (call first to arrange
visit). 🆆 alvear.es

🏠 **Bodega Pérez Barquero**
Avenida Andalucía 27. **Tel** 957 65 05
00. **Open** phone ahead to make an
appt, or e-mail info@perezbarquero.
com. 🆆 perezbarquero.com

The historic crest of the Bodega
Pérez Barquero

● Aguilar

Córdoba. **Road map** C2. ⛰ 13,500.
🚌 🚆 ℹ️ Calle Villa 1 (957 66 17 71).
🛒 Tue, Thu & Fri.

Ceramics, wine and olive oil
are important products in
Aguilar, which was settled
in Roman times. There are
several seigneurial houses,
and the eight-sided **Plaza
de San José**. Built in 1810, it
houses the town hall. Nearby
is a Baroque clock tower.

● Lucena

Córdoba. **Road map** D2. ⛰ 40,000.
🚌 ℹ️ Palacio de los Condes de Santa
Ana, Calle San Pedro 42 (957 51 32 82).
🛒 Wed. 🆆 turlucena.com

Lucena prospers from furniture
making and from its brass and
copper manufacturers, and
produces interesting ceramics.
Under the caliphs of Córdoba
(see p50) it was an important
trading and intellectual centre,
with a dynamic, independent,
Jewish community.

Iglesia de Santiago, with a
Baroque turret, was built on the
site of a synagogue in 1503.
The **Torre del Moral** is the only
remaining part of a Moorish
castle. Granada's last sultan,
Boabdil, was captured in 1483,
and imprisoned here. Nearby,
the 15th-century **Iglesia de
San Mateo** has a flamboyant
Baroque sacristy.

On the first Sunday in May
Lucena stages an elaborate
ceremony, which honours
the Virgen de Araceli.

● Cabra

Córdoba. **Road map** D2. ⛰ 21,000.
🚌 ℹ️ Calle Mayor 1 (957 52 34 93).
🛒 Mon. 🆆 turismo.cabra.eu

Set amid fertile fields and vast
olive groves, Cabra was an
episcopal seat in the 3rd century.
On a rise stands the former castle,
which is now a school. There are

Statue of Santo Domingo, Iglesia Santo
Domingo in Cabra

also some noble mansions
and the **Iglesia Santo Domingo**
with a Baroque façade.

Just outside the town,
the **Fuente del Río**, source of
the Río Cabra, is a pleasantly
leafy spot in which to picnic.

● Baena

Córdoba. **Road map** D2. ⛰ 20,000.
🚌 ℹ️ Virrey del Pino 5 (957 67 17 57).
🛒 Thu.

Baena's olive oil has been famed
since Roman times. At the top
of the whitewashed town is
Iglesia Santa María la Mayor.
On the Plaza de la Constitución
stands the handsome, modern
town hall. The **Casa del Monte**,
an arcaded mansion dating
from the 18th century, flanks
it on one side.

Easter week is spectacular,
when thousands of drummers
take to the streets (see p38).

Decoration on the façade of the 18th-century Casa del Monte, Baena

⑭ Jaén

The Moors knew Jaén as *geen*, meaning "way station of caravans". Their lofty fortress, later rebuilt as the Castillo de Santa Catalina, symbolizes Jaén's strategic importance on the route to Andalucía from the more austere Castile. For centuries this area was a battleground between Moors and Christians *(see pp52–3)*. The older, upper part of the city holds most interest. Around the cathedral and towards the Barrio San Juan are numerous seigneurial buildings, long winding streets and steep alleys. The city centre is filled with smart shops, and in the evenings the narrow streets near Plaza de la Constitución are filled with people enjoying the *tapeo* in the many bars.

🏛 Catedral
Plaza de Santa María. **Tel** 953 23 42 33.
Open 10am–2pm, 4–7pm Mon–Fri, (to 6pm Sat), 10am–noon, 4–6pm Sun.

Andrés de Vandelvira, responsible for many of Úbeda's fine buildings *(see pp158–9)*, designed the cathedral in the 16th century. Later additions include two 17th-century towers that flank the west front. Inside are carved choir stalls and a museum with art.

Every Friday, from 10:30am to noon and 5 to 6pm, worshippers can view the Lienzo del Santo Rostro. St Veronica is said to have used this piece of cloth to wipe Christ's face, which left a permanent impression.

🏛 Baños Arabes
Palacio Villardompardo, Plaza Santa Luisa de Marillac. **Tel** 953 24 80 68.
Open 9am–10pm Tue–Sat, 9am–3pm Sun. **Closed** public hols.

These 11th-century baths are known as the baths of Ali,

Horseshoe arches supporting the dome at the Baños Arabes

a Moorish chieftain. They were restored during the 1980s. The interior features horseshoe arches, ceilings decorated with tiny star-shaped windows, a hemispherical dome and two earthenware vats in which bathers once immersed themselves. The baths are entered

through an old mansion, the Palacio Villardompardo. The palace also houses the Museo de Artes y Costumbres Populares and the Museo Internacional de Arte Naïf Manuel Moral.

🏛 Capilla de San Andrés
Tucked away in a narrow alley next to a college lies the Capilla de San Andrés, a Mudéjar chapel. The chapel was founded in the 16th century, possibly on the site of a synagogue, by Gutiérrez González, who was treasurer to Pope Leo X and endowed with extensive privileges. A magnificent gilded iron screen by Maestro Bartolomé de Jaén is the highlight of the chapel.

🏛 Real Monasterio de Santa Clara
Founded in the 13th century, just after the Reconquest of the city by Christian forces, Real Monasterio de Santa Clara is one of the most ancient monasteries in Jaén. It has a lovely cloister, which dates from about 1581. The church has an *artesonado* ceiling and shelters a curious 16th-century bamboo image of Christ made in Ecuador. Sweet cakes are offered for sale by the nuns from the convent.

🏛 Iglesia San Ildefonso
This mainly Gothic church has façades in three different styles. One is Gothic, with a mosaic of the Virgin descending on Jaén during a Moorish siege in 1430. A second is partly Plateresque

---

Olive Oil

Olive oil is the life-blood of Jaén and its province. Since the Phoenicians, or possibly the Greeks, brought the olive tree to Spain it has flourished in Andalucía, particularly in Jaén, which today has an annual production of more than 200,000 tonnes of oil. Harvesting, mostly by hand, takes place from December onwards. Quality is controlled by a system known as *Denominación de Origen Controlada*. The best product, virgin olive oil, is made from the first cold-pressing, so that the full flavour, vitamins and nutrients of the oil are preserved.

Harvest time in one of the many olive groves in Andalucía

Shrine of Virgen de la Capilla in Iglesia San Ildefonso

Mighty ramparts of Castillo de Santa Catalina

(see p29) and the third, by Ventura Rodríguez in the late 18th century, is Neo-Classical. Inside, the high altar is by Pedro and José Roldán. There is also a chapel which enshrines the Virgen de la Capilla, Jaén's patron saint. The museum next door is devoted to the Virgin.

🏰 Castillo de Santa Catalina

Carretera al Castillo. **Tel** 953 12 07 33 (tourist centre), 953 23 00 00 (parador). **Open** daily. **Closed** public hols. 🅿

Hannibal is believed to have erected a tower on this rocky pinnacle, high above the city.

Later the Moors established a mighty fortress, only to lose it to the crusading King Fernando III in 1246. A larger castle was then built with huge ramparts. This has been restored and a medieval-style *parador* (inn) built next door.

It is worthwhile taking the sinuous road up to the Torre del Homenaje and the castle chapel. Even more rewarding are the stunning views of the city, and the surrounding landscape, including the Sierra Morena hills thick with olive trees and the mountains of the Sierra Nevada.

VISITORS' CHECKLIST

Practical Information

Jaén. **Road map** D2. 🚗 115,000. 🛈 Calle Maestra 8 (953 31 32 81). 🏛 Thu. 🎭 Semana Santa (Easter); Festividad de Nuestra Señora de la Capilla (11 Jun); Feria de San Lucas (18 Oct); Romería de Santa Catalina (25 Nov).

Transport

🚆 Paseo de la Estación s/n (902 43 23 43). 🚌 Plaza Coca de la Piñera s/n. 953 23 23 00.

🏛 Museo Provincial

Paseo de la Estación 29. **Tel** 953 10 13 66. **Open** mid-Jun–mid-Sep: 9am–3pm Tue–Sun & public hols; mid-Sep–mid-Jun: 9am–8pm Tue–Sat, 9am–3pm Sun & public hols.

This building incorporates the remains of the Iglesia de San Miguel and the façade of a 16th-century granary. A Palaeo-Christian sarcophagus and Greek and Roman ceramics are among the articles on display.

Nearby is the Plaza de las Batallas and a memorial to the defeats of Napoleon at Bailén (see p57) and of the Moors at Las Navas de Tolosa (see p52).

Sights at a Glance

1. Catedral
2. Baños Arabes
3. Capilla de San Andrés
4. Real Monasterio de Santa Clara
5. Iglesia San Ildefonso

For keys to symbols *see back flap*

The Moorish Castillo de la Mota and the ruined church crowning the hill above Alcalá la Real

⑫ Priego de Córdoba

Córdoba. **Road map** D2. ⚑ 23,000. ⚑ ℹ Plaza de la Constitución 3 (957 70 06 25). ⚑ Sat. ⚑ **turismode priego.com**

Priego de Córdoba lies on a fertile plain at the foot of La Tiñosa, the highest mountain in Córdoba province. It is a pleasant small town with an unassuming air, well away from the main routes, and yet it claims to be the capital of Córdoba Baroque. The title is easy to accept in view of the dazzling work of local carvers, gilders and ironworkers.

The town's labyrinthine old quarter was the site of the original Arab settlement. But the 18th century, when silk manufacture prospered, was Priego's golden age. During this time elegant houses were built and money was lavished on fine Baroque architecture, particularly churches.

A restored Moorish fortress, standing on Roman foundations, introduces visitors to the fine medieval quarter, **Barrio de la Villa**. Whitewashed buildings line its narrow streets and flower-decked squares. Paseo Colombia leads to the Adarve, a long promenade with views of the surrounding countryside.

The nearby **Iglesia de la Asunción** is an outstanding structure. Originally Gothic in style, it was converted to a Baroque church by Jerónimo Sánchez de Rueda in the 18th century. Its *pièce de résistance* is

the sacristy chapel, created in 1784 by local artist Francisco Javier Pedrajas. Its sumptuous ornamentation in the form of sculpted figures and plaster scrolls and cornices can be overwhelming. The main altar is in Plateresque style *(see p29)*.

The **Iglesia de la Aurora** is another fine Baroque building. At midnight every Saturday the cloaked brotherhood of Nuestra Señora de la Aurora, parades the streets singing songs to the Virgin and collecting alms.

Silk merchants built many of the imposing mansions that follow the curve around the Calle del Río. Niceto Alcalá Zamora was born at No. 33 in 1877. A brilliant orator, he became Spain's president in 1931, but was forced into exile

Fine statuary ornaments the 16th-century Fuente del Rey at Priego de Córdoba

during the Civil War. Today the house contains a museum about him and his life.

At the end of the street is the **Fuente del Rey**, or King's Fountain. This is a Baroque extravaganza, with three pools, and includes Neptune among its exuberant statuary.

May is one of the liveliest months to visit Priego. Every Sunday a procession celebrates the town's deliverance from a plague which devastated the population centuries ago.

⑬ Alcalá la Real

Jaén. **Road map** D2. ⚑ 22,000. ⚑ ℹ Palacio Abacial, Avenida de las Mercedes, s/n (953 10 28 68). ⚑ Tue.

Alcalá was a strategic point held by the military Order of Calatrava during Spain's Reconquest *(see pp52–3)*. On the hilltop of La Mota are the ruins of the Moorish **Fortaleza de la Mota**, built by the rulers of Granada in the 14th century, with later additions. Nearby are ruins of the town's former main church. There are splendid views over the countryside and the historic town, with its air of past glories. The Renaissance **Palacio Abacial** and **Fuente de Carlos V** are the chief attractions to be found around the plaza in the centre of the town.

⑭ Jaén

See pp152–3.

⓯ Andújar

Jaén. **Road map** D2. 🏛 40,000. 🚉
🚌 ℹ️ Torre del Reloj Plaza de Santa
Maria s/n (953 50 49 59). 🛒 Tue.

This strategically situated town
was once the site of Iliturgi, an
Iberian town that was destroyed
by Scipio's army in the Punic Wars
(*see p48*). A 15-arched bridge
built by the Roman conquerors
still spans the Guadalquivir river.

In the central plaza is the
Gothic **Iglesia San Miguel**, with
paintings by Alonso Cano. The
Iglesia Santa María la Mayor
features a Renaissance façade and
a splendid Mudéjar tower. Inside
is the painting *Christ in the Garden
of Olives* (c.1605) by El Greco.

The town is also renowned for
its potters, who still turn out
ceramics in traditional style. Olive
oil (*see p152*), which is produced
in Andújar, figures strongly in the
local cuisine.

Roman bridge spanning the Guadalquivir at Andújar

and the original statue of the
Virgin were destroyed in 1937 in
the Civil War (*see pp58–9*). For nine
months 230 civil guards held
out against Republican forces.
Twenty thousand men attacked
the sanctuary before it burned
down. Captain Santiago Cortés,
commander of the civil guard,
died from his battle wounds.
On the last Sunday in April,
thousands make a pilgrimage to
the sanctuary to pay homage
to the Virgin (*see p43*).

⓰ Santuario Virgen de la Cabeza

Padres Trinitarios. **Road map** D2.
Tel 953 54 90 15. **Open** daily. ♿
🍴 9am, 10am, 11am, noon, 1pm,
6pm (winter), 8pm (summer).
🌐 **santuariovirgencabeza.org**

North of Andújar, amid the oak
trees and bull ranches of the
Sierra Morena, is the Santuario
Virgen de la Cabeza. Within this
grim stone temple from the 13th
century, is a much-venerated
Virgin. According to tradition
her image was sent to Spain by
St Peter. Much of the building

Replica of the statue of the Virgin Mary,
Santuario de la Cabeza

⓱ Baños de la Encina

Jaén. **Road map** D2. 🚌 from Linares
& Jaén. **Tel** Avenida José Luis Messía 2.
953 61 33 38. **Open** Wed–Mon.
🌐 **bdelaencina.com**

Caliph al Hakam II (*see p50*)
ordered the construction of this
fortress, Castillo de Burgalimar,
in the foothills of the Sierra
Morena in AD 967. Rising above
the village, it is a daunting sight
with its 15 towers and soaring
ramparts. Its heights give views
across pastures and olive groves.

During the spring fair there is
a *romería* (*see p42*) to the town's
shrine of the Virgen de la Encina.
According to tradition, the Virgin
made a miraculous appearance
on an *encina* (holm oak tree).

⓲ La Carolina

Jaén. **Road map** E1. 🏛 15,500. 🚌
ℹ️ Plaza del Ayuntamiento 1 (953 66
00 34). 🛒 Tue & Fri.

Founded in 1767, La Carolina
was populated by settlers from
Germany and Flanders. This was
an ill-fated plan to develop the
area and to make it safer for
travellers. The person in charge,
Carlos III's minister, Pablo de
Olavide, had a palace built on

the main square. Just outside
town is a monument to a battle
at Las Navas de Tolosa in 1212.
Alfonso VIII, king of Castile, was
led by a shepherd over the hills
to Las Navas, where he crushed
the Moors. His victory began
the reconquest of Andalucía
(*see pp52–3*).

⓳ Desfiladero de Despeñaperros

Jaén. **Road map** E1. ℹ️ Visitors
Centre, Auto via de Andalucía (A4) km
262 Santa Elena, Jaén (953 66 43 58).

This spectacular pass in the
Sierra Morena is the main
gateway to Andalucía. Armies,
stage-coaches, mule-trains and
brigands all used the pass, so
hold-ups were common.

The four-lane Autovía de
Andalucía and a railway line
thread their way through the
chasm, which offers views
of rock formations – *Los Organos*
(the organ pipes) and the
Salto del Fraile (monk's leap).

⓴ Cástulo

Jaén. **Road map** E1. 🚌 from
Linares & Jaén. **Open** daily.
🌐 **viajealtiempodelosiberos.com**

Around 7 km (4 miles) from
Linares are the ruins of the
ancient city of Cástulo. Evidence
of human life dating to the
Neolithic period has been
discovered here along with traces
of late Neolithic-Chalcolithic huts
and tools from the Bronze Age.
The site's museum, the **Museo
Arqueológico de Linares**,
displays exhibits found in the
area. Highlights include the Ibero-
Roman León and the Patena de
Cristo, considered one of the
earliest representations of Christ.

㉑ Street-by-Street: Baeza

Nestling amid olive groves, beautiful Baeza is a small town, unusually rich in Renaissance architecture. In 2003 it was named a UNESCO World Heritage site. Called Beatia by the Romans and later the capital of a Moorish fiefdom, Baeza is portrayed as a "royal nest of hawks" on its coat of arms. It was conquered by Fernando III in 1226 – the first town in Andalucía to be definitively won back from the Moors – and was then settled by Castilian knights. An era of medieval splendour followed, reaching a climax in the 16th century, when Andrés de Vandelvira's splendid buildings were erected. In the early 20th century, Antonio Machado, one of his generation's greatest poets, lived here for some years.

★ Palacio de Jabalquinto
An Isabelline (see p28) style façade, flanked by elaborate, rounded buttresses, fronts this splendid Gothic palace.

Antigua Universidad
From 1542 until 1825, this Renaissance and Baroque building was the site of one of Spain's first universities.

Torre de los Aliatares is a 1,000-year-old tower built by the Moors.

To Úbeda

COMPAÑÍA

PLAZA SANTA CRUZ

BEATO ÁVILA

SAN FELIPE N

ROMANON

BARBACANA

MERCADERÍAS

PLAZA DE ESPAÑA

PASEO DE LA CONSTITUCIÓN

PASEO DE TUNDIDORES

O. NARVAEZ

BECERRA

GASPAR

Ayuntamiento
Formerly a jail and a courthouse, the town hall is a dignified Plateresque structure (see p29). The coats of arms of Felipe II, Juan de Borja and of the town of Baeza adorn its upper façade.

La Alhóndiga, the old corn exchange, has impressive triple-tier arches running along its front.

Casas Consistoriales Bajas

For hotels and restaurants in this region see pp217–18 and pp231–2

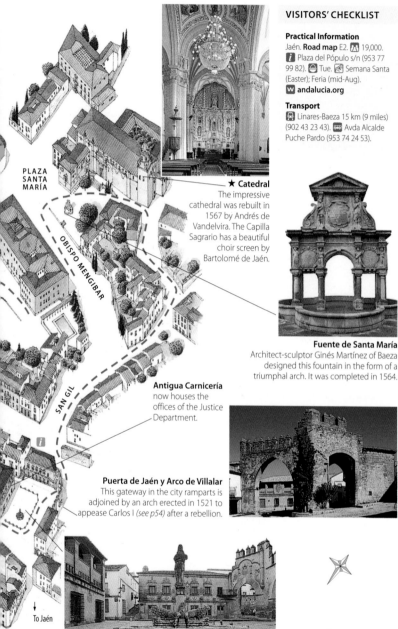

VISITORS' CHECKLIST

Practical Information
Jaén. **Road map** E2. 🚶 19,000.
ℹ️ Plaza del Pópulo s/n (953 77 99 82). 🔄 Tue. ⛪ Semana Santa (Easter); Feria (mid-Aug).
🌐 andalucia.org

Transport
🚉 Linares-Baeza 15 km (9 miles) (902 43 23 43). 🚌 Avda Alcalde Puche Pardo (953 74 24 53).

★ **Catedral**
The impressive cathedral was rebuilt in 1567 by Andrés de Vandelvira. The Capilla Sagrario has a beautiful choir screen by Bartolomé de Jaén.

Fuente de Santa María
Architect-sculptor Ginés Martínez of Baeza designed this fountain in the form of a triumphal arch. It was completed in 1564.

Antigua Carnicería
now houses the offices of the Justice Department.

Puerta de Jaén y Arco de Villalar
This gateway in the city ramparts is adjoined by an arch erected in 1521 to appease Carlos I *(see p54)* after a rebellion.

★ **Plaza del Pópulo**
The Casa del Pópulo, a fine Plateresque palace, now the tourist office, overlooks this square. In its centre is the Fuente de los Leones, a fountain with an Ibero-Roman statue flanked by lions.

PLAZA SANTA MARÍA

OBISPO MENGIBAR

SAN GIL

To Jaén

Key
ℹ️ Tourist information
— Suggested route

| 0 metres | 75 |
| 0 yards | 75 |

⏁ Úbeda

Perched on the crest of a ridge, Úbeda is a showcase of Renaissance magnificence. Thanks to the patronage of some of Spain's most influential men of the 16th century, such as Francisco de los Cobos, secretary of state, and his great nephew, Juan Vázquez de Molina, a number of noble buildings are dotted about the town. The Plaza de Vázquez de Molina is surrounded by elegant palaces and churches and is undoubtedly the jewel in the crown. The narrow streets of the old quarter contrast sharply with modern Úbeda, which expands north of the Plaza de Andalucía. In 2003 Úbeda became a UNESCO World Heritage Site.

Maestro Bartolomé's choir screen at Capilla del Salvador

⏁ Capilla del Salvador

Three architects, Andrés de Vandelvira (credited with refining the Renaissance style), Diego de Siloé and Esteban Jamete helped design this 16th-century landmark. It was built as the personal chapel of Francisco de los Cobos, whose tomb lies in the crypt.

Although the church was pillaged during the Civil War *(see pp58–9)*, it retains a number of treasures. These include a carving of Christ, which is all that remains of an altarpiece by Alonso de Berruguete, Maestro Bartolomé de Jaén's choir screen, and a sacristy by Vandelvira.

Behind the church are two other buildings dating from the 16th century – Cobos's palace, which is graced by a Renaissance façade, and the Hospital de los Honrados Viejos (Honoured Elders). At the end of Baja del Salvador is the Plaza de Santa Lucía. A promenade leads from this point along the Redonda de Miradores,

following the line of the old walls and offering views of the surrounding countryside.

⏁ Palacio de las Cadenas

Pl de Vázquez de Molina. **Tel** 953 75 04 40. **Open** 8am–2:30pm Mon– Fri.

Two stone lions guard Úbeda's town hall, which occupies this palace built for Vázquez de Molina by Vandelvira during the mid-16th century. The building gets its name from the iron chains *(cadenas)* once attached

Stone lions guarding the Palacio de las Cadenas

to the columns supporting the main doorway.

Crowning the corners of the Classical façade are carved stone lanterns. A museum of local pottery is in the basement. The building also houses the tourist information office.

⏁ Parador de Úbeda

Plaza de Vázquez de Molina s/n. **Tel** 953 75 03 45. **Patio Open** to non-guests daily. **W** parador.es

Built in the 16th century but considerably altered in the 17th century, this was the residence of Fernando Ortega Salido, Dean of Málaga and chaplain of El Salvador. The austere palace is now a hotel, which is also known as the Parador Condestable Dávalos in honour of a warrior famed during the Reconquest *(see pp52–3)*.

⏁ Santa María de los Reales Alcázares

Built on the site of an original mosque, this church, mainly dating from the 13th century, is being restored. Inside there is fine ironwork by Maestro Bartolomé. The Gothic cloister, with pointed arches and ribbed vaults, and a Romanesque doorway, are particularly noteworthy.

Near the church is the Cárcel del Obispo (Bishop's Jail), so called because nuns punished by the bishop were confined there. Today the building contains the town's courthouse.

⏁ Iglesia de San Pablo

The three doors of this church all date from different periods. The main entrance is in late Gothic

Statuary on the main entrance of Iglesia de San Pablo

Sun & public hols; mid-Sep–May: 10am–8:30pm Tue–Sat, 10am–5pm Sun & public hols.

This archaeological museum exhibits artifacts from Neolithic times to the Moorish era. The display includes tombstones from the 1st century AD and Moorish and Mudéjar works in wood and plaster. It is located in the 15th-century Casa Mudéjar, among the many palaces and churches gracing the streets of the old quarter.

🚍 Hospital de Santiago

Calle Obispo Cobos s/n. **Tel** 953 75 08 42. **Open** 10am–2pm, 5–9pm Mon–Sat, 10am–2pm, 6–9pm public hols. **Closed** Sun in Jul; Sat & Sun in Aug.

Created on the orders of the Bishop of Jaén around 1562, this colossal former hospital was designed by Vandelvira. The façade is flanked by square towers. Marble columns grace the patio with its central fountain. A staircase leads up to the gallery roofed by a frescoed ceiling.

Today the building houses the Palacio de Congresos y Exposiciones. At the entrance is an information office, and in a corner of the patio there is a stone-vaulted café.

style while the others are in transitional Romanesque and Isabelline. Inside is an apse, which dates from the 13th century and a beautiful 16th-century chapel by Vandelvira. The church is surmounted by a Plateresque tower (1537).

Nearby on Plaza de Vázquez de Molina is a monument to the poet and mystic San Juan de la Cruz (1549–91).

🏛 Museo Arqueológico

Casa Mudéjar, C/Cervantes 6. **Tel** 953 10 86 23. **Open** Jun–mid-Sep: 9am–3:30pm Tue–Sat, 10am–5pm

Nearby, on Avenida de la Constitución, is Úbeda's bullring, which is open during the *fiesta*.

Distinctive steeples above the Hospital de Santiago

Sights at a Glance

① Capilla del Salvador
② Palacio de las Cadenas
③ Parador de Úbeda
④ Santa María de los Reales Alcázares
⑤ Iglesia de San Pablo
⑥ Museo Arqueológico
⑦ Hospital de Santiago

0 metres 250
0 yards 250

For keys to symbols *see back flap*

Ruins of La Iruela, spectacularly situated above the road outside Cazorla

㉓ Cazorla

Jaén. **Road map** E2. 🏔 8,500. 🚍
i Paseo de Santa María, s/n (953 71 01 02). 🛒 Mon & Sat. 🎷 International Blues Festival (Jul).

Cazorla was wealthy in ancient times when the Romans mined the surrounding mountains for silver. Today it is better known as the jumping-off point for visiting the Parque Natural de Cazorla, Segura y Las Villas.

Modern buildings have proliferated, but it is pleasant to stroll along the crooked streets between Plaza de la Corredera and the charming Plaza Santa María. The ruined Iglesia de Santa María forms a picturesque backdrop to this popular meeting place. Above stands the **Castillo de la Yedra** which houses a folklore museum.

On the road leading to the park are the remains of **La Iruela**, a much-photographed fortress atop a rocky spur. On 14 May the locals pay homage to a former resident of Cazorla, San Isicio, one of seven apostles who preached Christianity in Spain before the arrival of the Moors.

🏛 **Castillo de la Yedra**
Folklore Museum: **Tel** 953 10 14 02 **Open** Jun–mid-Sep: 9am–3:30pm Tue–Sat, 10am–5pm Sun & public hols; mid-Sep–May: 10am–8:30pm Tue–Sat; 10am–5pm Sun & public hols.

㉔ Parque Natural de Cazorla, Segura y Las Villas

Jaén. **Road map** E2. 🚍 Cazorla.
i Paseo de Santa María, s/n, Cazorla (953 72 01 02).

First-time visitors are amazed by the spectacular scenery of this 214,336-ha (529,409-acre) nature reserve with its thick woodland, tumbling streams and abundant wildlife. Bristling mountains rise over 2,000 m (6,500 ft) above the source of the Guadalquivir River. The river flows north through a delightful valley before reaching the Tranco de Beas dam, where it turns to run down towards the Atlantic.

Cars are allowed only on the main road. Many visitors explore on foot, but the **Centro de Recepción e Interpretación de la Naturaleza** in the reserve can supply contacts for horse and bike hire companies and provides a lot of useful information. There are also opportunities for hunting and angling.

🏛 **Centro de Recepción e Interpretación de la Naturaleza**
Carretera del Tranco km 49, Torre del Vinagre. **Tel** 953 71 30 17. **Open** daily.

㉕ Segura de la Sierra

Jaén. **Road map** E1. 🏔 2,200. 🚍
i Paseo P Genaro Navarro 1 (953 48 07 84). 🌐 **seguradelasierra.es**

This tiny village at 1,200 m (4,000 ft) above sea level is dominated by its restored Moorish **castillo** (ask for keys in the village). From the ramparts there are splendid views of the harsh mountain ranges. Below is an unusual bullring, partly chipped out of rock. It sees most action at the *fiesta* in the first week of October.

Olive oil in the Segura de la Sierra area is one of four which bear Spain's prestigious *Denominación de Origen Controlada* label (*see p152*).

Moorish castillo at Segura de la Sierra, surrounded by olive groves

Wildlife in Cazorla, Segura and Las Villas

The nature reserve of Sierra de Cazorla, Segura and Las Villas protects a profusion of wildlife. Most is native to the region, but some species have been introduced or reintroduced for hunting. More than 100 species of birds live in Cazorla, some very rare. It is the only habitat in Spain, apart from the Pyrenees, where the lammergeier can be seen. The extensive forests are home to a range of plant life, such as the indigenous *Viola cazorlensis (see p25)*, which grows among rocks.

The **golden eagle** *(Aquila chrysaetus)*, king of the air, preys on small mammals living in the reserve.

Griffon vultures *(Gyps fulvus)* circle high above the reserve, descending rapidly when they catch sight of their prey.

The **lammergeier** *(Gypaetus barbatus)* drops bones from a height on to rocks to smash them and eat the marrow.

Landscape

The area's craggy limestone heights and riverside meadows are part of its attraction. Water trickles down the mountains, filling the lakes and brooks of the valley. This lush landscape provides ideal habitats for a diversity of wildlife.

Red deer *(Cervus elaphus)*, reintroduced to the area in 1952, are most commonly seen in the autumn months.

The **Spanish ibex** *(Capra pyrenaica)* is amazingly sure-footed on the rocky terrain. Today, the few that remain only emerge at dusk in order to feed.

Otters *(Lutra lutra)* live around lakes and streams and are active at dawn and dusk.

Wild boar *(Sus scrofa)* hide in woodland by day and forage at night for anything from acorns to roots, eggs of ground-nesting birds and small mammals.

CÁDIZ AND MÁLAGA

Andalucía's southern provinces offer striking contrasts. Beyond Málaga's suburbs are forested mountains with awesome natural wonders, such as the Garganta del Chorro. Behind the tourist resorts of the Costa del Sol is the Serranía de Ronda, habitat of elusive wildlife. Here, white Moorish towns command strategic hilltop locations. East of Gibraltar are the sherry towns of Cádiz province and the raw coastal strands of the Costa de la Luz.

In Málaga province the mountains fall steeply to the Mediterranean. The ancient port of Málaga town was a wintering place for English travellers in the 19th century; then in the 1960s, the narrow strip of coast to its east and west was claimed by the nascent tourist industry as the "Costa del Sol".

A rash of high-rise developments around the beaches of grey sand at its eastern end soon made the name "Torremolinos" synonymous with the excesses of cheap package holidays for the mass market. Meanwhile, further southwest at Marbella, an exclusive playground for international film stars and Arab royalty was taking shape. Gibraltar, a geographical and a historical oddity, is a decisive full stop at the end of

the Costa del Sol. The mountains of North Africa loom across the Strait of Gibraltar, and the spirit of the Moors can be felt very clearly in Tarifa and Cádiz – author Laurie Lee's city "sparkling with African light". Between these two towns is the Cádiz section of the Costa de la Luz ("Coast of Light") *(see p36)* which continues up north along the shores of Huelva province. Little developed, it is characterized by long stretches of windswept sand, popular with locals and windsurfers.

North of Cádiz is sherry country, with its hills and large vineyards. To taste sherry visit Jerez de la Frontera – once a link in a chain of towns on the frontier of the Christian war to reconquer Andalucía from its Muslim rulers.

Ronda with its 18th-century bridge spanning the Guadalevín river

◀ Whitewashed Moorish town near Estepona, Málaga

Exploring Cádiz and Málaga

With a network of excellent roads across the region, the mountains of Málaga province's interior are easily accessible to holiday-makers who are staying on the Costa del Sol. Day trips can be made from either Marbella or Torremolinos to the glorious Montes de Málaga and Grazalema nature reserves or to the Serranía de Ronda, with lunch stops at classic *pueblos blancos*. In the heart of this characteristic Andalucían landscape lies the captivating mountaintop town of Ronda, ensouled by clear, stark light and the lingering aura of Moorish times.

Further west, on the Atlantic coast beyond Tarifa where mass-market developers fear to tread, the same spirit lingers. The once great city of Cádiz and the small ports of El Puerto de Santa María, Chipiona and Sanlúcar de Barrameda all make excellent bases for exploring sherry country.

Outside dining at a restaurant close to the cathedral in Málaga

Key

━━ Motorway
── Major road
╌╌ Minor road
── Scenic route
╌╌ AVE train link
── Minor railway
━━ International border
━━ Provincial border

For additional map symbols *see back flap*

Sights at a Glance

1. Sanlúcar de Barrameda
2. Chipiona
3. Jerez de la Frontera
4. El Puerto de Santa María
5. *Cádiz pp168–71*
6. Medina Sidonia
7. Vejer de la Frontera
8. Barbate
9. Baelo Claudia
10. Tarifa
11. Los Alcornocales
12. *Gibraltar pp174–5*
13. La Línea de la Concepción
14. Sotogrande
16. Arcos de la Frontera
17. Ronda la Vieja
18. *Ronda pp178–9*
19. Parque Natural Sierra de las Nieves
20. Álora
21. Garganta del Chorro
22. Fuente de Piedra
23. Antequera
24. El Torcal
25. Archidona
26. Nerja
27. The Axarquia
28. Montes de Málaga
29. Málaga
30. Torremolinos
31. Benalmádena
32. Fuengirola
33. Marbella
34. Estepona
35. *Tangier pp186–7*
36. Ceuta
37. Melilla

Tour

15. Pueblos Blancos

Córdoba

Puente Genil

Granada

A92

N331

A92

FUENTE DE PIEDRA **22**

ARCHIDONA **25**

A365

Campillos

A384

A359

Almargen

ANTEQUERA **23**

A45

Teba

Embalse de Guadalhorce

A343

24 EL TORCAL

A367

A357

GARGANTA DEL CHORRO **21**

A356

Colmenar

Viñuela

Cuevas del Becerro

Carratraca

20 ÁLORA

AP46

MONTES DE MÁLAGA **28**

Vélez Málaga

THE AXARQUIA

27

Torrox

Motril

A366

El Burgo

Pizarra

MÁLAGA

A45

Alozaina

Cártama

A7

MÁLAGA **29**

Torre del Mar

26 NERJA

PARQUE NATURAL SIERRA DE LAS NIEVES **19**

Coín

Alhaurín el Grande

A366

Rincón de la Victoria

Ojén

TORREMOLINOS **30**

A376

A355

BENALMÁDENA **31**

AP7

FUENGIROLA **32**

MELILLA **37**

33 MARBELLA

Calahonda

San Pedro de Alcántara

P7

Costa del Sol

0 kilometres 20

0 miles 10

Getting Around

Málaga's international airport *(see p265)* is the busiest airport in Andalucía, and opened a third terminal in 2010. The main highway linking the Costa del Sol resorts is the A7/N340, with the AP7 toll road an option from Torremolinos to Guadiaro. After Algeciras, the road narrows and continues (N340 and A48) to Cádiz. The highway A376 from San Pedro de Alcántara northwards to Ronda is a sensationally beautiful route. The A382 and A384 cut across the north from Jerez towards Antequera. The route then continues as a dual carriageway, known as the A92, to Granada. A railway running along the Costa del Sol links Málaga, Torremolinos and Fuengirola. Another heads north from Málaga, stopping at Álora, El Chorro and Fuente de Piedra. Although you will find it possible to explore remote corners of Cádiz and Málaga provinces using the complex bus network, it requires some patience.

The beach of Nerja, situated at the foot of Sierra de Almijara on the Costa del Sol

Entrance to the Barbadillo *bodega* in Sanlúcar de Barrameda

❶ Sanlúcar de Barrameda

Cádiz. **Road map** B3. 🏠 62,000. 🚌
ℹ Calle Calzada Duquesa Isabel s/n (956 36 61 10). 🛒 Wed.

A fishing port at the mouth of the Guadalquivir river, Sanlúcar is overlooked by the Moorish **Castillo de Santiago**. The Parque Nacional de Doñana *(see pp134–5)*, over the river, can be reached by boat from the riverside quay. From here Columbus set off on his third trip to the Americas, in 1498, and in 1519 Ferdinand Magellan left the port intending to circumnavigate the globe.

However, Sanlúcar is now best known for its *manzanilla (see p34)*, a light, dry sherry from, among other producers, **Bodegas Barbadillo**.

Visitors can sip a *copita* (little glass) of *manzanilla* and enjoy the local shellfish, *langostinos*. There is also a museum on site, **Museo de Manzanilla**, which traces the history of the drink.

Sights in the town include the **Iglesia de Nuestra Señora de la O** *(see p28)*, which has superb Mudéjar portals.

🏠 **Bodegas Barbadillo**
C/Luis de Eguilaz 11. **Tel** 956 38 55 21.
📅 11am Tue–Sat in English. 🅿 ♿
🏛 Museo de Manzanilla: **Open** 10am–3pm daily. 🌐 barbadillo.net

❷ Chipiona

Cádiz. **Road map** B3. 🏠 17,000. 🚌
ℹ Calle Del Castillo 5 (956 92 90 65).
🛒 Mon. 🌐 turismochipiona.es

A lively little resort town, Chipiona is approached through sherry vineyards. It has a great beach

and a holiday atmosphere in the summer. Days on the beach are followed by a *paseo* along the quay or the main street of the Moorish old town, where many cafés and ice-cream parlours *(heladerías)* stay open well past midnight. There are also street entertainers and horse-drawn carriages. The **Iglesia de Nuestra Señora de Regla**, the main church, has a natural spring feeding a fountain, and an adjoining cloister decorated with 17th-century *azulejos*.

❸ Jerez de la Frontera

Cádiz. **Road map** B3. 🏠 186,000. ✈
🚆 🚌 ℹ Plaza del Arenal, Edificio Los Arcos (956 33 88 74). 🛒 Mon.
🌐 turismojerez.com

Jerez, the capital of sherry production, is surrounded by chalky countryside blanketed with long rows of vines. British merchants have been involved for centuries in producing and shipping sherry, and have created Anglo-Andaluz dynasties like Sandeman and John Harvey – names which can be seen emblazoned over the *bodega* entrances. A tour of a *bodega*, through cellars piled high with *soleras (see p35)*, will enable visitors to learn how to distinguish a *fino* from an *amontillado* and an *oloroso* sherry *(see p34)*.

Jerez has a second claim to world fame, the **Real Escuela Andaluza de Arte Ecuestre** – the school of equestrian art. On selected days, in a display of exquisite dressage, the horses dance to music amid colourful pageantry. Visitors can arrange to watch horses being trained.

Nearby is **La Atalaya Theme Centre**, including two museums: the magical **Palacio del Tiempo**, home to the most impressive clocks in Europe, and **El Misterio de Jerez**, which pays tribute to the history of sherry in the area.

The old city walls flank the Barrio de Santiago. On Plaza de San Juan is the 18th-century **Palacio de Pemartín**, the home of the **Centro Andaluz de Flamenco**, which, through exhibitions and audiovisual shows, offers an insight to this music and dance tradition *(see pp32–3)*. The 16th-century Gothic **Iglesia de San Mateo** is just one of several interesting churches nearby.

The partially restored, 11th-century **Alcázar** includes a well-preserved mosque, now a church. Just to the north of the Alcázar is the **Catedral del Salvador**, whose most interesting sight, *The Sleeping Girl* by Zurbarán, is in the sacristy.

🎭 **Real Escuela Andaluza de Arte Ecuestre**
Avenida Duque de Abrantes s/n.
Tel 956 31 96 35 (information, press 2 for English). **Open** 10am–2pm Mon–Fri. 🅿 ♿ 🌐 realescuela.org

🏰 **Alcázar**
Alameda Vieja s/n. **Tel** 956 14 99 55.
Open daily. **Closed** 25 Dec, 1 & 6 Jan.
🅿 ♿

🏛 **La Atalaya Theme Centre**
Calle Cervantes 3. **Tel** 902 18 21 00.
Open Mon–Fri for guided tours only.
🅿 📷 ♿

🏛 **Palacio de Pemartín**
Centro Andaluz de Flamenco, Plaza de San Juan 1. **Tel** 956 90 21 34. **Open** 9am–2pm Mon–Fri. **Closed** public hols.

Antique clock in Palacio del Tiempo, Jerez de la Frontera

❹ El Puerto de Santa María

Cádiz. **Road map** B3. 🏛 76,000. ✈
🚉 🚌 ℹ Palacio de Aranibar, Plaza de Alfonso X El Sabio 9 (956 48 37 14).
🗓 Tue. 🌐 **turismoelpuerto.com**

Sheltered from the Atlantic wind and waves of the Bay of Cádiz, El Puerto de Santa María is a tranquil town which has burgeoned as one of the main ports for the exportation of sherry in Andalucía. Sherry companies, such as **Terry** and **Osborne**, have *bodegas* here, which can be visited for tours and tasting.

Among the town's sites are the 13th-century **Castillo San Marcos** and a **Plaza de Toros** – one of the largest and most famous bullrings in Spain. The town's main square, the Plaza Mayor, is presided over by the 13th-century, Gothic **Iglesia Mayor Prioral**, which is worth a look for its unusual choir.

Scattered around the town are several fine old *palacios*, or stately houses, adorned with the coats of arms of wealthy families who prospered in the port during colonial times.

The waterfront is lined with quite a few first-rate seafood restaurants, among them La Resaca (the Hangover), where, when it is dark, dancers perform fiery flamenco.

🏰 **Castillo San Marcos**
Plaza Alfonso X, El Sabio. **Tel** 956 85 17 51. **Open** for tours (in English): Jul–Sep: 11:30am Wed–Mon; Oct–Jun: 11:30am Tue, Thu & Sat. ♿ 🅿️

🎪 **Plaza de Toros**
Plaza Elias Ahuja s/n. **Tel** 956 86 11 88. **Open** daily. ♿

🍷 **Bodegas Osborne**
Calle de los Moros 7. **Tel** 956 86 91 00. **Open** daily (reservation required). ♿ 🅿️

🍷 **Bodegas Terry**
C/ San Ildefonso 3 . **Tel** 956 15 15 00. **Open** Mon–Fri (phone to arrange). **Closed** public hols. ♿ 🅿️

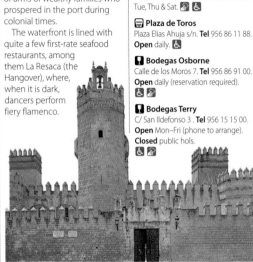

El Puerto de Santa María's 13th-century Castillo San Marcos

Bodegas of Jerez

Touring *bodegas* and tasting sherry is one of the major reasons for visiting Jerez. The tourist office here will supply a list of *bodegas* offering tours, and a tour time-table. The most comprehensive tours are those that are offered by González Byass, Pedro Domecq and Sandeman.

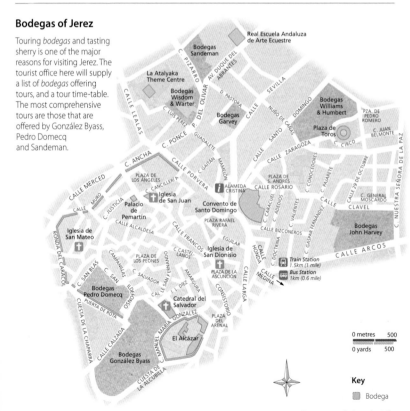

Key

🟦 Bodega

For map symbols *see back flap*

❺ Cádiz

Jutting out of the Bay of Cádiz, and almost entirely surrounded by water, Cádiz can lay claim to being Europe's oldest city. Legend names Hercules as its founder, although history credits the Phoenicians with establishing the town of Gadir in 1100 BC. Occupied by the Carthaginians, Romans and Moors in turn, the city also prospered after the Reconquest *(see pp52–3)* on wealth taken from the New World. In 1587 Sir Francis Drake raided the port in the first of many British attacks in the war for world trade. In 1812 Cádiz briefly became Spain's capital when the nation's first constitution was declared here *(see p56)*.

Terracota bust of a Roman goddess in the Museo de Cádiz

Exploring Cádiz

Writers have waxed lyrical over Cádiz for centuries:" … the most beautiful town I ever beheld … and full of the finest women in Spain," gushed Lord Byron in 1809. Modern Cádiz is a busy port, with a few ugly suburbs to get through before arriving at the historic centre. This is situated on a peninsula that juts sharply into the sea, and consists of haphazardly heaped, Moorish-style houses.

The joy of visiting Cádiz is to wander the harbour quayside, with its well-tended gardens and open squares, then plunging into the centre *(see p170–71)*.

The old town is full of narrow, dilapidated alleys, where flowers sprout from rusting cans mounted on walls beside religious tile paintings. Markets pack into tiny squares, alive with the bartering of fish and vegetables, and street vendors selling pink boiled shrimps in paper cones.

The pride of Cádiz is Los Carnavales *(see p43)*. Under the dictator Franco, Cádiz was the only city where the authorities failed to suppress the anarchy of carnival.

🏛 Cádiz Cathedral

Plaza Fray Félix. **Tel** 956 28 61 54. **Open** 10am–6:30pm Mon–Sat; 1–6:30pm Sun (10am–2pm public hols).

Known as the Catedral Nueva (New Cathedral) because it was built over the site of an older one, this Baroque and Neo-Classical church is one of Spain's largest. Its dome of yellow tiles looks like gilt glinting in the sun. The carved stalls inside came from a Carthusian monastery. In the crypt are the tombs of the composer Manuel de Falla (1876–1946) and writer José Maria Pemán (1897–1981), both natives of Cádiz. The cathedral's treasures are stored in a museum in Plaza Fray Félix and include jewel-studded monstrances of silver and gold, and notable paintings.

🏛 Museo de Cádiz

Plaza de Mina s/n. **Tel** 856 10 50 23. **Open** mid-Jun–mid-Sep: 9am–3pm Tue–Sun; mid-Sep–mid-Jun: 9am–8pm Tue–Sat, 9am–3pm Sun. **Closed** 1 Jan, 1 May, 25 Dec. ♿

On the ground floor there are archaeological exhibits charting the history of Cádiz, including statues of Roman emperors, such as Trajan, and Phoenician stone sarcophagi. Upstairs is one of Andalucía's largest art galleries, displaying works by Rubens, Murillo and Zurbarán, as well as paintings by recognized contemporary Spanish artists. On the third floor is a collection

Cádiz Cathedral

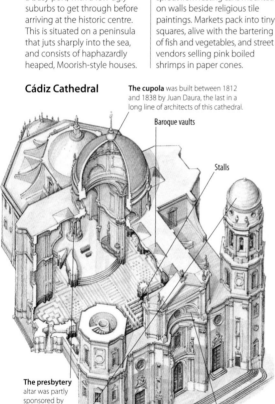

The cupola was built between 1812 and 1838 by Juan Daura, the last in a long line of architects of this cathedral.

Baroque vaults

Stalls

The presbytery altar was partly sponsored by Isabel II *(see pp56–7)*.

Neo-Classical towers

Neo-Classical façade

of puppets made for village *fiestas* around Andalucía. There are also some more recent ones satirizing current political figures.

🎭 Oratorio de San Felipe Neri

Calle Santa Inés s/n. **Tel** 956 80 70 18. **Open** Tue–Sun; mass on Sun at 1pm Sep–Jun and at noon Jul & Aug.

On 19 March 1812 a major event took place in this 18th-century Baroque church: the proclamation of a liberal constitution for Spain *(see p56)*. As Napoleon's troops besieged Cádiz during the Peninsular War, the members of the provisional parliament assembled in the church to draft a document that would inspire radicals throughout Europe. In its limitations of the power of the monarch and its provisions for citizens to enjoy unprecedented rights, the constitution was ahead of its time and ultimately doomed to fail. No sooner had the French been driven out of Spain in 1814 than it was repealed by Fernando VII.

Commemorative plaques on the Oratorio de San Felipe Neri

The Baroque Torre Tavira, the highest watchtower in Cádiz

🏛 Torre Tavira

Calle Marqués del Real Tesoro 10. **Tel** 956 21 29 10. **Open** daily. **Closed** 1 Jan & 25 Dec. 🅿 📷

In the mid-1700s, when much of Spain's trade with the Americas passed through the port of Cádiz, the city's merchants built themselves watchtowers from which to observe the coming and going of vessels – either for commercial interest in the cargoes or for their own amusement. More than 100 such towers remain as part of Cádiz's skyline, but only this one is open to the public.

Baroque in style, the tower rises above what was once the home of the Marqués de Ricaño (now a music academy); it stands in the centre of the Old Town and is its highest point, reaching 45 m (150 ft) above sea level. Its penultimate floor contains the first camera

VISITORS' CHECKLIST

Practical Information
Cádiz.
Road map B4. 🏛 150,000.
ℹ Avenida José León de Carranza, s/n, at corner of Avenida de La Coruña (956 28 56 01). 🚌 Mon. 🎭 Los Carnavales (Feb), Semana Santa (Easter).
w cadizturismo.com

Transport
🚉 Plaza de Sevilla s/n (902 24 05 05). 🚌 Plaza de la Hispanidad s/n (956 80 70 59).

obscura installed in Spain, but it is also worth visiting for the simple pleasure of the views over the rooftops and the sea from its four balconies.

Environs
At the northern lip of the Bay of Cádiz is Rota, a town best known for its Spanish-US naval base but which also claims to have the highest population of chameleons in Spain. There is a walled old town quarter and some very fine beaches.

The southern limit of the bay is marked by the small island of Sancti Petri, believed by archaeologists to be the site of a Temple of Hercules, built by the Phoenicians in the 12th century BC over the mythical burial site of the hero-turned-god.

Much of the bay lying between these two points forms the Bahia de Cádiz Nature Reserve; a shifting population of migratory wildfowl uses this area as a staging post between the Straits of Gibraltar and the Doñana National Park *(see pp134–5)*.

Catamaran Crossing

Rather than drive up the isthmus into Cádiz, you can travel by ferry across the bay from El Puerto de Santa María *(see p167)* and to and from Rota. A fast catamaran is part of the public transportation system and provides a regular service roughly every 30 minutes. The catamaran takes 30 minutes to cross the bay and is accessible for disabled travellers. It is identified as the B-042 line and time-tables for the service can be found on the website (Tel: 902 45 05 50; www.catamaran bahiacadiz.es/horarios.php).

A catamaran crossing the Bay of Cádiz

A 90-Minute Walk Around Historic Cádiz

This walk begins at the *Ayuntamiento* (town hall) and takes in 3,000 years of Cádiz history, most of which is defined by the surrounding sea. The route starts on the eastern flank at the Bay of Cádiz. It heads into the heart of the city's warren of small alleys and squares via the stunning topiary gardens by the university. You are rarely out of sight of the sea, passing Cádiz's fish market, its most famous fish restaurant, its beach spa and the Atlantic seafront. The walk ends at the city's monumental cathedral, with its golden-coloured dome overlooking the ocean.

⑤ The Murallas de San Carlos, overlooking the Bay of Cádiz

A café-lined lane near the central Plaza San Juan de Dios

Plaza San Juan de Dios to Parque Genovés

The pretty palm-lined Plaza San Juan offers many cafés and shops. The Neo-Classical Ayuntamiento ①, built in 1799, is chiefly the work of architect Torcuato Benjumeda. Head north from the square, taking Calle Nueva ②, part of Cádiz's busy shopping district. Nueva runs into Calle San Francisco up to Plaza de San Francisco ③,

one of many tiny neighbourhood squares. Turn right into Isabel La Catolica, which becomes Calle Rafael de la Viesca and, via Doctor Zurita, enters the Plaza de España. The militaristic Monumento a las Cortes ④, erected in 1912, has special resonance for the people of Cádiz, and Spain itself. In 1812, Cádiz was home to a short-lived alternative parliament to Madrid, but this attempt to establish democratic rule was crushed by the monarchy. Across the plaza, turn left into Fernando El Catolico, which leads to the seafront Murallas (walls) de San Carlos ⑤, overlooking the Bay of Cádiz and the town of Puerto de Santa María opposite, an interesting destination in its own right. At the Murallas, follow Calle Honduras ⑥ left, hugging Cádiz's sea walls. You pass the Alameda Apodaca ⑦, one of numerous gardens boasting vast dragon trees, and the Baluarte (battlement) de la Candelaria ⑧, now a contemporary arts centre. Turn left again into Avenida Carlos III, passing the Universidad and the lovely Parque Genovés ⑨, with its avenue of symmetrical topiary trees, open-air theatre and café.

⑨ Taking a stroll in leafy Parque Genovés

Tips for Walkers

Starting point: Plaza San Juan de Dios.
Length: 4 km (3 miles)
Getting there: Plaza San Juan de Dios is next to the port and a few minutes' walk from rail and bus stations.
Stopping-off points: The family-owned Bar Terraza on the Plaza de la Catedral s/n has outdoor seating with a fantastic view of the cathedral.

For hotels and restaurants in this region see pp218–19 and pp232–6

Parador to Playa de la Caleta

At the end of the gardens is Cádiz's modern parador hotel ⑩. From here, visitors can head into the heart of the Old Town. Turn left into Calle Benito Perez Galdos, passing Plaza de Falla and the gaudy, pink Gran Teatro Falla ⑪, both named after famous local composer Manuel de Falla, interred in the cathedral. The Neo-Mudéjar theatre was finished in 1919, after 30 years' construction, and is busiest during Cádiz's wild February Carnival (see p43). Calle Galdos changes name here to Calle

⑱ One of the bell towers of the Catedral de Santa Cruz overlooking the city

into Plaza Topete and the city's bustling market, with stalls preparing delicious fresh seafood snacks.

Cross the square to Calle Libertad and into Desamparados, then turn right into the leafy Plaza de la Cruz Verde ⑭, which, via Calle Maria Arteaga, joins Calle Rosa to reach the city's most famous beach, Playa de la Caleta, its 19th-century bathing station ⑮ (now government offices) and a nautical college. The beach overlooks the old harbour and two small forts, one of which, San Sebastián, was once the 1100 BC Phoenician settlement of Gadir and site of a temple to Kronos.

Caleta to Catedral

From Caleta, Calle de Nájera joins the Campo del Sur seafront, but it is worth turning left into Calle Venezuela into the fishermen's quarter and down to San Felix and the most famous fish restaurant in the region, El Faro (open: 1pm) ⑯. Both the restaurant and the tapas bar here live up to the local saying, "Don't leave Cádiz before eating at El Faro." Take Felix up to the seafront and turn left into Campo del Sur ⑰, where lovely pastel-colour buildings stretch to the magnificent Cádiz Catedral ⑱, begun in 1722 and finished only in 1838. Several architects contributed to its wonderful mix of Baroque, Rococo and Neo-Classical styles. The views from its bell towers repay the climb. Calle Pelota, opposite, leads back to Plaza San Juan de Dios.

Key

••• Walk route

0 metres 300
0 yards 300

Sacramento, the busiest of the shopping streets, and you pass the Oratorio de San Felipe Neri ⑫ and the unusual 18th-century Torre Tavira ⑬, named after its first keeper, Antonio Tavira. At 45 m (150 ft) above sea level, this lookout and camera obscura is the highest viewpoint in the city. At Calle Alcala Sacramento, turn right

⑬ Cádiz cathedral seen from Torre Tavira

For keys to map symbols see back flap

Carved *retablo*, Iglesia de Santa María la Coronada, Medina Sidonia

❻ Medina Sidonia

Cádiz. **Road map** B4. �︎ 11,500. 🚌
ℹ️ Plaza Iglesia Mayor s/n (956 41 24 04). 🚉 Mon.

As you drive along the N440, between Algeciras and Jerez, Medina Sidonia appears startlingly white atop a conical hill. The town was taken from the Moors in 1264 by Alfonso X, and during the 15th century the Guzmán family were established as the Dukes of Medina Sidonia to defend the territory between here and the Bay of Cádiz. After the Reconquest *(see pp52–3)*, the family grew rich from investments in the Americas, and Medina Sidonia became one of the most important ducal seats in Spain. Many parts of the town's medieval walls still

stand and cobbled alleys nestle beneath them.

The **Iglesia de Santa María la Coronada** is the town's most impressive building. Begun on the foundations of a castle in the 15th century, after the Reconquest, it is a fine example of Andalucían Gothic. Inside is a collection of religious works of art dating from the Renaissance, including paintings and a charming *retablo* with beautifully carved panels.

❼ Vejer de la Frontera

Cádiz. **Road map** B4. 🚍 13,000.
ℹ️ Avenida Los Remedios 2, Parque Municipal Los Remedios (956 45 17 36). 🌐 **vejerdelafrontera.co.uk**

Attractively located on a hilltop above Barbate, Vejer de la Frontera was one of the first places occupied by the Muslim invaders in 711, shortly after they had defeated the Visigoths in battle close by (the exact site is not known).

The oldest part of town is enclosed by an irregular wall that is protected by three towers and entered by four gates. Within the walled area are the Arab castle and the parish church, the Iglesia Parroquial del Divino Salvador, which was built on the site of a mosque between the 14th and 16th centuries, in a mixture of Gothic and Mudejar architecture. Later buildings

outside the walls include the Palacio del Marqués de Tamaron, which is a 17th- to 18th-century stately home.

The lighthouse on Cabo de Trafalgar, near Barbate on Costa de la Luz

❽ Barbate

Cádiz. **Road map** B4. 🚍 22,000.
ℹ️ Paseo Marítimo 5 (956 06 36 13). 🌐 **barbate.es**

The largest coastal settlement between Cádiz and Tarifa, Barbate stands at the mouth of the eponymous river, in an area of marshes and saltflats. There is not much of interest in the town itself, but two small tourist resorts attached to it are worth visiting.

A short way south down the coast is **Zahara de los Atunes**, which has grown up along one of the coast's best beaches. The epithet of "the tuna fish" is a reminder of an important industry in these waters. Barbate's culinary speciality is *mojama*, tuna that has been cured in the same way as *jamón serrano*. Inland from Zahara, around the main N340 coast road, are large swathes of wind turbines generating electricity for the national grid. The road north out of Barbate

The fortified walls surrounding the Old Town of Vejer de la Frontera

For hotels and restaurants in this region see pp218–19 and pp232–6

The characteristic turbines of a windfarm north of Tarifa

Windfarms

North of Tarifa, the wind blows with such reliable force that it is used to drive wind turbines to generate electricity. Spain has the world's second-highest installed capacity of windpower after Germany, and the country aims to meet 20 per cent of its energy needs from renewable resources by 2020. Critics argue that windpower works only when the wind is strong enough and that the turbines are unsightly. Another objection, that the blades of the turbines are a hazard to birds, hasn't been substantiated by evidence.

(past the fishing port) climbs over a headland fringed by cliffs and planted with dense pine woods to drop down to the small holiday resort of **Los Caños de Meca**, which began as a hippy hideaway in the 1970s and still has a carefree feel to it.

On a short sand spit nearby stands a lighthouse marking the **Cabo de Trafalgar** (Cape Trafalgar), which gave its name to the naval battle fought on 21 October 1805. Early in the morning of that day, Britain's Admiral Nelson decided to take on the combined fleet of Spanish and French ships that had left Cádiz two days earlier. The British were outnumbered and outgunned but defeated the enemy without the loss of a single ship. Nelson, however, was struck by a musket ball late in the battle and died soon after.

9 Baelo Claudia

Bolonia, Cádiz. **Road map** B4. **Tel** 956 10 67 97. **Open** Apr–mid-Jun: 9am–7:30pm Tue–Sat, 9am–2:30pm Sun & hols; mid-Jun–mid-Sep: 9am–2:30pm Tue–Sun & hols; mid-Sep–Mar: 9am–5:30pm Tue–Sat, 9am–2:30pm Sun & hols. (free to EU citizens). **juntadeandalucia.es/cultura/museos**

The Roman settlement of Baelo Claudia was established on the seashore in the 2nd century BC and gradually grew in importance through trade with North Africa and its fish salting and pickling works. Emperor Claudius (41–54 AD) elevated Baelo Claudia to the status of municipality, but its prestige was short-lived, since it was effectively destroyed by an earthquake in the 2nd century and finally abandoned in the 6th century. The ruins, which include a theatre, a necropolis and several erect columns, are in a picturesque spot next to a beautiful beach beside the small settlement of Bolonia.

Statue of Trajan at Baelo Claudia

10 Tarifa

Cádiz. **Road map** B4. 16,000. Paseo de la Alameda s/n (956 68 09 93). Tue. **tarifaweb.com**

Europe's wind- and kitesurfing capital *(see p36)* takes its name from Tarif ben Maluk, an 8th-century Moorish commander.

The 10th-century **Castillo de Guzmán el Bueno** is the site of a legend. In 1292, Guzmán, who was defending Tarifa from the Moors, was told his hostage son would die if he did not surrender. Rather than give in, he threw down his dagger for the captors to use.

Castillo de Guzmán el Bueno
Calle Guzmán el Bueno. **Tel** 956 68 46 89. **Open** Winter: Tue–Sun; summer: daily.

11 Parque Natural de Los Alcornocales

Cádiz and Málaga. **Road map** B4. Carretera Ctra C–2112 km 1, Alcalá de los Gazules – Benalup Casas Viejas (956 41 86 14); Parque Natural de los Alcornocales (856 58 75 08).

This nature reserve is named after the *alcornocales*, cork oak trees that are prevalent in many parts of it. They are easily identified because they have been stripped of their lower bark, leaving the vivid red heartwood showing. The far south of the natural park is crossed by deep valleys called *canutos*, in which rare vestiges of Europe's ancient fern-rich forests cling on.

Apart from its wildlife, the area has a few towns worth visiting, including Jimena de la Frontera, Castellar de la Frontera and Medina Sidonia *(see p172)*, and several caves holding prehistoric paintings.

Cork trees in the Parque Natural de Los Alcornocales

⑫ Gibraltar

Native Gibraltarians are descendents of British, Genoese
Jews, Portuguese and Spanish who remained after the Great
Siege *(see p56)*. Britain seized Gibraltar during the War of the
Spanish Succession in 1704, and was granted it "in perpetuity"
by the Treaty of Utrecht *(see p56)* nine years later. As the
gateway to the Mediterranean, the Rock was essential to
Britain in colonial times. Tensions over Gibraltar have now
eased, with more co-operation between Spain and Britain
expected in the future. Each year, around 4 million people
stream across the frontier at La Línea to visit this speck of
England bolted on to Andalucía. Pubs, fish and chips, pounds
sterling and bobbies on the beat all contrast with Spain.

The Keep
The lower part of this Moorish
castle, built in the 8th century, is
still used to house Gibraltar's
prison population.

Siege Tunnels
Soldiers' barracks and storerooms
fill 50 km (31 miles) of tunnels.

KEY

① **The airport runway** currently crosses over the main road from La Línea to Gibraltar.

② **Spanish border and customs**

③ **The Apes' Den** is home to Gibraltar's tailless apes; legend has it that the British will keep the Rock only as long as the apes remain.

④ **Europa Point,** on the southernmost tip, looks across the Strait of Gibraltar to North Africa.

⑤ **The 100-Ton Gun** was put here in 1884; it took two hours to load and it could fire shells weighing 910 kg (2,000 lb).

⑥ **A cable car** runs from the centre of the town to the Top of the Rock, Gibraltar's summit, which, at 450 m (1,475 ft) high, is often shrouded in mist.

St Michael's Cave
During World War II these caves served as a bombproof military hospital. These days classical concerts are performed here.

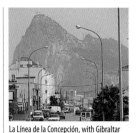

La Línea de la Concepción, with Gibraltar in the distance

⑬ La Línea de la Concepción

Cádiz. Road map C4. 🚹 60,000.
🚌 🚶 Avenida de 20 Abril s/n (956 78 41 35). 🚌 Wed.

La Línea is a town on the Spanish side of the border with Gibraltar. Its name, "The Line", refers to the old walls that once formed the frontier, but were demolished during the Napoleonic wars to prevent the French using them for defence. Now it is a lively trading town, with several hotels patronized by people who want to avoid the higher prices of Gibraltar hotels.

The elegant marina at Sotogrande

⑭ Sotogrande

Cádiz. Road map C4. 🚹 2,000.
🚌 San Roque. 🚶 Palacio de los Gobernadores, Calle Rubín de Celis s/n (956 69 40 05). 🚌 Sun.

Just above Gibraltar, on the Costa del Sol, Sotogrande is an exclusive residential seaside town, popular with wealthy Gibraltarians, who commute to the Rock. The marina is filled with expensive yachts and lined with excellent seafood restaurants.

Nearby there are several immaculately manicured golf courses (see p36).

Gibraltar Museum
This museum, built on the foundations of Moorish baths, houses an exhibition of Gibraltar's history under British rule.

⓯ A Tour Around the Pueblos Blancos

Instead of settling on Andalucía's plains, where they would have fallen prey to bandits, some Andalucíans chose to live in fortified hilltop towns and villages. The way of life in these *pueblos blancos* – so called because they are whitewashed in the Moorish tradition – has barely changed for centuries. Touring the *pueblos blancos,* which crown the mountains rising sharply from the coast, will show visitors a world full of references to the past. Yet today they are working agricultural towns, not just tourist sights.

③ **Zahara de la Sierra** This fine *pueblo blanco,* a tightly huddled hillside village below a castle ruin, has been declared a national monument.

④ **Grazalema** At the heart of the Parque Natural de la Sierra de Grazalema, this village has the highest rainfall in Spain. Lush vegetation fills the park.

② **Ubrique**
This town, nestling at the foot of the Sierra de Ubrique, has become a flourishing producer of leather goods.

Sevilla

Cádiz, Jerez

El Bosque •

• Benamahoma

A372

A373

Embalse de los Hurones

Benaocaz

A374

Parque Natural Sierra de Grazalema

① **Arcos de la Frontera**
This strategically positioned town has been fortified for centuries. From the commanding heights of this stronghold, there are fine views over the Guadalete valley.

Charco de los Hurones •

CA5221

Sierra de Ubrique

Cortes de la Frontera

A373

⑧ **Jimena de la Frontera**
An expanse of cork and olive trees blankets the hills leading up to this village. A ruined Moorish castle, which is open to visitors, overlooks the surroundings where wild bulls graze peacefully.

CA503

A375

Río Hozgarganta

Parque Natural de los Alcornocales-Sierra del Aljibe

Río Guadiaro

La Saučeda •

CA3331

A369

⑦ **Gaucín**
From here there are unsurpassed vistas over the Mediterranean, the Atlantic, the great hump of Gibraltar and across the strait to the Rif mountains of North Africa.

0 km

0 miles   05

Embals de Zah

CA

⑤ Setenil
The streets of this white town are formed from the ledge of a gorge, carved from tufa rock by the river Trejo.

MA486

●Ronda la Vieja

A376

⑥

● La Cueva de la Pileta

A369

⑥ Ronda
With the Tajo gorge as an efficient moat, Ronda was one of the last towns recaptured from the Moors. It later became the cradle of modern bullfighting *(see pp178–9)*.

Key

▬ Tour route
▭ Other roads

Tips for Drivers

Tour length: 205 km (135 miles).
Stopping-off points: Ronda has a wide range of hotels and restaurants. Arcos de la Frontera has a parador *(see p218)*, other hotels and restaurants. Gaucín, Jimena de la Frontera and Zahara de la Sierra also have places to stay and eat. Grazalema has a resort for families and Setenil a couple of bars and a hotel. Ubrique has two hotels and several B&Bs.

⑯ Arcos de la Frontera

Cádiz. **Road map** B3. 🏠 30,000.
🚌 *i* Calle Cuesta de Belén 5 (956 70 22 64). 🗓 Fri.

Arcos has been inhabited since prehistoric times. Its strategic position encouraged settlement, first as the Roman town of Arcobriga, and later as the stronghold of Medina Arkosh under the Caliphate of Córdoba *(see p50)*. It was captured by Alfonso X's *(see p52)* Christian forces in 1264.

An archetypal white town, it has a labyrinthine Moorish quarter that twists up to its ruined castle. At its centre is the Plaza de España, one side of which gives views across sunbaked plains. Fronting the square is the superb **Iglesia de Santa María de la Asunción**, a late Gothic-Mudéjar building worth seeing for its extravagant Baroque choir stalls and Renaissance altarpiece. A small museum displays the church treasures. More striking is the massive 14th-century Gothic **Parroquia de San Pedro**. Its thick-set tower provides a view over the sheer drop down to the Guadalete river. Nearby is the **Palacio del Mayorazgo** with an ornate Renaissance façade. The **Ayuntamiento** is also worth seeing, particularly to view its beautiful Mudéjar ceiling.

🏛 **Palacio del Mayorazgo**
Calle San Pedro 2. **Tel** 956 70 30 13 (Casa de Cultura).
Open 10am–2pm Mon–Fri. ♿

🏛 **Ayuntamiento**
Plaza del Cabildo 1.
Tel 956 70 49 50.
Open Mon–Fri.
Closed public hols.

Roman theatre set amid the ruins of Acinipo (Ronda la Vieja)

⑰ Ronda la Vieja

Málaga. **Road map** C3. 🚉 🚌 Ronda.
Tel 952 21 36 40 & 630 42 99 49.
i Avenida de Blas Infante, s/n (952 18 71 19). **Open** times vary – check
W facebook.com/acinipoenclave
arqueologico. Cuevas de la Pileta: by guided tour (twice daily).
W turismoderonda.es

Ronda la Vieja is the modern name for the remains of the Roman city of Acinipo, 12 km (7 miles) northwest of Ronda *(see pp178–9)*. An important town in the 1st century AD, it later declined, unlike the growing town of Ronda, which was called Arunda by the Romans.

The ruins are sited on a hillside where only a fraction of the town has been excavated. The town's most significant sight is the theatre, but lines of stones also mark foundations of houses, and of the forum and other public buildings.

Along the C339, 22 km (12 miles) from Ronda la Vieja, are the Cuevas de la Pileta, the site of pre-historic cave paintings dating from about 25,000 BC *(see p47)*.

The Gothic-Mudéjar Iglesia de Santa María de la Asunción

⑱ Street-by-Street: Ronda

One of the most spectacularly located cities in Spain, Ronda sits on a massive rocky outcrop, straddling a precipitous limestone cleft. Because of its impregnable position this town was one of the last Moorish bastions, finally falling to the Christians in 1485. On the south side perches a classic Moorish *pueblo blanco (see p176)* of cobbled alleys, window grilles and dazzling whitewash – most historic sights are in this old town. Across the gorge in El Mercadillo, the newer town, is one of Spain's oldest bullrings.

★ **Puente Nuevo**
Building the "New Bridge" over the nearly 100 m (330 ft) deep Tajo gorge was a feat of civil engineering in the late 18th century.

To El Mercadillo, Plaza de Toros and Parador de Ronda *(see p219)*

Convento de Santo Domingo was the local headquarters of the Inquisition.

SANTO DOMINGO

CALLE ARMIÑAN

TENORIO

Casa del Rey Moro
From this 18th-century mansion, built on the foundations of a Moorish palace, 365 steps lead down to the river.

Key

— Suggested route

| 0 metres | 75 |
| 0 yards | 75 |

Mirador El Campillo

PLAZA DEL CAMPILLO

★ **Palacio Mondragón**
Much of this palace was rebuilt after the Reconquest *(see pp52–3)*, but its arcaded patio is adorned with original Moorish mosaics and plasterwork.

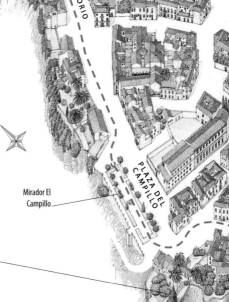

For hotels and restaurants in this region see pp218–19 and pp232–6

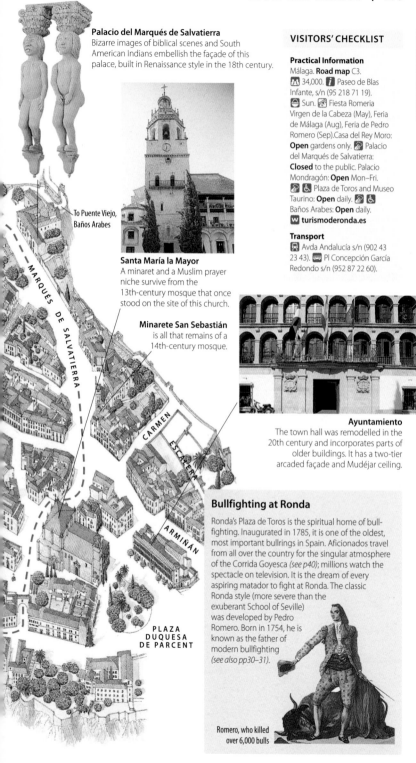

Palacio del Marqués de Salvatierra

Bizarre images of biblical scenes and South American Indians embellish the façade of this palace, built in Renaissance style in the 18th century.

To Puente Viejo,
Baños Arabes

MARQUÉS DE SALVATIERRA

Santa María la Mayor

A minaret and a Muslim prayer niche survive from the 13th-century mosque that once stood on the site of this church.

Minarete San Sebastián

is all that remains of a 14th-century mosque.

CARMEN

ESCALERA

ARMIÑÁN

PLAZA
DUQUESA
DE PARCENT

Ayuntamiento

The town hall was remodelled in the 20th century and incorporates parts of older buildings. It has a two-tier arcaded façade and Mudéjar ceiling.

Bullfighting at Ronda

Ronda's Plaza de Toros is the spiritual home of bull-fighting. Inaugurated in 1785, it is one of the oldest, most important bullrings in Spain. Aficionados travel from all over the country for the singular atmosphere of the Corrida Goyesca *(see p40)*; millions watch the spectacle on television. It is the dream of every aspiring matador to fight at Ronda. The classic Ronda style (more severe than the exuberant School of Seville) was developed by Pedro Romero. Born in 1754, he is known as the father of modern bullfighting *(see also pp30–31)*.

Romero, who killed over 6,000 bulls

⓳ Parque Natural Sierra de las Nieves

Málaga. **Road map** C3. ℹ️ Calle Jacaranda 1, Cortes de la Frontera (952 15 45 99).

One of Andalucía's least accessible areas, this UNESCO biosphere reserve southeast of Ronda extends between Parauta (to the east), Tolox (west), El Burgo (north) and Istán (south). Interestingly, it features both extreme highs and lows, reaching up to the peak of Torrecilla (1,919 m/ 6,295 ft) and down to one of the world's deepest potholes, GESM, which is 1,100 m (3,608 ft) deep. The sierra is popular for caving and rock climbing, and it also has some moderate to difficult signposted walking trails.

A short way south, near Ojén, is the beautiful Refugio de Juanar, which offers walks through mixed woodland to a viewpoint overlooking the coast.

Olive groves between the villages of Álora and Antequera

⓴ Álora

Málaga. **Road map** C3. 🚻 13,000. 🚉 🚌 ℹ️ Plaza Fuente de Arriba 15 (952 49 61 00). 🔄 Mon. 🌐 **alora.es**

Situated in the Guadalhorce river valley, Álora is an important agricultural centre. It is a classic white town (pueblo blanco, see pp176–7), perched on a hillside overlooking wheat fields, citrus orchards and olive groves.

The town's cobbled streets radiate from the 18th-century **Iglesia de la Encarnación**. At the weekly market, stalls of farm produce and clothing fill nearby streets. On the higher of Álora's twin hills stands the **Castillo**, with a cemetery of niche tombs set in neat blocks.

🏰 Castillo Árabe
Calle Ancha. **Tel** 952 49 55 77 (tourist office). **Open** daily.

㉑ Garganta del Chorro

Málaga. **Road map** C3. 🚉 El Chorro. 🚌 Parque Ardales. ℹ️ Plaza Fuente de Arriba 15 (952 49 61 00).

Up the fertile Guadalhorce valley, 12 km (7 miles) on from Álora, is one of the geographical wonders of Spain. The Garganta del Chorro is an immense gaping chasm 180 m (590 ft) high, slashing through a limestone mountain. In some places, where the Guadalhorce river hurtles through the gorge, waters foaming white, it is only 10 m (30 ft) wide. Visitors can access the Caminito del Rey walkway, which is attached to the walls of the gorge over 100 m (330 ft) above the river. A limited number of hikers is allowed at any one time, so reservations are essential.

🏞️ Caminito del Rey
Open Tue–Sun. 🌐 **caminodelrey.info**

㉒ Fuente de Piedra

Málaga. **Road map** C3. 🚉 🚌 ℹ️ Calle Cerro del Palo s/n (952 71 25 54).

The largest of several lakes in an expanse of wetlands north of Antequera, the Laguna de la Fuente de Piedra teems with bird life, including huge flocks of flamingos. In March, every year, up to 25,000 of them arrive to breed before migrating back to West Africa. However, if there is drought in the region, there will be fewer birds breeding.

The Garganta del Chorro, rising high above the Guadalhorce river

Apart from flamingos, you will also be able to admire cranes, herons, bee-eaters, snow-white egrets, as well as many species of ducks and geese. Their numbers have been on the increase since conservation and anti-hunting laws were introduced and the area declared a sanctuary. A road off the N334 leads to the lake side, from where visitors can watch the birds. Be advised that restraint is required: it is forbidden to join the waders in the lake. Information is available from a visitors' centre near the village of Fuente de Piedra.

Limestone formations in the Parque Natural del Torcal

The triumphal 16th-century Arco de los Gigantes, Antequera

❸ Antequera

Málaga. **Road map** D3. 🏔 42,000. 🚌 Plaza San Sebastián 7 (952 70 25 05). 🌐 **antequera.co.uk**

This busy market town has long been strategically important; first as Roman Anticaria, and later as a Moorish border fortress defending Granada.

The **Iglesia de Nuestra Señora del Carmen**, with its massive Baroque altarpiece, is not to be missed. To the west of here, at the opposite end of the town, is the 19th-century **Plaza de Toros**, with its museum of bullfighting.

High on a hill overlooking the town is the **Castillo Arabe**, a 13th-century Moorish castle. Visitors cannot go inside, but can walk round the castle walls – the approach is through the 16th-century **Arco de los Gigantes**. There are fine views from the

Torre del Papabellotas. In the town below, the 18th-century **Palacio de Nájera** is the setting for the Municipal Museum, whose star exhibit is a 2,000-year-old statue of a Roman boy.

On the outskirts of town are three large prehistoric **dolmens** that may have been the burial chambers of tribal leaders. Two of them – Viera and Menga – stand together, the latter the oldest and most impressive of all, dated at between 4,000 and 4,500 years old. A short distance away is the Dolmen de Romeral, which has a vaulted central chamber.

🎪 Plaza de Toros
Crta de Sevilla. **Tel** 952 70 81 42. **Open** Tue–Sun. Museo Taurino: **Open** Tue–Sun.

🏛 Palacio de Nájera
Coso Viejo. **Tel** 952 70 83 00. **Open** 10am–2pm, 4:30–6:30pm Tue–Sat, 10am–2pm Sun. 🕮 🕮 Tue.

🏛 Dolmens:
Tel 952 71 22 06. **Open** Apr–mid-Jun: 9am–7:30pm Tue–Sat; mid-Jun–mid-Sep: 9am–3:30pm Tue–Sat; mid-Sep–Mar: 9am–5:30pm Tue–Sat; all year: 9am–3:30pm Sun & public hols. 🕮

❹ El Torcal

Málaga. **Road map** D3. 🚌 🚌 Antequera. ℹ Ctra C3310, 10 km (6 miles) south of Antequera (952 24 33 24).

A huge exposed hump of limestone upland battered into bizarre formations by wind and rain, the **Parque Natural del Torcal** is very popular with hikers. Most follow a network of footpaths leading from a visitors'

centre in the middle; short walks (up to two hours) are marked by yellow arrows; longer walks are marked in red. There are caves, canyons, mushroom-shaped rocks and other geological curiosities to see. The park also boasts fox and weasel populations, and colonies of eagles, hawks and vultures. It also protects rare plants and flowers.

❺ Archidona

Málaga. **Road map** D3. 🏔 8,200. 🚌 🚌 ℹ Plaza Ochavada 2 (952 71 44 80). 🕮 Mon.

This small town is worth a stop to see its extraordinary **Plaza Ochavada**. This is an octagonal square built in the 18th century in a French style, but which also incorporates traditional Andalucían features.

From the **Ermita Virgen de Gracia** on a hillside above the town, there are commanding views over rolling countryside.

The 18th-century, octagonal Plaza Ochavada in Archidona

㉖ Nerja

Málaga. **Road map** D3. 🏔 18,000. 🚌
🛈 Calle Carmen 1 (ground floor of Ayuntamiento) (952 52 15 31). 🛒 Tue.
🖥 nerja.org

This fashionable resort at the eastern extremity of the Costa del Sol lies at the foot of the beautiful mountains of the Sierra de Almijara, and is perched on a cliff above a succession of sandy coves. The main area for tourist activity in the resort centres around the promenade, running along a rocky promontory known as **El Balcón de Europa** (the Balcony of Europe). Spread along its length is a hotel and cafés with outdoor tables. There are sweeping views up and down the coast. On the edges of town, holiday villas and apartments proliferate.

Due east of the town are the **Cuevas de Nerja**, a series of vast

The town of Nerja overlooking the sea from El Balcón de Europa

caverns of considerable archaeological interest, which were discovered in 1959. Wall paintings *(see p46)* found in them are believed to be about 20,000 years old. Unfortunately most are closed to public view, but a few of the many cathedral-sized chambers are open to the public. One of these has been

turned into an impressive underground auditorium large enough to hold audiences of several hundred. Concerts are held there in the summer.

🏛 **Cuevas de Nerja**
Carretera de las Cuevas de Nerja.
Tel 952 52 95 20. **Open** daily. **Closed**
1 Jan, 15 May. 🎫 🖥 cuevadenerja.es

㉙ Málaga

Málaga. **Road map** D3. 🏔 650,000.
✈ 🚉 🚌 🛈 Plaza de la Marina 11
(951 92 60 20). 🛒 Sun.
🖥 malagaturismo.com

A thriving port, Málaga is Andalucía's second largest city. Initial impressions tend to be of ugly suburbs and high-rise blocks, but this belies a city that is rich with history, and is filled with monuments.

Façade detail, Málaga Cathedral

Malaca, the Phoenician *(see pp46–7)* city, was an important trading port on the Iberian peninsula. After Rome's victory against Carthage in 206 BC *(see p48)*, it became a major port for Roman trade with Byzantium. Málaga's heyday came after 711, when it fell to the Moors and became their main port serving Granada. It was recaptured by the Christians in 1487. The Moors left behind were expelled *(see pp54–5)* after a rebellion.

Following a long decline, the city flourished again during the 19th century, when Málaga wine became one of Europe's popular drinks. Unfortunately, phylloxera, the vine disease that ravaged the vineyards of Europe, ended the prosperity of its vineyards.

The old town at the heart of Málaga radiates from the **catedral**. It was begun in 1528 by Diego de Siloé, but it is a mix of styles. Its construction was interrupted by an earthquake in 1680. The half-built second tower, abandoned in 1765, is the reason for its nickname: La Manquita (the one-armed one). Málaga's **Museo Carmen Thyssen** has a fine collection of 13th–20th century Spanish art while the **Centre Pompidou** has an impressive collection of 20th and 21st-century art-works. The **Museo Automovilístico y de la Moda**

has a fascinating collection of over 90 cars through the ages. The **Museo de Picasso** displays works by the native artist and the **Casa Natal de Picasso**, where the painter spent his early years, is now the headquarters of the Picasso Foundation. On the hill directly behind the Alcazaba are the ruins of the 14th-century Moorish **Castillo de Gibralfaro**.

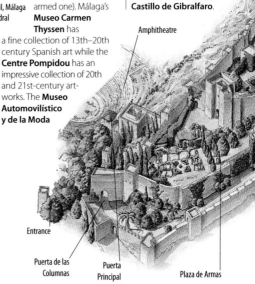

Amphitheatre

Entrance

Puerta de las Columnas

Puerta Principal

Plaza de Armas

🕗 The Axarquia

Málaga. **Road map** D3. 🔢 Avenida de la Constitución 1 (952 55 36 85). 🔲 competa.es

The hills behind Torre del Mar and Nerja make up the pretty upland region of the Axarquia, whose main town, **Vélez-Málaga**, has a few old streets and the remains of a castle to explore.

A better base for excursions is the attractive sweet wine-producing town of **Cómpeta**, 20 km (12 miles) from the coast by winding mountain roads. From here, there is an interesting "Mudejar route" down the hill and up the valley to **Archez** and **Salares**, villages whose church towers are undisguised brick minarets dating from the 15th and 13th centuries respectively.

Two other villages worth visiting are **Frigiliana**, close to the coast and easily accessible from Nerja; and **Comares** (north east of Vélez-Málaga), perched on top of an impressive outcrop of rock from which there are superb views.

Narrow street in the Barrio de San Sebastián, Vélez-Málaga

🕗 Montes de Málaga

Málaga. **Road map** D3. 🚌 to Colmenar. 🔢 Lagar de Torrijos, on C345 at km 544,3 (951 04 21 00).

To the north and east of Málaga are the beautiful hills of Montes de Málaga. A wide area is undergoing reforestation and forms the **Parque Natural de Montes de Málaga**. Wildlife thrives in the strongly scented undergrowth of lavender and wild herbs. Occasionally, there are glimpses of wild cats, stone martens, wild boars, eagles and other birds of prey.

Walkers can follow marked trails. A farmhouse has been restored and converted into an ethnological museum. Along the C345 road between Málaga and the park, there are sensational views down to the sea.

Eastwards, on the road to Vélez Málaga, is the unspoilt beach of Rincón de la Victoria (see p37).

🏛 **Museo Carmen Thyssen**
Plaza Carmen Thyssen. **Tel** 952 21 75 11. **Open** 10am–8pm Tue–Sun.

🏛 **Centre Pompidou Malaga**
Pasaje Doctor Carillo Casaux, s/n Muelle Uno. **Tel** 951 92 62 00. **Open** 9:30am–8pm Wed–Mon (11am–10pm 15 Jun–15 Sep). 🖼

🏛 **Museo Automovilístico y de la Moda**
Avenida Sor Teresa Prat 15. **Tel** 951 13 70 01. **Open** 10am–7pm Tue–Sun. 🖼

🏛 **Museo de Picasso**
Calle San Agustín 8. **Tel** 952 12 76 00. **Open** 10am–6pm Tue–Sun. **Closed** 1 & 6 Jan, 25 Dec. 🖼

🏛 **Casa Natal de Picasso**
Plaza de la Merced 15. **Tel** 951 92 60 60. **Open** 9:30am–8pm daily. **Closed** public hols.

🏰 **Castillo de Gibralfaro**
Tel 952 12 20 20. **Open** 9am–6pm daily (to 8pm summer). 🖼

🏰 **Alcazaba**
Calle Alcazabilla s/n. **Tel** 952 22 72 30. **Open** 9am–6pm daily. **Closed** 1 Jan, 24, 25 & 31 Dec.

🏛 **Museo Arqueológico**
Calle Alcazabilla. **Tel** 951 91 19 04. **Open** mid-Jun–mid-Sep: 9am–3pm Tue–Sun; mid-Sep–mid-Jun: 9am–8pm Tue–Sat, 9am–3pm Sun. 🖼
🔲 museosdeandalucia.es

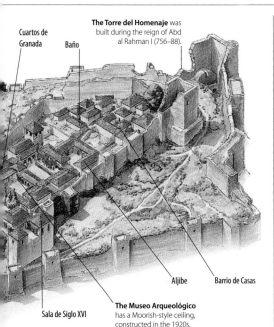

Cuartos de Granada

Baño

The Torre del Homenaje was built during the reign of Abd al Rahman I (756–88).

Aljibe

Barrio de Casas

Sala de Siglo XVI

The Museo Arqueológico has a Moorish-style ceiling, constructed in the 1920s.

Málaga's Alcazaba

Málaga's vast Alcazaba was built between the 8th and 11th centuries on the site of a Roman town. The two are curiously juxtaposed, with the Roman amphitheatre, discovered in 1951 and now almost fully excavated, just outside the entrance. The remains of Moorish walls can be seen, but the real attraction is the Museo Arqueológico, housing collections of Phoenician, Roman and Moorish artifacts, including fine ceramics.

Torremolinos, the capital of the Costa del Sol's tourist industry

⑳ Torremolinos

Málaga. **Road map** D3. 🚆 50,000.
🚌 🚉 *i* Plaza de Andalucía s/n
(952 37 95 12). 🕐 Thu.
w ayto-torremolinos.org

Torremolinos grew from a village in the 1950s to one of the busiest resorts on the Costa del Sol, where British and, to a lesser extent, German holiday-makers enjoyed their cheap package holidays. It also developed its red-light district and a raffish nightlife to provide "recreation" for sailors of the US navy in port at Málaga.

The town was cleaned up as part of a scheme that spent huge sums on new squares, a promenade, green spaces and enlarging the beach with millions of tonnes of golden sand.

Although Torremolinos still has scores of English bars run by expatriates, the atmosphere is now decidedly less down-market, especially at Carihuela beach, towards the adjoining resort of Benalmádena.

㉛ Benalmádena

Málaga. **Road map** D4. 🚆 66,000. 🚌
🚌 *i* Antonio Machado (952 44 24 94).

Benalmádena hosts an array of great attractions, including the impressive **Castillo de Colomares** built between 1987 and 1994 as homage to Christopher Columbus. The monument reflects architectural styles that influenced Spanish culture, including Byzantine, Romanesque and Arabic, and carved into the structure are representations of Spain's history. Only the exterior may be visited.

Europe's largest Buddhist monument, the Benálmadena **Stupa**, is also located here.

🏛 Castillo de Colomares

Carretera del Sol (El Viñazo). **Tel** 952 44 88 21. **Open** 10am–2pm daily, (also 4–7pm Apr–Jun & Sep–Oct, 5–9pm Jul & Aug, 4–6pm Nov–Mar).

🏛 Stupa

Calle Muérdago s/n, El Retamar. **Tel** 606 27 53 75. **Open** 10am–2pm, 3:30–7pm Tue–Sat; 10am–7:30pm Sun. 🖼

㉜ Fuengirola

Málaga. **Road map** C4. 🚆 53,000.
🚌 🚉 *i* Avda Jesús Santos Rein 6 (952 46 74 57). 🕐 Tue, Sat & Sun.
w fuengirola.org

The town of Fuengirola is another package-holiday resort, although some of the wilder elements of its mostly British clientele have moved on to newer pastures. Nowadays Fuengirola attracts mainly families.

During the mild winter months, retired people from the UK come to stroll along the promenade, go to English bars and waltz the afternoons away at hotel tea dances.

Boxes of fresh fish, Fuengirola

㉝ Marbella

Málaga. **Road map** C4. 🚆 120,000.
🚌 *i* Glorieta de la Fontanilla s/n, Paseo Maritimo (952 76 87 60).
🕐 Mon & Sat (Puerto Banús).
w marbella.es

Marbella is one of Europe's most exclusive holiday resorts. Royalty, film stars and other members of the jet set spend

Yachts and motorboats moored in the exclusive marina of Marbella

19th-century lithograph of the harbour at Málaga

Life in the Sun

The idealized image of the Costa del Sol before tourism is of idyllic fishing villages where life was always at an easy pace. It is true to say that local economies have turned away from fishing and agriculture, and that the natural beauty of this coast has been marred by development. Any measured view, however, should consider the situation described by Laurie Lee, the writer who in 1936 wrote of "… salt-fish villages, thin-ribbed, sea-hating, cursing their place in the sun". Today, few Andalucíans curse their new-found prosperity.

their summers here, in smart villas or at one of Marbella's luxury hotels. In winter, the major attraction is the golf (*see pp36–7*).

As well as extensive modern developments, Marbella boasts a well-preserved, charming Old Town. A number of streets lead from the main road, Avenida Ramón y Cajal, to Plaza de los Naranjos, the main square, surrounded by orange trees (hence its name).

The remains of the town's Arab walls loom over adjacent Calle Carmen, which leads to the 17th-century Iglesia de Nuestra Señora de la Encarnación. Nearby is the **Museo del Grabado Contemporaneo** (Museum of Contemporary Engravings), which contains works by Miró and Picasso.

On the other side of Avenida Ramón y Cajal is the Paseo de la Alameda, a park with benches decorated with colourful ceramics. From here, the road to the seafront, Avenida del Mar, is lined with sculptures made from designs by famous painter Salvador Dalí.

Heading west, Avenida Ramón y Cajal becomes the A7/N340. The first stretch is known as the "Golden Mile" because of its real-estate value. At the other end of the Golden Mile is Puerto Banús, the most exclusive marina in Spain.

Beyond Puerto Banús is San Pedro de Alcántara, really a separate town but officially part of Marbella. It is quiet, with a sleepy atmosphere, especially

in the Plaza de la Iglesia, the town square. Most of the smart holiday developments are on the town's fringes, set amid a number of golf courses.

🏛 Museo del Grabado Contemporáneo
C/Hospital Bazan s/n. **Tel** 952 76 57 41. **Open** Mon–Sat. **Closed** public hols. 🖼

🔢 Estepona

Málaga. **Road map** C4. 🚏 46,000. 🚌
🛈 Plaza de las Flores, s/n (952 80 20 02). 🚩 Wed & Sun. 🌐 **estepona.es**

This former fishing village, situated midway between Marbella and Gibraltar, has been altered, but not totally overwhelmed, by tourist developments. Now a popular resort, it is not particularly attractive at first sight, with big

The leafy Plaza de las Flores hidden in Estepona's backstreets

hotels and apartment blocks fronting the town's busy main tourist area. Behind, however, there are endearing pockets of all that is quintessentially Spanish – orange trees lining the streets, and the lovely **Plaza Arce** and **Plaza de las Flores** –peaceful squares where old men sit reading newspapers while around them children kick footballs about. There are also a few good, relatively inexpensive fish restaurants and tapas bars serving traditional delicacies. The beach is pleasant enough and evenings in the town tend to be quiet, which makes the resort popular with families with young children. Not far away from Estepona, however, is a popular nudist beach called the Costa Natura (*see pp36–7*).

Relaxing in peaceful San Pedro de Alcántara

㉟ Tangier

Tangier is only 45 minutes by fast ferry from Tarifa, making it a perfect day trip. Despite its proximity, this ancient Moroccan port, founded by the Berbers before 1000 BC, will be a sharp culture shock for those used to life in Europe. Tangier is vibrant with eastern colour, and the vast, labyrinthine Medina, the market quarter, pulsates with noise. From their workshops in back alleys, craftsmen make traditional goods for busy shops and stalls in the crowded streets. Yet behind wrought-iron railings the traveller will see tranquil courtyards decorated with mosaics, cool fountains and mosques.

View into the labyrinthine Medina from the Grand Socco

Sights at a Glance

① Dar El Makhzen
② Kasbah
③ Hôtel Continental
④ Grand Mosque
⑤ Rue es Siaghin
⑥ Grand Socco
⑦ American Legation

🏛 Dar El Makhzen

Place de la Kasbah. **Tel** 212 39 93 20 97. **Open** Wed–Mon. 🎫

Sultan Moulay Ismail, who unified Morocco in the 17th century, had this palace built within the Kasbah. The sultans lived here until 1912. It is now a museum of crafts such as ceramics, embroidery and ironwork. The exhibits are arranged round a central courtyard and in cool rooms with tiled ceilings. There are illuminated Korans in the Fez Room and a courtyard in the style of Andalucían Moorish gardens.

🏯 Kasbah

The Kasbah or citadel, where the sultans once held court, is at the Medina's highest point. It is separated from its alleys by sturdy walls and four massive stone gateways. From the battlements there are views over the Strait of Gibraltar.

The Kasbah encloses the Dar El Makhzen, the treasury house, the old prison and the law courts. Villas once owned by American and European celebrities, such as Paul Bowles, the author of *The Sheltering Sky*, are also within the Kasbah walls.

For keys to symbols *see back flap*

Façade of the Dar El Makhzen, the museum of Moroccan arts

🏨 Hôtel Continental

Rue Dar El Baroud. **Tel** 212 39 93 10 24. **Open** daily.

Numerous intrigues have been played out in this hotel overlooking the port. Today it is a fine place to sit and drink tea.

C Grand Mosque

Green and white minarets rise above this massive edifice built in the 17th century by Sultan Moulay Ismail. An exquisitely carved gateway suggests more treasures within – non-Muslims, however, are forbidden from entering any mosque.

The carved façade of Tangier's
Grand Mosque

Rue es Siaghin

The Medina's "Silversmith's Street"
was Tangier's main thoroughfare
in the 1930s and still offers a
staggering array of merchandise;
shop owners will offer you mint
tea in a bid to get you to buy.

Grand Socco

Traders from the Rif mountains
come to barter their goods at
this busy main square at the
heart of Tangier. The square's
official name, Place du 9 Avril
1947, commemorates a visit by
Sultan Muhammad V.

American Legation

Rue du Portugal. **Tel** 212 39 93 53 17.
Open 10am–5pm Mon–Fri.
legation.org

This former palace was the
USA's first diplomatic mission.
It was the American Embassy
until 1961 and is now a
museum with an exhibit
devoted to writer Paul Bowles.

❸❻ Ceuta

Road map C4. 76,000. from
Algeciras (see p265). Calle Edrisis,
Baluarte de los Mallorquines (856 20
05 60). **ceuta.si**

The closest of Spain's two North
African enclaves to Europe is
worth visiting if you want to dip
your toe into North Africa
without leaving Spain (although
you will need to show an identity
card or passport on entering), or
if are on your way to Morocco.
Ceuta, only 19 km (12 miles) from
mainland Spain, is dominated by
a hill called Monte Hacho, on
which there is a fort occupied by
the Spanish army. The city has
Phoenician and Arab remains,
churches dating from the 17th
to the 19th centuries and
several museums, including the
Museo de la Legión, dedicated
to the Spanish Foreign Legion.
   Ceuta's shops offer the
chance to indulge in some tax-
free shopping. Both Ceuta and
Melilla are surrounded by high
fences, as they are European
entry points for illegal immigrants
from parts of Africa.

Museo de la Legión

Avda Deán Navarro Acuña 6. **Tel** 956
52 62 19. **Open** 10am–1pm Mon–Sat.

European architectural influence in the
North African enclave of Ceuta

❸❼ Melilla

Road map E5. 69,000. from
Málaga or Almería. See p265 for travel
info. Palacio de Exposiciones y
Congresos, Calle Fortuny 21 (952 97
61 51). **melillaturismo.com**

Spain's second North African
enclave, settled by Spain in
1497, is located 150 km (90
miles) due south of Adra (in
Almería), across the sea, on
the Moroccan coast. It takes
a little effort to get there, as
Melilla is a six hour ferry ride
from mainland Spain, but it
is worth it as there is plenty to
see, including the only Gothic
architecture in Africa and
samples of Modernisme, the
Catalan version of Art Nouveau
architecture. Modern-day
Melilla prides itself on being a
place of peaceful co-existence
between its main four
component cultures: Christian,
Muslim, Jewish and Hindu.
   All the principal sights are
located in **Melilla La Vieja** (Old
Melilla), a cluster of four fortified
areas separated by moats or
walls, built in the 14th century
on a hammer-head promontory
jutting out into the sea.
   The 19th- and 20th-century
parts of the city, however,
are equally worth strolling
around in, since they include
an abundance of splendid
Modernisme and Art Deco
buildings. There are around
900 period edifices in Melilla.
There is also a small beach.

The International Era

From 1932 until its incorporation
into Morocco in 1956, Tangier was
an international zone, tax free and
under the control of a committee
of 30 nations. This was an era that
was characterized by financial fraud,
espionage, large-scale smuggling,
outrageous sexual licence and
profligacy by wealthy tax exiles,
such as heiress Barbara Hutton.
Celebrities such as Henri Matisse,
Jack Kerouac and Orson Welles
added colour to the scene.

Wealthy American socialite Barbara
Woolworth Hutton in Tangier

GRANADA AND ALMERÍA

Eastern Andalucía is dominated by the Sierra Nevada, Iberia's highest range and one of Spain's premier winter sports venues. At its foot is Granada, once a Moorish kingdom, with a royal palace, the Alhambra, straight out of *One Thousand and One Nights*. Ruined fortresses, relics of a warring past, dominate the towns of Granada province. In Almería's arid interior, film directors have put to use atmospheric landscapes reminiscent of Arabia or the Wild West.

At the point where the mountains of the Sierra Nevada meet the plain, 670 m (2,200 ft) above sea level, nestles the ancient city of Granada, founded by the Iberians. For 250 years it was the capital of a Moorish kingdom whose borders enclosed both Almería and Málaga provinces. On a ridge overlooking the city rises the royal citadel of the Alhambra, a complex of palaces and water gardens.

The mountainous terrain of Granada province is starkly impressive. Amid the ravines, crags and terraced fields of Las Alpujarras on the southern flank of the Sierra Nevada, the villages seem to cling to the sheer slopes. Along the coastal strip of Granada province, avocados and custard apples flourish in the subtropical climate. Hotels, villas and holiday apartment blocks are also much in evidence here.

East of Granada, the landscape becomes more arid. Around the town of Guadix, founded in Phoenician and Roman times, thousands of people live in cave-houses. A statue of an Iberian goddess from pre-Roman times was found at Baza, and at Los Millares, near Almería, there are traces of a 4,000-year-old settlement. In contrast, just outside Guadix is one of Europe's major solar power plants, the Andasol solar power station.

Almería, a flourishing port in the Moorish era, has been revitalized by a new form of agriculture. Plastic greenhouses now cover hectares of its surrounding province, producing fruit and vegetables all year round.

Along the sparsely populated coast of Cabo de Gata, little-visited villages and bays doze in year-round sunshine.

The Renaissance castle of La Calahorra at the foot of the Sierra Nevada

◄ Street view in Alpujarras de la Sierra, with the Sierra Nevada mountains in the background

Exploring Granada and Almería

Granada and the Alhambra are the obvious highlights of this region, but are only a part of its appeal. Improved roads make it easy to reach most places within a few hours, and from Granada it is possible to explore the Sierra Nevada, plunge into the clear waters of the Costa Tropical, or wander through beautiful, spectacularly situated old towns, such as Montefrío and Alhama de Granada. From Almería it is a short hop to the Arizona-like country around Tabernas, where spaghetti westerns were made, or to the secluded beaches of the Parque Natural de Cabo de Gata. Each town and whitewashed village that lies in between has its own charm.

The Alhambra, with the snow-covered Sierra Nevada mountain range in the background

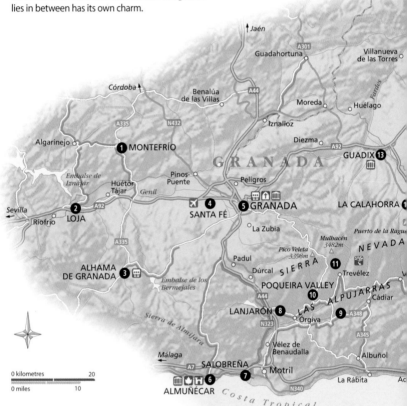

Sights at a Glance

1. Montefrío
2. Loja
3. Alhama de Granada
4. Santa Fé
5. *Granada pp194–202*
6. Almuñécar
7. Salobreña
8. Lanjarón
9. Poqueira Valley
10. Sierra Nevada
11. La Calahorra
12. Guadix
13. Baza
14. Vélez Blanco
15. Tabernas
16. Roquetas de Mar
17. *Almería pp206–7*
18. Parque Natural de Cabo de Gata
19. San José
20. Níjar
21. Sorbas
22. Mojácar

Tour

9. Las Alpujarras

Key

▬▬ Motorway
▬ Major road
▬▬ Minor road
▬ Scenic route
▬▬ Major railway
▬ Minor railway
▬▬ Provincial border
△ Summit

For additional map symbols *see back flap*

Avenida de Andalucía, the main street in Lanjarón

Spaghetti-western-style landscape near Tabernas

Getting Around

The A92 runs east to Guadix and then turns south to Almería. The A92N continues east from Guadix towards Lorca. The N340 follows the coast via Almería and the Costa Tropical. The N323 links the coast with Granada and the A348 connects the villages of the Alpujarras. There are three trains a day between Granada and Almería, but no coastal rail service. Frequent buses run from both cities to towns on main routes.

Whitewashed houses on the edge of the gorge at Alhama de Granada, surrounded by olive groves

❶ Montefrío

Granada. **Road map** D3. 🏚 7,000. 🚌
ℹ️ Plaza de España 1 (958 33 60 04).
🛒 Mon.

Montefrío is the archetypal
Andalucían town, which,
approached by road from the
south, offers wonderful views of
tiled rooftops and whitewashed
houses running up to a steep
crag. The village is surmounted
by remains of Moorish
fortifications and the
16th-century Gothic
Iglesia de la Villa, which
is attributed to Diego de
Siloé. Located in the
centre of town stands
the **Iglesia de la
Encarnación**, in Neo-
Classical design; the
architect Ventura
Rodríguez (1717–85)
is credited with its
design. Montefrío is
also famed for the
high quality of its
pork products.

❷ Loja

Granada. **Road map** D3. 🏚 21,000.
🚊 🚌 ℹ️ Edificio Espacio Joven
Calle Comedias 2 (958 32 15 20).
🛒 Mon. 🌐 lojaturismo.com

A ruined Moorish fort rises
above the crooked streets of
the old town of Loja, which
was built at a strategic point on
the Río Genil. The Renaissance
Templo de San Gabriel (1566)
has a striking façade, designed
by Diego de Siloé. Known as
"the city of water", Loja also has

some beautiful fountains. East
of the town, the fast-flowing
Río Genil cuts through **Los
Infiernos** gorge. Sample local
trout in **Riofrío**, to the west.

❸ Alhama de Granada

Granada. **Road map** D3. 🏚 6,000.
🚌 ℹ️ Carrera de Francisco
Toledo 10 (958 36 06 86). 🛒 Fri.
🌐 turismodealhama.com

Alhama is a charming, small
town balanced above a
gorge. It was known as Al
hamma (hot springs) to
the Arabs. Their baths
can still be seen in
Hotel Balneario on
the edge of the town.
Alhama's fall to the
Christians in 1482 led
to the final humiliation
of the Nasrid
kingdom at Granada
in 1492 (see p52).
The 16th-century
Iglesia de Carmen
has a number of very
fine paintings inside its dome,
which had to be restored after
damage incurred during the
Spanish Civil War (see
pp58–9). Narrow, imma-
culately white-washed
streets lead to the **Iglesia
de la Encarnación**, founded
by the Catholic Monarchs (see
pp52–3) in the 16th century.
Some of the vestments
worn by the present-day
priests are said to have
been embroidered by
Queen Isabel herself. The

Belfry of Templo de San
Gabriel at Loja

church also has a Renaissance
bell tower designed by Diego de
Siloé. Nearby is the 16th-century
Hospital de la Reina, now an
exhibition centre for local artists
housing a fine artesonado ceiling.

🏨 **Hotel Balneario**
Calle Balneario. **Tel** 958 35 00 11.
Open Mar–Nov.

🏨 **Hospital de la Reina**
Calle Vendederas s/n. **Tel** 958 36 06 86
(tourist office). **Open** 9am–3pm Mon–
Fri. Contact Tourist Office to visit (open
8am–3pm Mon–Fri) and for tours of
other local sights.

❹ Santa Fé

Granada. **Road map** D3. 🏚 12,500.
🚌 ℹ️ Arco de Sevilla, Calle Isabel la
Católica 7 (958 51 31 10). 🛒 Thu.

The army of the Catholic
Monarchs camped here as it lay
siege to Granada (see p52). The
camp burned down, it is said,
after a maid placed a candle too
close to a curtain in Isabel's tent.
Fernando ordered a model
town to be built. Its name, "holy
faith", was chosen by the
devout Isabel. In 1492 the
Moors made a formal
surrender at Santa Fé
and here, in the same
year, the two
monarchs backed
Columbus's voyage of
exploration (see p131). An
earthquake destroyed
some of the town in 1806.
A Moor's severed head,
carved in stone,
decorates the spire of

Spire-tip of the
church, Santa Fé

the parish church.

❺ Granada

See pp194–202.

❻ Almuñécar

Granada. **Road map** D3. 22,000. Avenida Europa s/n (958 63 11 25). Fri. **turismoalmunecar.es**

Almuñécar lies on southern Spain's most spectacular coast, the **Costa Tropical** *(see p37)*, where mountains rise to over 2,000 m (6,560 ft) from the shores of the Mediterranean Sea. The Phoenicians founded the first settlement, called Sexi, at Almuñécar, and the Romans built an aqueduct here. When the English writer Laurie Lee made his long trek across Spain in 1936, he described Almuñécar as "a tumbling little village fronted by a strip of grey sand, which some hoped would be an attraction for tourists". On returning in the 1950s, he found a village still coming to terms with the Spanish Civil War *(see pp58–9)*, which he recounts in his novel *A Rose for Winter*.

Almuñécar is now a holiday resort. Above the old town is the **Castillo de San Miguel**. In its shadow are botanic gardens, the **Parque Ornitológico** and a Roman fish-salting factory. Phoenician artifacts are displayed

Castillo de San Miguel, overlooking the village of Almuñécar

in the **Museo Arqueológico Cueva de Siete Palacios**.

🏰 Castillo de San Miguel
Tel 650 02 75 84. **Open** Tue–Sun.

🐦 Parque Ornitológico
Plaza de Abderraman s/n. **Tel** 958 63 56 17. **Open** daily.

🏛 Museo Arqueológico Cueva de Siete Palacios
Calle Cueva de Siete Palacios s/n. **Tel** 607 86 54 66. **Open** Tue–Sun.

❼ Salobreña

Granada. **Road map** E3. 10,500. Plaza de Goya s/n (958 61 03 14). Tue & Fri. **ayto-salobrena.org**

From across the coastal plain, Salobreña looks like a white liner sailing above a sea of waving sugar cane. Narrow streets wend their way up a hill first fortified by the Phoenicians. The hill later became the site of the restored **Castillo Arabe**, which gives fine views of the Sierra Nevada *(see p203)*. Modern developments, bars and restaurants line part of this resort's lengthy beach.

🏰 Castillo Arabe
Falda del Castillo, Calle Andrés Segovia. **Tel** 958 61 03 14. **Open** daily.

❽ Lanjarón

Granada. **Road map** E3. 24,000. Avda de Madrid s/n (958 77 04 62). Tue & Fri. **lanjanet.com**

Scores of snow-fed springs bubble from the slopes below the Sierra Nevada, and Lanjarón, on the threshold of Las Alpujarras *(see pp204–5)*, has a long history as a spa. From June to October visitors flock to the town to take the waters and, under medical supervision, enjoy various water treatments for arthritis, obesity, nervous tension and other ailments. Lanjarón bottled water is sold all over Spain.

The town occupies a lovely site, but it can seem melancholic. The exception to this is during the early hours of the festival of San Juan *(see p39)* when a water battle takes place. Anybody who dares venture into the streets gets liberally doused.

🏨 Balneario
Balneario de Lanjarón. **Tel** 958 77 04 54. **Open** daily. **Closed** mid-Dec–mid-Jan. **hotelbalneariolanjaron.com**

The village of Salobreña viewed across fields of sugar cane

❺ Granada

The guitarist Andres Segovia (1893–1987) described Granada as a "place of dreams, where the Lord put the seed of music in my soul". It was ruled by the Nasrid dynasty *(see pp52–3)* from 1238 until 1492 when it fell to the Catholic Monarchs. Before the Moors were expelled, artisans, merchants, scholars and scientists all contributed to the city's reputation as a centre for culture. Under Christian rule the city became a focus for the Renaissance. After a period of decline in the 19th century, Granada has become the subject of renewed interest and efforts are being made to restore parts of it to their past glory.

Entrance to the Moorish mihrab in the Palacio de la Madraza

Façade of Granada cathedral

⛪ Catedral

C/Gran Via 5. **Tel** 958 22 29 59.

On the orders of the Catholic Monarchs, work on the cathedral began in 1523 to Enrique de Egas's Gothic-style plans. It continued under the Renaissance maestro Diego de Siloé, who also designed the façade. Corinthian pillars support his circular Capilla Mayor. Under its dome, windows of 16th-century glass depict Juan del Campo's *The Passion*. The west front was designed by local Baroque artist Alonso Cano. His grave and many of his works are housed in the cathedral. By the entrance arch are wooden statues of the Catholic Monarchs carved by Pedro de Mena in 1677.

⛪ Capilla Real

C/Oficios 3. **Tel** 958 22 92 39.

The Royal Chapel was built for the Catholic Monarchs between 1505 and 1507 by Enrique de Egas. A magnificent *reja* (grille) by Maestro Bartolomé de Jaén encloses the mausoleums and high altar. The *retablo* by the sculptor Felipe de Vigarney has

reliefs depicting the fall of Granada *(see pp52–3)*. Carrara marble figures of Fernando and Isabel repose next to those of their daughter Juana la Loca (the Mad) and her husband Felipe el Hermoso (the Handsome), both by sculptor Bartolomé Ordóñez.

Steps lead down to the crypt where their corpses are stored in lead coffins. In the sacristy there are many art treasures, including paintings by Van der Weyden and Botticelli. Glass cases house Isabel's crown and Fernando's sword.

🏛 Palacio de la Madraza

Calle Oficios 14. **Tel** 958 99 63 50.
Open daily. ♿

Originally an Arab university, this building later became the city hall. The façade dates from the 18th century. Inside is a Moorish hall with a finely decorated mihrab. Today the Palacio is part of the University of Granada.

🏛 Corral del Carbón

Calle Mariana Pineda s/n. **Tel** 958 22 59 90. **Open** 10:30am–1:30pm, 5–8pm Mon–Fri; 10:30am–2pm Sat. ♿

This galleried courtyard is a unique relic of the Moorish era.

Originally it was a storehouse and inn for merchants who mainly dealt in coal.

In Christian times it was a venue for theatrical performances. Today it houses government offices.

🏛 Casa de los Tiros

Calle Pavaneras 19. **Tel** 958 22 06 29.
Open Jun–mid-Sep: 9am–3:30pm Tue–Sat, 10am–5pm Sun & public hols; mid-Sep–May: 10am–8:30pm Tue–Sat, 10am–5pm Sun & public hols.

This fortress-like palace was built in Renaissance style in the 16th century. It was once the property of a family who were awarded the Generalife after the fall of Granada *(see pp52–3)*; among their possessions was a sword belonging to Boabdil *(see p53)*. The sword is represented on the façade. The building owes its name to the muskets projecting from its battlements, *tiros* being the Spanish word for shot.

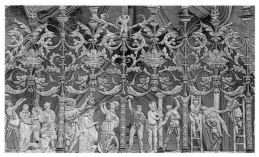

Reja by Maestro Bartolomé de Jaén enclosing the altar of the Capilla Real

🔲 Mirador de San Nicolás

From this square visitors can enjoy splendid sunset views. Tiled rooftops drop away to the Darro river, on the far side of which stands the great complex of the Alhambra; the Sierra Nevada provides a suitably dramatic backdrop.

🔲 El Bañuelo

Carrera del Darro 31. **Tel** 958 02 78 00. **Open** 10am–2pm Tue–Sat. **Closed** public hols.

These brick-vaulted Arab baths, located near the Darro river, were built in the 11th century. Roman, Visigothic and Arab capitals were all incorporated into the baths' columns.

🏛 Museo Arqueológico

Carrera del Darro 43. **Tel** 958 57 52 02 (tourist office). **Closed** for renovations.

The Renaissance Casa de Castril, which has a Plateresque portal, houses this museum of Iberian, Phoenician, Roman and Arab antiquities and artifacts.

Cupola in the sanctuary of the Monasterio de la Cartuja

🏛 Palacio Carlos V

Alhambra. **Tel** 958 56 35 08. **Open** Tue–Sun (opening hours vary month by month so call ahead).

This Italian Renaissance palace in the Alhambra is the masterpiece of Pedro Machuca, a student of Michelangelo. It houses the Museo Hispano-Musulmán and the Museo de Bellas Artes. The highlight of the Muslim art collection is a most exquisite 15th-century vase from the Alhambra, which has brilliant blue and gold designs.

🔲 Alhambra

See pp198–9.

🔷 Monasterio de la Cartuja

Tel 958 16 19 32. **Open** 10am–1pm, 4–8pm daily. 🎨

A Christian warrior, El Gran Capitán, donated the land on which this monastery was built in 1516. A cupola by Antonio Palomino tops the sanctuary. The Churrigueresque sacristy (see p29) is by mason Luis de Arévalo and sculptor Luis Cabello.

Sights at a Glance

① Catedral
② Capilla Real
③ Palacio de la Madraza
④ Corral del Carbón
⑤ Casa de los Tiros
⑥ Mirador de San Nicolás
⑦ El Bañuelo
⑧ Museo Arqueológico
⑨ Palacio Carlos V
⑩ Alhambra

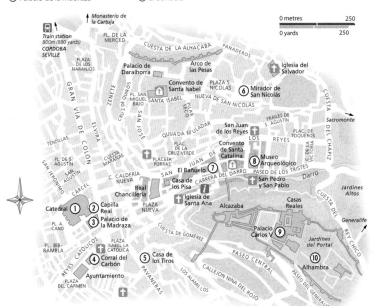

Street-by-Street: The Albaicín

This corner of Granada, clinging to the hillside opposite the Alhambra, is where one feels closest to the city's Moorish ancestry. A fortress was first built here in the 13th century and there were once over 30 mosques, some of which can still be traced. Along narrow, cobbled alleys stand *cármenes*, villas with Moorish decoration and gardens, secluded from the world by their high walls. In the evening, when the scent of jasmine lingers in the air, take a walk up to the Mirador de San Nicolás. From here the view over a maze of rooftops and the Alhambra glowing in the sunset is magical.

Albaicín Street
Steep and sinuous, the Albaicín streets form a virtual labyrinth. Many street names start with *Cuesta*, meaning slope.

Real Chancillería
Commissioned by the Catholic Monarchs, the Royal Chancery dates from 1530. Its patio is attributed to de Siloé.

Casa de los Pisas displays works of art belonging to the Knights Hospitallers, founded by Juan de Dios in the 16th century.

Key

 — Suggested route

| 0 metres | 50 |
| 0 yards | 50 |

★ Iglesia de Santa Ana
At the end of the Plaza Santa Ana stands this 16th-century brick church in Mudéjar style. It has an elegant Plateresque portal and, inside, a coffered ceiling.

Carrera del Darro
The road along the Río Darro leads past fine façades and crumbling bridges. At the top end, several bars offer views of the Alhambra.

VISITORS' CHECKLIST

Practical Information
Granada. **Road map** D3. ⚂
250,000. ℹ️ Santa Ana 4 (958 57
52 02); Plaza del Carmen s/n (958
24 82 80). 🗓️ Sat & Sun. 🎭 Día
de la Cruz (3 May), Corpus Christi
(May/Jun). 🌐 **granadatur.com**

Transport
✈️ 12 km (7 miles) SE of city. 🚉
Avenida de Andalucia s/n (902 43
23 43). 🚌 Carretera de Jaen s/n
(902 42 22 42).

★ Museo Arqueológico
The ornate façade of this museum has Plateresque carvings, including reliefs of mythological figures.

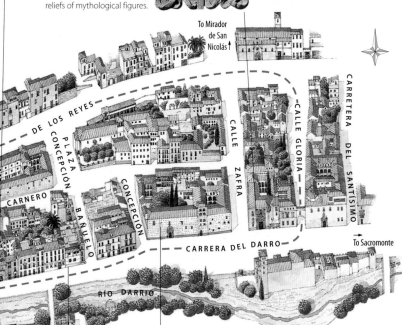

To Mirador de San Nicolás ↑

DE LOS REYES

PLAZA CONCEPCIÓN

CARNERO

BAÑUELO

CONCEPCIÓN

CALLE ZAFRA

CALLE GLORIA

CARRETERA DEL SANTISIMO

CARRERA DEL DARRO

To Sacromonte →

RÍO DARRIO

Convento de Santa Catalina de Zafra was founded in 1521.

★ El Bañuelo
Star-shaped openings in the vaults let light into these well-preserved Moorish baths, which were built in the 11th century.

Sacromonte

Granada's gypsies (Roma) formerly lived in the caves honeycombing this hillside. Travellers such as Washington Irving (*see p57*) would go there to enjoy spontaneous outbursts of flamenco. Today, virtually all Roma have moved away, but touristy flamenco shows of variable quality are still performed here in the evenings (*see p244*). A Benedictine monastery, the Abadía del Sacro-monte, sits at the very top of the hill. Inside, the ashes of San Cecilio, Granada's patron saint, are stored.

Gypsies dancing flamenco, 19th century

Granada: Alhambra

A magical use of space, light, water and decoration characterizes this most sensual piece of architecture. It was built under Ismail I, Yusuf I and Muhammad V, caliphs when the Nasrid dynasty *(see p52)* ruled Granada. Seeking to belie an image of waning power, they constructed their idea of paradise on Earth. Modest materials were used (tiles, plaster and timber), but they were superbly worked. Although the Alhambra suffered from decay and pillage, including an attempt by Napoleon's troops to blow it up, it has undergone extensive restoration and its delicate craftsmanship still dazzles the eye.

★ Salón de Embajadores
The ceiling of this sumptuous throne room, built between 1334 and 1354, represents the seven heavens of the Muslim cosmos.

★ Patio de Arrayanes
This pool, set amid myrtle hedges and graceful arcades, reflects light into the surrounding halls.

KEY

① Patio de Machuca

② Sala de la Barca

③ Washington Irving's apartments

④ Jardín de Lindaraja

⑤ Baños Reales

⑥ **The Sala de las Dos Hermanas**, with its honeycomb dome, is regarded as the ultimate example of Spanish Islamic architecture.

⑦ Puerta de la Rawda

⑧ **The Palacio Carlos V** *(see p54)*, a fine Renaissance building, was added to the Alhambra in 1526.

Entrance

Patio del Mexuar
This council chamber, completed in 1365, was where the reigning sultan listened to the petitions of his subjects and held meetings with his ministers.

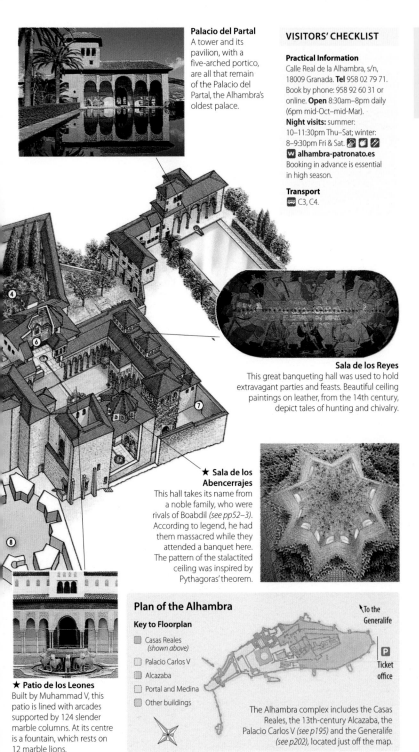

Palacio del Partal
A tower and its pavilion, with a five-arched portico, are all that remain of the Palacio del Partal, the Alhambra's oldest palace.

VISITORS' CHECKLIST

Practical Information
Calle Real de la Alhambra, s/n, 18009 Granada. **Tel** 958 02 79 71. Book by phone: 958 92 60 31 or online. **Open** 8:30am–8pm daily (6pm mid-Oct–mid-Mar).
Night visits: summer: 10–11:30pm Thu–Sat; winter: 8–9:30pm Fri & Sat. 🅿 💳 ♿
W **alhambra-patronato.es**
Booking in advance is essential in high season.

Transport
🚌 C3, C4.

Sala de los Reyes
This great banqueting hall was used to hold extravagant parties and feasts. Beautiful ceiling paintings on leather, from the 14th century, depict tales of hunting and chivalry.

★ **Sala de los Abencerrajes**
This hall takes its name from a noble family, who were rivals of Boabdil (see pp52–3). According to legend, he had them massacred while they attended a banquet here. The pattern of the stalactited ceiling was inspired by Pythagoras' theorem.

Plan of the Alhambra

Key to Floorplan

- 🟦 Casas Reales (shown above)
- ⬜ Palacio Carlos V
- ⬜ Alcazaba
- ⬜ Portal and Medina
- ⬜ Other buildings

↖To the Generalife

P Ticket office

The Alhambra complex includes the Casas Reales, the 13th-century Alcazaba, the Palacio Carlos V (see p195) and the Generalife (see p202), located just off the map.

★ **Patio de los Leones**
Built by Muhammad V, this patio is lined with arcades supported by 124 slender marble columns. At its centre is a fountain, which rests on 12 marble lions.

Granada: Generalife

Located northeast of the Alhambra, the Generalife was the country estate of the Nasrid kings. Here, they could escape the intrigues of the palace and enjoy tranquillity high above the city, a little closer to heaven. The name Generalife, or Yannat al Arif, has various interpretations, perhaps the most pleasing being "the garden of lofty paradise". The gardens, begun in the 13th century, have been modified over the years. They originally contained orchards and pastures for animals. The Generalife provides a magical setting for Granada's yearly International Music and Dance Festival *(see p39)*.

Patio de la Acequia
This enclosed oriental garden is built round a long central pool. Rows of water jets make graceful arches above it.

Sala Regia

Jardines Altos
(Upper Gardens)

The Escalera del Agua is a staircase with water flowing gently down it.

Entrance

The Patio de los Cipreses, otherwise known as the Patio de la Sultana, was the secret meeting place for Soraya, wife of the Sultan Abu l-Hasan, and her lover, the chief of the Abencerrajes.

The Patio de Polo was the courtyard where palace visitors, arriving on horseback, would leave their horses.

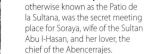

Patio del Generalife
Leading up from the Alhambra to the Generalife are the Jardines Bajos (lower gardens). Above them, just before the main compound, is the Patio del Generalife.

◀ Picturesque town of Picena in Las Alpujarras

The majestic peaks of the Sierra Nevada towering, in places, over 3,000 m (9,800 ft) above sea level

❾ Las Alpujarras

See pp204–5.

❿ Poqueira Valley

Barranco de Poqueira, Granada. **Road map** E3. 🅸 Plaza de la Libertad 7, Pampaneira (958 76 31 27).

Many visitors to the Alpujarras get no further than this deep, steep-sided valley above Orgiva, and it is certainly the best place to head for on a short visit. It contains three pretty, well-kept villages climbing the slope. In ascending order, they are: **Pampaneira**, **Bubion** and **Capileira**. All these villages are perfect examples of the singular architectural style of the Alpujarras, which has its closest relation in the Atlas Mountains of Morocco. The whitewashed houses of each village huddle together seemingly randomly ("a confused agglomeration of boxes" as the writer Gerald Brenan described them), with flat grey gravel roofs sprouting a variety of eccentrically tall chimneys. The streets between the houses are rarely straight, often stepped and tapering, and they sometimes disappear into short tunnels.

The countryside between the villages makes excellent walking or horse-riding country. The slopes are still divided by dry-stone walls into terraced fields that are fed by an ingenious irrigation system that distributes the melt water from the mountains above. Dilapidated mills and old threshing floors are other signs of a vanishing way of life.

⓫ Sierra Nevada

Granada. **Road map** E3. 🚌 from Granada. 🅸 Parque Nacional Sierra Nevada Centro de Visitantes "El Dornajo", Carretera de Sierra Nevada Km 23, Güéjar Sierra (958 98 02 46). 🌐 **sierranevada.es/en**

Fourteen peaks, more than 3,000 m (9,800 ft) high, crown the heights of the Sierra Nevada. The snow lingers until July and begins falling again in late autumn. Europe's highest road (closed to traffic) runs past a ski resort at 2,100 m (6,890 ft), and skirts the two highest peaks, **Pico Veleta** at 3,398 m (11,145 ft) and **Mulhacén** at 3,482 m (11,420 ft). The altitude and closeness to the Mediterranean of this mountain range account for its array of fauna and flora. It is a habitat for golden eagles, rare butterflies and over 60 species of flowers unique to the area.

The Sierra Nevada was declared a national park in 1999 and access to it restricted. The park authorities run guided minibus excursions to the higher slopes from its checkpoints on the two sides of the Sierra Nevada: Hoya de la Mora (above the ski station on the Granada side) and Hoya del Portillo (above Capileira in the Alpujarras). The Sierra Nevada observatory is located on the northern slopes at an elevation of 2800 m (9,186 ft).

⓬ La Calahorra

Granada. **Road map** E3. 🚌 Guadix. 🅸 Town Hall, Plaza Ayuntamiento 1 (958 67 70 98). **Open** 10am–1pm, 4–6pm Wed.

Immensely thick walls encircle this castle, perched on a hillock above the village. Rodrigo de Mendoza, son of Cardinal Mendoza, ordered La Calahorra to be built for his bride between 1509 and 1512, using architects and craftsmen from Italy. Inside is a Renaissance courtyard with a staircase and Carrara marble pillars.

The castle of La Calahorra above the village of the same name

For hotels and restaurants in this region see p219 and pp236–7

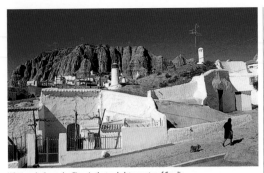

Whitewashed cave dwellings in the troglodyte quarter of Guadix

⓭ Guadix

Granada. **Road map** E3. 🚹 20,100.
🚌 🚍 ℹ️ Avenida de la Constitución
15–18 (958 66 28 04). 🛒 Sat.
🌐 **guadix.es**

The troglodyte quarter, with
2,000 inhabited caves, is the
town's most remarkable sight.
The **Museo de Alfarería** and
**Centro de Interpretación
Cuevas de Guadix** show how

people live underground. Around
2,000 years ago Guadix had iron,
copper and silver mines. The
town thrived under the Moors
and after the Reconquest (see
pp52–3), but declined in the
18th century. Relics of San
Torcuato, who established the
first Christian bishopric in
Spain, are kept in the cathedral
museum. The **Catedral**, begun
in 1594, was finished between

1701 and 1796. Near the
9th-century **Alcazaba**, the
Mudéjar **Iglesia de Santiago**
has a fine coffered ceiling.
Palacio de Peñaflor, dating
from the 16th century, has
been fully restored.

🏛 **Museo de Alfarería**
C/San Miguel 59 (958 66 47 67). **Open**
10:30am–2pm, 4:30–8pm daily. 🏚

🏛 **Centro de Interpretación
Cuevas de Guadix**
Ermita Nueva s/n. (958 66 55 69).
Open 10am–2pm, 4–6pm Mon–Fri
(5–7pm in summer), 10am–2pm
Sat. 🏚

⓮ Baza

Granada. **Road map** E2. 🚹 20,000.
🚍 ℹ️ Calle Alhóndiga 1, under
museum (958 86 13 25). 🛒 Wed.

Impressive evidence of ancient
cultures based around Baza came
to light in 1971, when a large,
seated, female figure was found
in a necropolis. She is the Dama

⓭ A Tour of Las Alpujarras

Las Alpujarras lie on the southern slopes of the Sierra
Nevada. The villages in this area cling to valley sides
clothed with oak and walnut trees. Their flat-roofed
houses are distinctive and seen nowhere else in
Andalucía. Local food is rustic. A speciality is *plato
alpujarreño*: pork fillet, ham, sausage and blood sausage,
accompanied by a pinkish wine from the Contraviesa
mountains. Local crafts include handwoven rugs (see
p242) and curtains with Moorish-influenced designs.

④ **Trevélez**
Trevélez, in the shadow of Mulhacén,
is built in typical Alpujarran style and
is famous for its cured hams.

② **Poqueira Valley**
Three villages typical of Las
Alpujarras in this river valley
are Capileira, Bubión and
Pampaneira (see p203).

▲ *Mulhacén*
3,479 m
11,410 ft

Juviles

Pórtugos
Pitres

① **Orgiva**
This is the largest town of the
region, with a Baroque church
in the main street and a lively
Thursday market.

③ **Fuente Agria**
People come here from far and
wide to drink the iron-rich,
naturally carbonated waters.

Lanjarón
Granada

Sierra de l

de Baza (see p47), believed to represent an Iberian goddess, and estimated to be 2,400 years old. Subsequently, she was removed to the Museo Arqueológico in Madrid but a replica can be seen in the **Museo Arqueológico** in Baza. The Renaissance **Colegiata de Santa María**, nearby, has a Plateresque entrance and a fine 18th-century tower.

During the first few days of September a riotous fiesta takes place (see p40). An emissary, El Cascamorras, is despatched from the neighbouring town of Guadix to try to bring back a coveted image of the Virgin from Baza's **Convento de la Merced**. He is covered in oil and chased back to Guadix by youths, also covered in oil. There, he is taunted again for returning empty-handed.

⑭ Museo Arqueológico
Plaza Mayor s/n. **Tel** 958 86 19 47. **Open** 11am–2pm Tue–Sun (also 6–7:30pm Thu–Sat).

⑮ Vélez Blanco

Almería. **Road map** F2. 🅰 2,200. 🚌 Vélez Rubio. 🛈 Marqués de los Vélez s/n (950 41 95 85). 🗓 Wed.

Dominating this pleasant little village is the mighty **Castillo de Vélez Blanco**. It was built from 1506 to 1513 by the first Marquis de Los Vélez, and its interior richly adorned by Italian craftsmen. Unfortunately for the visitor its

The village of Vélez Blanco, overlooked by a 16th-century castle

Renaissance splendour has since been ripped out and shipped to the Metropolitan Museum of New York. There is, however, a reconstruction of one of the original patios.

A blend of Gothic, Renaissance and Mudéjar styles (see pp28–9) can be seen in the **Iglesia de Santiago**, located in the village's main street.

Just outside Vélez Blanco is the **Cueva de los Letreros**, which contains paintings from around 4000 BC. One image depicts a horned man holding sickles; another the Indalo, a figure believed to be a deity with magical powers, still used as a symbol of Almería.

🏰 Castillo de Vélez Blanco
Tel 607 41 50 55. **Open** 10am–2pm, 5–8pm Wed–Sun (Oct–Mar: 4–6pm).

🏛 Cueva de los Letreros
Camino de la Cueva de los Letreros. **Tel** 694 46 71 36. **Open** Wed, Sat, Sun & public hols by appointment. 🕵

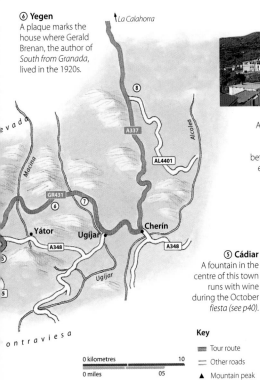

⑥ Yegen
A plaque marks the house where Gerald Brenan, the author of South from Granada, lived in the 1920s.

↑ La Calahorra

⑦ Válor
Aben Humeya, leader of a rebellion by Moriscos (see p54), was born in this village. A commemorative battle between Moors and Christians is staged each year in mid-September (see p40).

⑧ Puerto de la Ragua
This pass, which leads across the mountains to Guadix, is nearly 2,000 m (6,560 ft) high and often snowbound in winter.

⑤ Cádiar
A fountain in the centre of this town runs with wine during the October fiesta (see p40).

Yátor Ugíjar Cherín

Tips for Drivers

Tour length: 85 km (56 miles). **Stopping-off points:** Orgiva and Trevélez have bars, restaurants and hotels. Bubión has hotels and one good restaurant (see p236). Capileira has bars and restaurants. Orgiva is the last petrol stop before Cádiar.

Key
▬ Tour route
═ Other roads
▲ Mountain peak

0 kilometres 10
0 miles 05

⑱ Almería

A colossal fortress bears witness to Almería's golden age, when it was an important port for the Caliphate of Córdoba. Known as al Mariyat (the Mirror of the Sea), the city was a centre for trade and textile industries, with silk, cotton and brocade among its chief exports. After the city fell to the Catholic Monarchs *(see pp52–3)* in 1489, it went into decline for the next 300 years. During the 19th and early 20th centuries, mining and a new port revived the city's fortunes, but this period ended abruptly with the start of the Civil War *(see pp58–9)*. Today a North African air still pervades the city, with its flat-roofed houses, desert-like environs and palm trees and regular ferry services still link the city with Morocco.

The 10th-century Alcazaba in Almería's old town

🏛 Alcazaba

C/Almanzor s/n. **Tel** 950 80 10 08. **Open** Tue–Sun. **Closed** 1 Jan, 25 Dec.

Fine views are offered by this 1,000-year old Moorish fortress. It has been restored and within its walls are pleasant gardens and a Mudéjar chapel. It was the largest fortress built by the Moors and covered an area of more than 25,000 sq m (269,000 sq ft). The walls extend for 430 m (1,410 ft). Abd al Rahman III started construction in AD 955, but there were considerable additions later. The fort withstood two major sieges but fell to the Catholic Monarchs in 1489. Their coat of arms can be seen on the Torre del Homenaje, which was built during the monarchs' reign.

In the past, a bell in the Alcazaba was rung to advise the farmers in the surrounding countryside when irrigation was allowed. Bells were also rung to warn the citizens of Almería when pirates had been sighted off the coast. It is inadvisable for visitors to wander around the Alcazaba district alone or after dark.

🏛 Iglesia San Juan

C/Calle San Juan & Calle Gen Luque. **Tel** 950 23 30 07. **Open** Apr–Sep: 7–7:30pm daily; Oct–Mar: 6–6:30pm Sat–Thu.

Traces of Almería's most important mosque can still be seen – one wall of the present church is Moorish. Inside is a 12th-century mihrab, a prayer

niche with cupola. The church, built over the mosque, was damaged in the Spanish Civil War and abandoned until 1979. It is now restored.

🏛 Catedral

Plaza de la Catedral 8. **Tel** 678 27 97 50. **Open** Mon–Sat.

From North Africa, Berber pirates would often raid Almería. Consequently, the cathedral looks more like a fortress than a place of worship, with four towers, thick walls and small windows. A mosque once stood on the site. It was later converted to a Christian temple, but destroyed by an earthquake in 1522. Work began on the present building in 1524 under the direction of Diego de Siloé. Juan de Orea designed the Renaissance façade. He also created the beautifully carved walnut choir stalls. The naves and high altar are Gothic.

🏛 Plaza Vieja

Also known as the Plaza de la Constitución, this is a 17th-century arcaded square. On one side is the Ayuntamiento, a building with a cream and pink façade dating from 1899.

🏛 Puerta de Purchena

Located at the heart of the city, the Puerta de Purchena was once one of the main gateways in the city walls. From it run a

The pedestrianized 17th-century Plaza Vieja, surrounded by elegant arcades

number of shopping streets, including the wide Paseo de Almería. A tree-lined thoroughfare, this is the focus of city life, with its cafés, Teatro Cervantes and nearby food market.

Centro Rescate de la Fauna Sahariana

C/General Segura 1. **Tel** 950 28 10 45. **Open** call ahead for an appointment.

At the rear of the Alcazaba, this rescue centre shelters endangered species from the Sahara, in particular different kinds of gazelle. Having flourished in Almería's arid climate, some animals have been shipped to restock African nature reserves.

Museo de Almería

Carretera de Ronda 91. **Tel** 950 10 04 09. **Open** mid-Jun–mid-Sep: 9am–3pm Tue–Sat, 9am–3pm Sun & public hols; mid-Sep–mid-Jun: 9am–8pm Tue–Sat, 9am–3pm Sun & public hols. (free for EU citizens).

Almería's two main prehistoric civilizations, Los Millares and El Algar, are explained in this

Brightly coloured entrance to a gypsy cave in La Chanca district

archaeological museum that has 900 exhibits chosen from a collection of 80,000 pieces.

Environs

One of the most important examples of a Copper Age settlement in Europe, **Los Millares**, lies 17 km (10.5 miles) north of Almería. As many as 2,000 people occupied the site from around 2700 to 1800 BC (see pp46–7). Discovered in 1891, remains of houses,

defensive ramparts and a necropolis that contains more than 100 tombs have since been uncovered.

The community here lived from agriculture but also had the capability to forge tools, arms and adornments from copper, which was mined in the nearby of Sierra de Gador.

Los Millares

Santa Fé de Mondújar. **Tel** 677 90 34 04. **Open** 10am–2pm Wed–Sun. (Groups of 12 or more call ahead.)
w andalucia.org

Sights at a Glance

1. Alcazaba
2. Iglesia San Juan
3. Catedral
4. Plaza Vieja
5. Puerta de Purchena
6. Centro Rescate de la Fauna Sahariana

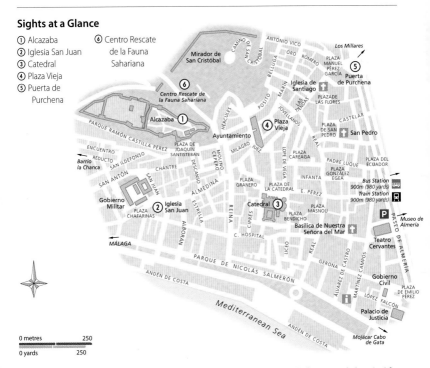

0 metres   250
0 yards   250

For keys to symbols see back flap

Spaghetti Westerns

Two Wild West towns lie off the N340 highway west of Tabernas. Here, visitors can re-enact classic film scenes or watch stunt men performing bank hold-ups and saloon brawls. The Poblados del Oeste were built during the 1960s and early 1970s when low costs and eternal sunshine made Almería the ideal location for spaghetti westerns. Sergio Leone, director of *The Good, the Bad and the Ugly*, built a ranch here and film-sets sprang up in the desert. Local gypsies played Indians and Mexicans. The deserts and Arizona-style badlands are still used occasionally for television commercials and series, and by film directors such as Steven Spielberg.

Still from *For a Few Dollars More* by Sergio Leone

⓰ Tabernas

Almería. **Road map** F3. ⛰ 3,000.
🚌 ℹ on main road: N340, km 464
(950 52 50 30). 🏛 Wed.

A Moorish hilltop fortress presides over the town of Tabernas and the surrounding dusty, cactus-dotted landscape of eroded hills and dried-out riverbeds. The harsh, rugged scenery has figured in many so-called spaghetti westerns.

Not far from Tabernas is a solar energy research centre, where hundreds of heliostats follow the course of southern Andalucía's powerful sunshine.

⓱ Roquetas de Mar

Almería. **Road map** F3. ⛰ 34,000.
ℹ Avenida de las Marinas 2 (950 33 32 03).

Much of Almería's southern coastal plain is given over to massive plastic greenhouses in which vegetables and flowers are raised for export. Interrupting the greenhouses is the resort of Roquetas de Mar, which has a 17th-century castle and a squat lighthouse, both used for exhibitions. Roquetas also has an aquarium with tropical and Mediterranean species of fish.

🗾 **Aquarium**
Avda Reino de España.
Tel 950 16 00 36. **Open** 10am–6pm
Wed–Fri, 10am–7pm Sat & Sun. 🐾
🌐 aquariumroquetas.com

⓲ Almería

See pp206–7.

⓳ Parque Natural de Cabo de Gata

Almería. **Road map** F3. 🚌 to San José. ℹ Centro de Visitantes de las Amoladeras, Carretera Cabo de Gata km 6 (950 16 04 35). Park **Open** daily.

Towering cliffs of volcanic rock, sand dunes, salt flats, secluded coves and a few fishing settlements can be found in the 290 sq km (112 sq m) Parque Natural de Cabo de Gata. The end of the cape, near the Arrecife de las Sirenas (Sirens' Reef), is marked by a lighthouse. The park includes a stretch of sea-bed about 2 km (1.2 miles) wide, which allows protection of the marine flora and fauna; the clear waters attract divers and snorkellers.

The area of dunes and saltpans between the cape and the Playa de San Miguel is a habitat for thorny jujube trees. Thousands of migrating birds stop here en route to and from Africa. Among the 170 or so bird species recorded in the park there are flamingoes, avocets, Dupont's larks and griffon vultures. Attempts to reintroduce the monk seal, which died out in the 1970s, however, have now ceased. At the northern end of the park, where there is a cormorants' fishing area, is Punta de los Muertos, ("dead man's point"); this takes its name from the bodies of shipwrecked sailors that are said to have washed ashore there.

⓴ San José

Almería. **Road map** F3. ⛰ 1,000. 🚌
ℹ Avenida de San José 27 (950 38 02 99). 🏛 Sun (Easter & summer).

Located on a fine, sandy bay, San José is a small but fast-growing sea resort within the Parque Natural de Cabo de Gata. Rising behind it is the arid **Sierra de Cabo de Gata**, a range

Lighthouse overlooking the cliffs of the Parque Natural de Cabo de Gata

The harbour at the traditional fishing village of La Isleta

of bleak grandeur. Nearby are fine beaches, including Playa de los Genoveses *(see p37)*. Along the coast are **Rodalquilar**, a town once important for gold-mining, and **La Isleta**, a fishing hamlet.

㉑ Níjar

Almería. **Road map** F3. 3,000. 🚌
ℹ️ Fundición s/n, Rodalquilar (671 59 44 19). 🚪 Wed.

Set amid a lush oasis of citrus trees on the edge of the Sierra Alhamilla, Níjar's fame stems from the colourful pottery and the *jarapas*, handwoven rugs and blankets, that are made here. The town's historic quarter is typical of Andalucía, with narrow streets and wrought-iron balconies.

The **Iglesia de Nuestra Señora de la Anunciación,** dating from the 16th century, has a coffered Mudéjar ceiling, delicately inlaid. The barren plain between Níjar and the sea has begun to blossom thanks to irrigation.

In Spanish minds, the name of Níjar is closely associated with a poignant and violent incident that occurred here in the 1920s, and later became the subject of a play by Federico García Lorca.

㉒ Sorbas

Almería. **Road map** F3. 3,000. 🚌
ℹ️ Centro de Visitantes los Yesares, Calle Terraplen, 9 (950 36 45 63). 🚪 Thu.

Balanced on the edge of a deep chasm, Sorbas overlooks the Río de Aguas, which flows far below.

There are two buildings in this village worth a look: the 16th-century **Iglesia de Santa María** and a 17th-century mansion said to have once been a summer retreat for the Duke of Alba.

Another point of interest for visitors is the traditional, rustic earthenware turned out and sold by Sorbas' local potters.

Located near to Sorbas is the peculiar **Yesos de Sorbas** nature reserve. This is an unusual region of karst, where water action has carved out hundreds of subterranean galleries and chambers in the limestone and gypsum strata. Speleologists are allowed to explore the caves, but only if they are granted permission by Andalucía's environmental department. On the surface, the green, fertile valley of the Río de Aguas cuts through dry, eroded hills. Local wildlife in this area includes tortoises and peregrine falcons.

㉓ Mojácar

Almería. **Road map** F3. 7,000. 🚌
ℹ️ Plaza del Frontón 1 (950 61 50 25). 🚪 Wed & Sun.

From a distance, the village of Mojácar shimmers like the mirage of a Moorish citadel, its white houses cascading over a lofty ridge near to the sea. The village was taken by the Christians in 1488 and the Moors were later expelled. In the years after the Spanish Civil War *(see pp58–9)* the village fell into ruin, as much of its population emigrated. In the 1960s Mojácar was discovered by tourists, giving rise to a new era of prosperity. The old gateway in the walls is still here, but otherwise the village has been completely rebuilt.

Pensión façade in the picturesque village of Mojácar

Blood Wedding At Nijar

Bodas de Sangre (Blood Wedding), a play by Federico García Lorca *(see p59)*, is based on a tragic event that occurred in 1928 near the town of Níjar. A woman called Paquita la Coja agreed, under pressure from her sister, to marry a suitor, Casimiro. A few hours before the ceremony, however, she fled with her cousin. Casimiro felt humiliated and Paquita's sister, who had hoped to benefit from the dowry, was furious. The cousin was found shot dead and Paquita half-strangled. Paquita's sister and her husband, Casimiro's brother, were found guilty of the crime. Shamed by this horrific scenario, Paquita hid from the world until her death in 1987. Lorca never visited Níjar, but based his play on newspaper reports.

The dramatist Federico García Lorca (1899–1936)

TRAVELLERS' NEEDS

Where to Stay **212–219**

Where to Eat and Drink **220–237**

Shops and Markets **238–243**

Entertainment in Andalucía **244–247**

Outdoor Activities
  and Specialist Holidays **248–251**

WHERE TO STAY

Some of the most charming places to stay in Spain are in Andalucía. They range from restored atmospheric castles to family guesthouses, and luxurious hotels to organic farms deep in the countryside. For budget travellers there are pensions and youth hostels, and for hikers there are mountain refuges. A night or two in a B&B is an increasingly popular option in rural areas.

Apartments and village houses throughout the region are let by the week for self-catering holidays. Andalucía's climate is also ideal for camping (except Nov–Mar), which can be a cheaper alternative.

The hotel listings on pages 216–19 are organized into different themes, with DK Choices highlighted. See Recommended Hotels on page 215 for more information.

The Monasterio de San Francisco in Palma del Río *(see p218)*

Where to Look

In Seville, the most appealing places to stay are mainly in the centre of town, especially around the Santa Cruz district *(see pp74–87)*, where there is a broad range of hotels. As in most cities, the cheapest hotels tend to be small family-run pensions.

Parking is always a problem in the town centre, so if you drive, you may have to book into a hotel with secure private parking, or look around the city's outer suburbs. You can ask your hotel to direct you to attended car parks in the city. A reasonable alternative is to stay in a town close to Seville, such as Carmona *(see pp136–7)*.

Granada has two main hotel districts: around the Alhambra *(see pp198–9)*, which is quiet, and around the centre, which is livelier, noisier and usually cheaper. Central hotels make the best base for going out on the town at night.

In Córdoba the Judería *(see pp144–5)* is the most convenient place to stay if you plan to get around on foot. If you drive, you may prefer a hotel on the outskirts of the city.

Hotels in Andalucía's coastal resorts are mainly the modern chains that cater for package holiday-makers, although there are also many small, family-owned seaside hotels favoured by Spanish and foreign visitors alike. If you want somewhere

more relaxing, there are good small hotels a short way inland. Look out for them in the white towns between Arcos de la Frontera *(see p177)* and Ronda *(see pp178–9)*, and around Cazorla *(see p160)*.

Two small private chains have a growing network of hotels in western Andalucía: the luxury Fuerte group and the budget Tugasa chain.

Hotel Grading and Facilities

Hotels in Andalucía are awarded categories and stars by the regional tourist authorities. Hotels (H is the abbreviation) are assigned between one and five stars and pensions (P) between one and two stars. The star-rating system assesses the quantity of facilities a hotel has (such as whether there is a lift, a restaurant or air conditioning) rather than the quality of service to expect. Most hotels in the region have restaurants that can be used by

Moorish-style patio at the Parador de Carmona *(see p217)*

◀ Stained glass windows at Atarazanas market, Málaga

non-residents. Hotel-Residencias (HR), however, do not have dining rooms, although they may serve breakfast.

Paradors

Paradors are government-run hotels that fall into the three- to five-star classifications. The best ones occupy historic monuments, such as castles, monasteries, palaces and old hunting lodges, but a number of paradors have been purpose-built in attractive settings. Though a parador may not always be the best hotel in town, it can be counted on to deliver a predictable level of comfort: regional dishes will always be on the menu and rooms are usually comfortable and spacious.

If you are travelling around the paradors during high season, or intending to stay in smaller paradors, it is advisable to book ahead through parador agents *(see p214)*.

Prices

Hotels are obliged by law to display their range of prices at the reception desk and in every room. As a rule, the more stars a hotel has, the more you pay. Rates for a double room start at €45 per night in a cheap one-star pension and can average as high as €275 or more; some are even €600 in a five-star hotel.

Prices vary according to the room, the region and season. Rural hotels are generally cheaper than city ones. All the prices quoted on pages 216–19 are based on the rates for high season. High season at the beach is usually July and August, but it can also run from April to October. Inland, the peak season is September, October and from mid-March to June. City hotels charge inflated rates during major *fiestas*, such as Semana Santa *(see p42)* in Seville. Easter is a popular travel period for the Spanish themselves, and it is usually included in the

Ceramic tiling and Moorish arches at the famous Alfonso XIII in Seville *(see p216)*

high-season price range, so be sure to enquire about availability and prices in advance.

Note that most hotels in Andalucía will quote prices per room and meal prices per person without *IVA* (VAT).

Booking and Checking In

You do not need to book ahead if you are travelling off-season in rural Andalucía, unless you want to stay in a particular hotel. On the other hand, it is essential to reserve rooms by phone, through a travel agent or on the Internet if you travel in high season. You will also need to book if you want a specific room, with a good view, with a double bed (twin beds are the norm), or away from a noisy road. Hotels in many coastal resorts close in the winter, so check that where you want to stay is open.

Some hotels will request a deposit of 20–25 per cent for booking during peak times, or for a long stay. This can be arranged by credit card and phone, even in smaller hotels. Others will hold your booking until an agreed arrival time. Try to make cancellations at least a

Five-star hotel restaurant sign

week in advance, or you may lose all or some of your deposit. A reserved room will be held only until 6pm unless you can inform the hotel that you are going to arrive late.

When you book in you will be asked for your passport or identity card, to comply with police regulations. It will be returned to you when your details have been copied.

You are usually expected to check out of your room by noon or to pay for another night. Most hotels are happy to keep your luggage for you until later that day.

Minimalist interior of Hospes Palacio de Bailio in Córdoba *(see p217)*

The Marbella Club Hotel an exclusive beachside hotel in Marbella *(see p218)*

Paying

Most hotels, except the most basic of bed and breakfasts, accept payment by credit card. In some large hotels you may be asked to sign a blank credit card slip on arrival. This is against Spanish law, and you are advised to refuse to sign.

No hotel in Andalucía takes cheques, even when backed by a guarantee card or drawn on a Spanish bank, and few accept traveller's cheques.

In Spain it is customary to tip the porter and the chambermaid in a hotel by €1–2. The usual amount to tip in hotel restaurants is 5–10 per cent of the bill, although some restaurants will have included a service charge already.

Self-Catering

Villas and holiday flats let by the week are plentiful along the Costa del Sol and the coasts of Granada and Almería. Most cities will also have holiday let accommodation in central, well-furnished apartments that may be cheaper than a comparable hotel and give you the option of preparing your own meals. The local tourism office can supply information about letting agencies.

Inland, an increasing number of village and farm houses are also being let all over the region. In the UK, a number of private companies, among them **James Villa Holidays**, act as agents for owners of apartments and houses. Many

agents belong to an organization called the **RAAR** (Red Andaluza de Alojamientos Rurales or Andalucían Rural Accommodation Network), through which it is possible to make direct bookings.

Prices charged for self-catering accommodation sometimes vary considerably: prices are determined by location, the season and type of property. A four-person villa with a pool typically costs as little as €240 for a week if it is inland and over €950 per week if it is in a prime coastal location.

Another possibility is a *villa turística* (holiday village), which is half hotel, half holiday apartments. Guests can hire rooms with kitchens and use the restaurant.

Bed and Breakfast

Andalucía's 500 or more *casas rurales* offering bed and breakfast range from stately *cortijos* (manor houses) to small organic farms. Do not necessarily expect the usual full hotel service or a long list of facilities. However, you are likely to be met with a friendly welcome and be spoiled with good home cooking.

DIRECTORY

Hotels

Asociación de Hoteles Rurales de Andalucía (AHRA)
C/Cueva de Viera 2.
Centro del Negocio CADI,
Edificio Málaga
3ª planta local 8,
29200 Antequera,
Málaga.
Tel 952 70 51 28.
W ahra.es

Asociación de Hoteles de Sevilla
Calle San Pablo 1,
Casa A Bajo,
41001 Seville.
Tel 954 22 15 38.
W hotelesdesevilla.com

Fuerte Hotels
W fuertehoteles.com

Tugasa Hotels
W tugasa.com

Paradors

Central de Reservas
Calle José Abascal 2–4,
28003 Madrid.
Tel 902 54 79 79.
W parador.es

Keytel
The Foundry,
156 Blackfriars Road,
London SE1 8EN UK.
Tel (020) 7199 6360.
W keytel.co.uk

Self-Catering and Bed & Breakfast

James Villa Holidays
Tel (0800) 074 01 22.
W jamesvillas.co.uk

RAAR
Sagunto 8-10-3,
04004 Almería.
Tel 950 28 00 93.
W raar.es

Youth Hostels

Central de Reservas de Inturjoven
Virgen de la Victoria 46,
41011 Seville. **Map** 3 A4.
Tel 955 18 11 81.
W inturjoven.com

Mountain Refuges

Federación Andaluza de Montañismo
Calle Santa Paula 23, 2°
Planta, 18001 Granada.
Tel 958 29 13 40. **Open:**
8:30am–2:30pm 4–7pm
Mon–Fri. W fedamon.
com

Camping

Camping and Caravanning Club
Tel (024) 76 47 54 48.
W campingand
caravanningclub.co.uk

Club de Camping y Caravanning de Andalucía

Calle Francisco Carrión
Mejías 13, 41003 Seville.
Tel 954 22 77 66.
W irdecampings.com

Federación Andaluza de Campings
Carretera de los Filtros 55,
18008 Granada. **Tel** 958 22
35 17. W campings
andalucia.es

Disabled Travellers

Can Be Done
Congress House, 14 Lyon
Road, Harrow HA1 2EN,
UK. **Tel** (020) 8907 2400.
W canbedone.co.uk

Viajes 2000
Tel 954 28 11 77.
W viajes2000.com

Outdoor pool at the historic Alcazar de la Reina hotel in Carmona (see p217)

A stay at a bed and breakfast can be booked through **RAAR**, which specializes in farmstays and rural accommodation, the owners' association, or directly. If you are booking from abroad you may be asked to send a 10 per cent deposit and to stay for at least two nights.

Youth Hostels and Mountain Refuges

To use Andalucía's extensive network of *albergues juveniles* (youth hostels) you have to buy an international Youth Hostel Association card from a hostel or show a YHA card from your country. Bed and breakfast costs between €12 and €18 per person. You can book a bed or room in a hostel directly or through the central booking office of Inturjoven – **Central de Reservas de Inturjoven**.

If you backpack in remote mountain areas, you can stay in *refugios*, which are shelters with basic kitchens and dormitories. The *refugios* are marked on all good large-scale maps of the mountains and national parks. They are administered by the **Federación Andaluza de Montañismo**.

Camping

There are more than 110 camp sites across the region of Andalucía, many of them along the coasts but there are also some outside the major cities

and in popular countryside areas. Most have electricity and running water; some also have launderettes, restaurants, shops, play areas for children and pools.

It is wise to take a camping *carnet* (card). It can be used to check in at sites, and it also gives you third-party insurance. *Carnets* are issued by the AA, the RAC, and by camping and caravanning clubs. A map of all the region's camp sites, with links to their websites, is available from the **F.A.C. (Federación Andaluza de Campings)**.

Logo for a five-star hotel

Disabled Travellers

Hotel managers will advise on wheelchair access and staff will always assist, but few hotels are equipped for the disabled. However, some of the youth hostels are. **RADAR** (see p256), the Royal Association for Disability and Rehabilitation, publishes a useful booklet

called *Holidays and Travel Abroad*, and Accessible Tourism publishes a fact sheet for disabled travellers in Spain.

In Spain, the Confederación Coordinadora Estatal de Minusválidos Físicos de España, also known as **Servi-COCEMFE** (see p256), and **Viajes 2000** have details of hotels with special facilities in Andalucía.

Can Be Done arranges accessible accommodation, transport and other help for visitors all over Europe.

Recommended Hotels

The hotels listed on pages 216–19 cover the best boutique, luxury, bed and breakfast, inn and historic accommodation types in Seville and Andalucía. They are listed by price within each area. Boutique hotels have character and high design elements, while luxury hotels encompass the finest of Seville and Andalucía's upscale hotels. Bed and breakfasts offer a friendly ambience, with cosy rooms and a hearty breakfast, while inns are quaint places oozing charm. The region is also full of historic accommodation as many monasteries and mansions have been converted into hotels.

Throughout the listings, certain hotels have been marked as DK Choice. These offer a particularly special experience – for their beautiful surroundings, excellent service, outstanding rooms, top-notch amenities, historical interest, or a combination of these.

Elegantly furnished room at the Marbella Club Hotel (see p218)

Where to Stay

Seville
El Arenal

Petit Palace Canalejas €
Boutique **Map** 5 B3
C/Canalejas 2, 41001
Tel 954 22 64 00
Ⓦ en.petitpalacecanalejassevilla.com
Housed in a pretty 20th-century building, this hotel has modern rooms at reasonable rates. Rooms have hydromassage showers, and some have small balconies.

Taberna del Alabardero €€
Historic **Map** 5 B3
C/Zaragoza 20, 41001
Tel 954 502 721
Ⓦ tabernadelalabardero.es
Rooms here boast antiques and stylish fabrics. The cosy central patio has a stained-glass roof. The restaurant serves excellent Andalucían cuisine.

Gran Melia Colon €€€
Luxury **Map** 5 B3
C/Canalejas 1, 41001
Tel 954 50 55 99
Ⓦ solmelia.com
Expect elegant rooms and attentive service at this centrally located hotel. The rooftop terrace has a hot tub and solarium. Popular with celebrities.

Santa Cruz & Parque María Luisa

Hispano Luz Confort €
B&B **Map** 6 D5
C/Miguel Mañara 4, 41004
Tel 955 63 80 79
Close to the Real Alcázar, this modern hotel has well-equipped rooms, some with balconies. Bike rental is available.

La Casa del Maestro €€
Historic **Map** 6 E2
C/Niño Ricardo 5, 41003
Tel 954 50 00 07
Ⓦ lacasadelmaestro.com
Centred on a traditional plant-filled patio, this delightful yellow-ochre guesthouse has spacious, vibrantly decorated rooms and a rooftop terrace with a solarium.

Hotel Inglaterra €€
Historic **Map** 5 C3
Plaza Nueva 7, 41001
Tel 954 22 49 70
Ⓦ hotelinglaterra.es
This chic hotel opposite the town hall has superb antique furnishings and Andalucían tiles. Enjoy a cocktail in the rooftop terrace bar.

Alfonso XIII €€€
Historic **Map** 6 D5
C/San Fernando 2, 41004
Tel 954 91 70 00
Ⓦ hotel-alfonsoxiii-seville.com
A regal hotel featuring spectacular Mudéjar architecture and opulent furnishings. There's a fitness centre, sauna and an outdoor swimming pool. In the evening visitors can enjoy a cocktail on the terrace.

DK Choice

Casa Numero Siete €€€
Boutique **Map** 6 E3
C/Virgenes 7, 41004
Tel 954 22 15 81
Ⓦ casanumero7.com
Discover sheer luxury in a 19th-century mansion right in the heart of Seville's evocative old quarter. The decor and furnishings at this small but immaculate boutique guesthouse include antiques and family heirlooms. Relax in the elegant lounge.

Las Casas del Rey de Baeza €€€
Boutique **Map** 6 E2
Plaza Jesús de la Redención 2, 41003
Tel 954 56 14 96
Ⓦ hospes.com
This hotel has chic bedrooms. The rooftop pool offers a respite from the hot Seville summer. Lovely open-air patio and spa.

EME Catedral Hotel €€€
Luxury **Map** 6 D4
C/Alemanes 27, 41004
Tel 954 56 00 00
Ⓦ emecatedralhotel.com
Four restaurants, a cocktail bar, a panoramic terrace, pool and spa are the key attractions at this superb hotel. In a great location, it offers unparalleled views.

La Macarena

Patio de la Alameda €
B&B **Map** 2 D3
Alameda de Hercules, 56, 41002
Tel 954 90 49 99
Ⓦ patiodelaalemeda.com
Rooms at this delightful B&B are stylishly furnished with details such as mosaic tiled bathrooms. Family rooms (up to four people) are available. The terrace has a bar with views of the historic surroundings.

Alcoba del Rey de Sevilla €€
Boutique **Map** 2 D4
C/Becquer 9, 41002
Tel 954 91 58 00
Ⓦ alcobadelrey.com
Intricate glassware, colourful tiles and silk cushions define the decor of this charming hotel. Rooftop solarium with Jacuzzi.

Hotel Boutique Casa Romana €€
Boutique **Map** 1 C5
C/Trajano 5, 41002
Tel 954 91 51 70
Ⓦ hotelcasaromana.com
Roman and Andalucían themes merge in this imaginative hotel. The elegant rooms border a bright central patio. The rooftop terrace has a large Jacuzzi.

Triana

Ribera de Triana Hotel €€
Luxury **Map** 3 A1
Plaza Chapina, 41010
Tel 954 26 80 00
Ⓦ hotelriberadetriana.com
This upmarket hotel with modern decor, a rooftop pool and terrace offers stunning city views, and first-rate technological amenities.

La Cartuja

Eurostars Torre Sevilla €€€
Luxury **Map** 1 5A
Gonzalo Jiménez Quesada, 2, Torre Sevilla, Isla de la Cartuja, 41092
Tel 954 46 06 60
Ⓦ eurostarshotels.com
The hotel in this soaring tower, the tallest building in Andalucía, offers stunning views. The tastefully decorated, comfortable rooms have spacious bathrooms.

Comfortable furnishings at Casa Numero Siete, Seville

Huelva and Sevilla

ALCALÁ DE GUADAÍRA: Hotel Oromana €
Historic **Map** B3
Avda de Portugal, 41500
Tel 955 68 64 00
W hoteloromana.com
Set in a converted 1920s mansion in the Oromana Nature Reserve, this atmospheric and friendly hotel has a great on-site restaurant. Pets allowed.

DK Choice

ARACENA: Finca Buen Vino €€
B&B **Map** B2
Carretera N-433, km 95 Los Marines, 21208
Tel 959 12 40 34
W fincabuenvino.com
This hilltop guesthouse, set amid citrus and olive groves bordering a lovely natural park, is famed for its cuisine and cookery courses. All rooms are spacious and individually furnished. Self-catering cottages are also available. Expect great service.

ARACENA: Hotel Convento Aracena €€
Boutique **Map** B2
C/Jesus y Maria 19, 21200
Tel 959 12 68 99
W hotelconventoaracena.es
Strategically located by the castle of Aracena, this restored 17th-century convent is surrounded by peaceful gardens and cloisters. It has an outdoor pool and a spa.

CARMONA: Alcazar de la Reina €
Historic **Map** B2
C/Hermana Concepción Orellana 2, 41410
Tel 954 19 62 00
W alcazar-reina.es
This stately hotel has elegant, large rooms with lovely views. There is a welcoming interior courtyard as well as an outdoor pool.

DK Choice

CARMONA: Parador de Carmona €€
Luxury **Map** B2
C/Alcazar s/n, 41410
Tel 954 14 10 10
W parador.es
This is a classic Spanish parador. Originally a Moorish fortress, it has a stunning hilltop location and majestic interiors decorated with tapestries and antiques. The rooms are comfortable and stylish. Relax in the outdoor pool (summer only).

CAZALLA DE LA SIERRA: Las Navezuelas €
Inn **Map** B2
Ctra Cazalla-Ed A-432, km 43.3 Pedrosa, 41370
Tel 954 88 47 64
W lasnavezuelas.com
A family-run cortijo (farmhouse), in the Sierra del Norte mountains, with simple rooms and home-made meals. The sun terrace has a pool (summer only) and garden.

EL ROCÍO: Complejo Pequeño Rocio €€
Inn **Map** B3
Avenida de la Canaliega s/n, 21750
Tel 959 44 20 40
W complejopequenorocio.es/hotel
This lovely complex has 22 rooms, centered around a garden and pool. Rooms have a sitting area with a sofa, TV and fridge. Free Wi-Fi in public areas.

ISLA CRISTINA: Sensimar Isla Cristina Palace €€€
Luxury **Map** A3
Avenida del Parque s/n, 21420
Tel 959 34 44 99
W hotelsensimarislacristina.com
At this deluxe beachside hotel and spa all rooms have private balconies overlooking the pool or ocean. Adults only.

MAZAGÓN: Parador de Mazagón €€€
Luxury **Map** A3
Ctra San Juan-Matalascañas km 31, 21130
Tel 959 53 63 00
W parador.es
Well-appointed parador in a stunning location overlooking Mazagón beach on the Atlantic Coast. The indoor and outdoor pools are open all year round.

SANLÚCAR LA MAYOR: Exe Gran Hotel Solucar €
Luxury **Map** B2
Ctra Nacional Sevilla-Huelva A-472 s/n, 41800
Tel 955 70 34 08
W exegranhotelsolucar.com
This comfortable hotel has a seasonal outdoor pool and a beautiful courtyard.

Córdoba and Jaén

BAEZA: Hotel Fuentenueva €
Historic **Map** E2
C/Carmen 15, 23440
Tel 953 74 31 00
W fuentenueva.com
All rooms at this hotel located in a 16th-century building have hydromassage baths. There is a rooftop terrace and pool.

Stylish interiors at Hospes Palacio de Bailio in Córdoba

CAZORLA: Molino de la Farraga €
Historic **Map** E2
Camino de la Hoz, 23470
Tel 953 72 12 49
W molinolafarraga.com
A restored 200-year-old mill with a farm and a vegetable garden. The rooms have traditional decor. There is a large botanical garden in which the distant murmur of the Cerezuelo river can be heard.

CÓRDOBA: Hotel Maestre €
Inn **Map** C2
C/Romero Barros 4–6, 14003
Tel 957 47 24 10
W hotelmaestre.com
This charming, traditional hotel has a central flower-filled patio, and clean, simple rooms. Free Wi-Fi.

CÓRDOBA: Hospedería del Atalia €€
Boutique **Map** C2
C/Buen Pastor 19, 14003
Tel 957 49 66 59
W hospederiadelatalia.com
In the heart of the Jewish Quarter, this hotel has individually decorated rooms, combining chic, modern styles with Moorish tiles on the walls. There is a rooftop terrace with views of the Mezquita.

CÓRDOBA: Eurostars Palace €€€
Luxury **Map** C2
Paseo de la Victoria s/n, 14004
Tel 957 76 04 52
W eurostarshotels.com
Just outside the historic centre of Córdoba, this hotel has stylish rooms equipped with a sofa, minibar, satellite TV and spa tub.

CÓRDOBA: Hospes Palacio de Bailio €€€
Boutique **Map** C2
C/Ramirez de las Casas Deza 10–12, 14001
Tel 957 49 89 93
W hospes.com
Magnificent 17th-century palace with beautiful gardens. Many of the original features have been preserved and walls are adorned with original artwork and frescos.

JAÉN: Parador de Jaén   €€
Luxury   Map D2
Castillo de Santa Catalina s/n
Tel 953 23 00 00
🅦 parador.es
Hilltop parador set in an 18th-century castle with traditional Arabic decor and rooms that offer panoramic views.

LINARES: Hotel Baviera   €
Boutique   Map E2
La Virgen 25, 23700
Tel 953 60 71 15
🅦 hotelbavieraandalucia.es
This pleasant hotel has charming rooms. Some of the bathrooms include a hydromassage tub.

PALMA DEL RÍO: Monasterio de San Francisco   €
Historic   Map C2
Avda del Pío XII 35, 14700
Tel 957 71 01 83
🅦 intergrouphoteles.com
A romantic hotel set in a restored 15th-century monastery. Rooms are spacious and clean and organic meals are available.

ÚBEDA: Zenit El Postigo   €
Inn   Map E2
C/Postigo 5, 23400
Tel 953 75 00 00
🅦 elpostigo.zenithoteles.com
Modern hotel with fireplace, pool and garden. Rooms are spacious and comfortable. There is a social lounge with a fireplace for chilly winter nights. Free Wi-Fi.

ZUHEROS: Zuhayra   €
Inn   Map D2
C/Mirador 10, 14870
Tel 957 69 46 93
🅦 zercahoteles.com
This friendly hotel has neat rooms with modern amenities and lovely views of the surrouding natural beauty.

Cádiz and Málaga

ARCOS DE LA FRONTERA: Casa Grande   €
Historic   Map B3
C/Maldonaldo 10, 11360
Tel 956 70 39 30
🅦 lacasagrande.net
A whitewashed 18th-century mansion with a hilltop location, offering great views of the Andalucían countryside below. Each room has unique decor with antique furnishings. Family rooms are available here. Good breakfast spread.

View from the roof terrace at Casa Grande, Arcos de la Frontera

CÁDIZ: Hotel Playa Victoria   €€
Boutique   Map B4
Glorieta Ingeniero La Cierva 4, 11010
Tel 956 20 51 00
🅦 palafoxhoteles.com
Eco-friendly seafront hotel with avant-garde interior furnishings. The seasonal outdoor pool has direct access to the beach.

CAÑOS DE MECA: La Breña   €€
Boutique   Map B4
Avda Trafalgar 4, 11149
Tel 956 4373 68
🅦 en.hotelbrena.com
Rooms are simple but spacious, and some have sea views. A lovely terrace overlooks the ocean. Excellent beach location.

CASTELLAR DE LA FRONTERA: Casa Convento La Almoraima   €
Historic   Map C4
Ctra. Algeciras-Ronda s/n, Finca la Almoraima, 11350
Tel 956 69 30 02
🅦 laalmoraimahotel.com
A former monastery has been converted into a modern hotel with antique furnishings and an inner patio.

CORTES DE LA FRONTERA: Casa Rural Ahora   €
Inn   Map C3
Bda El Colmenar 29490
Tel 952 15 30 46
🅦 casaruralahora.com
A rural hideaway with chic rustic furnishings and decor nestled in a valley beside a stream. There is a wellness centre with a spa.

GIBRALTAR: Rock Hotel   €€
Historic   Map C4
3 Europe Road, Gibraltar
Tel +350 20 07 30 00
🅦 rockhotelgibraltar.com
A 70-year-old colonial-style cliffside hotel with a nostalgic aura and stately guest rooms. Enjoy outstanding views of the Bay and Straits of Gibraltar as well as the Spanish mainland.

GRAZALEMA: Hotel Fuerte Grazalema   €
Inn   Map C3
Baldio de los Alamillos, Ctra A-372, km 53, 11610
Tel 956 13 30 00
🅦 fuertehoteles.com
A comfortable rural hotel located inside the wooded Grazalema Nature Reserve. Ideal for walking, cycling or horse-riding breaks. Good children's facilities. The on-site restaurant serves regional dishes.

MÁLAGA: Salles Hotel   €€
Luxury   Map D3
C/Marmoles 6, 29007
Tel 952 07 02 16
🅦 salleshotels.com
Well-appointed hotel in the heart of Málaga with superb city views. Visitors can enjoy the rooftop pool in summer. Free Wi-Fi.

MARBELLA: Hotel Fuerte Marbella   €€€
Luxury   Map C4
C/El Fuerte, 29602
Tel 952 86 15 00
🅦 fuertehoteles.com
Marbella's very first purpose-built luxury hotel features lush gardens and two outdoor pools and a fitness centre with an indoor pool. Close to the beach.

MARBELLA: Marbella Club Hotel   €€€
Luxury   Map C4
Bulevar Príncipe Alfonso von Hohenlohe, 29600
Tel 952 82 22 11
🅦 marbellaclub.com
A deluxe beachside hotel with lush gardens, swimming pools, world-class golf course and spa. The Kids' Club offers a music room, dance studio, an enchanted forest and other forms of entertainment.

MIJAS: Hotel Hacienda Puerta del Sol   €
Luxury   Map C3
Ctra Fuengirola-Mijas km 4, 29650
Tel 952 48 64 00
🅦 hhpuertadelsol.es/en
Stylish hotel with an exceptional range of sports amenities, and both covered and open-air pools. It has family rooms.

NERJA: El Carabeo   €€
Boutique   Map D3
C/Hernando de Carabeo 34, 29780
Tel 952 52 54 44
🅦 hotelcarabeo.com
A lovely British-owned hotel. Rooms are furnished with antiques and original artworks.

OJÉN: Posada del Angel €
Inn **Map** C3
C/Mesones 21, 29610
Tel *952 88 18 08*
W laposadadelangel.net
This charming Andalucían hotel with Moorish touches features individually decorated rooms. Enjoy breakfast on the patio.

PUERTO DE SANTA MARÍA: Monasterio de San Miguel €
Historic **Map** B3
C/Virgen de los Milagros 27, 11500
Tel *956 54 04 40*
W monasteriosanmiguelhotel.com
A former Capuchin monastery with many original features. Rooms are large and simply furnished. There is a pleasant courtyard.

RINCÓN DE LA VICTORIA: Molino de Santillan €€
Historic **Map** D3
Ctra de Macharaviaya km 3, 29730
Tel *952 40 09 49*
W centrosantillan.com
This cosy converted former *finca* is set high on a hilltop. It features a library, yoga rooms, tennis court, saltwater pool, gardens and nature trails.

RONDA: Parador de Ronda €€€
Historic **Map** C3
Plaza España, 29400
Tel *952 87 75 00*
W parador.es
Located at the edge of the iconic gorge of Ronda, this parador has bright, stylish rooms – top floor suites have fine views – and a huge garden.

SANLÚCAR DE BARRAMEDA: Hotel Barrameda €
Boutique **Map** B3
Ancha 10, 11540
Tel *956 38 58 78*
W hotelbarrameda.com
Smart hotel overlooking plaza Cabildo. Some of the modern rooms have private terraces.

TARIFA: Hurricane Hotel €€
Boutique **Map** B4
Ctra N-340 Km 78, 11380
Tel *956 68 49 19*
W hotelhurricane.com
Laidback hotel with lush gardens, two pools and health facilities such as gym, sauna and massage services. Great on-site restaurant.

VEJER DE LA FRONTERA: La Casa del Califa €€
Boutique **Map** B4
Plaza de España, 16 11150
Tel *956 44 77 30*
W califavejer.com
An intimate and charming hotel with individually decorated rooms. Excellent service.

Light and spacious suite at La Bobadilla, Loja

Granada and Almería

ALMERÍA: Hotel Catedral €
Historic **Map** F3
Plaza de la Catedral 8, 04002
Tel *950 27 81 78*
W hotelcatedral.net
A converted manor house with spacious and comfortable rooms. There are great views from the roof terrace.

GRANADA: Posada del Toro €
Inn **Map** D3
C/Elvira 25, 18010
Tel *958 22 73 33*
W posadadeltoro.com
A renovated 19th-century inn that blends old charm and modern comforts. Wi-Fi in all rooms.

GRANADA: Casa 1800 €€€
Boutique **Map** D3
C/Benalua 11, 18010
Tel *958 21 07 00*
W hotelcasa1800granada.com
Romantic hotel in a converted 17th-century mansion. The façade features the original Renaissance-style murals.

DK Choice

GRANADA: Parador de Granada €€€
Luxury **Map** D3
C/Real de la Alhambra, 18009
Tel *958 22 14 40*
W parador.es
Lovingly restored from an old convent, this parador enjoys an incomparable location right inside the grounds of the impressive Alhambra Palace. Elegantly appointed rooms. Book ahead.

LOJA: La Bobadilla €€€
Luxury **Map** D3
Ctra Salinas-Villanueva de Tapia (A-333), km 65.5, 18300
Tel *958 32 18 61*
W barcelolabobadilla.com
All rooms and suites have unique decor at this hotel in a quiet location, perfect for relaxation.

MECINA BOMBARÓN: Casas Rurales Benarum €
B&B **Map** E3
Av. Jose Antonio Bravo 60, 18450
Tel *958 85 11 49*
W benarum.com
Plush bungalows in the mountains of Alpujarra with all modern comforts. Facilities include Jacuzzis and Finnish saunas.

MOJÁCAR: Parador de Mojácar €€
Luxury **Map** F3
Paseo del Mediterráneo 339, 04638
Tel *950 47 82 50*
W parador.es
Dazzling white beachside parador with comfortable rooms that offer Mediterranean views.

MONACHIL: La Almunia del Valle €€€
Boutique **Map** E3
Camino de la Umbria, 18193
Tel *958 30 80 10*
W laalmuniadelvalle.com
Friendly boutique hotel located high in the Sierra Nevada. Lovely gardens and pool (summer only).

ORGIVA: Taray Botánico €
B&B **Map** E3
Ctra A-348 Tablete-Abuñol km 18, 18400
Tel *958 78 45 25*
W hoteltaray.com
A lovely whitewashed rural hotel with an olive and orange tree-filled garden. Free parking.

PECHINA: Hotel Balneario de Sierra Alhamilla €
Historic **Map** F3
C/Los Baños s/n, 04259
Tel *950 31 74 13*
W balneariosierraalhamilla.es
This well-restored 18th-century spa hotel in the Sierra Alhamilla offers spa treatments.

SAN JOSÉ: Cortijo el Sotillo €€
Historic **Map** F3
Ctra San Jose, 04118
Tel *950 61 11 00*
W cortijoelsotillo.es
Farmhouse set in Cabo de Gata Natural Park. Enjoy the quiet of the nearby unspoilt beaches.

WHERE TO EAT AND DRINK

One of the joys of eating out in this region is the sheer sociability of the Andalucíans. Family and friends, often with children in tow, start early with tapas, and usually continue eating until after midnight. The food has a regional bias – the best restaurants have grown from taverns and tapas bars serving fresh, home-cooked food. The places to eat listed on pages 228–37 have been selected for their excellent cuisine and conviviality. There is a guide to regional food on pages 222–3, and to tapas, with a glossary on pages 224–5. Pages 226–7 illustrate typical drinks of the region.

The dining room of El Churrasco restaurant, Córdoba *(see p232)*

Andalucían Cuisine

The food of Andalucía falls into two categories: coastal and inland. Five of the region's eight provinces have stretches of coastline and a sixth, Seville, has a tidal river and several seaports (Cádiz, Sanlúcar, Barbate and Zahara among them) nearby. Coastal cooking includes a huge variety of fish and shellfish. The most famous fish dish is *pescaíto frito* (fried fish). Although fish is integral to the Spanish diet, meat dishes such as veal and chops also make regular appearances on menus across the region.

Inland, rich stews with hams and sausages, and game, pork, lamb and chicken dishes are served. Vegetables and salads are excellent, as is Andalucía's signature dish, *gazpacho*, a cold soup made from fresh tomatoes, cucumber and peppers.

Meal Times

In Spain, *desayuno* (breakfast), is a light meal, usually consisting of toasted bread with butter and jam and *café con leche* (milky coffee). A more substantial breakfast follows between 10 and 11am – a *bocadillo* or *mollete* (a baguette or roll) with ham, sausage or cheese, or a slice of *tortilla de patatas* (potato omelette). *Churros* (fried dough strips) are sold mainly from stalls in autumn and winter.

It is common for Andalucíans to stop in a bar for a beer or wine with tapas around 1pm. By 2 or 2:30pm offices close for *almuerzo* (lunch), the main meal of the day, eaten between 2 and 3pm, followed by a *siesta* hour. By 5:30pm or 6pm cafés, *salones de té* (tea rooms) and *pastelerías* (pastry shops) fill up for la *merienda* (tea): pastries and cakes with coffee, tea or juice.

Tapas bars become busy by 8:30pm. *La cena* (supper) is eaten from about 9pm, although some places begin service earlier for tourists.

Spaniards tend to lunch out on weekdays and dine out at weekends. Sunday lunch is usually a family affair.

How to Dress

Spanish people dress smartly, especially in city restaurants. In the beach resorts, dress is casual, although shorts at night are frowned upon.

Reading the Menu

The Spanish word for menu is *la carta*. The Spanish *menú* means a fixed-price menu of the day. The day's specialities are often chalked on a board or clipped to the menu. Some finer restaurants offer a *menú de degustación*, which allows you to sample six or seven of the chef's special dishes.

La carta will start with *sopas* (soups), *ensaladas* (salads), *entremeses* (hors d'oeuvres), *huevos y tortillas* (eggs and omelettes) and *verduras y legumbres* (vegetable dishes).

Main courses are *pescados y mariscos* (fish and shellfish) and *carnes y aves* (meat and poultry). Paella and other rice dishes often come as the first course. Follow rice with meat, or start with *serrano* ham or salad and follow with paella. It is quite normal to order just one or two courses from any part of the menu.

Desserts and puddings are grouped as *postres*, but fresh fruit is the preferred choice for desserts in Andalucía.

Traditional interior of Casa Plácido in Santa Cruz, Seville *(see p228)*

Children

Children are generally very welcome, but there are seldom special facilities such as high chairs or colouring sheets available for them. *Ventas*, or country restaurants, are the exception; they often have play areas.

Smoking

Smoking is not permitted inside public areas, including in restaurants, cafés and bars. Smoking on outside terraces is still allowed.

Wheelchair Access

Since restaurants are rarely designed for wheelchairs, you (or hotel staff) should call to book and to discuss access to restaurant and toilets. Spanish law requires all new-build public buildings to have wheelchair access, so newer restaurants will offer easier disabled access and facilities such as adapted toilets and wheelchair space in dining areas.

Wine Choices

Dry sherry *fino* wines are perfect with shellfish, *serrano* ham, olives, soups and first courses. Wines to accompany

Stylish dining room of the exclusive Oriza, Seville *(see p229)*

meals are usually from Ribera del Duero, Rioja, Navarra or Penedés. A tapas bar might serve Valdepeñas or La Mancha wines. *Oloroso* wines are often drunk as a digestif. *(See also What to Drink pp226–7 and The Land of Sherry pp34–5.)*

What it Costs

The cheapest places to eat are usually tapas bars and smaller, family-run establishments *(bar-restaurantes)*. A *menú del día* is offered in the majority of restaurants. It is usually three courses and priced well below choices from *la carta*. Ordering from *la carta* in a restaurant can push your final bill way above average, especially if you choose pricey items like *ibérico* ham and fresh seafood. If you find "bargain prices" for swordfish, hake, sole and other fish, then it is probably frozen. Expect shellfish such as lobster and large prawns, and fish such as sea bass and bream, to be priced by weight. The bill *(la cuenta)* includes service charges and sometimes a small cover charge. Prices on the menus do

not include ten per cent *IVA* (VAT), which, as a rule, is added when the bill is totalled. Tipping is just that, a discretionary gratuity. The Spanish rarely tip more than five per cent, often just rounding up the bill.

Credit cards are accepted in restaurants everywhere, but do not expect to pay by credit card in smaller tapas bars or cafés.

Recommended Restaurants

The restaurants featured in this guide have been selected for a variety of criteria including their good value, food, location and atmosphere. A wide range of establishments has been included – from no-frills dining spots, down-to-earth tapas bars and restaurants specializing in seafood to sophisticated and stylish diners featuring tasting menus prepared by leading and popular Spanish chefs. Seville offers a number of tempting options for both carnivores and vegetarians.

Note that establishments labelled DK Choice are places that have been highlighted in recognition of an exceptional feature – exquisite food, a unique menu, an inviting ambience, an unusual location or simply for great value. Most of these places are popular with locals and visitors, so be sure to book well in advance.

Outdoor tables at the popular El Modesto tapas bar in Santa Cruz, Seville *(see p228)*

The Flavours of Andalucía

Andalucía is vast, bordered on one side by the Mediterranean and on the other by the Atlantic. Inland are lofty mountains, undulating hills, endless olive groves and bright fields of sunflowers. The cuisine is as varied as the terrain, with a huge array of seafood, meat and game, and sun-ripened fruit and vegetables. The *tapeo* (tapas-bar-hopping) is a regional institution and, around Granada, these little morsels are still often served free with drinks. In the cities and along the Costa de Sol, new culinary trends and international influences have brought on a storm of fashionable gastrobars, but in other inland areas traditional recipes still prevail.

Olives and olive oil

Choosing from a selection of tapas

Tapas

The *tapeo*, or tapas crawl, is an intrinsic part of daily life in Andalucía. Each bar is usually known for a particular speciality: one might be well known for its home-made *croquetas* (potato croquettes, usually filled with ham or cod), while another will serve exceptional hams, and yet another might make the best *albóndigas* (meatballs) in the

neighbourhood. Tapas are often accompanied by a glass of chilled, dry *fino* sherry, or perhaps a cold draught beer (*una caña*). Tapas were once free, but that tradition has largely died out.

Seafood

It is not surprising, given its extensive coastline, that southern Spain offers every

imaginable variety of seafood, including cod, hake, prawns, crayfish, clams, razor clams, octopus, cuttlefish, squid, sole and tuna. Almost every seaside resort will offer *pescaíto frito*, originally a Málaga dish, made with whatever fish is freshest that day. In Cádiz, they are served in a paper cone, and in nearby Sanlúcar you must not miss the sweet and juicy *langostinos* (king prawns).

Jamón Ibérico bellota   Morcilla with onion   Morcilla with rice   Salchichón Ibérico bellota

Chorizo rosario picante

Lomo embuchado

Selection of delicious Spanish *embutidos* (cured meats)

Regional Dishes and Specialities

Andalucía embodies many of the images most closely associated with Spain – the heady rhythms of flamenco, striking white villages, bull fighting and, of course, tapas. You can easily make a meal of these delectable treats, and most bars have an excellent range. Don't miss the mouthwatering hams (*jamón*) from Jabugo and Trevélez which are famed throughout Spain, or the platters of freshly fried fish liberally doused with lemon juice. An ice-cold sherry (the word comes from Jerez, where most sherry is produced) is deliciously refreshing in the searing summer heat and is the most popular tipple at southern fiestas. While pork, particularly cured ham remains the most appreciated local meat, duck, beef and lamb are also favourites, subtly flavoured with aromatic bay leaves.

Pomegranates

Gazpacho This chilled soup combines ripe tomatoes, breadcrumbs, cucumbers, garlic, vinegar, olive oil and peppers.

Andalucían market stall displaying fresh local produce

Meat and Game

Pork (*cerdo*) is king in Andalucía. The famous hams of Jabugo (in the southwest) and Trevélez (near Granada) are among the finest produced in Spain, and are made with free-range, black-footed pigs fed on a diet of acorns. Beef (*ternera*) is also popular; endless fields full of glossy black bulls (some of

Prawns and sardines on display at the fishmarket

which are raised for bull-fighting but most for meat) are a common sight, and one of the most popular local dishes is *rabo de toro* (bull's tail). All kinds of cured meats are made here, often to traditional recipes that have remained unchanged for centuries. In the wild inland Sierras, you will find an abundance of game in season, along with the traditional country staples of lamb (*cordero*) and rabbit (*conejo*).

Fruit and Vegetables

The undulating Andalucían fields and hillsides are densely covered with beautiful olive groves, and the best oils are graded as carefully as fine wines. Olive oil is liberally used in Andalucían cuisine, and the typical southern breakfast is toasted country

bread topped with thin slices of tomato and drizzled with olive oil – utterly delicious. The hot climate is perfect for fruit and vegetables, including luscious peaches, papayas, persimmons, mangoes and oranges, as well as tomatoes, asparagus, aubergines (eggplants) and artichokes. The chilled tomato soup, *gazpacho*, is a classic, but *salmorejo*, which is thicker and topped with a sprinkling of chopped boiled eggs and ham, is even tastier.

ON THE MENU

Chocos con habas Cuttlefish is cooked with beans, white wine and plenty of bay leaves.

Pato a la Sevillana Succulent duck, cooked slowly with onion, leeks, carrots, bay leaf and a dash of sherry, this is a speciality of Seville.

Rabo de Toro An Andalucían classic, made with chunks of bull's tail, slowly braised with vegetables, bay leaf and a dash of sherry until tender.

Salmorejo Cordobés A creamy tomato dip thickened with breadcrumbs.

Torta de Camarones Delicious fritters filled with tiny, whole shrimps from Cádiz.

Tortilla del Sacromonte A speciality of Granada: omelette with brains, kidney or other offal, peppers and peas.

Huevos a la Flamenca Eggs are baked in a terracotta dish with tomato sauce, ham and chorizo sausage.

Pescaíto Frito A seaside favourite, this is a platter of small fish tossed in batter and quickly fried in olive oil.

Tocino de Cielo This is a creamy custard dessert with a caramel topping. Its name means "heavenly lard".

Choosing Tapas

Tapas, sometimes called *pinchos,* are small snacks that originated in Andalucía in the 19th century to accompany sherry. Stemming from a bartender's practice of covering a glass with a saucer or *tapa* (cover) to keep out flies, the custom progressed to a chunk of cheese or bread being used, and then to a few olives being placed on a platter to accompany a drink. Once free of charge, tapas are usually paid for nowadays, and a selection makes a delicious light meal. Choose from a range of appetizing varieties, from cold meats to elaborately prepared hot dishes of meat, seafood or vegetables.

Mixed
green olives

Patatas bravas is a piquant dish of fried potatoes with a spicy red sauce.

Albóndigas (meatballs) are a hearty tapa, often served with a spicy tomato sauce.

Almendras fritas are fried, salted almonds.

Banderillas are canapés skewered on toothpicks. The entire canapé should be eaten at once.

Calamares fritos are squid rings and tentacles which have been dusted with flour before being deep fried in olive oil. They are usually served garnished with a piece of lemon.

Jamón serrano is salt-cured ham dried in mountain *(serrano)* air.

ON THE TAPAS BAR

Aceitunas Olives

Alcachofas Artichokes, typically served pickled in vinegar

Almejas Clams

Berenjenas rebozadas Battered and fried aubergines (eggplants)

Boquerones al natural Fresh anchovies in garlic and olive oil. Often served fried as well

Buñuelos de bacalao Salted cod fritters

Cacahuetes Peanuts

Calamares a la romana Fried squid rings

Callos Tripe

Caracoles Snails in broth

Carne en salsa Meat in a thick tomato sauce

Champiñones Button mushrooms fried and served in a light sauce with garlic and parsley

Chipirones a la plancha Grilled cuttlefish with a garlic and parsley sauce

Chopitos Cuttlefish fried in batter

Chorizo al vino Chorizo sausage cooked in red wine

Chorizo diablo Chorizo served flamed with brandy

Costillas Spare ribs

Criadillas Bulls' testicles

Croquetas Croquettes

Ensaladilla Rusa "Russian salad", with potatoes, vegetables and mayonnaise

Gambas pil pil Spicy, garlicky fried king prawns (shrimp)

Habas con jamón Tender broad beans fried with *jamón serrano*

Magro Pork in a paprika and tomato sauce

Tapas Bars

Even a small village will have at least one bar where the locals go to enjoy drinks, tapas and conversation with friends. On Sundays and holidays, favourite places are packed with whole families enjoying the fare. In larger towns it is customary to move from bar to bar, sampling the specialities of each. A tapa is a single serving, whereas a *ración* is two or three. Tapas are usually eaten standing or perching on a stool at the bar rather than sitting at a table, for which a surcharge is generally made.

Choice of tapas at a busy bar

Chorizo, a popular sausage flavoured with paprika and garlic, may be eaten cold or fried and served hot.

Salpicón de mariscos is a luxurious cold salad of assorted fresh seafood in a zesty vinaigrette.

Gambas a la plancha is a simple but flavourful dish of grilled prawns (shrimp).

Tortilla española is the ubiquitous Spanish potato omelette, often made with onion, and served cold.

Queso manchego is a sheep's-milk cheese from La Mancha.

Pollo al ajillo consists of small pieces of chicken (often wings) sautéed and then simmered with a garlic-flavoured sauce.

Manitas de cerdo Pig's trotters

Mejillones Mussels

Merluza a la romana Hake fried in a light batter

Migas Breadcrumbs, fried and flavoured with savoury ingredients

Montaditos Mini sandwiches made with a variety of fillings

Morcilla Black (blood) pudding

Muslitos del mar Crab-meat croquette, skewered onto a claw

Orejas de cerdo Pig's ears

Paella Rice dish made with meat, fish and/or vegetables

Pan de ajo Garlic bread

Patatas a lo pobre Potato chunks sautéed with onions and red and green peppers

Patatas alioli Potato chunks in a garlic mayonnaise

Pescaíto frito Fish given a light dusting of flour and fried

Pescaditos Small fried fish

Pimientos Fried green peppers

Pimientos rellenos Stuffed peppers, usually with tuna

Pinchos morunos pork kebabs, Moorish-style

Pulpo Baby octopus

Quesos Spanish cheeses

Rabo (or cola) de toro Bull's tail

Revueltos Scrambled eggs with asparagus or mushrooms

Salmonetes Red mullet

Sardinas Sardines, fried or grilled

Sepia a la plancha Grilled cuttlefish

Sesos Brains, usually lamb or calf

Truita de patates Catalan name for *tortilla española*

Verdura a la plancha Grilled vegetables

What to Drink in Andalucía

Andalucía is the third-largest of Spain's wine regions and produces some of the world's best-known wines; particularly sherry *(see pp34–5)*. Wine is such a large part of the culture that festivals celebrating the *vendimia* (grape harvest) are held all over the region *(see p40)*. Bars and cafés are an institution in Andalucía, and much social life takes place over morning coffee. Start the day with coffee at the counter in a café, have sherry or beer at midday, wine with lunch, and finish lunch or dinner with coffee and a *copa* of brandy.

Autumn grape harvest or *vendimia* celebrated all over Andalucía

Fino from Jerez

Manzanilla from Sanlúcar

Fino from Montilla

Fino

Fino is Andalucía's signature drink. Ask for *un fino*, or *una copa de vino fino*. Depending on where you are, you may be served a dry, pale sherry from Jerez de la Frontera *(see p166)*, a dry Montilla-Moriles wine from Córdoba province, or a dry Manzanilla, a sherry from Sanlúcar de Barrameda *(see p166)*. You can also ask for *fino* by name: for instance, Tío Pepe, a sherry from the González Byass *bodega* in Jerez; Gran Barquero, which comes from Montilla *(see p151)*; or Solear, a Manzanilla from the Barbadillo *bodega* in Sanlúcar. Manzanilla is the favoured drink during the Feria de Abril in Seville *(see p42)*.

Fino wine has a higher degree of alcohol than table wines (around 15 per cent). When drunk, it should have a fresh aroma and be dry and light to the palate. It is usually served chilled, in a small-stemmed glass with a rim narrower than its base. (Hold it by the base, not around the middle.) However, in some rustic bars, *fino* comes in a tall, straight glass known as a *copita* or a *vasito*.

Fino is most often drunk with first courses and tapas, and its dry taste is a perfect accompaniment to dishes such as *jamón serrano (see pp224–5)*.

Wine

Andalucía produces a few young white table wines, notably Castillo de San Diego, Marqués de la Sierra and wines from El Condado *(see p133)*. Most table wines – *tinto* (red), *blanco* (white) and *rosado* (rosé) – come from other parts of Spain. In more up-market establishments these tend to be Rioja, Ribera del Duero, Navarra and Penedés. Look for the label showing the wine's *denominación de origen* (guarantee of origin and quality). Recent vintages, or *cosecha* wines, are the least expensive; *crianza* and *reserva* wines are aged and more expensive. *Cava*, sparkling wines made by *méthode champenoise*, are usually from Catalonia but Andalucían *bodegas* have begun producing *cava* as well.

Tapas bars tend to serve ordinary Valdepeñas and La Mancha wines. People often dilute these with some *gaseosa*, a fizzy, slightly sweet lemonade. The resulting mixture – known as *tinto de verano* ("summer red wine") – is actually very refreshing.

Castillo de San Diego

Beer

Several brands of lager beers are brewed in Andalucía. These all come in bottles, though quite a few of them are available on draught, too. People often drink draught beers with tapas, especially in summer. Ask for *una caña*. One very good local beer, among the best in Spain, is Cruzcampo. Another, which may perhaps be more familiar to non-Spaniards, is San Miguel.

Una caña de cerveza

Cruzcampo in a bottle

Anise brandy
(aguardiente)

Moscatel from
Málaga

Lepanto *coñac*
from Jerez

Coffee

In the morning, the Spanish tend to drink café con leche, half hot milk, half coffee, often served in a glass instead of a cup. Children and insomniacs might prefer to have a *leche manchada* instead, prepared with just a "shadow" of coffee and lots of hot milk. Another option is a *cortado*, which is mainly coffee, with a tiny amount of milk. After dinner, you should drink café solo, a black espresso-style coffee, which is served in a tiny cup, though it sometimes comes in a short glass.

Spanish coffee is made in espresso machines from coffee beans dark-roasted (torrefacto) with a little sugar to give it a special flavour.

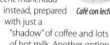

Café con leche

Café solo

Other Drinks

Herbal teas or *infusiones* can be ordered in most bars and cafés. *Poleo-menta* (mint), *manzanilla* (camomile), and *tila* (limeflower) are among the best. *Zumo de naranja natural* (freshly squeezed orange juice) is excellent but expensive and not always available. *Mosto* is grape juice. Tap water throughout Spain is safe to drink, but Andalucíans are discerning about the taste of their water and buy it bottled from natural springs, such as Lanjarón (see p193); it can be bought either *sin gas* (still) or *con gas* (bubbly). Fresh goat's milk is also available in most villages.

Mineral water
from Lanjarón

Fresh orange juice

Camomile tea
(*manzanilla*)

Other Aperitifs and Digestifs

Anise brandy, which is often called *aguardiente*, the name for any distilled spirit, can be sweet or dry. It is drunk from breakfast (desayuno) to late afternoon tea (la merienda) and is sometimes accompanied by little cakes, especially during festivities. It is also drunk after dinner as a digestif. *Tinto de verano* is a summer drink of red wine with ice and *gaseosa*. *Sangría* is a red-wine punch with fruit.

With tapas, instead of *fino*, try one of the mellow apéritif wines, such as *amontillado*, *oloroso* or *palo cortado* (see p35), made in Jerez and Montilla. With your dessert try a *moscatel*; the best known of these is a Málaga wine made from Pedro Ximénez or muscatel grapes. Alternatively try a sweet "cream" sherry from Jerez. After dinner, have a brandy with coffee. Spanish brandy comes mainly from the sherry *bodegas* in Jerez and is called *coñac* in bars. Most *bodegas* produce at least three labels and price ranges, often displayed on shelves whose levels correspond to quality. A good middle-shelf brandy is Magno; top-shelf labels are Lepanto and Larios 1886.

If you are going on, say, to a nightclub, it is customary to switch to tall drinks – whisky with ice and water, gin and tonic or rum and soda. Rum is made on the south coast, where sugar cane is grown. A strawberry flavoured gin, Puerto de Indias, made in Carmona, has gained in popularity as the preferred gin for mixed cocktails.

Amontillado from Jerez, an
apéritif wine

Hot Chocolate

Hot chocolate

Chocolate, originally from Mexico, was imported to Europe by conquistadors. *Tchocolatl*, a bitter, peppery drink made from cocoa, was drunk by the Aztec Indians during religious celebrations. Nuns, living in the colonies, adapted it by adding sugar to the cocoa, creating a sweeter drink more acceptable to European tastes. In the 16th century, chocolate became increasingly popular. Spain had a monopoly on the export of cocoa beans and the "formula" for chocolate was a state secret for over a century. In the 1830s, the English writer, Richard Ford, described chocolate as "for the Spanish what tea is for the English". For many Spaniards this is still the case.

Indian making
tchocolatl

Where to Eat and Drink

Seville

El Arenal

Bodeguita Casablanca €
Traditional **Map** 5 C5
C/Adolfo Rodriguez Jurado 12, 41002
Tel *954 22 41 14* **Closed** *Sat eve, Sun*
Traditional family-run tapas bar with no-frills decor of tiles and barrel tables. Very popular with regular clientèle.

La Brunilda Tapas €
Modern **Map** 5 B3
C/ Galera 5, 41001
Tel *954 22 04 81* **Closed** *Sun eve, Mon*
Bright, modern bar with excellent tapas. Try the *solomillo de buey y patatas al tomillo* (ox sirloin with thyme potatoes).

El Aguador de Velazquez €€
Fusion **Map** 5 C3
C/ Albareda 14, 41001
Tel *954 22 47 20*
Tucked away on a backstreet, El Aguador is a delight. The menu ranges from regional favourites to adaptations of Asian and Mexican dishes.

El Burladero €€
Fine Dining **Map** 5 B3
C/ Canalejas 1, 41001
Tel *954 50 55 99*
Set inside the 19th-century Hotel Gran Melía Colón, with bull-fighting memorabilia and a varied menu. Try the *cola de toro* (oxtail) in eight different ways.

Enrique Becerra €€
Historic **Map** 5 C4
C/ Gamazo 2, 41001
Tel *954 21 30 49* **Closed** *Sun*
Sample delicious *albóndigas de cordero a la yerbabuena* (lamb meatballs with mint) or *pastel de queso, beicon y alcauciles* (cheese, bacon and artichoke pie) at this renovated 19th-century mansion.

Petit Comité €€
Traditional **Map** 5 C5
Calle Dos de Mayo 30, 41001
Tel *954 22 95 95* **Closed** *Mon, Tue lunch*
This cosy restaurant with eclectic decor serves creative cuisine. The risotto here is excellent, or try the *cochinillo confitado con manzana y cebollitas francesas* (roast piglet with caramelised apple and French shallots). Reservations are highly recommended.

DK Choice

Taberna del Alabardero €€
Traditional **Map** 5 B3
C/ Zaragoza 20, 41001
Tel *954 50 27 21*
Savour a flavoursome meal in this beautiful eating spot set in an old, refurbished mansion, which is also home to a culinary school. Tuck into one of the popular dishes, or try their *menu de degustación* (tasting menu) for best value.

Santa Cruz & Parque María Luisa

El Modesto €
Traditional **Map** 6 E4
C/ Cano y Cueto 5 (Plaza de la Carne), 41004
Tel *954 41 68 11*
A classic establishment with tables overlooking Jardines de Murillo. Try the delicious home-made paellas or *gambas al ajillo* (shrimp cooked in oil with garlic and chilli peppers).

Price Guide
Prices categories include a three-course evening meal for one including a half bottle of house wine and all extra charges.
€ under €25
€€ €25 to 45
€€€ over €45

Albarama €€
Fusion **Map** 5 C3
Plaza de San Francisco 5, 41004
Tel *954 22 97 84*
This stylish but casual gastro-bar with a commanding plaza location serves delicious, innovative dishes, such as *hamburguesa de atún con tartar de aguacate* (tuna burger with avocado tartar sauce).

Becerrita €€
Fine Dining **Map** 6 F3
C/ Recaredo 9, 41004
Tel *954 41 20 57* **Closed** *Sun eve*
An intimate restaurant offering gourmet creations. Good selection of meat, fish and seafood and a great wine list.

Casa Plácido €€
Traditional **Map** 6 E4
Mesón del Moro 5, 41004
Tel *954 56 39 71*
Small tapas bar decorated with traditional tiles, bullfight posters and hanging hams. Sample *fino* from the barrel and excellent *tortillas* (potato omelettes).

Casa Robles €€
Seafood **Map** 6 D4
C/ Álvarez Quintero 58, 41004
Tel *954 21 31 50*
Prize-winning restaurant adorned with statues and coloured tiles. Great fish and shellfish selection, plus an impressive wine list. Don't miss the home-made desserts.

Corral del Agua €€
Traditional **Map** 6 D5
Callejón del Agua 6, 41004
Tel *954 22 48 41* **Closed** *Sun*
Cool patio dining and two air-conditioned dining rooms with vibrant decor feature antiques and paintings, close to the Real Alcázar gardens. Try the *menu del dia* (daily menu) for best value.

Doña Elvira €€
Regional **Map** 6 D5
Plaza de Doña Elvira 6, 41004
Tel *954 22 73 88*
With links to the Don Juan legend, this traditional Sevillian restaurant offers dining indoors or al fresco under shady trees. It serves great innovative salads, paella, seafood and meat dishes.

Spacious dining area at Casa Robles, Seville

A rich selection of tapas on offer at fusion restaurant Oriza, Seville

Donaire Azabache €€
Traditional **Map** 6 D4
Calle Santo Tomás 11, 41004
Tel *954 22 47 02* **Closed** *Sun eve*
Close to the Archivo de Indias, this restaurant offers an array of Andalucían dishes in a pleasant setting. The rooftop terrace offers wonderful views of the city centre.

Hard Rock Café €€
Fine Dining **Map** 6 D5
Calle San Fernando 3, 41004
Tel *954 22 01 26*
Sample American cuisine in this restaurant, surrounded by the memorabilia of famous musicians.

Mama Bistro €€
Fusion **Map** 6 D4
Calle Mateos Gago 9 B, 41004
Tel *954 22 73 09* **Closed** *Tue, Wed lunch*
This modern bistro with traditional roots has good vegetarian options. Reservations required.

Oriza €€
Fusion **Map** 3 C3
C/ San Fernando 41, 41004
Tel *954 22 72 54* **Closed** *Sun eve*
Avant-garde cuisine based on the best products and local flavours, set in an early 20th-century mansion. Sample the superb *bacalao* (salted cod) and *merluza* (hake). Also on offer are great meat dishes and desserts.

La Quinta Braseria €€
Historic **Map** 6 E2
Plaza Padre Jeronimo de Cordoba 1, 41004
Tel *954 60 00 16* **Closed** *Sun eve, Mon*
Elegant restaurant with excellent choices. Start with the *croquetas de pollo y trufa negra* (chicken and black truffle croquettes) or the tartare, followed by one of the juicy grilled meat selections. Book in advance.

San Marco €€
Italian **Map** 6 E4
Mesón del Moro 6, 41004
Tel *954 21 43 90*
A uniquely atmospheric restaurant located in the old Arab Baths. Come here for first-rate Italian pasta dishes. One of three branches in the city.

El Traga €€
Traditional **Map** 6 E3
Calle Aguilas 6, 41004
Tel *854 52 14 94*
Modern tapas bar, which serves contemporary Andalucían cuisine. Try the tuna ceviche and the lamb shank with truffled pumpkin puree and red cabbage. Be sure to order the deconstructed cheesecake. Good wine selection.

DK Choice

Vinería San Telmo €€
Fusion **Map** 6 E4
Paseo Catalina de Ribera 4, 41004
Tel *954 41 06 00*
A charming establishment with tables on a pleasant square. Innovative twists to regional favourites will delight, such as *trigo cremoso con boletus y aceite de trufa* (creamy bulghur risotto with boletus mushrooms and truffle oil), but make sure you leave room for the fabulous home-made desserts.

San Fernando €€€
Fine Dining **Map** 6 D5
C/ San Fernando 2, 41004
Tel *954 91 70 44*
A first-rate restaurant inside the Alfonso XIII Hotel. Try the truffle and wild mushroom risotto or go for the delicious *solomillo* (beef) Wellington.

La Macarena

Contenedor €€
Market-to-Table **Map** 2 E4
C/ San Luis 50, 41003
Tel *954 91 63 33*
Top-value eating spot serving traditional dishes using fresh market produce. Good service.

Eslava €€
Seafood/Regional **Map** 1 C4
C/ Eslava 3, 41002
Tel *954 90 65 68* **Closed** *Sun eve, Mon*
A no-frills, popular restaurant featuring creative Andalucían cuisine. Great seafood and salads, and an inventive choice of tapas.

Triana

Cervecería la Gamba Blanca €
Traditional **Map** 3 A3
C/ Febo 20, 41010
Tel *954 28 29 40* **Closed** *Sun eve*
This tapas bar with traditional decor serves several seafood specialities, as well as meat, cheese and vegetable dishes.

Gastro Bar María Trifulca €
Seafood **Map** 3 A2
Plaza Del Altozano, 1, 41010
Tel *681 20 04 00*
The views are incredible from this tower, which was once a maritime station. Book a table on the rooftop terrace and try one of the rice dishes with langoustine and Scarlet shrimp.

Vega 10 €
Market-to-Table **Map** 3 B3
C/ Rosario Vega 10, 41010
Tel *954 23 77 48* **Closed** *Sun*
Offering a seasonal choice of creative dishes made with fresh ingredients, this restaurant also has a daily-changing tapas menu.

Elegant place settings at Taberna del Alabardero, Seville

For more information on types of restaurants *see p221*

Abades Triana €€€
Seafood **Map** 3 B3
C/ Betis 69, 41010
Tel 954 28 64 59
Enjoy superb international and
Mediterranean cuisine at this
riverside eatery with pretty views.

Huelva and Sevilla

ALMONTE: El Tamborilero €
Market-to-Table **Map** B3
C/ Unamuno 15, 21730
Tel 959 40 69 55 **Closed** Sun; 1–15
Jul
An atmospheric former *bodega*
(wine cellar) with traditional
decor and a chef who invites you
into the kitchen to choose from
their selections of the day.

DK Choice

**ALMONTE: Aires de Doñana
(La Choza del Rocío)** €€
Regional **Map** B3
Avda de la Canaliega 1, 21730
Tel 959 44 22 89 **Closed** Mon
A converted *choza* (thatched
hut), this beautifully decorated
restaurant enjoys splendid
terrace views across the Doñana
parkland's woods, reeds and
waterways. Specialities include
revuelto marismeño (scrambled
eggs with local herbs) and
cabrito lechal (suckling kid).

**BORMUJOS: La Choza
de Manuela** €
Grill **Map** B2
Calle Menendez Pidal 2, 41930
Tel 959 72 60 92 **Closed** Mon
A complex of thatched-roof
huts and terraces, this is the
go-to place for excellent, good-
value grilled meats and fish
served in generous portions

Bright and inviting dining room at El Tamborilero, Almonte

CARMONA: Goya €
Traditional **Map** B2
C/ Prim 2, 41410
Tel 954 14 30 60
Unassuming Sevillian eating spot
off the city's main square. Try the
baked lamb. The tapas bar does
good tortillas.

**CARMONA: El Molino de
la Romera** €€
Historic **Map** B2
C/ Sor Angela de la Cruz 8, 41410
Tel 954 14 20 00 **Closed** Mon
Converted from a 16th-century
Moorish mill and granary, this
evocative restaurant specializes
in delicious regional dishes.

**CARMONA: Parador Alcázar
del Rey Don Pedro** €€
Regional **Map** B2
C/ del Alcázar s/n, 41410
Tel 954 14 10 10
Chic parador restaurant with a
vaulted, antique-furnished dining
room. First-rate regional dishes
use fresh market produce.

CARMONA: La Yedra €€
Traditional **Map** B2
Calle General Freire 6, 41410
Tel 954 14 45 25 **Closed** Sun eve,
Mon
A romantic restaurant with a
charming courtyard. The excellent
Mediterranean cuisine is meticu-
lously prepared. Some dishes are
modern takes on regional classics.
Be sure to try the exquisite
homemade desserts.

**EL ROCÍO: Restaurante
Toruño** €
Regional **Map** B3
Plaza Acebuchal 22, 21750
Tel 959 44 24 22
Inviting restaurant with terrace
boasting excellent views. Try the
berenjenas gratinadas (aubergine
gratin), or one of the rice dishes.

Appetizing tapas at El Molino de
la Romera, Carmona

GERENA: Casa Salvi Tapas €
Regional/Fusion **Map** B2
Miguel de Cervantes 46, 41860
Tel 955 78 32 72
Choose from a vast selection of
tapas and *raciones* and enjoy
your meal in the shady plaza or
one of the charming dining
rooms. Superb value.

HUELVA: Azabache €€
Traditional **Map** A3
Calle Vazquez Lopez 22, 21001
Tel 959 25 75 28 **Closed** Sat eve,
Sun
This restaurant features a varied
menu based on top-quality,
ingredients. It serves traditional
cuisine as well as innovative
versions of local dishes. Excellent
seafood and good options for
vegetarians. Extensive wine list.

HUELVA: Las Meigas €€
Seafood **Map** A3
Avda Guatemala 44, 21003
Tel 959 27 19 58 **Closed** Sun
Top-notch restaurant serving
fresh Atlantic seafood. Try the
scrumptious *pulpo a la gallega
con cachelos* (Galician-style
octopus with sliced potato).

HUELVA: El Portichuelo €€
Regional **Map** A3
C/ Vázquez López 15, 21001
Tel 959 24 57 68
Unpretentious and centrally
located, El Portichuelo dishes out
traditional Andalucían fare made
from the freshest market produce.
Warm and friendly service.

HUELVA: Taberna La Botánico €€
Seafood **Map** A3
Avenida Andalucía 5, 21459
Tel 959 39 95 61 **Closed** Sun
This restaurant is known for its
freshly caught fish and seafood,
which is cooked to perfection. The

fresh tomato and mozarella salad is extremely flavourful. Attentive staff and good value for money.

ISLA CRISTINA: Casa Rufino €€
Seafood **Map** A3
Avda de la Playa s/n, 21410
Tel *959 33 08 10* **Closed** *Jan*
A beachside haven for seafood lovers, serving a variety of fresh fish. Try the *rape en salsa de pasas* (angler fish in raisin sauce).

JABUGO: Meson Cinco Jotas €€
Traditional **Map** A2
Ctra San Juan del Puerto, 21290
Tel *959 12 10 71*
Unpretentious eating joint in the birthplace of Spain's greatest *jamón* (ham). Sample the home-cured *jabugo* and cod with prawns and olives.

LA RINCONADA: El Pela €
Traditional **Map** B2
Plaza de Rodriguez Montes 2, 41300
Tel *955 79 70 39* **Closed** *Wed*
Simple, no-frills Sevillian restaurant where breakfast is served with delicious *pan prieto de la Algaba* (local speciality bread). Warm and friendly service.

MATALASCAÑAS: Los Pepes €€
Seafood **Map** A3
Sector N Parcela 43, Paseo Marítimo de Matalascañas
Tel *959 44 10 64*
Sunny *chiringuito* (beach bar) with a beachside terrace. Try the *lubina a la sal* (sea bass baked in salt) and *langosta* (fresh lobster), or one of the first-rate *guisos* (stews).

OSUNA: El Mesón del Duque €
Regional **Map** C3
Plaza de la Duquesa 1, 41640
Tel *620 19 47 87* **Closed** *Wed, second week in May*
A fine traditional eating spot with a terrace, offering Andalucían specialities. Tapas include home-made *albóndigas* (meatballs).

OSUNA: Doña Guadalupe €€
Regional **Map** C3
Plaza de Guadalupe 6-8, 41640
Tel *954 81 05 58* **Closed** *Sat, Sun*
Family-run restaurant with outdoor terrace dining. Sample classic regional fare such as *perdíz con arroz* (partridge cooked with rice).

PALOS DE LA FRONTERA: El Bodegón €
Traditional **Map** A3
C/ Rábida 46, 21810
Tel *959 53 11 05* **Closed** *Tue; 15–30 Sep*
An eco-conscious restaurant with indoor and patio dining options. Bite into the juicy *solomillo a la brasa* (oak grilled sirloin steak).

Paintings of landscapes decorating the walls of the dining room at Casa Juanito, Baeza

Córdoba and Jaén

BAEZA: Casa Juanito €€
Regional **Map** E2
Av del Alcalde Puché Pardo 57, 23440
Tel *953 74 00 40*
This is a cozy family-run eatery. Olive oil-based dishes include *cabrito con habas* (young goat with broad beans). Fabulous home-made desserts.

DK Choice

BAEZA: Palacio de Gallego Restaurante & Boutique €€€
Regional **Map** E2
Calle Santa Catalina 5, 23440
Tel *667 76 01 84* **Closed** *Tue*
Set in the peaceful courtyard of a historic building in the old town centre, close to the cathedral, the Palacio de Gallego offers a fine selection of meats and fish, grilled while you watch. The excellent wine list spans all the regions of Spain. Don't forget to save room for dessert.

BAILÉN: Zodiaco Libra €€
Traditional **Map** D2
Carretera Nailén-Motril km 294, 23710
Tel *953 67 10 58*
A popular restaurant that serves cold summer soups on a lovely garden terrace. Great shrimp and asparagus *revuelto* (scrambled egg) dishes.

CAZORLA: Meson Leandro €€
Traditional **Map** E2
C/ Hoz 3, 23470
Tel *953 72 06 32* **Closed** *Wed & 15–30 Jun*
Michelin-recommended restaurant in a lovely Jaén village bordering a national park, and renowned for its *carne a la piedra* (stone-baked meat) dishes.

CÓRDOBA: Horno San Luis €
Market-to-Table **Map** C2
Calle Cardenal Gonzalez, 14003
Tel *665 05 37 83*
Housed in a historic *panaderia* (bread bakery), this two-storey restaurant serves innovative and creative dishes. In the evening, it turns into a cocktail bar.

CÓRDOBA: Taberna Sociedad de Plateros €
Traditional **Map** C2
C/ María Auxiliadora 25, 14002
Tel *957 47 03 04*
Iconic 1930s establishment often frequented by celebrities. The skylit patio is decorated with *azulejos* (glazed tiles). Try the *revuelto* (scrambled eggs).

CÓRDOBA: La Almudaina €€
Traditional **Map** C2
Campo Santo de los Mártires 1, 14004
Tel *957 47 43 42* **Closed** *Sun eve*
Excellent restaurant in a former bishop's palace. Traditional dishes include *salmorejo* (chilled tomato and bread soup) and *solomillo al foie* (pork sirloin with paté).

CÓRDOBA: El Blasón €€
Traditional **Map** C2
C/ José Zorrilla 11, 14008
Tel *957 48 06 25* **Closed** *Sun*
Centrally located restaurant with an elegant tiled patio. The menu features amazing *guisos* (stews), inventive seafood dishes and delectable home-made desserts.

CÓRDOBA: Casa Pepe de la Judería €€
Regional **Map** C2
C/ Romero 1, 14003
Tel *957 20 07 44* **Closed** *last 2 weekends of May*
An enduring favourite since 1928. Dine in the beautiful flower-filled patio and savour the traditional Córdoban pork dish, *flamenquin*.

For more information on types of restaurants *see p221*

CÓRDOBA: El Churrasco €€
Grill **Map** C2
C/ Romero 16, 14003
Tel 957 29 08 19 **Closed** Aug;
24 Oct; 24, 25 & 31 Dec
Indulge in romantic patio dining
under a lemon tree. Enjoy the
charcoal-grilled steaks or one of
a range of vegetarian dishes.
Tapas menu also available.

CÓRDOBA: Regadera €€
Traditional **Map** C2
Calle Ronda de Isasa 10, 14002
Tel 957 10 14 00
Situated, just steps from the
riverfront, Regadera serves
excellent food at great prices. Try
the rabo de toro con espuma de
patata (oxtail with potato foam).

**CÓRDOBA: San Miguel
Casa El Pisto** €€
Traditional **Map** C2
Plaza San Miguel 1, 14002
Tel 957 47 01 66 **Closed** Sun
Sterling family-run eating spot
with tiled floors and traditional
decor. Sample Iberian cured
meats and pisto (ratatouille).

CÓRDOBA: Caballo Rojo €€€
Fine Dining **Map** C2
C/ Cardenal Herrero 28, 14003
Tel 957 47 53 75
Recognized by the Michelin guide,
this charming eating place is right
next to the Mezquita. Discover
Basque-, Moorish- and Sephardic-
influenced dishes such as cordero
con miel (lamb with honey) and
the delicious monkfish mozárabe.

JAÉN: Antaño €
Traditional **Map** D2
C/ de la Rioja 5, 23009
Tel 953 22 46 51 **Closed** 1 Jan,
25 Dec
No-frills restaurant with a large
summer terrace. Try the cazuela
(fish stew) or bacalao en alioli (cod
in garlic and mayonnaise sauce).

JAÉN: Taberna Don Sancho €
Traditional **Map** D2
Avda de Andalucía 17, 23005
Tel 953 26 40 21
Good-value friendly restaurant
with a creative take on classic
dishes. Ask for the delicious cod
with blueberries. Great service.

JAÉN: Casa Vicente €€
Fine Dining **Map** D2
C/ Cristo Rey 3, 23007
Tel 953 23 22 22 **Closed** Sun &
Mon eve
Elegant Michelin-recommended
mansion restaurant, which serves
local favourites like guiso de
cordero (lamb stew) and pimientos
rellenos de mariscos (shellfish-
stuffed peppers).

JAÉN: Casa Antonio €€€
Modern **Map** D2
C/ Fermín Palma 3, 23008
Tel 953 27 02 62 **Closed** Sun eve,
Mon, Aug
Chic restaurant with a lovely
terrace serving contemporary
versions of traditional dishes. The
menu changes frequently but
the excellent cochinillo (suckling
pig) features regularly.

PALMA DEL RÍO: El Refectorio €€
Historic **Map** C2
Avda Pío XII 35, 14700
Tel 957 71 01 83
Dine in the old rectory of
a converted 15th-century
monastery. Traditional dishes
include game in winter. Try the
wild boar cooked in acorn flour.

DK Choice

**ÚBEDA: Parador
Condestable Dávalos** €€
Historic **Map** E2
Plaza Vázquez de Molina, 23400
Tel 953 75 03 45
One of Úbeda's finest and most
sumptuous spots, this stylish
restaurant is located in a grand
16th-century parador. Savour
the outstanding cabrito guisado
con piñones (stewed kid with
pine nuts) and seasonal game
dishes. A wonderful historic
setting, traditional decor and
mouth-watering food.

ÚBEDA: El Seco €€
Traditional **Map** E2
C/ Corazón de Jesus 8, 23400.
Tel 953 79 14 52
Sink into a cosy dining room
and savour homely dishes such
as bacalao al seco (salted cod in
cream sauce). Good service.

Cádiz and Málaga

ALGECIRAS: Maridaje €
Vegetarian/Seafood **Map** C4
Calle Buen Aire 9, 11201
Tel 646 48 64 08 **Closed** Sun
This sleek restaurant serves tasty
tapas. Try the surtido de atun, a
plate of tuna prepared in various
ways. Good selection of wines.

ALGECIRAS: La Cabaña €€
Traditional **Map** C4
Avda Agua Marina 5, 11203
Tel 956 66 73 79 **Closed** Mon
Traditional restaurant with indoor
and terrace dining, and live music
some nights. Dishes include pulpo
gallego (Galician-style octopus).

**ARCOS DE LA FRONTERA:
Bar La Cárcel** €
Traditional **Map** B3
C/ Dean Espinosa, 18, 11630
Tel 956 70 04 10
A very popular restaurant
with rustic decor. Ask for the
aubergine with honey and goat's
cheese, or try the carne en Pedro
Ximénez (wine-marinated meat).

BENAHAVÍS: Los Abanicos €€
Regional **Map** C4
C/ Málaga 15, 28679
Tel 952 85 50 22 **Closed** Tue,
Christmas
Popular for Sunday lunches, this
restaurant specializes in regional
dishes with excellent paletilla de
cordero (shoulder of lamb).

BENAOJÁN: Molino del Santo €€
Market-to-Table **Map** C3
Bda Estación s/n, 29370
Tel 952 16 71 51 **Closed** Dec–Feb
With a great location amidst
wooded mountain countryside,
this place serves dishes prepared

Vibrant interior at El Churrasco, Córdoba

Elegant place settings at Casa Paco, Coín

with fresh market vegetables and local chorizo, ham and game. Gourmet barbeques in summer.

CÁDIZ: Freiduría Cervecería Las Flores
Seafood   €   **Map** B4
Plaza Topete 4, 11001
Tel *956 22 61 12*
Simple restaurant specializing in *mariscos* (shellfish) and fresh *pescaíto frito* (fried fish platter) – make your choice and see it cooked on the spot.

CÁDIZ: Balandro
Seafood   €€   **Map** B4
Alameda Apodaca 22, 11004
Tel *956 22 09 92*
Set in a converted 18th-century mansion overlooking the Bay of Cádiz, this place offers excellent boned and grilled gilthead and a good selection of meat dishes.

CÁDIZ: El Faro
Seafood   €€   **Map** B4
C/San Felix 15, 11011
Tel *956 21 10 68*
Atmospheric seafood restaurant in the port district. Do not miss the *tortillitas de camarones* (shrimp fritters), or try one of the various taster menus available.

CÁDIZ: Ventorillo del Chato
Seafood   €€   **Map** B4
Via Augusta Julia, 11011
Tel *956 25 00 25*   **Closed** *Sun eve (except in Aug)*
Lovely 18th-century seaside inn specializing in local fresh fish. Try the *pasta negra fresca y frutos del mar* (fresh black pasta with seafood).

CASARES: Venta Garcia
Traditional   €   **Map** C4
Ctra de Casares (MA 546) km 7, 29690
Tel *952 89 41 91*
Charming restaurant set in a scenic white roadside villa that offers great terrace views. The scallops are delicious and so is the *guiso de pescado* (fish stew).

COÍN: Casa Paco
Traditional   €€   **Map** C3
C/Maria Moreno 2, 29100
Tel *952 45 03 49*   **Closed** *Mon eve, Tue*
Large country inn with a range of menus. Try the *boquerones* (fresh anchovies) and feast on *langostinos* (king prawns) and rice dishes. Popular for wedding receptions.

ESTEPONA: La Alborada
Seafood   €€   **Map** C4
Puerto Deportivo de Estepona, 29680
Tel *952 80 20 47*   **Closed** *Wed*
Stylish marine restaurant serving tasty paellas and *pescaíto frito* (Andalucían fried fish platter). Good selection of desserts.

FUENGIROLA: Moochers Jazz Café
Crèpes   €   **Map** C4
C/la Cruz 17, 39640
Tel *952 47 71 54*
A warm and lively restaurant with soft, candlelit interiors and live music in the evening. Moochers specializes in vegetarian crèpes but seafood and chicken are also served. Rooftop dining in summer.

Original wine press at La Fructuosa restaurant, Gaucín

FUENGIROLA: Vegetalia
Vegetarian   €   **Map** C4
C/Santa Isabel 8, Los Boliches 29640
Tel *952 58 60 31*   **Closed** *Sun, Jul–Aug*
Finnish-owned vegetarian restaurant with a good lunchtime buffet. Indulge in delicious home-made desserts and juices.

GAUCÍN: La Fructuosa
Moroccan/Spanish   €€   **Map** C4
C/Convento 67, 29480
Tel *617 69 27 84*   **Closed** *Mon, Tue, lunch Wed–Sun*
Comfortable Spanish-Moroccan-style restaurant with ceiling beams and an old wine press. Savour the views while sampling the fresh goat's cheese and honey.

GIBRALTAR: The Waterfront Bistro
      €€   **Map** C4
Queensway Quay, Units 4/5 Ragged Staff Wharf, Marina Bay
Tel *350 20 04 56 66*   **Closed** *Good Fri; 25, 26, 31 Dec; 1 Jan*
A waterside eating spot with idyllic sunset views. Sink your teeth into the Cajun chicken, T-bone steaks and grilled sea bass. There are also good vegetarian choices.

GIBRALTAR: Rib Room
Fine Dining   €€€   **Map** C4
Rock Hotel, 3 Europa Road
Tel *350 20 07 30 00*
An iconic restaurant in one of Gibraltar's most distinguished hotels, Rib Room serves delicious modern British cuisine with Iberian and Moroccan influences.

JEREZ DE LA FRONTERA: Reino de Leon Gastrobar
Fusion   €   **Map** B3
C/Latorre, 8, 11402
Tel *956 32 29 15*
Chic modern restaurant with interesting choices such as *chupa-chups cremosos de cheddar con regaliz* (creamy cheddar lollipops with liquorice). Finish with one of the inventive gin and tonics.

Diners enjoying the seaview at Garum, Marbella

JEREZ DE LA FRONTERA:
Bar Juanito   €€
Traditional   **Map** B3
C/Pescadería Vieja 8, 11403
Tel *956 33 48 38*   **Closed** *Sun*
Atmospheric tapas bar and
restaurant with bullfighting and
flamenco decorations, serving
large portions of tapas; be sure
to try the local artichokes.

LA LINEA: La Marina   €€
Seafood   **Map** C4
Paseo Marítimo, La Atunara s/n, 11300
Tel *956 17 15 31*   **Closed** *Mon; 24,
31 Dec*
Large seaside restaurant with
nautical decor. Enjoy great bay
views while savouring delicious
chirlas marineras (clams).

LOS BARRIOS: Mesón El Copo €€
Seafood   **Map** C4
*Calle La Almadraba 2 (Palmones),
11369*
Tel *956 67 77 10*   **Closed** *Sun*
This first-rate beachside
restaurant serves fresh local
urta (sea bream) and *gallineta*
(Atlantic red fish), as well as
great home-made desserts.

The elegant Parador Gibralfaro
restaurant, Málaga

MÁLAGA: Antigua Casa
de la Guardia   €
Historic   **Map** D3
Alameda Principal 18, 29015
Tel *952 21 46 80* **Closed** *Sun (except
Holy Week, Feria & Dec)*
One of Málaga's oldest and
most atmospheric wine cellar
bars. Their speciality tipple is
dark, rich Pedro Ximénez wine
served directly from the barrel.

MÁLAGA: Mesón Cortijo
de Pepe   €
Traditional   **Map** D3
Plaza de la Merced 2, 29012
Tel *952 22 40 71*   **Closed** *Tue*
Popular tapas bar that serves
succulent *calamarares a la romana*
(squid fried in batter) and *gambas
a la plancha* (grilled prawns).

DK Choice

MÁLAGA: El Tintero II   €
Seafood   **Map** D3
Playa del Dedo s/n (El Palo), 29018
Tel *952 20 68 26*
Without a doubt the noisiest
restaurant on the Costa del
Sol. However, the beachside
location, sweeping views across
the bay and magnificent choice
of fish dishes make El Tintero II
a must visit. There is no menu.
You simply need to point at the
dish you want as waiters pass
by announcing them. Go for the
grilled *salmonetes* (red mullet) or
rape (angler fish) in a rich garlic
sauce. Great value for money.

MÁLAGA: Café de Paris   €€
Fusion   **Map** D3
C/Velez Málaga s/n, 29016
Tel *952 22 50 43*   **Closed** *Sun,
Mon eve*
This stylish restaurant serves
modern Spanish-Mediterranean
dishes such as parmesan rice
and tasty pigeon and sirloin with
duck paté, plus innovative tapas.

MÁLAGA: Mesón Astorga   €€
Traditional   **Map** D3
C/Gerona 11, 29006
Tel *952 34 25 63*   **Closed** *Sun*
Classic Malagueno restaurant
with dishes prepared from fresh
market produce. Sample the
almejas (clams) and *boqueroncitos*
(baby anchovies), and try the
fried aubergine with sugar
cane honey.

MÁLAGA: Parador Gibralfaro €€
Regional   **Map** D3
Camino de Gibralfaro s/n, 29006
Tel *952 22 19 02*
Elegant restaurant in Málaga's
spectacular hilltop parador,
serving traditional fare such as
zoque and *gazpachelo* (standard
and fish versions of *gazpacho*).

MANILVA: Macues   €€
Seafood   **Map** C4
*Plaza Delfín s/n, Puerto Deportivo de
la Duquesa*
Tel *952 89 03 95*   **Closed** *Mon, Sat
lunch*
Stylish place serving *dorada a la
sal* (bream baked in salt) – a
regular favourite – and charcoal-
grilled steaks for meat lovers.

MARBELLA: Altamirano   €€
Seafood   **Map** C4
Plaza Altamirano 3, 29601
Tel *952 82 49 32* **Closed** *Wed; 8 Jan–
15 Feb*
Good value family-friendly
option with a garden for alfresco
dining. Specialities range from
fritura malagueña (fried fish
platter) and *besugo a la brasa*
(barbecued sea bream).

MARBELLA: Garum   €€
Fusion   **Map** C4
Avda de la Fontanilla, 29600
Tel *952 85 88 58*
Finnish-run restaurant with an
enclosed beachside terrace. Try
tasty pumpkin, *albóndigas* (meat-
balls), smoked lamb and steaks.

MARBELLA: Santiago €€
Seafood **Map** C4
Avda Duque de Ahamada 5, 29602
Tel *952 77 00 78*
Great seafood institution dishing out *almejas* (clams), *lubina* (sea bass) and a variety of paellas. Good tapas selection at the bar.

MARBELLA: Paco Jiménez €€€
Traditional **Map** C4
Plaza Naranjos 11, 29601
Tel *952 77 36 10* **Closed** *lunch, Mon*
Opt for a table on the balcony overlooking the lovely Plaza de Naranjos. The menu features an array of seafood and meat dishes.

MARBELLA: Skina €€€
Fusion **Map** C4
C/Aduar 12, 29601
Tel *952 76 52 77* **Closed** *Sun, Mon, 9–15 Dec, 7 Jan–3 Feb*
This Michelin-starred chic, intimate, old-town restaurant has an eclectic mix of dishes, ranging from rabbit terrine to sole with artichokes and tomato.

MIJAS: El Mirlo Blanco €€
Traditional **Map** C3
Cuesta de la Villa 13, 29650
Tel *952 48 57 00* **Closed** *Tue, 11 Jan–11 Feb*
Established Basque restaurant serving dishes such as *txangurro* (stuffed spider crab) and *kokotxas de bacalao pil pil* (cod cheeks in hot garlic, chilli and olive oil).

NERJA: Restaurante Jacky €€
International **Map** D3
C/Chaparil 6 (Edificio Corona), 29780
Tel *952 52 11 38*
Intimate, quality restaurant offering French and Mediterranean cuisine. Try the excellent *menu de degustación,* or the quail stuffed with foie gras.

PUERTO DE SANTA MARÍA: Pantalán G €€
Seafood **Map** B3
Avenida de la Libertad s/n, Puerto Sherry, 11500
Tel *956 87 18 65* **Closed** *Sun eve*
Port-side restaurant offering a delectable assortment of meat, fish and seafood. Meat lovers should try the *Tomahawk Steak de Buey.* There is a good selection of vegetables as well.

PUERTO DE SANTA MARÍA: El Faro de El Puerto €€€
Seafood **Map** B3
Avda de Fuentebravia km 0.5, 11500
Tel *956 87 09 52* **Closed** *Sun eve (except Aug)*
Refined family-run restaurant set in lush gardens serving delicious *lomo de pargo con berenjenas* (red snapper with aubergine). Extensive choice of wines.

RONDA: Tragatapas €
Modern **Map** C3
Calle Nueva 4, 29400
Tel *952 87 72 09*
Cosy and unassuming, Tragatapas offers inventive tapas such as goat's cheese and asparagus, marinated salmon and sautéed mushrooms.

RONDA: Pedro Romero €€
Traditional **Map** C3
C/Virgen de la Paz 18, 29400
Tel *952 87 11 10*
Named after a 17th-century matador, this restaurant serves excellent *rabo de toro* (braised oxtail) and *perdiz con alubias* (partridge with kidney beans).

RONDA: Puerta Grande Ronda €€
Fine Dining **Map** C3
Calle Nueva 10, 29400
Tel *952 87 92 00* **Closed** *dinner, Tue*
A traditional restaurant serving Andalucían dishes, some with

Michelin-starred Skina in Marbella

innovative interpretations. Try one of the paellas, or the *lomo de venado en salsa de frambuesas y moras* (venison loin in a raspberry and blackberry sauce) and finish with the pavlova.

SAN FERNANDO: Venta de Vargas €
Traditional **Map** B4
Plaza Juan Vargas s/n, 11100
Tel *956 88 16 22*
Former haunt of flamenco icon Cameron de la Isla. The menu here includes *chocos de la bahía* (cuttlefish from the bay). Live flamenco every now and then.

SANLÚCAR DE BARRAMEDA: Casa Bigote €€
Seafood **Map** B3
C/Pórtico Bajo de Guia 10, 11540
Tel *956 36 26 96* **Closed** *Sun*
Set beside the Guadalquivir estuary, this traditional restaurant serves fresh seafood and regional hams. Exceptional *lomo de atún* (tuna steak) and king prawns.

TARIFA: Arte-Vida €€
Seafood **Map** B4
Ctra Cádiz-Málaga (N 340) km. 79.3, 11380
Tel *956 68 52 46*
Chic restaurant with views across the straits, specializing in fresh seafood, salads and pizzas. The café serves great coffee and cakes.

TARIFA: Meson de Sancho €€
Traditional **Map** B4
Ctra Cádiz-Málaga (N 340) km 94, 11380
Tel *956 68 81 27*
Cosy Andalucían inn serving first-rate dishes and fantastic breakfasts. Order the sea bream cooked in cognac or the *pierna de cordero* (leg of lamb).

The well-stocked wine cellar at El Faro de El Puerto, Puerto de Santa María

For more information on types of restaurants *see p221*

DK Choice

TORREMOLINOS:
Nuevo Lanjarón   €
Traditional   **Map** D3
C/Europa 10, 29620
Tel *952 38 87 74*   **Closed** *Mon*
This long-established family-run
place is probably the best value
restaurant on the Costa del Sol.
Choose from a variety of
inexpensive set menus that
include fish and meat dishes. Try
the exquisite *estofado de ternera*
(veal stew) or the generous
fritura malagueña (fried fish
platter), followed by home-
made flan. Good service.

TORREMOLINOS: Yate El
Cordobés   €
Seafood   **Map** D3
Paseo Marítimo s/n (Bajondillo) 29620
Tel *952 38 49 56*
Sample local seafood dishes
ranging from *espetos de sardinas*
(charcoal-cooked fresh sardines)
to *mero en adobo* (grouper
marinated in vinegar).

TORREMOLINOS: Casa Juan
los Mellizos   €€
Seafood   **Map** D3
C/San Ginés 20, 29620
Tel *952 37 35 12*
Excellent value fish dishes at this
family-run establishment. The
bouillabaisse and fried sea-food
platter, as well as the creamy rice
dishes, are popular draws.

TORREMOLINOS: Frutos   €€
Traditional   **Map** D3
Avda de la Riviera 80, 29620
Tel *952 38 15 40*   **Closed** *Sun eve*
A typical grand old Costa del
Sol restaurant. Enjoy classic
dishes such as *judiones a la
Granja* (Castilian style white
beans) and a wide selection
of fresh fish.

VEJER DE LA FRONTERA:
Venta Pinto   €€
Seafood   **Map** B4
C/La Barca de Vejer s/n, 11150
Tel *956 45 08 77*
Traditional restaurant with
specialities including *perdiz roja
asada* (roasted red partridge) and
rodaballo al horno con alcaparras
(baked turbot with capers).

ZAHARA DE LOS ATUNES:
Restaurante Zoko   €
Seafood   **Map** B4
Calle Real 14, 11393
Tel *657 86 44 57*   **Closed** *Wed*
Specialities here include *salmorejo
con aguacate y langostinos* (thick
gazpacho dip with langoustines
and avocado) and the *mini-fajita
de atun* (mini tuna fajita).

Granada and Almería

ALMERÍA: Rincón de
Juan Pedro   €
Traditional   **Map** F3
C/Federico Castro 2, 04003
Tel *950 27 81 67*   **Closed** *Mon*
A very popular tapas bar, offering
generous portions of pungent
hams, chorizos and cheeses, as
well as local specialities such as
trigo a la cortijera (wheat berry
and sausage stew).

ALMERÍA: Bodega Bellavista €€
Regional   **Map** F3
*Urbanización Bellavista, Calle
Partenón 1, 04130*
Tel *950 29 71 56*   **Closed** *Sun eve &
Mon*
This charming traditional
restaurant is located close to
the airport. It offers classic
regional seafood – shellfish
dominates the menu – and
meat dishes, using fresh market
produce. Great wine list.

ALMERÍA: Casa Sevilla   €€
Seafood   **Map** F3
C/Rueda López s/n, 04004
Tel *950 27 29 12*   **Closed** *Sun*
Sociable family restaurant serving
fresh seafood. Go for the *tempura
de bacalao sobre arroz meloso de
hongos* (cod tempura on a bed of
creamy mushroom rice). Monthly
wine tastings.

ALMERÍA: Club de Mar   €€
Seafood   **Map** F3
Playa de Almadrabillas, 1, 04007
Tel *950 23 50 48*   **Closed** *Tue*
Chic restaurant with a seafront
terrace in Almería's prestigious
yacht club. It is renowned for its
zarzuela de pescado y marisco
(bouillabaise) and *fritura de
pescado* (fried fish platter).

ALMERÍA: Taberna Nuevo
Torreluz   €€
Fusion   **Map** F3
Plaza Flores 1, 04001
Tel *950 23 43 99*   **Closed** *Sun,
Mon eve*
Elegant restaurant with creative
dishes, varied tapas and *raciones*.
Delicious breakfasts. Friendly
service and fantastic location

ALMERÍA: Valentin   €€
Seafood   **Map** F3
C/Tenor Iribarne 19, 04001
Tel *950 26 44 75*   **Closed** *Mon, Sep*
A popular Michelin-recommended
marisquería (restaurant specializing
in shellfish) where everything is
market fresh.

BUBIÓN: Teide   €
Traditional   **Map** E3
C/Carretera s/n,18412
Tel *958 76 30 37*   **Closed** *Second
fortnight in Jun*
A charming stone-built restaurant
with a tree-shaded garden, Teide
serves home-cooked food such as
migas (fried breadcrumbs with
garlic) and *choto asado* (roast kid).

Seafood restaurant Casa Juan los Mellizos in Torremolinos

CARBONERAS: El Cabo €€
Seafood Map F3
Paseo Marítimo 67, 04140
Tel *950 13 06 24* **Closed** *Mon*
Beachside restaurant close to Cabo
de Gata National Park. Try seafood
dishes such as squid stuffed with
spinach and pine nuts.

**GRANADA: Antigua Bodega
Castañeda** €
Traditional Map E3
C/Elvira 5, 18010
Tel *958 22 97 06*
Authentic tapas bar with barrels,
beams and colourful tiles. Feast
on Trevélez mountain ham, squid
and sardines, and enjoy a chilled
fino on the side.

**GRANADA: Restaurante
Carmela** €
Modern Map E3
*Calle Colcha, 13 (Corner of
Pavaneras), 18009*
Tel *958 22 57 94*
Cheery restaurant serving playful
versions of classic Andalucían
cuisine. Start with *croquetas de
morcilla con cebolla caramelizada*
(black pudding croquettes with
caramelized onions).

GRANADA: Tragalios €
Modern Map E3
Calle San Matías 21, 18009
Tel *685 19 37 41* **Closed** *15 Jan–
5 Feb, Mon*
Colourful restaurant with
innovative interpretations of
regional fare, including Iberian
pork, aged beef, fresh fish and
plenty of local produce.

**GRANADA: Carmen del
San Miguel** €€
Traditional Map E3
Plaza Torres Bermejas 3, 18009
Tel *958 22 67 23* **Closed** *Sun eve,
all day Sun in summer*
Attractive terrace restaurant
overlooking the Alhambra,
serving up traditional dishes made
from fresh market produce.

GRANADA: Chikito €€
Regional Map E3
Plaza del Campillo 9, 18009
Tel *958 22 33 64* **Closed** *Wed*
Attractive tapas bar-restaurant
built on the site of a former
Garcia Lorca haunt. Be brave and
dig into the tortilla Sacromonte –
omelette with marrow, brains,
herbs and bull's testicles!

**GRANADA: Mirador de
Mirayma** €€
Traditional Map E3
C/Pianista Gracia Carrillo 2, 18010
Tel *958 22 82 90* **Closed** *Sun eve*
This delightful patio restaurant
inside the Albaicín offers great

Charming outdoor seating at the popular Ruta del Veleta, Granada

city views. Try the fresh *remojón*
(salad with salted cod, olives and
orange) and *salmorejo* (soup).

DK Choice

**GRANADA: Restaurante
Damasqueros** €€
Modern Map E3
C/Damasqueros 3 (El Realejo), 18009
Tel *958 21 05 50* **Closed** *Sun eve,
Mon*
An award-winning tapas bar,
Restaurante Damasqueros
serves modern interpretations
of traditional fare. The rack of
lamb with *migas* (fried
breadcrumbs), grapes and
melon is a tasty favourite, and
you can't go wrong with one
of the risottos or *guisos* (stews).

GRANADA: Ruta del Azafrán €€
Fusion Map E3
Paseo del Padre Manjón 1, 18010
Tel *958 22 68 82* **Closed** *24 Dec*
This neat, modern restaurant
beside the Darro River serves
an eclectic range of dishes,
including seafood, vegetarian,
Italian and Arabic food.

Place settings at upmarket restaurant
La Finca, Loja

GRANADA: Ruta del Veleta €€€
Fusion Map E3
*Ctra Sierra Nevada 136, km 5,4. Cenes
de la Vega, 18190*
Tel *958 48 61 34* **Closed** *Sun eve*
Feast on dishes such as roast kid,
seasonal game and good seafood
at this popular regional restaurant.

**HUÉRCAL DE ALMERÍA:
Marhaba** €€
Fusion Map F3
Calle Antonio Cano 28, 04009
Tel *950 53 06 36* **Closed** *Sun & Mon*
Moroccan cuisine with Spanish
influences is well presented in
this elegant restaurant.

LOJA: La Finca €€€
Traditional Map D3
*Hotel La Bobadilla, Ctra Salinas-
Villanueva de Tapia (A-333), km 65.5,
18300*
Tel *958 32 18 61* **Closed** *Sun & Mon
May–Jul*
Delicious seafood, meat and
vegetable dishes – all made using
local ingredients – are served here.

MOTRIL: Tropical €€
Regional Map E3
Avda Rodriguez Acosta 23, 18600.
Tel *958 60 04 50* **Closed** *Sun, Jun*
Friendly seaside inn serving
classic Andalucían fare. Try the
lobster and rice stew.

**ROQUETAS DE MAR:
Alejandro** €€€
Seafood/Fusion Map F3
Avda Antonio Machado 32, 04740
Tel *950 32 24 08* **Closed** *Sun, Mon*
Boasting a Michelin star, this
restaurant specializes in exquisite
seafood fusion dishes. Splash out
on the shellfish tasting menu.

VERA: Terraza Carmona €€
Regional Map F3
C/del Mar 1, 04620
Tel *950 39 07 60* **Closed** *Mon*
Award-winning restaurant
specializing in regional dishes such
as seasonal wild boar with olives.

For more information on types of restaurants *see p221*

SHOPS AND MARKETS

Shopping in Andalucía is a highly pleasurable business, particularly if you approach it in a typically Spanish manner. Here, shopping fits in with the climate, always respects the siesta and is meant to be an unhurried, leisurely activity, punctuated with frequent breaks for coffee and tapas.

While a number of European chain stores and franchises appear all over Spain, the towns and villages of the south are refreshingly full of shops and businesses that are unique to the area. The region is renowned for its high-quality, traditional arts and crafts, and there is an overwhelming choice of ceramics, leather goods, marquetry, jewellery in filigree silver, flamenco-inspired accessories and sweets and biscuits.

World-famous wines can be had from the *bodegas* of Jerez, Montilla, Málaga and Sanlúcar de Barrameda. A visit to a *bodega*, an experience in itself, is the best way to become familiar with the variety of wines on offer.

Many shops still provide a charming personal service. Although few assistants speak English, most are very obliging.

Calle Sierpes, one of the busiest shopping streets in Seville

When to Shop

Spanish shops tend to close during the afternoon siesta (except for department stores and touristy souvenir shops in the large towns). Most shops open at 9:30am and close at 1:30pm. They usually reopen about 4:30pm or 5pm, and stay open until around 8pm. These times will obviously vary from shop to shop; boutiques, for example, rarely open before 10am. Times also tend to vary during summer – some shops close altogether in the afternoon heat, while others will stay open later than usual, in order to take full advantage of the large numbers of visitors.

Many shops – especially if they are in small towns – close on Saturday afternoons. This practice, however, is now gradually disappearing. Sales generally take place in January and July, though shops may also sometimes offer pre-Christmas discounts or start their sales in late December.

How to Pay

It is still customary among Spaniards to pay in cash. While many shops, especially the larger stores, now accept major credit cards, few take traveller's cheques.

You are entitled to exchange goods if you can produce a receipt, although this does not apply to items bought in a sale. Large shops and department stores tend to give credit notes rather than cash refunds. It is a good idea to check the shop's policy with a sales assistant before you buy anything.

One of several styles of plate made in Seville

VAT Exemption

Visitors to Spain who come from countries outside the European Union can claim a refund of sales tax (*IVA*, pronounced "eeva" in Spanish) on items bought at large department stores such as **Cortefiel** and **El Corte Inglés**. For each item that you purchase costing more than €90.16 you need to collect a form from the store's central cash desk. You should have this stamped both as you leave Spain and on re-entering your own country. You then need to return the stamped form to the shop where the purchase was made, which, in turn, will send you a cheque refunding the sales tax on the items you bought.

An array of fans at Albanicos Díaz, Calle Sierpes, Seville

Stylish hats from Sombrerería Herederos de J Russi in Córdoba

Shopping in Seville

Seville is a charming city in which to shop, offering the buyer a unique concoction of old-style regional crafts and good modern design.

The district that surrounds Calle Tetuán and the pedestrianized Calle Sierpes (see p78) is the place to visit for the best of Seville's old and new shops. This is a smart area of bustling streets, where you will find an eclectic range of goods.

For stylish, fashion-forward attire for the whole family, head to **Massimo Dutti**. Stylish **Loewe** makes exquisite luggage and leather bags, clothes and accessories in striking colours, while **Purificación Garcia** sells chic clothes.

The streets around the Plaza Nueva are full of shops such as **Nuria Cobo**, **Paco Rodriguez** and **Adolfo Domínguez**, selling stylish, tailored clothes and shoes; and quaint shops that sell religious objects. Ornate earrings, colourful headpieces and other one-of-a-kind acces-sories can be found in **Naif Tocados**. For typically Andalusian items, such as elaborate fans, go to **Albanicos Diaz**; for top-quality cordobés hats to **Maquedano** and for hand-embroidered shawls, to **Juan Foronda**.

Around the Barrio de Santa Cruz is a range of interesting shops. Among these are **Casa Rodríguez** and **Velasco**, which specialize in trimmings for church robes and religious

images. For the most exquisite baby clothes, head for **Larrana** and look for Agua de Sevilla perfumes in **El Corte Inglés**. The **Botellas y Latas** is a small grocers stocking gourmet Spanish food and wines. The Calle Hernando Colón has a few curious shops for collectors of everything from old children's toys to stamps, while **El Postigo**, in the El Arenal area, is an arts and crafts centre with a good selection of handmade items on sale.

Sevillarte, which is close to Real Alcázar (see pp86–7), and **Martián** sell attractive ceramics for both utility and decoration.

For some of Andalucía's finest ceramics, head for Triana (see p106). Look out in particular for **Cerámica Triana**, **Antonio Campos** and the many small work-shops along the Calle Covadonga.

Triana is also a good area for purchasing flamboyant flamenco outfits,

Colourful, hand painted tiles at Cerámica Santa Ana

while at **Juan Osete** you can buy a marvellous range of feria accessories. Anyone who claims to be a serious collector of antiques must make a point of calling at **Antigüedades El Museo**, which has a fine collection of furniture, decorative art and jewellery.

At **FÉLIX** you can find historical posters from spring festivals and bullfights of years gone by.

Muebles Ceballos, situated on the busy Calle de la Feria, is one of several shops in the Seville area that specializes in traditionally made wicker-work items.

Córdoba

Córdoba presents plenty of options for the shopper. Perhaps the most fascinating shopping area is within the old narrow streets of the Judería (see p144). Here the **Zoco Municipal** runs an interesting selection of craft workshops making Córdoban specialities such as filigree silver jewellery, hand-painted ceramics, leather-ware and wonderful, award-winning painted masks. Ceramics, leatherware and woodwork can also be found at **Artesanos Cordobeses**. The area surrounding the Mezquita (see p148) is packed with souvenir shops, which apart from the expected tourist trinkets, sell a range of fine handicrafts. Of these, **Meryan** specializes in embossed leather goods.

At the guitar workshop of **Manuel Reyes Maldonado** you can purchase highest quality, custom-built guitars, many of which end up in the hands of internationally renowned musicians.

One of the most celebrated hat-makers in the whole of Spain is the **Sombrerería Herederos de J Russi**. You can purchase a typical, flat-topped córdobes hat here for a great deal less than the price that would be asked in Madrid or Seville.

Manuel Reyes Maldonado in his guitar workshop in Córdoba

Marquetry in the making in a
Granada workshop

Granada

The characteristically cold winters
ensure that shops in Granada
keep a range of winter clothes
and shoes. **Zara** stocks both
menswear and womenswear,
and **Cortefiel** is a quality department store specializing in
clothing. With the Sierra
Nevada close by, skiwear
is sold in some depart-
ment stores as well
as specialist shops.

The city centre
is full of surprises,
among them the
Mercado Árabe, a
long gallery packed
with shops that sell
Moroccan-inspired
clothing and acces-
sories. **Artesanía Beas**
specializes in marquetry, while
Mantillas Granada offers handmade lace *mantillas*. **El Artesano
Granada** has handmade leather
bags and accessories. For
Flamenco-inspired ornaments,
head to **Cándido Puerto
Artesanía y Complementos**,
which sells handmade *mantillas*,
fans and earrings. In the streets
around the Gran Vía are *platerías* –
smart shops selling silverware.

Basketware from Alhama
de Granada

Andalucía

In Andalucía people frequently
make special trips to towns
famed for one particular item,
such as olive oil, wine, rugs or
furniture. If you have time to
explore, the region offers many
local, handmade specialities.

The finest virgin olive oils
come from Baena *(see p151)*
and Segura de la Sierra *(see
p160)*. Some of the best olive
oil in Sevilla province is sold
in the village of Ginés. Many
monasteries make and sell
their own sweets and biscuits.

There are several *bodegas*
which are worth a visit, namely
those in Jerez *(see p166)*, in
Sanlúcar de Barrameda *(see
p166)*, in Montilla *(see p151)* and
in Málaga town *(see p182*.
Botijos – spouted
ceramic drinking
jugs – are a local
speciality of the
town of La Rambla,
30 km (19 miles)
south of Córdoba.
In Córdoba
province, Lucena
(see p151) is a good
place to buy ceramics
and wrought ironwork.
Ronda *(see pp178–9)* has a
few shops selling rustic-style
furniture. In Guarromán in Jaén
province, antique furniture is
sold at **Antigüedades Trastos
Viejos**, which is housed in an
old *cortijo* (farmhouse).

In Granada province, the
villages of Las Alpujarras *(see
p204)* are famous for *jarapas*,
(rag rugs), basketwork and
locally grown medicinal herbs.

Fruit and vegetable market in
Vélez Blanco *(see p205)*

Just north of Granada, in the
small village of Jún, **Cerámica
Miguel Ruiz Jiménez** collects
and sells some of the finest
ceramics and pottery made all
over Andalucía.

Exquisite hand-embroidered
shawls are sold by **Ángeles
Espinar** in Villamanrique de
Condesa, outside Seville.

Markets

The markets held in most
Andalucían towns offer a
wonderful opportunity to try
local food specialities, including
a wide range of sausages,
cheeses and cured ham.

Most markets tend to sell a
little of everything. However,
Seville does have a few
specialized markets. These
include an antiques and bric-
a-brac market, which is held
in Calle Feria on Thursdays.

On Sundays, Los Pájaros pet
market takes place in Plaza del
Alfalfa, and stamps and coins
are traded at Plaza del Cabildo.
All manner of bric-a-brac are
sold on Charco de la Pava in La
Cartuja, and a bigger *rastro* (flea
market) is held in the Parque
Alcosa, northeast of the centre.

The food markets in Plaza
de la Encarnación and El Arenal
are both very good.

Córdoba has an absorbing
flea market on Saturdays and
Sundays at the 16th-century
arcaded Plaza de la Corredera.

On the Costa del Sol, bric-a-
brac markets and car boot sales
are popular. The best are held
on Tuesday and Saturday mornings at Fuengirola fairground.

Pottery stall at the Plaza de la Corredera market in Córdoba

DIRECTORY

Seville

DEPARTMENT STORES

El Corte Inglés
Pl Duque de la Victoria 10.
Map 1 C5 (5 C2).
Tel 954 59 70 00.
🆆 elcorteingles.es

Cortefiel
C/Tetuan 18–20.
Map 5 C3.
Tel 954 21 24 76.
🆆 cortefiel.com

FASHION AND ACCESSORIES

Adolfo Domínguez
Pl Duque de la Victoria 8.
Map 1 C5 (5 C2).
Tel 954 21 68 86.
🆆 adolfodominguez.com

Loewe
Plaza Nueva 12.
Map 3 B1 (5 C3).
Tel 954 22 52 53.
🆆 loewe.com

Maquedano
Calle Sierpes 40.
Map 3 C1 (5 C3).
Tel 954 56 47 71.
🆆 maquedano.com

Massimo Dutti
Velazquez 13.
Map 3 C1 (5 C3).
Tel 954 22 57 72.
🆆 massimodutti.com

Naif Tocados
Calle San Eloy 27.
Map 3 B1 (5 C3).
Tel 677 78 20 67.
🆆 naiftocados.es

Purificación García
Plaza Nueva 8.
Map 3 B1 (5 C3).
Tel 954 50 11 29.
🆆 purificacion garcia.com

CHILDREN'S CLOTHES

Larrana
Calle Blanca de los Ríos 4.
Map 3 C1 (6 D3).
Tel 954 21 52 80.
🆆 larrana.es

SHOES

Nuria Cobo
C/Méndez Núñez esq,
Rosario 16.
Map 3 B1 (5 C3).
Tel 954 21 13 24.
🆆 nuriacobo.com

Paco Rodríguez
C/Tetuán 5–7.
Map 3 C1 (5 C3).
Tel 954 21 66 06.
🆆 calzadospa corodriguez.com

FLAMENCO

Albanicos Díaz
Calle Sierpes 71.
Map 3 C1 (5 C3).
Tel 954 22 81 02.
🆆 abanicsodesevilla.net

Juan Foronda
Calle Sierpes 79.
Map 3 C1 (5 C3).
Tel 954 21 40 50.
🆆 juanforonda.com

Juan Osete
Calle de Castilla 10.
Map 3 A1.
Tel 954 34 33 31.

Roberto Garrudo
C/ Córdoba 9.
Map 3 C1 (6 D3).
Tel 954 21 84 19.

RELIGIOUS OBJECTS

Casa Rodríguez
Calle Francos 35.
Map 3 C1 (6 D3).
Tel 954 22 78 42.
🆆 casa-rodriguez.es

Velasco
Calle Chapineros 4 (off
Calle Francos).
Map 3 C1 (5 C3).
Tel 954 21 83 38.

ARTS AND CRAFTS

Antonio Campos
C/Alfarería 22, Triana.
Map 3 A2.
Tel 651 88 19 20.
🆆 alfareriantonio campos.blogspot.com.es

Cerámica Triana
Calle Callao 14, Triana.
Map 3 A2 (1 A4).
Tel 954 33 21 79.

FÉLIX
Avda de la Constitución,
26 Sevilla, 41001.
Map 3 C2 (5 C4).
Tel 954 21 80 26.

Martián
Calle Sierpes 74.
Map 3 C1 (5 C3).
Tel 954 21 34 13.

Muebles Ceballos
Calle Feria 49
(near Calle de Relator).
Map 2 D4.
Tel 954 90 17 54.

El Postigo
Calle Arfe s/n. **Map** 3 B2
(5 C4). **Tel** 954 56 00 13.
🆆 mercadodeartesania elpostigo.com

Sevillarte
Calle Vida 13. **Map** 3 C2 (6
D5). **Tel** 954 21 03 91.
🆆 sevillarte.com

ART AND ANTIQUES

Antigüedades El Museo
Plaza del Museo 4. **Map** 1
B5 (5 B2). **Tel** 954 56 01 28.
🆆 antiguedades elmuseo.com

FOOD AND WINE

Botellas y Latas
Calle Regina 14.
Map 2 D5 (2 D1).
Tel 954 29 31 22.

Córdoba

ARTS AND CRAFTS

Artesanos Cordobeses
Calle Judios, s/n (Zoco).
Tel 957 20 40 33.
🆆 artesaniade cordoba.com/en

Manuel Reyes Maldonado
Calle Armas 6.
Tel 957 47 91 16.

Meryan
Calleja de las Flores 2.
Tel 957 47 59 02.
🆆 meryancor.com

Sombrerería Herederos de J Russi
Calle Conde de Cárdenas
1, Gondomar 4.
Tel 957 47 79 53.
🆆 rusiherederos.com

Zoco Municipal
Calle Judíos s/n.
Tel 957 29 05 75.

Granada

FASHION, SHOES AND ACCESSORIES

El Artesano Granada
Calle Salamanca 11.
Tel 661 11 91 02.

Cándido Puerto Artesanía y Complementos
Calle Salamanca 13.
Tel 958 25 49 95.
🆆 mantones.com

Cortefiel
Gran Vía de Colón 1.
Tel 958 22 35 47.
🆆 cortefiel.es

Zara
Calle Recogidas 10–12.
Tel 958 25 25 04.

ARTS AND CRAFTS

Artesanía Beas
Calle de Santa Rosalía 20.
Tel 958 81 37 58.
🆆 artesaniabeas.com

Mantillas Granada
Carretera de Murcia 120,
Albaicín. **Tel** 958 27 13 28.
🆆 mantillasgranada.com

Mercado Árabe
La Alcaicería.

Andalucía

Ángeles Espinar
Calle Pascual Márquez 8,
Villamanrique de
Condesa, Sevilla.
Tel 955 75 56 20
(call ahead).
🆆 angeles espinar.com

Antigüedades Trastos Viejos
Autovía E5 km 280,
Aldea de los Rios 1,
Guarromán, Jaén.
Tel 953 61 51 26.
🆆 trastosviejos.com

Cerámica Miguel Ruiz Jiménez
Camino Viejo de Jún s/n,
Jún, Granada.
Tel 958 41 40 77.

What to Buy in Andalucía

The strong and vibrant culture of Andalucía is reflected in the items available in the region's markets and shops. Andalucía has a long tradition of arts and crafts, so its towns and villages produce a surprising range of unique, often exquisite, handmade goods. Many towns have specialities; for example, Granada is famous for marquetry and Moorish-style painted ceramics; Seville for fans and *mantillas*; Jerez, Montilla and Málaga for their renowned wines; while Córdoba specializes in filigree silver, leather work and guitars.

Traditional glazed earthenware pots from Úbeda *(see pp158–9)* in the province of Jaén

The Ceramics of Andalucía

The rich, terracotta soil of Andalucía has been utilized for centuries in the creation of practical and decorative ceramics. The variety encompasses simple earthenware cooking dishes *(cazuelas)*, drinking jugs *(botijos)*, pots *(tinajas)*, decorative painted tiles *(azulejos)*, and kitchen and tableware. You can buy them from workshops or, more cheaply, from local markets.

Ceramic plate painted in traditional colours

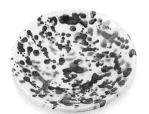
Plate from Ronda spattered in blue and green

Bowl from Córdoba in a traditional design

Replicas of 18th-century tiles from Triana *(see p104)*

Leather Goods

Leather goods such as bags and belts can be bought all over Andalucía. Embossed leather, however, is a speciality of the city of Córdoba *(see pp144–50)*.

Rugs

Andalucían rug-making skills have developed over centuries. The most famous rug-making area is in the Alpujarras *(see pp204–5)*, where rugs are made in various fibres, including cotton and wool, and in colour schemes in which earth colours and blues predominate.

Inlaid Boxes

Marquetry is produced in Granada *(see pp194–202)*. Craftsmen make furniture, boxes, and other items inlaid with ivory and coloured woods in Moorish designs.

Handmade Fans

A classic souvenir from Andalucía, a fan is useful in the searing heat. The most exclusive are wooden, carved and painted by hand.

Castanets

Castanets, a classic flamenco musical instrument, can be bought in a medley of sizes, made of wood or plastic.

Guitars

In the land of flamenco, guitars are a speciality. Workshops in Córdoba produce top-quality, custom-made guitars, many of which are destined for famous guitarists.

Mantillas

A *mantilla* is a headdress of lace draped over a large and ornate comb which is crafted from tortoiseshell or made in plastic.

The Flavours of Andalucía

Andalucían gastronomy reflects locally grown produce. An astonishing range of olive oils is available, and the region's grapes are made into sherry vinegars, as well as some of Spain's most distinctive wines (*see p226*). Almonds are used to make delicious sweets, such as turrón, a type of nougat.

Olive oil from the provinces of Córdoba and Sevilla

Sherry wine vinegars produced by sherry *bodegas*

Yemas, sweets produced by nuns in the Convento de San Leandro *(see p81)*

Marmalade from the Convento de Santa Paula *(see p94)* in Seville

Herbs and Spices

Almost 800 years of Moorish occupation in Andalucía left a distinctive mark on the region's cuisine. Many dishes are flavoured with fragrant spices once imported from the East, such as cumin, coriander, paprika, and strands of saffron. Markets are the best place to buy exotic spices and locally grown herbs, which are sold loose by weight.

Saffron threads

Pimentón (paprika)

Coriander seeds

Cumin seeds

ENTERTAINMENT IN ANDALUCÍA

In Andalucía there is almost always a lively buzz in the streets, and activities such as bar-hopping and people-watching can provide enough entertainment in themselves to fill up any spare moment of your holiday.

But there is also plenty more going on. Southern Spain boasts a busy programme of traditional fiestas *(see pp42–3)*, as well as a variety of annual cultural festivals *(see pp38–41)*, theatre performances and sporting fixtures. There is also music and dance in abundance – Andalucía is, after all, the home of flamenco.

Given the mild climate, many events take place out of doors; in summer, when daytime temperatures can soar to up to 45°C (113°F), they do not start until late in the evening, when the air is cooler. Many cultural events and concerts begin at around midnight.

Flamenco guitarist playing at a festival at the Teatro de la Maestranza, Seville

Practical Information

Tourist information offices are the best places to find out what is on locally, but there are also two useful listings magazines worth looking out for: *El Giraldillo* (published in Seville) and *Qué Hacer/What's On* (published in Málaga). Both appear monthly, cover all of Andalucía and are free.

Each major city has its own commercial websites offering a wealth of local information, but certain websites covering the whole of Spain, notably **Guía del Ocio**, are also worth consulting; just choose the province in which you are interested from the drop-down menu.

Booking Tickets

It is usually possible to book tickets for major sports events, operas, concerts and festivals in advance at the venue's booking office, by phone or online. Alternatively, use an agency that specializes in booking tickets for all entertainments, such as **Ticketmaster** and **Entradas.com.**

Flamenco

Seville and Jerez de la Frontera claim to be the birthplaces of flamenco, the traditional music and dance of Andalucía *(see pp32–3)*. Both cities have *tablaos*, bars and restaurants with floor-shows where the admission usually includes dinner or at least a drink. In Seville, it is best to look for venues in the Barrio de Santa Cruz. A good starting point is the **Museo del Baile Flamenco** *(see p79)* or **La Casa de la Memoria de Al Andalus**, both of which feature intimate, quality performances.

Jerez has a **Centro Andaluz de Flamenco**, as well as several *tablaos*. In Granada, there are traditional flamenco venues in Sacromonte *(see p197)* and the Albaicín – among them, **Sala Albayzín** and **Zambra María La Canastera**. Córdoba also has some flamenco bars, notably **El Cardenal** and **La Bulería**.

The two main flamenco festivals are Seville's **Bienal de Flamenco**, which is held in theatres all over the city in even-numbered years, and Córdoba's **Concurso Nacional de Arte Flamenco**, which happens every third year (2019, 2022 and so on).

Theatre

Most drama staged in Andalucía is in Spanish, but there are occasional performances by visiting international companies or mime artists. The theatre season includes not only plays, but also classical music, dance and opera. Seville's main theatres are the **Teatro de la Maestranza** *(see p72)*, the **Teatro Lope de Vega** *(see p101)* and the **Teatro Central**.

In Córdoba, the place to go is the **Gran Teatro**. Granada's two main theatres are the **Teatro Alhambra** and the **Teatro Isabel La Católica**. Málaga has the **Teatro Cánovas** and the **Teatro Cervantes**.

Gran Teatro, Córdoba, one of the city's leading venues for theatre

Rosario Flores, a famous Andalucían singing star, performing at one of her concerts

Cinema

Most foreign films shown in main-stream cinemas in Andalucía are usually dubbed into Spanish. Original-version (VO for *version original*) films are shown in cinemas such as **Avenida 5 Cines** in Seville, the **Filmoteca de Andalucía** in Córdoba and the **Complejo Cinematográfico Gran Marbella** on the Costa del Sol. From June to late August, you can also attend a *cine de verano*, an open-air "summer cinema".

Opera and Classical Music

In Seville, most operas, including those by prestigious international companies, are performed at either the **Teatro Lope de Vega** *(see p101)* or the **Teatro de la Maestranza** *(see p72)*. For something less highbrow, Spain has its own brand of operetta, *zarzuela*.

As for classical music, all the main cities maintain their own orchestras (such as the **Real Orquesta Sinfónica de Sevilla**). Granada is great for classical music. As well as having the **Centro Cultural Manuel de Falla** as a venue, it hosts the **Festival Internacional de Música y Danza** *(see p39)*, during which concerts are held against the backdrop of the Alhambra.

Other Live Music

Touring international rock and pop stars mostly play their Spanish dates in Madrid or Barcelona, but they sometimes make it to Seville or other cities in Andalucía. Such concerts usually take place in football stadiums and bullrings. Spain has its own thriving rock-pop scene. Andalucían musicians, in particular, have drawn on their flamenco roots to create distinctive fusions between musical genres.

Two other great influences on the contemporary music of Andalucía are North Africa and Latin America. Jazz also has a devoted public in Andalucía: Seville has the **Naima Jazz Café** and Granada has the **Festival de Jazz**. To find out where the up-and-coming acts are playing, ask around or keep an eye out for flyers.

La tuna, traditional singers in Santa Cruz, Seville

Another interesting musical tradition is represented by *la tuna*: groups of students dressed as minstrels playing lutes and mandolins and singing serenades in streets and squares.

Nightlife

Nights out in Andalucía begin late and can easily go on until dawn. The first stop is often a *bar de copas* (also called a *pub*), which differs from a tapas bar in that no food is served and spirits replace wine and beer for drinking. Some such bars have DJs at weekends. The next stop is a *discoteca*, which may open at midnight but not fill up for a couple of hours. There are clubs in the city centres, but many are on industrial estates or outside of town, where the noise won't bother residents.

Where to go depends on your age, your musical tastes and your sexual orientation – each city has a few gay and lesbian clubs. If you aren't concerned about being seen in the hippest places, reliably fun areas to go bar-hopping in are the Santa Cruz quarter in Seville, the Judería in Córdoba and around the Plaza del Realejo and the lower Albaicín (especially the Carrera del Darro and the Paseo de los Tristes) in Granada.

The summer nightlife of the holiday resorts on the Costa del Sol is completely different from that of the cities of Andalucía. Here you'll still find *bares de copa* and *discotecas*, but also many places geared to foreign tourists.

For a smart night out, try one of Andalucía's casinos. Don't dress too casually, and take your passport with you.

A display of flamenco dancing in a bar in Seville

Real Escuela Andaluza de Arte Ecuestre, Jerez de la Frontera

Bullfighting

The **Maestranza** bullring *(see p72)* in Seville is mythical among bullfighting fans, and some of the most important bullfights in Spain are held here during the Feria de Abril *(see p42)*. Ronda *(see pp178–9)*, Córdoba and Granada also have their own bullrings and a renowned season.

The season usually runs from April to October. Tickets are sold at the bullring's booking office.

Tile for Seville's Betis football club

Football

Football is the most popular spectator sport in Spain. Seville has two rival teams, FC Sevilla, based at the **Estadio Ramón Sánchez Pizjuán**, and Betis, who play at the **Estadio Benito Villamarín**. Other successful teams in the region are Cádiz, Málaga and Recreativo de Huelva (the oldest football club in Spain).

The Spanish football league has three divisions, with league matches being played on Sunday (sometimes Saturday) evenings from September to June. During the season, teams also compete in an eliminatory tournament for the Copa del Rey (King's Cup) and for international trophies; such matches are usually played mid-week. Important fixtures are televised, although some are only shown on pay-per-view channels. To see a live game, it is advisable to book ahead at the stadium or online.

Entertainment for Children

In Spain, children go wherever adults go at just about any time of day or night. If you want to take yours for a treat, there are several options. **Isla Mágica** *(see p108)* in Seville is Andalucía's biggest theme park, while **Tivoli World** is the largest amusement park on the Costa del Sol. Every city and strip of coast has its water park designed specifically for older children *(see p249)*. A cable car, the **Teleférico Benalmádena**, takes off from beside Tivoli World to the top of Mount Calamorro, 800 m (2,600 ft) above sea level. There is another good cable-car ride in Gibraltar *(see pp174–5)*. In Seville, a boat trip down the river can be fun, as can be the trip across the Bay of Cádiz in a catamaran *(see p169)*. Horse and carriages travel round the streets in Marbella, Córdoba and Seville, and most beach resorts also have road trains.

In Córdoba, children can let off steam at **Ciudad de los Niños**, a large park with more than 30 slides, swings, trampolines and other attractions. It is located directly behind El Parque Zoológico de Córdoba and access is free with a zoo entry pass. The park is free for kids under the age of five.

The desert in the centre of Almería region was once used as a film set for westerns *(see p208)*, and kids love the shootouts staged by the small Wild West town of **Oasys Parque Temático Mini-Hollywood**, near Tabernas. Another good show – this time of performing horses – is put on by the **Real Escuela Andaluza de Arte Ecuestre** *(see p166)* in Jerez de la Frontera. Jerez also has Andalucía's best collection of exotic animals in the **Zoobotánico Jerez**; the safari park **Selwo Aventura**, outside Estepona, is also good. There are aquariums at Roquetas del Mar *(see p208)* in Almería and Benalmádena, a town that also offers **Selwo Marina**, Andalucía's only dolphinarium and ice penguinarium. The **Acuario de Sevilla** in Seville is another large aquarium.

The port of Gibraltar from the vantage point of a cable car

DIRECTORY

Practical Information

El Giraldillo
W elgiraldillo.es

Guía del Ocio
W guiadelocio.com

Booking Tickets

Entradas.com
Tel 902 65 65 79.
W entradas.com

Ticketmaster
Tel 902 48 84 88.
W ticketmaster.es

Flamenco

SEVILLE

Bienal de Flamenco
Tel 955 47 28 22.
W labienal.com

Casa de la Memoria de Al Andalus
C/ Cuna 6. **Map** 3 C1 (6 D2).
Tel 954 56 06 70.

CÓRDOBA

La Bulería
Calle Pedro López 3.
Tel 957 48 38 39.

El Cardenal
Calle Buen Pastor 2.
Tel 691 21 79 22.
W tablaocardenal.es

Concurso Nacional de Arte Flamenco
Tel 957 48 02 37.

GRANADA

Sala Albayzín
Carretera de Murcia, Mirador San Cristóbal. **Tel** 958 80 46 46. W flamen coalbayzin.com

Zambra María La Canastera
Camino del Sacromonte 89. **Tel** 958 12 11 83.
W granadainfo.com/canastera

JEREZ DE LA FRONTERA

Centro Andaluz de Flamenco
Palacio Pemartin, Plaza San Juan 1. **Tel** 956 90 21 34. W centroandaluz deflamenco.es

Theatre

SEVILLE

Teatro Central
C/ José Gálvez 6, Isla de la Cartuja. **Map** 1 C2. **Tel** 955 54 21 55. W juntade andalucia.es/cultura/teatros/teatro-central

CÓRDOBA

Gran Teatro
Avenida Gran Capitán 3.
Tel 957 48 02 37.
W teatrocordoba.es

GRANADA

Teatro Alhambra
Calle Molinos 56.
Tel 958 02 80 00.

Teatro Isabel La Católica
Calle Acera del Casino 7.
Tel 958 22 29 07.

MÁLAGA

Teatro Cánovas
Plaza de El Ejido 5.
Tel 951 30 89 02.

Teatro Cervantes
Calle Ramos Marín.
Tel 952 22 41 09.
W teatrocervantes.com

Cinema

SEVILLE

Avenida 5 Cines
Marqués de Paradas 15.
Tel 954 29 30 25.

CÓRDOBA

Filmoteca de Andalucía
Medina y Corella 5. **Tel** 957 10 36 27. W filmotecade andalucia.es

MARBELLA

Complejo Cinematográfico Gran Marbella
Av Julio Iglesias s/n. **Tel** 951 19 66 65. W cineste atrogoya.com

Opera and Classical Music

SEVILLE

Real Orquesta Sinfónica de Sevilla
Tel 954 56 15 36.
W rossevilla.es

Teatro de la Maestranza
Paseo de Colón 22. **Map** 3 B2 (5 C5). **Tel** 954 22 33 44. W teatrodelamae stranza.es

GRANADA

Centro Cultural Manuel de Falla
Paseo de los Mártires.
Tel 958 22 21 88.
W manueldefalla.org

Festival Internacional de Música y Danza
Corral del Carbón, 2ª planta Mariana Pineda s/n.
Tel 958 27 62 00.
W granadafestival.org

Other Live Music

SEVILLE

Naima Jazz Café
Calle Trajano 47. **Map** 1 C5 (5 C1). **Tel** 954 38 24 85.

GRANADA

Festival de Jazz de Granada
Calle Mariana Pineda 8.
Tel 958 21 59 80.
W jazzgranada.es

Nightlife

SEVILLE

Bar 1987
Alameda de Hércules 93.

Gran Casino Aljarafe
Avenida de la Arboleda, Tomares. **Tel** 902 42 42 22. W grancasinoaljarafe.com

Rejoneo
Calle Betis 31.
Tel 658 80 90 03.

BENALMÁDENA

Casino Torrequebrada
Avenida del Sol. **Tel** 952 57 73 00. W casino torrequebrada.com

GRANADA

Paripé
Calle Moras 1.
Tel 629 42 38 55.

MARBELLA

Casino Nueva Andalucía
Hotel Andalucía Plaza.
Tel 952 81 40 00.
W casinomarbella.com

PUERTO DE SANTA MARÍA

Casino Bahía de Cádiz
Tel 956 87 10 42.
W casinobahiade cadiz.es

Bullfighting

CÓRDOBA

Plaza de Toros
Avenida de Gran Vía Parque. **Tel** 957 23 25 07.

GRANADA

Plaza de Toros
Avenida Doctor Olóriz 25.
Tel 958 27 24 51.

Football

Estadio Benito Villamarín (Betis)
Avenida Heliópolis, Seville. **Tel** 902 19 19 07.
W realbetisbalompie.es

Estadio Ramón Sánchez Pizjuán (Sevilla FC)
Avenida Eduardo Dato, Seville. **Map** 4 F2.
Tel 902 51 00 11.
W sevillafc.es

Entertainment for Children

BENALMÁDENA

Selwo Marina
Parque de la Paloma.
Tel 902 19 04 82.
W selwomarina.es

Teleférico Benalmádena
Explanada de Tivoli.
Tel 902 19 04 82.
W teleferico benalmadena.com

Tivoli World
Avda de Tivoli s/n.
Tel 952 57 70 16.
W tivoli.es

CÓRDOBA

Ciudad de los Niños
Avenida de Linneo s/n.
Tel 650 54 78 65.

ESTEPONA

Selwo Aventura
Avda Selwo s/n, Autovía A7 km 162.5.
Tel 902 19 04 82.
W selwo.es

JEREZ DE LA FRONTERA

Zoobotánico Jerez
C/ Madreselva s/n.
Tel 956 14 97 85.
W zoobotanico jerez.com

SEVILLE

Acuario de Sevilla
Muelle de las Delicias, Area Sur, Puerto de Sevilla.
Tel 955 44 15 41.
W acuariosevilla.es

TABERNAS

Oasys Parque Temático Mini-Hollywood
Carretera Nacional 340A, Km 464, Tabernas, Almería.
Tel 902 53 35 32.
W oasysparque tematico.com

OUTDOOR ACTIVITIES AND SPECIALIST HOLIDAYS

Andalucía has a perfect climate for enjoying a range of outdoor activities, with comparatively few cold or wet days, and reliable sunshine most of the year. Its coastline offers a great variety of water sports – from windsurfing on the Atlantic coast, to scuba diving in the clear, calm waters of the Mediterranean. Away from the seashore, there are many golf courses and some great countryside – mostly hilly or mountainous – suitable for hiking and horse riding. In winter, skiers head for Europe's southernmost winter-sport resort on the slopes of the Sierra Nevada.

Walking and Trekking

Andalucía has a huge variety of landscapes suitable for walking: from coastal fringes, through forests, to mountain ranges. Spring is the best time to be outdoors: temperatures are mild, and the landscape blossoms with wildflowers. Mid-summer is best avoided because of the extreme heat and the risk of dehydration.

Two popular areas for hiking are the Alpujarras *(see pp204–5)* and the Sierra de Grazalema *(see p176)*, but all of the region's nature reserves have marked footpaths.

Always carry a good map. The Spanish army (Servicio Geográfico del Ejército) produces a useful series of 1:50,000 maps, but the best are the 1:25,000-series maps published by the Centro Nacional de Información Geográfica (CNIG). Wear good walking shoes, preferably boots, and long trousers to avoid lacerations from spiky Mediterranean shrubs. Bring a hat and, if you are going to be gaining altitude, a warm jacket. Always carry drinking water.

For more advice, contact the **Federación Andaluza de Montañismo**. Companies such as **Authentic Adventures** *(see Specialist Holidays p250)* and **Spanish Steps** offer guided walks through the region.

Cycling

Andalucía's terrain is mainly mountainous, which discourages all but the hardiest cyclist. Added to this, there are few quiet backroads to use as alternatives to busy main roads. However, the trend of converting disused railway lines into "green ways" *(vía verdes)* has created 12 traffic-free cycling routes, such as the 55 km (34 mile) Via Verde del Aceite (Olive Oil Green Way) between Jaén and Alcaudete. To locate green ways, see the **Fundación de los Ferrocarriles Españoles** website. If you want to go on an organized cycling holiday with accommodation arranged for you, try **Biking Andalucía**.

Fishing

Andalucía offers good seafishing off its coasts as well as rather more limited opportunities for freshwater

Fishing at a beach on Andalucía's Mediterranean coast

fishing in its scattered reservoirs and rivers, such as in the Cazorla Nature Reserve *(see p160)*. For information about where to go and permits needed, contact the regional fishing association, the **Federación Andaluza de Pesca Deportiva**.

Wildlife and Birdwatching

The best place to get close to Andalucía's wildlife is the Doñana National Park *(see pp134–5)*, but other nature reserves in the region also offer good opportunities for wildflower- and bird-spotting. Contact **Iberian Wildlife** for tours. Several companies run whale-watching trips out of Tarifa harbour *(see p173)*; among them is the **Foundation for Information and Research on Marine Mammals**.

Equestrian Sports

The horse forms a proud part of Andalucía's traditions, as can be seen during Seville's April

Hiking down from the Sierra Nevada through the Alpujarras

feria *(see p42)*, the pilgrimage to El Rocío *(see p42)* and many other fiestas. The undisputed equestrian capital of Andalucía is Jerez de la Frontera *(see p166)*, home of the Real Escuela Andaluza de Arte Ecuestre, which stages shows on Tuesdays and Thursdays featuring dancing horses.

A day's trek on horseback can be a splendid way to get to know the countryside of Andalucía. There are stables everywhere that will organize anything from a brief outing to an extended riding holiday. Two of them are **Dallas Love** in the Alpujarras and **Los Alamos** on the Costa de la Luz. For all things to do with horses, the organization to contact is the **Federación Andaluza de Hípica**.

Horse riding on the deserted Atlantic beach of Zahara, near Cádiz

The stunning golf course at La Cala de Mijas, near the beaches of Málaga

Golf

Andalucía boasts more than 90 golf courses, mainly concentrated on the Costa del Sol (also known as the "Costa Golf", *see pp36–37*) and around the major cities. Most have 18 holes and are open to non-members on payment of a green fee; advance booking is recommended.

The largest golf club in Andalucía is **La Cala Resort**, which has three 18-hole courses and one six-hole course. Another outstanding course is the **Barceló Montecastillo Golf Resort**, in Jerez de la Frontera, which is used for the Volvo Masters and other important tournaments. To find your nearest golf course, consult the **Federación Andaluza de Golf**.

Tennis

Tennis is extremely popular in Andalucía. To find out where to play, ask around locally. Many large hotels have courts available for the use of guests, and there are also private clubs you can join. An inexpensive option is to book a court at the local sports centre. For more information, contact the **Federación Andaluza de Tenis.**

Water Sports

Water sports such as kayaking and waterskiing are available at all major resorts along the coast. Sea-going boats can be hired at most of the marinas. For information about sailing in the waters off Andalucía, contact the **Real Federación Española de Vela**.

Tarifa *(see p173)* has ideal conditions for wind- and kite-surfing; the Hurricane Hotel *(see p219)* will point you towards lessons and equipment rental.

The headlands at La Herradura, on the coast of Granada province, and around the Cabo de Gata in Almería are known for their scuba diving. The **Federación Española de Actividades Subacuáticas** will direct you to the nearest dive school, where you can try an introductory dive or sign up for an intensive course.

Andalucía also has ten water parks *(parques acuáticos)* especially aimed at children, with slides and wave pools. They are at Torre del Mar, Torremolinos, Granada, Mijas, Córdoba, Seville, Almuñecar (on the coast of Granada), Puerto de Santa María, Huelva and Vera (in Almería).

Air Sports

To find out where and how to hang-glide, balloon or parachute over Andalucía, contact the **Federación Andaluza de los Deportes Aéreos**.

Because of its normally reliable weather conditions, Andalucía is considered a good place for parachuting: **Skydive Spain** has its own drop zone near Seville and runs beginners' courses as well as taking clients on tandem jumps. For balloon trips, check the **Balloon Flights Spain** website for details.

Skiing

The **Sierra Nevada** *(see p203)* is Europe's southernmost skiing resort. Its base station is at 2,100 m (6,890 ft), and its highest run starts from 3,300 m (10,800 ft). The resort has 80 pistes, with a longest continual run of almost 6 km (4 miles) down the Pista del Águila.

Kite-surfing, a popular activity on the beaches of windy Tarifa

The impressive and atmospheric Arab baths in Granada

Naturism

Topless bathing is tacitly accepted at all resorts, most of which also have one or more discreet, officially recognized naturist beaches in a cove away from the main beach. **Vera Playa Club** in Almería is a hotel specifically for nudists, and **Costa Natura** near Estepona is a residential "village" also dedicated to naturism. For further information about naturism, contact the **Asociación Naturista-Nudista de Andalucía**.

Spas and Spa Hotels

Andalucía's traditional spas are mainly small, out-of-the-way towns where springs of thermal or medicinal waters supply hotels-cum-sanatoriums that treat patients with a range of ailments. The main ones are Alhama de Almería, Sierra Alhamilla (Almería), Alhama de Granada, Alicun de las Torres (Granada), Graena (near Guadix), Lanjarón (in the Alpujarras), San Andrés (Jaén), Carratraca (Málaga), Fuente Armaga at Tolox (Málaga) and Fuente Amarga at Chiclana in Cádiz. Contact the **Asociación Nacional de Estaciones Termales** for details.

Spa hotels have seen a huge growth in popularity. These tend to be larger, luxury properties and are often located beachside or complemented with a golf course. The spa facilities are normally reserved for the use of hotel guests and tend to focus more on pampering and beauty treatments rather than providing health-enhancing therapy. The spa at **Gran Hotel**

Guadalpin Banus (Puerto Banus, Marbella coast) specializes in Oriental Spa treatments, with Japanese and Chinese influences as well as meditation, yoga and pilates classes. Guests at the **Hotel La Fuente de la Higuera**, in Ronda, can choose from a range of facials, wraps and massages or have a soak in the Turkish baths. **Villa Padierna Palace Hotel** in Marbella focuses more on well-being, offering slimming and anti-stress treatments. The serenity spa at **Las Dunas**, in Estepona, uses Ligne St Barth products from the French Caribbean in its pampering treatments. The **Marbella Club Hotel** (see p218) has a beachfront spa that offers Thalasso, body and beauty treatments, including a seashell facial massage. The Elysium Spa at **NH Sotogrande** offers treatments such as hydromassage and a colour-therapy relaxation room.

Arab Baths

When Andalucía was under the sway of the Moors, it had many public bathhouses – the equivalent of Turkish baths. Although the last one closed in the 17th century, private companies have been recreating their own "Arab baths", with hot and cold rooms and massages, in Seville, Córdoba, Málaga and Granada. Sessions need to be reserved – and, in some cases, paid for – in advance.

Specialist Holidays

A good way to spend a week or two in Andalucía while learning something useful at the same time is to go on a special-interest holiday. If you want to get deep into the heart of Andalucía, you could try a flamenco dancing workshop at **La Fuente Centro Flamenco** in Granada. Beginner, intermediate and advanced levels are available.

Cooking is another way to learn something about your surroundings. **Annie B's Spanish Kitchen** runs residential courses in Mediterranean cooking, while at **Finca Buen Vino** you will be taught how to prepare Andalucían cuisine, including dishes with North African influences.

Learning to speak Spanish is another obvious way to make a holiday yield tangible benefits, but keep in mind that you may pick up an Andaluz accent rather than the more neutral pronunciation of central Spain. Many private companies run courses in Spanish lasting from a week to several months, but a safe option is to make arrangements with the organization in charge of promoting the Spanish language, the **Instituto Cervantes**.

Other subjects on offer are not directly related to Andalucía. **Authentic Adventures** will teach you painting and photography, as well as taking you for interesting guided walks, and the **Complejo Turístico Salitre** in the mountains behind Estepona will introduce you to the delights of the night sky from its observatory.

An artist painting the coastal scene at Nerja, on the Costa del Sol

DIRECTORY

Walking and Trekking

Federación Andaluza de Montañismo
Calle Santa Paula 23,
2° Planta, Granada.
Tel 958 29 13 40.
ⓦ fedamon.com

Spanish Steps
Calle Carreteria 6,
Cómpeta (Málaga).
Tel 952 55 32 70.
ⓦ spanish-steps.com

Cycling

Biking Andalucía
Apartado de Correos 346,
Orgiva (Granada).
Tel 676 00 25 46.
ⓦ bikingandalucia.com

Fundación de los Ferrocarriles Españoles
ⓦ ffe.es/viasverdes

Fishing

Federación Andaluza de Pesca Deportiva
Calle Diego Fernández
Herrera 19, 2ª Planta,
Puerta B, Jerez de la
Frontera (Cádiz).
Tel 956 18 75 85.
ⓦ fapd.net

Wildlife and Birdwatching

Foundation for Information and Research on Marine Mammals
Pedro Cortés 4, Tarifa.
Tel 956 62 70 08.
ⓦ firmm.org

Iberian Wildlife
Tel 918 98 91 95.
ⓦ iberianwildlife.com

Equestrian Sports

Los Alamos
La Zarzadilla 23, San
Ambrosio Apartado 113,
Vejer de la Frontera (Cadiz).
Tel 956 43 10 47.
ⓦ losalamosriding.
co.uk

Dallas Love
Bubión (Alpujarras).
Tel 608 45 38 02.
ⓦ spain-horse-riding.
com

Federación Andaluza de Hípica
C/ O'Donnell nº 16, 3º
41001, Sevilla.
Tel 954 21 81 46.
ⓦ fah.es

Golf

Barceló Montecastillo Golf Resort
Ctra Jerez-Arcos km 6,
Jerez de La Frontera.
Tel 956 15 12 00.
ⓦ barcelo.com

La Cala Resort
Urb La Cala Golf s/n, Mijas
Costa. **Tel** 952 669 016.
ⓦ lacala.com

Federación Andaluza de Golf
Tel 952 22 55 90.
ⓦ rfga.org

Tennis

Federación Andaluza de Tenis
Tel 954 44 44 33.
ⓦ fatenis.com

Water Sports

Federación Española de Actividades Subacuáticas
Avenida Dr. Miguel Ríos
Sarmiento s/n, Centro de
Tecnificación de Tenis
41020, Sevilla. **Tel** 932 00
67 69. ⓦ fedas.es

Real Federación Española de Vela
Tel 915 19 50 08.
ⓦ rfev.es

Air Sports

Balloon Flights Spain
ⓦ balloonflightsspain.
com

Federación Andaluza de los Deportes Aéreos
Estadio de la Cartuja,
Seville. **Tel** 954 32 54 38.
ⓦ feada.org

Skydive Spain
Aerodromo La Juliana,
Carretera A474, Bolullos
de la Mitación. **Tel** 955 76
60 56. ⓦ skydivespain.
com

Skiing

Sierra Nevada
Tel 902 70 80 90.
ⓦ sierranevada.es

Naturism

Asociación Naturista-Nudista de Andalucía
ⓦ anna-nudismo.es

Costa Natura
Carretera de Cádiz
km 151, Estepona.
Tel 952 80 80 65.
ⓦ costanatura.com

Vera Playa Club
Calle Aguamarga 1
(Almería). **Tel** 950 46 70 27.
ⓦ veraplaya.es

Spas and Spa Hotels

Asociación Nacional de Estaciones Termales
Tel 902 11 76 22.
ⓦ balnearios.org

Las Dunas Health & Beach Spa
Urb. La Boladilla Baja,
Ctra de Cadiz km 163.5,
29689 Estepona, Marbella.
Tel 951 08 20 90.
ⓦ healthouse-naturhouse.com

Gran Hotel Guadalpin Banus
C/Edgar Neville s/n,
Nueva Andalucía,
Puerto Banus, Marbella.
Tel 952 89 97 00.
ⓦ granhotelguadalpin.
com

Hotel La Fuente de la Higuera
Partido de los Frontones,
29400 Ronda, Málaga.
Tel 952 16 56 08.
ⓦ hotellafuente.com

NH Sotogrande
Autovía A-7, Salida 130,
11310 Cádiz.
Tel 956 69 54 44.
ⓦ nh-hotels.com

Villa Padierna Palace Hotel
Carretera de Cádiz, km
166, Marbella. **Tel** 902 20
06 76. ⓦ villapadierna
palacehotel.com

Arab Baths

Córdoba
Calle Corregidor Luis de
la Cerda 51.
Tel 957 48 47 46.
ⓦ cordoba.hammam
alandalus.com

Granada
Calle Santa Ana 16.
Tel 958 22 99 78.
ⓦ granada.hammam
alandalus.com

Málaga
Plaza de los Mártires 5.
Tel 952 21 50 18.
ⓦ malaga.hammam
alandalus.com

Seville
Calle Aire 15.
Tel 955 01 00 25.
ⓦ airedesevilla.com

Specialist Holidays

Annie B's Spanish Kitchen
Calle Viñas 11, Vejer de
la Frontera. **Tel** 620 56 06
49. ⓦ anniebspain.com

Authentic Adventures
Tel 01453 823 328 (in
the UK). ⓦ authentic
adventures.co.uk

Complejo Turístico Salitre
Carretera Comarcal 373
Algatocín, Málaga.
Tel 952 11 70 05.
ⓦ turismosalitre.com

Finca Buen Vino
Los Marines 21208,
Huelva. **Tel** 959 12 40 34.
ⓦ fincabuenvino.com

La Fuente Centro Flamenco
Carretera de la Sierra s/n
18413 Capileira (Granada).
ⓦ flamencolafuente.
com

Instituto Cervantes
Tel 914 36 76 00.
ⓦ cervantes.es

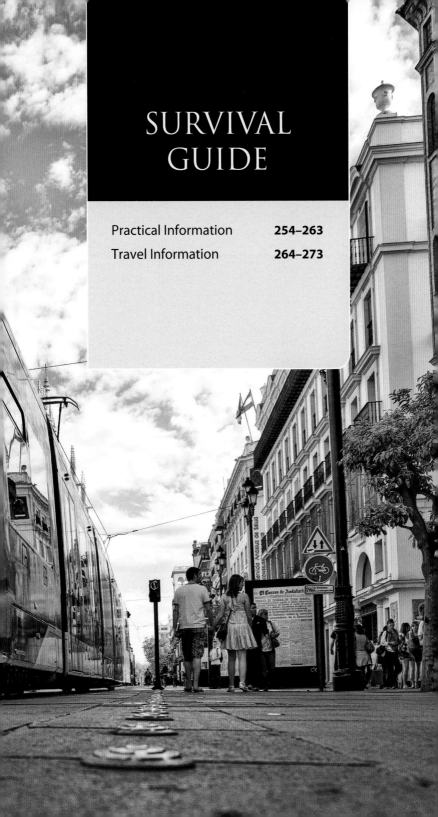

SURVIVAL GUIDE

Practical Information   254–263
Travel Information   264–273

PRACTICAL INFORMATION

The economy of Andalucía is heavily dependent on tourism. The rich variety of natural attractions and its cultural heritage draw a large number of visitors to the area throughout the year. Many have even settled in this evocative region, home of all things quintessentially Spanish: rich terracotta landscapes, olive groves, flamenco dancing, and *corridas* (bullfights).

Andalucía has successfully staged numerous high-profile sporting events such as the Sierra Nevada Ski Championships, the UEFA Cup final and the European Grand Prix, which have led to an increase in the number of tourist facilities and an improved infrastructure. The *Junta de Andalucía* has tourist offices across the region, offering a wealth of brochures, maps and leaflets.

Try not to do too much at once, but savour the particular delights of one or two places. Adjust to the slower pace and, in summer, do your sightseeing early in the day before the heat becomes unbearable.

Guided horse-drawn carriage tours, operating in Andalucía's main cities

When to Go

Any season is perfect for a visit to Andalucía. Spring boasts balmy weather and numerous festivals, including the Holy Week processions and Feria de Abril *(see p38)*, as well as local fairs in all towns, and the start of the bullfighting season. Summer is hot in the region's interior so it is the perfect time to head to the vast coastline, while autumn offers pleasant weather for sightseeing or rural excursions. Winter is mild in most areas, except in the Sierra Nevada *(see p203)* where you can hit the ski slopes.

Visas and Passports

Visas are not required for citizens of EU countries. Visitors from the US, Canada, Australia and New Zealand do not need a visa for stays of up to 90 days. For longer visits, apply to your Spanish consulate for a permit *(visado)* several months in advance. Visitors from all other countries are legally required to obtain a visa before travelling to Spain. Check the requirements with your Spanish consulate.

Your hotel will take your passport details on arrival. If you lose your passport, or need legal advice while in Spain, contact your embassy or consulate.

Travel Safety Advice

Visitors can get up-to-date travel safety information from the **UK Foreign and Commonwealth Office**, the **US State Department** and the **Australian Department of Foreign Affairs and Trade**.

Tourist Information

All of Andalucía's major cities have several *Oficinas de Turismo* (tourist offices). *Turespaña* provides information on Spain at a national level, while offices run by the *Junta de Andalucía* cover Andalucía as a region. Local tourist offices usually have details only of their environs.

Most tourist offices are well organized, offering brochures covering all kinds of services. They have a range of leaflets listing local festivals and can also offer suggestions on nightlife and shows, as well as outdoor activities. For guided tours, the tourist office will be able to direct you to a number of multilingual agencies, such as *El Legado Andalusi* ("The Legacy of Al- Andalus"), which highlights Andalucía's heritage through exhibitions and self-guided cultural tours *(see p272)*. The Andalucía tourism website (www.andalucia.org) has a useful app which can be used on mobile devices.

Admission Charges

Many sights offer free entry to Spanish residents and members of the European Union. Others

Many monuments and museums offer free or discounted entry

◀ Metro-Centro tram in Seville's city centre

charge a moderate fee (with relevant ID, seniors, students and children receive discounts). Large groups should make advance reservations, and may be offered a discount. In Granada, Córdoba, Baeza, Úbeda and Jaén, a *bono turístico* (tourist pass) allows entrance to various monuments and museums for a reduced fixed rate. At many sights, credit card payments are not accepted.

Opening Hours

The majority of museums and monuments are operated by the *Junta de Andalucía* and are usually open 10am–8pm from mid-September to May, and 9am–3pm from June to mid-September, staying open during the siesta. Most are open Sunday and public holidays 10am–3pm, but close all day Monday. Ticket offices close an hour before the sight closes. Many churches open only for Mass, but in small towns a caretaker will often let visitors in between religious services. Hours for Mass vary, but tend to be to 8pm on Sunday, and between 7 and 9pm on weekdays.

Language

The Costa del Sol has many multilingual residents and establishments. In major city centres people working in the service industry will have at least a basic level of English, but in rural towns you are likely to hear mainly Spanish. Most people are accommodating and will try their best to communicate with you.

Etiquette and Smoking

In Spain, strangers usually greet each other on meeting in doorways and lifts – and even when passing on the street in small towns. When introduced to someone, expect to shake hands. Once they are familiar, men embrace and pat each other on the shoulder, and female friends greet each other with a hug or kiss on both cheeks. Spaniards rarely drink alcohol without nibbles until after dinner. The waiter will not bring the bill until you ask for it, and generally

Visitors outside a church in the town of El Rocío in Andalucía

the bill for a round of drinks is not shared. The Spanish tend to dress smartly, so wearing very casual clothes and shoes will readily identify you as a tourist. However, few venues have a strict dress code so smart-casual attire is accepted. Smoking is not allowed in public indoor spaces. In bars and restaurants smoking is permitted in the outdoor areas.

Visiting Churches

In most towns, tourists are welcome in the church during a service as long as they are quiet and respectful. Dress codes in Spanish churches are not as strict as in other Catholic countries, but avoid skimpy shorts and bare shoulders. There is usually no admission charge, except in larger cathedrals, although a donation may be

expected. Tourist offices and hotels are usually able to provide details of churches holding services in English.

Public Conveniences

Public toilets are scarce. However, there is a bar on virtually every corner that is legally bound to allow you to use its toilets. Another option is to head to a department store, like El Corte Inglés. Ladies should look for a "D" *(Damas)* or "M" *(Mujeres)* on the door; while men's rooms are marked with an "H" *(Hombres)* or a "C" *(Caballeros)*.

Watch out for signs in public toilets within older buildings that state *"No tirar papel al WC"* (do not flush paper or other objects down the toilet).

Taxes and Tipping

If you are not a European Union resident, you can reclaim the VAT *(IVA* in Spanish) paid on goods bought in any authorized shop in Spain. When you spend a minimum of €90.16 in the same shop on the same day *(see p238)*, ask for information on how to claim your refund. See www.premiertaxfree.com

Tipping tends to be an issue of discretion in Spain. A service charge *(servicio)* is usually included *(see p221)* in the bill, but in more upmarket restaurants you are expected to tip around five per cent in addition. It is also common to round up the fare for taxi drivers.

Upmarket restaurant in Seville where tipping is expected in addition to the bill

Travellers with Special Needs

Modern buildings generally have adequate provision for disabled visitors, with lifts, ramps and special toilet facilities. However, entry to some historical monuments may be restricted so check ahead with the local tourist office or monument staff. Some historic centres have pedestrian zones and bicycle lanes, which can be used, with caution, by wheelchairs.

Disability Rights UK, a UK-based charity, and the **Comité de Entidades Representantes de Personas con Discapacidad (CEADIS)** in Seville can provide travel information for disabled users. In Madrid, **Servi-COCEMFE** advises on suitable accommodation *(see p215)*.

All public transport in Seville is wheelchair accessible, with electronic ramps or same-level entry onto buses and Metro-Centro trams.

Senior Travellers

There are many options for both leisurely and more active holidays for senior travellers. Health spas are popular choices, as are walking holidays. There are substantial discounts for travellers over the age of 55 staying in four-star hotels, during the off-peak season. US-based **Road Scholar** specializes in offering group travel experiences for seniors.

Gay and Lesbian Travellers

In general, Spain openly accepts gays and lesbians. However, discretion is still advisable in rural

A Gay Pride Parade weaving its way through the streets of Málaga

Local market stall with a colourful display of fresh produce

towns and public places. Andalucía has a dynamic gay scene, with clubs, bars, hotels and associations throughout the region, particularly in larger cities.

Colegas, an association that promotes gay and lesbian rights, has centres in Córdoba and Seville. The **International Gay & Lesbian Travel Association** has an online directory of gay- and lesbian-friendly travel businesses and tour operators.

International Student Identity Card

Travelling on a Budget

Most large towns have a **Centro de Documentación e Información Juvenil**, which provides information for students and young people. A valid International Student Identification Card (ISIC card) entitles you to some price reductions, including museum entrance fees and travel.

Many museums and monuments offer free entry one day a week, so it is worth checking this in advance.

To dine on a budget, order the *menú del día* (a two–three-course meal at a fixed price) or choose tapas instead of dishes from *la carta*. Another way to save would be to opt for locally brewed beer or house wines.

Youth hostels provide shared minimal facilities for a bargain price, while family-run budget hotels offer more privacy.

Responsible Travel

There are a growing number of hotels and guesthouses with an emphasis on green tourism. **Andeco** promotes ecotourism in Andalucía, while **Top Rural** lists accommodation throughout the countryside. **Glamping Hub** provides a glamorous but green way of camping, offering many destinations in Andalucía.

Every town and city has local markets and shops that promote their regional produce, and local activities and festivals to provide entertainment. Local farmers belong to cooperatives, which sell their produce in the markets *(Mercado de Abastos)*. Locally grown meats and fresh fish from regional waters are also sold here, but there will also be some imported produce.

Organically grown produce is referred to as *ecológico*; while organic meats are defined as *de corral, ecológica* or *orgánica*, and will be marked as such in stores and markets. Market stalls that exclusively sell organically grown goods can be difficult to find in bigger cities. However, on the second Saturday of every month, an organic market, Feria Ecológica de Productores Locales, is held in the Plaza Alameda de Hercules in Seville.

Every town and city has local artisan shops. On Sunday mornings, Seville's Art Market features works from local professional artists. Seasonal markets also feature regional artisans, with one of the most impressive being the *Mercado de Belenes* (Market of Nativity Scenes), held every December in the Plaza de San Francisco. Here you will find stalls offering intricately detailed, handmade nativity characters. Local activities and festivals such as Holy Week processions, fairs and music festivals promoting local artists provide unique entertainment.

Time

Spain is one hour ahead of Greenwich Mean Time (GMT) and British Summer Time, except for brief periods in spring and autumn when clock changes are not synchronized.

The 24-hour clock is used for written and official purposes but not in speech. The morning is referred to as *por la mañana* and the afternoon, *por la tarde*. Afternoon starts after siesta time, at around 5pm.

Electricity

The current in Spain is 220V-AC with two-pin, round-pronged plugs. Adaptors can be found in many local hypermarkets, supermarkets and electrical stores. If you can, take one with you to be on the safe side. Many hotels now use the key/card system for switching on the electricity supply in rooms.

Conversion Chart

Imperial to Metric
1 inch = 2.54 centimetres
1 foot = 30 centimetres
1 mile = 1.6 kilometres
1 ounce = 28 grams
1 pound = 454 grams
1 pint = 0.6 litres
1 gallon = 4.6 litres

Metric to Imperial
1 centimetre = 0.4 inches
1 metre = 3 feet, 3 inches
1 kilometre = 0.6 miles
1 gram = 0.04 ounces
1 kilogram = 2.2 pounds
1 litre = 1.8 pints

DIRECTORY

Embassies and Consulates

Australian Embassy
Torre Espacio, Paseo de la Castellana 259D, Planta 24, 28046 Madrid. **Tel** 913 53 66 00. w **spain. embassy.gov.au**

British Consulate
Edificio Eurocom, Calle Mauricio Moro Pareto 2, 29006 Málaga. **Tel** 902 10 93 56. w **gov.uk/ government/world/ spain**

Canadian Consulate
Edificio Horizonte, Plaza de la Malagueta 2, 1st floor, 29016 Málaga. **Tel** 952 22 33 46. w **international.gc.ca**

US Consulate
Plaza Nueva, 8-8 dupl, 2nd floor, Seville. **Map** 3 B1 (5 C3). **Tel** 954 21 87 51. w **madrid. usembassy.gov**

Travel Safety Advice

Australian Department of Foreign Affairs and Trade
w **dfat.gov.au**
w **smartraveller.gov.au**

UK Foreign and Commonwealth Office
w **gov.uk/foreign- travel-advice**

US Department of State
w **travel.state.gov**

Tourist Information

Oficinas de Turismo
w **andalucia.org**
Almería
Parque Nicolás Salmerón s/n. **Tel** 950 17 52 20.

Córdoba
Plaza del Triunfo s/n. **Tel** 902 20 17 74.

Granada
Calle Santa Ana 4. **Tel** 958 57 52 02.

Jaén
Calle Maestra 8. **Tel** 953 31 32 81 .

Málaga
Pasaje de Chinitas 4. **Tel** 951 30 89 11.

Seville
Avenida de la Constitución 21. **Map** 3 C2 (5 C4). **Tel** 954 78 75 78.

Plaza San Francisco 19, Edificio Laredo, Seville. **Map** 3 C3 (5 C3).**Tel** 954 23 44 65.w **turismo. sevilla.org**

Spanish Tourist Office (UK)
6th Floor, 64 North Row, London W1K 7DE. **Tel** 020 7317 2011.w **spain.info**

Travellers with Special Needs

Comité de Entidades Representantes de Personas con Discapacidad (CEADIS)
Pabellón de la Fundación ONCE, Isla de la Cartuja C/ Leonardo Da Vinci 13. **Tel** 954 46 11 92. w **cermiandalucia.es**

Disability Rights UK
Ground Floor, CAN Mezzanine, 49–51 East Road, London N1 6AH, UK. **Tel** (020) 7250 8181. w **disabilityrightsuk.org**

Servi-COCEMFE
C/Luis Cabrera 63, 28002 Madrid. **Tel** 917 44 36 00. w **cocemfe.es**

Senior Travellers

Road Scholar
11 Avenue de Lafayette, Boston, MA 02111-1746. **Tel** 1 800 454 5768 (outside US 1 978 323 4141). w **roadscholar.org**

Gay and Lesbian Travellers

Colegas
Tel 954 50 13 77. w **colegaweb.org**

International Gay & Lesbian Travel Association
w **iglta.org**

Travelling on a Budget

ALMERÍA
Centro de Información Juvenil
C/ Marín 2–2. **Tel** 950 21 13 67. w **injuve.es**

CÓRDOBA
La Casa de la Juventud
Campo Madre de Dios s/n, 14010. **Tel** 957 76 47 07. w **injuve.es**

GRANADA

Centro de Información Juvenil
Avenida de Madrid 5, Granada. **Tel** 958 20 46 52. w **injuve.es**

JAÉN

Centro de Información Juvenil
Avenida de Andalucia 47– 5ª, Planta. **Tel** 953 21 91 56.

MÁLAGA

Centro de Información y Asesoramiento Juvenil (INFOJOVEN)
Calle Roger de Flor 1, Málaga. **Tel** 951 92 60 67. w **juventud.malaga.eu**

SEVILLE

Instituto Andaluz de la Juventud
Calle Bilbao, 8–10, Seville. **Tel** 955 03 57 16. w **informajoven.org**

Responsible Travel

Andeco
Avenida Ramón y Cajal nº4, Marbella (Málaga). **Tel** 952 77 09 54. w **ecoturismo enandalucia.org**

Glamping Hub
Marion St, Denver, Colorado.**Tel** (415) 800 3004. w **glamphinghub. com**

Top Rural
Paseo de la Castellana 79, Madrid. **Tel** 911 23 83 11. w **toprural.com**

Personal Security and Health

Andalucía is, by and large, a safe place for visitors. Women travelling alone tend not be hassled, but may have to put up with so-called compliments from men of all ages. Pickpockets and bag-snatchers, however, are very common in cities, so be cautious around tourist spots and on crowded transport. If you must carry valuable items, avoid putting them all in the same place. Wear a money belt and do not keep your wallet in an easily accessible place. If you become ill during your stay, go to a pharmacy, where someone should be able to advise you. Organize travel insurance before leaving for Spain as it is difficult to obtain and more expensive once there.

Mounted police officers from the *Policía Nacional*

Police

There are three types of police in Spain – the *Guardia Civil*, the *Policía Nacional* and the *Policía Local*. When approaching police on the street, remember that it is illegal to be without ID.

In rural areas you will usually encounter the green-uniformed *Guardia Civil*, who patrol the country highways and will help if your car breaks down *(see p271)*. They also set up random road blocks to check for drink driving or other infractions. The *Policía Nacional*, who wear

Ambulance displaying the emergency number

Marked car of the *Policía Nacional*

Fire engine marked with contact number

a dark blue uniform, have many responsibilities, such as dealing with visitors' permits and documentation and they are also the best to turn to when reporting a crime.

The *Policía Local* handle the day-to-day traffic policing of towns and cities.

What to Be Aware Of

The abundance of street-life means that you will rarely find yourself alone or in a position to be harassed.

There are no particularly notorious areas of Seville to be avoided. Just act streetwise: do not use maps late at night and try to look like you know where you are going.

When visiting the Sacromonte caves in Granada to see flamenco performances *(see p197)*, go in a group and keep an eye on your belongings. In cities such as Seville, Granada and Córdoba, beware of Roma (gypsies) who will try to read your palm or offer a sprig of rosemary, then demand compensation (petty change doesn't suffice). Your refusal to pay results in their outrage, and you can have a difficult time getting away from them.

Make sure that you take official taxis displaying a licence number, although illegal cabs are rare.

In an Emergency

The telephone number for medical emergency services is **061**. Report all serious crime to the local police, and for the fire brigade dial **112**.

Lost and Stolen Property

Pickpockets are common in crowded areas. Beware of people trying to distract you while someone else snatches your bag or wallet. Wear bags and cameras across your body, not on your shoulder, and take special care of mobile phones and laptops. At ATMs be cautious of loitering strangers. Take a photocopy of your passport and leave the original in the hotel safe. Park in a secure car park, storing valuables out of view.

Report any incident to the police *(poner una denuncia)* as soon as possible (within 24 hours), particularly if you wish to obtain a statement *(denuncia)* for an insurance claim.

Health Precautions

Beware of the sun, particularly in the summer months when temperatures can reach up to 45° C (113° F). Try to avoid walking in the midday sun and stay in the shade whenever possible. Use sunscreen, wear a hat and be sure to drink plenty of water.

In rural areas, take any signs showing a bull or saying *toro bravo* (fighting bull) seriously. These bulls are extremely dangerous animals and should not be approached.

Hospitals and Pharmacies

For minor ailments, visit a pharmacy *(farmacia)*, where pharmacists can dispense a wide range of medication over the counter, but for many drugs you will need a doctor's prescription.

Farmacias have a green or red neon cross outside and are found in most towns. A few are open 24 hours, but most open 12 hours a day. Some close for *siesta*. At least one will be *de guardia* – ready to dispatch out of hours. The opening rota is posted on the door of all *farmacias* and also in local newspapers.

For urgent medical assistance, go to the nearest *Urgencias* – the emergency ward of a hospital or clinic.

All the cities have several hospitals each, while the Costa del Sol has a hospital situated on the main coastal highway (N340) just east of Marbella.

For private care, contact your insurance company for a list of centres covered by your plan.

All public hospitals will have volunteer interpreters who speak English and occasionally other languages. Keep in mind this is generally done via speaker phone.

The Cruz Roja (Red Cross) has an extensive network throughout Spain and runs an ambulance service. Your hotel and embassy or consulate can provide a list of English-speaking doctors and dentists. Dental procedures are safe and are generally much cheaper than the UK and US.

Spanish pharmacy signs

Travel and Health Insurance

All EU nationals are entitled to Spanish social security cover. Before travelling, you must obtain the **European Health Insurance Card** (see www.ehic.org.uk). Show your card or policy to receive medical care. In some cases you may have to pay first and be reimbursed later. For private medical care, make sure you have your policy on you when you request assistance.

Travel insurance is advisable, and should be arranged before your trip. Carry all documentation with you.

If you need a lawyer, ask your embassy or consulate *(see p257)* to recommend one. Not all lawyers speak English, but police stations may be able to offer a volunteer interpreter *(intérprete)*. Otherwise you may need to hire a *Traductor Oficial* or *Jurado* to state your case and undertake legal work.

DIRECTORY

Local Police Stations

Almería
Tel 950 62 30 40.

Córdoba
Tel 957 29 07 60.

Granada
Tel 954 24 82 11.

Málaga
Tel 952 06 18 70.

Seville
Tel 954 28 93 00.

In an Emergency

Ambulance
Tel 061 and 112.

Fire Brigade
Tel 112.

Police
Tel 112.

Lost and Stolen Property

Almería
Oficina de Objetos Perdidos
Avenida del Mediterráneo 255.
Tel 950 62 14 98.

Córdoba
Comisaría de Policía
Avenida de los Ángeles Custodios.
Tel 957 48 00 16.

Granada
Ayuntamiento
Plaza del Carmen 5.
Tel 958 24 81 03.

Málaga Oficina de Objetos Perdidos
Calle Victoria 15.
Tel 951 92 61 11.

Seville Oficina de Objetos Perdidos
Calle Manuel Vázquez Sagastizábal 3.
Map 6 F5.
Tel 955 47 22 77.

Hospitals

Cruz Roja
Hospital Victoria Eugenia,
Avenida de la Cruz Roja,
Seville. Map 2 E4.
Tel 954 35 14 00.

Hospital Costa del Sol
Autovía A-7 km 187,
Marbella, Málaga.
Tel 951 97 66 69.

Hospital General
Avenida de las Fuerzas Armadas 2,
Granada.
Tel 958 02 00 00.

Hospital Reina Sofía
Avenida Menéndez Pidal s/n, Córdoba.
Tel 957 01 00 00.

Hospital Torrecardenas
Paraje de Torrecardenas s/n, Almería.
Tel 950 01 60 00.

Hospital Universitario Virgen del Rocio
Avenida Manuel Siurots s/n, Seville.
Tel 955 01 20 00.

Pharmacies

Almería
Carretera de Ronda 325.
Tel 950 25 35 57.
Open 24 hours.

Córdoba
Calle Lope de Hoces 7.
Tel 957 29 33 57.

Granada
Calle Reyes Catolicos 5.
Tel 958 26 26 64.

Málaga
Calle Mesonero Romanos 2.
Tel 952 61 08 36.

Seville
María Auxiliadora 6.
Tel 954 41 62 61.
Open 24 hours.

Travel and Health Insurance

Asociación Profesional de Traductores e Intérpretes
Apartado de Correos 55,
47080 Valladolid.
Tel 652 15 54 06.
W aptij.es

European Health Insurance Card (EHIC)
Bridge House,
152 Pilgrim St, Newcastle
Upon Tyne NE1 6SN.
Tel 0845 605 0707
(from abroad
+44 191 218 1999).
W europeanhealth
card.org.uk

Banking and Currency

Andalucía has an extensive bank network with plenty of ATMs, and finding a bank is not a problem except in the most remote villages. Banks in larger cities have the best exchange rates. Other options for changing currency include bureaux de change and hotels, though the latter often have poor exchange rates and charge higher fees. Alternatively, credit cards are widely accepted.

You can take any amount of foreign currency into Spain, but sums worth over €6,000 should be declared at customs when you enter the country.

Changing Money

Most banks have a foreign exchange desk *casa de cambio*, and in building societies a *caja de ahorros*. While Málaga airport has 24-hour exchange facilities and at Seville airport the Iberia Airlines information desk offers money changing, the rates are generally higher in airports. You can change money at El Corte Inglés department stores, travel agents and hotels, although their rates are not favourable and fees vary.

It is better to take enough euros for your initial needs before travelling, and to shop around for the best rates at your leisure after you arrive.

You must show your passport or driver's licence to change money.

Banking Hours

Banks open from 8:30am to 2pm Monday to Friday. A few banks open on Thursday evenings and Saturday mornings in the winter months. During a town's annual *feria* week (see pp42–3) banking hours are reduced, and on public holidays all banks remain closed (see p41).

ATMs

ATMs are readily available in Andalucía. Look for the logo on your card to find an appropriate machine. ATMs have various language options. Check with your bank regarding foreign transaction fees and inform them prior to travel. Spanish banks may impose a fee (€2–3 per transaction), but exchange rates are better.

Debit and Credit Cards

Credit cards such as **American Express**, **Visa** and **MasterCard**, as well as debit cards bearing the Cirrus or Maestro logo are widely accepted all over Spain. Contactless payments are also accepted in many establishments. Very few banks will convert traveller's cheques to euros. However, prepaid currency cards, such as those issued by **Travelex**, can be used to obtain cash from ATMs and to pay for goods in most shops, restaurants and hotels.

Wiring Money

To wire money, you can use a bank or an international service such as **Western Union** or **MoneyGram**. If using a bank, go to a large central office where they may have more experience. To receive money through a bank you will need a local bank account.

For both sending and receiving money, Western Union is available at all central **Correos** post offices. MoneyGram is available at select stores or public telephone offices (*locutorios*).

A branch of the BBVA bank, Seville

The Euro

The euro (€) is the common currency of the European Union. It went into general circulation on 1 January 2002, initially for 12 participating countries. Spain was one of those countries. EU members using the euro as sole official currency are known as the Eurozone. Several EU members have opted out of joining this common currency. Euro notes are identical throughout the Eurozone countries, each one including designs of fictional architectural structures and monuments. The coins, however, have one side identical (the value side), and one side with an image unique to each country. Note that the €500 note has been discontinued, but it is still valid and can be exchanged at any bank in the Eurozone.

Bank Notes

Euro bank notes have seven denominations. The €5 note (grey in colour) is the smallest, followed by the €10 note (pink), €20 note (blue), €50 note (orange), €100 note (green), €200 note (yellow) and €500 note (purple). All notes show the stars of the European Union.

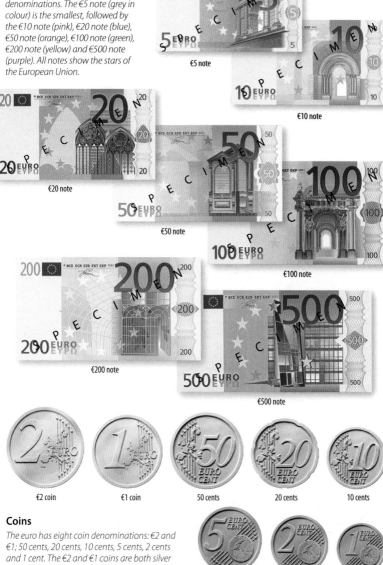

€5 note

€10 note

€20 note

€50 note

€100 note

€200 note

€500 note

€2 coin

€1 coin

50 cents

20 cents

10 cents

Coins

The euro has eight coin denominations: €2 and €1; 50 cents, 20 cents, 10 cents, 5 cents, 2 cents and 1 cent. The €2 and €1 coins are both silver and gold in colour. The 50-, 20- and 10-cent coins are gold, while 5-, 2- and 1-cent coins are bronze.

5 cents

2 cents

1 cent

Communications and Media

The telephone system in Spain is run by Movistar. It is efficient, but one of the most expensive in Europe. Public phones are scarce, but you will find some *locutorios* (public telephone call centres). Wi-Fi is available in most hotels, as well as in many bars and public places.

Spain's postal service can be slow but letters posted at central post offices will arrive at their destination faster. Digital TV and radio provide options for regional and international programmes. Newspapers, both in hard copy and online, are plentiful in Andalucía.

International and Local Telephone Calls

Public phone booths *(cabinas telefonicas)* and public telephones in bars are disappearing. If you locate a pay phone, they either use coins or phonecards, which are available from most newsstands and tobacconists *(estancos)*. Phonecards are priced by their value in call units.

Accessing Wi-Fi on a laptop at an outdoor café

Mobile Phones

4G signal coverage is generally good across Andalucía, though it might prove patchy in more rural areas. Since roaming charges have been abolished for EU member states it is much cheaper for visitors from the EU to use mobile phones abroad. If you are from outside the EU and anticipate making many calls while you are in Andalucía it might be a good idea to obtain a Spanish SIM and phone number. Make sure that your phone is unlocked to insert the Spanish pre-paid SIM card, or buy a pre-pay phone that comes with a number of minutes included. **Orange, Vodafone**, **Movistar** and **Yoigo** are common suppliers, and their products can be found at El Corte Inglés stores *(see p241)* or at **Phone House**.

Internet

Wi-Fi is available in nearly all hotels, and is usually free. There is free Wi-Fi in many restaurants, bars and cafés, and also in some parks and plazas, such as Plaza de España in Seville, and at railway stations. **Starbucks** can be found in nearly every major city, offering free Wi-Fi. For an up-to-date map of Wi-Fi hotspots, download the Free WiFi – Wiman app.

There are still some Internet cafés in Andalucía, although they are not plentiful. Generally, they offer other services as well, such as document printing and mobile phone SIM cards. In Seville, the only centrally located Internet café is **Internet Sevilla Locutorio**, in front of the university. Most local libraries also offer computers with free Internet access.

Postal Services

The Spanish postal service between major cities is fairly efficient, but between smaller towns it can be slow. Letters posted at a central post office usually arrive in reasonable time; although for important or urgent mail use the *certificado* (registered) and *urgente* (express) mail services.

Main post offices open all day Monday to Saturday; local post offices open mornings only. A *poste restante* service in central offices enables you to collect letters or parcels. A passport or other form of identification is needed but there is no collection fee.

Buy stamps *(sellos)* at any post office and at *estancos* (state-run tobacconists), displaying a yellow and blue sign.

International couriers such as **DHL** and **UPS** guarantee urgent delivery worldwide. Call the central office to arrange a pick up.

Reaching the Right Number

When dialling within a city, province or to another province, dial the entire number – the province is indicated by the initial numbers: Seville 954, 955; Málaga 951, 952; Córdoba 957; Cádiz 956; Granada 958; Huelva 959; Jaén 953; Almería 950.

- International calls: dial 00, wait for tone, dial country and area codes and number.
- Movistar directory enquiries are on 11886.
- International directory enquiries are on 025.
- To connect directly with the operator in your country dial 900 followed by the country code 990061 (Australia); 990015 (Canada); 990011 (USA); or 990044 for the UK.

A DHL delivery truck on a street in Seville

Kiosk selling newspapers and magazines

Addresses

In speech, on maps and in written information, Spaniards often drop the *Calle* in street names, so that Calle Mateos Gago becomes just Mateos Gago. Other terms, such as *Plaza (Pza), Callejón, Carretera (Ctra)* and *Avenida (Avda)*, remain unchanged.

In addresses, a *s/n (sin número)* after the street name indicates that the building has no number. Outside towns, an address may say "Carretera Córdoba–Málaga km 47" – this means the sight is on the motorway near to the kilometre sign.

Newspapers and Magazines

The most important national papers are *El País* (the socialist paper with a daily Andalucían version), *ABC* (conservative), and *El Mundo* (independent). Local papers such as *Ideal* in Granada, *Diario de Sevilla*, the *Córdoba Diario*, *Almería Diario*, or the *Málaga Sur*, have extensive listings of local cultural and sporting activities. An English version of *Sur* is distributed free in Málaga, Granada, Almería and Cádiz on Fridays or is viewable online at www.surinenglish.com.

The English paper *Costa del Sol News* can be purchased weekly in kiosks along the Málaga coast. Almería province also has an English newspaper, *Costa Almería News*, published

on Friday. The local listings magazines are the *Giraldillo* in Seville and the *Guía del Ocio* in Granada *(see p244). FIND* has complete cultural listings and nightlife for the Costa del Sol and *La Tribuna*, Córdoba's weekly free sheet, publishes useful practical information. Málaga has *Qué Hacer/What's On*. The online guide www. guiadelocio.com has current listings of events and activities for all provinces of Spain.

Television and Radio

In 2010, Spain eliminated the use of all analogue TV signals, and changed completely to digital TV as the standard signal, providing around 30 TV channels for free. Two are state channels, TVE1 and TVE2, and the main private ones are Antena 3, Cuatro and Telecinco. In addition, Andalucía has Canal Sur and Canal 2 Andalucía. Canal Plus is a cable TV company showing films, sport and documentaries. Subtitled foreign films are listed by the letters V.O. *(Versión Original)*.

The best radio news programmes are broadcast on Radio Nacional de España. BBC World Service frequencies and listings can be found on their website, www.bbc.co.uk/ worldservice. With the all-digital signal, most programmes are available in their original language simply by changing the TV language setting.

Canal Sur logo

DIRECTORY

Mobile Phones

Movistar
w movistar.es

Orange
w orange.es

Phone House
w phonehouse.es

Vodafone
w vodafone.es

Yoigo
w yoigo.com

Internet

Biblioteca Corredera
Centro Cívico Centro, Plaza de la Corredera, s/n, Córdoba.
Tel 957 49 68 82.

Cybercafe Abakan
Calle Marcos 19, Almería.

Internet Sevilla Locutorio
Calle Fernando 35, Seville.

Locutorio Duquesa
Calle Duquesa, Granada.

Meeting Point
Plaza de la Merced 29, Málaga.

Starbucks
Av Constitucion 11, Seville.
Tel 954 21 80 05.

Postal Services

General Information
Tel 902 19 71 97.
w correos.es

Almería
Calle San Juan Bosco 35.
Tel 950 62 04 33.

Córdoba
C/ José Cruz Conde 15.
Tel 957 49 63 42.

Granada
Puerta Real 2.
Tel 958 22 11 38.

Málaga
Avenida de Andalucía (El Corte Inglés).
Tel 952 36 43 80.

Seville
Avenida de la Constitución 32.
Map 3 C2 (5 C4).
Tel 954 22 47 60.

Couriers

DHL
Tel 902 12 24 24.
w dhl.es

UPS
Tel 902 88 88 20.
w ups.com

TRAVEL INFORMATION

Andalucía is well served by a wide range of transport. Each year sees the arrival of thousands of flights, mostly from European countries, though some are from further afield. Most flights from beyond Europe stop in Madrid or Barcelona before arriving at Andalucía's busiest airport, Málaga. Located a short plane or ferry ride from Morocco, Málaga serves as a gateway to Africa. Seville airport also caters to international flights.

Seville and Málaga have good rail links, and the AVE high-speed train between major cities is often quicker than flying (including checking-in time). There are coaches from northern Europe and regional services in Andalucía. Ferries sail from Plymouth and Portsmouth to Santander and Bilbao; with a 10-hour drive to Andalucía. Driving is not recommended in summer when the number of cars on the road peaks.

One of Andalucía's biodiesel-fuelled buses

Green Travel

Andalucía, has extensive recycling initiatives, solar and wind energy and biodiesel-fuelled buses. Most cab companies now have fleets of hybrid cars. An efficient pubic transport network makes it fairly easy to get around the region without a car. Trains and coaches are modern and comfortable, with extensive and reliable services. Many historic city centres have very limited access for vehicles, with large pedestrianized zones, bicycle lanes and a bike hire scheme (see p273).

Rural Andalucía has a large network of natural parks and trails as well as rivers and lakes for water sports, although depending on your itinerary a car may be necessary.

Arriving by Air

Most of Europe's major airlines, as well as some Middle Eastern and American lines, run scheduled flights to Málaga, Andalucía's main airport. A large portion of the traffic, however, is made up of budget airlines and cheap charter flights, which bring in thousands of holiday-makers. Over-booking can be a problem in summer and flights are often delayed. Seville airport is much less busy and is convenient for travellers staying inland. Granada, Jerez and Almería offer limited domestic and international flights too.

Fares and Package Deals

Fares vary widely and peak travel depends on the destination: May, June, September and October for Seville; June to August for the coast, and December to February for the Sierra Nevada. Book directly through an airline, or via online search engines such as www.kayak.co.uk or www.momondo.com, which compare numerous servers to get the best deal, or

for a complete service visit your local travel agent.

Almost all package deals to Andalucía focus on beach holidays. However, some tour operators also offer city breaks, which can be cheaper in the winter. **Tour Andalucia** offers small group tours originating in Málaga and **Euro Adventures (EA Tours)** offer food and wine package holidays starting in Costa del Sol, then following an itinerary, travelling by coach along the Costa del Sol to Seville, Córdoba, Granada and Cádiz. Low-cost airlines also offer cheap deals.

Seville Airport

Seville airport is 4 km (2.5 miles) north of the city centre. **Iberia** and **Air Europa** fly to numerous domestic and international destinations. **easyJet, Ryanair** and **Vueling Airlines** offer low-cost flights, and charter flights also operate out of Seville.

Los Amarillos runs a daily bus service between Prado de San Sebastián and the airport, approximately every 30 minutes from 4:30am to midnight. Taxis to or from the city centre cost between €22 and €31.

Seville airport, conveniently situated just outside the city

Modern interior of the ticket hall, Seville airport

Málaga Airport

Málaga airport has links to about 120 international destinations. Scheduled flights are available from **British Airways**, Iberia, **easyJet**, Ryanair, Virgin and Vueling. The *tren de cercanías (see p266)* runs into Málaga and down the coast to Fuengirola, every 20 minutes, from 6am to 11pm. The No. 19 bus, which runs every 30 minutes from 6:30am to midnight, also travels into Málaga.

Jerez Airport

Around 8 km (5 miles) northwest of the city, Jerez airport has flights to and from some destinations in the UK and Germany, as well as to Barcelona, Palma de Mallorca and Madrid. Trains and buses connect the airport to Jerez, Seville and Cádiz.

Granada Airport

Granada's airport is 17 km (10.5 miles) southeast of the city on the main road to Málaga. Facilities and flights are rather limited, but there are regular flights to Palma de Mallorca, Barcelona and Madrid, as well as limited services to Melilla, Milan and Bologna.

Gibraltar Airport

This airport can be a useful arrival point when visiting the south-west of Andalucía. Flights are operated by British Airways, **Monarch Airlines** and easyJet,

with services from Heathrow, Gatwick, Luton and Manchester. The airport has few amenities.

Almería Airport

Located 9 km (6 miles) west of the city, Almería's airport has limited facilities. Flights are offered to Barcelona, Madrid, Seville, Palma de Mallorca, Brussels, Manchester and Melilla with Air Europa, Air Berlin, easyJet, Ryanair and Monarch Airlines.

Airport Car Hire

Major airports are well served with car hire companies such as **AVIS**, **Enterprise**, **Hertz** and **Europcar**. **Holiday Autos** is a budget option, best booked online. Hire your car prior to your visit during high-season.

An FRS fast ferry on the Tangier–Tarifa route

Getting to North Africa

Most nationalities need only a valid passport to visit Morocco for a stay up to 90 days. For further information contact the **Consulate of Morocco**. Morocco time is 1 hour behind Spain.

Acciona Trasmediterranea, **FRS** and **BALEARIA** operate ferries from Algeciras to Ceuta; FRS, Balearia and **Intershipping** run from Algeciras to Tangier. FRS and Direct Ferries have fast ferries (35–45 mins) from Tarifa to Tangier. Acciona Trasmediterranea runs from Almería to Melilla in 8 hours. FRS also has a high-speed Gibraltar–Tangier Med route.

By air, Iberia, **Royal Air Maroc (RAM)**, Air Europa and Air Nostrum operate from Spain's mainland to various destinations in North Africa. **Helicópteros Inaer** runs a helicopter shuttle service between Málaga and Ceuta.

Travelling by Train

Owing to the natural bottleneck of the Pyrenees, train connections between Spain and the rest of Europe are a little restricted. However, a subsidiary of Spain's national network, **RENFE**, runs a service that links Madrid and Barcelona to France, Italy, Austria and Switzerland. RENFE offers routes throughout the country, on a variety of trains, and at a high level of service. The high-speed AVE *(Tren de Alta Velocidad Española)* linking Seville, Córdoba and Madrid, and Málaga to Madrid (via Córdoba) has cut down journey times by almost half, and is extremely efficient.

AVE high-speed trains at Santa Justa railway station, Seville

Arriving by Train

Trains coming from other European countries to Spain terminate in either Madrid or Barcelona. From Barcelona it is about 5 hours to Seville by high-speed AVE; from Madrid it takes around 3 hours travelling by AVE.

Andalucía's most important stations are Málaga, Córdoba and Seville's Santa Justa. Connections to all major Andalucían towns and with Barcelona and Madrid (including over 20 AVE high-speed trains) run daily.

European and American rail passes, including EurRail and Inter-Rail, are accepted on the RENFE network, subject to the usual conditions. However, keep in mind that on certain trains you may find a supplement is payable.

Major stations are accessible to disabled passengers. It is possible for passengers to arrange in advance for assistance in the station, through RENFE's subsidiary company, **Atendo**.

Train Travel in Spain

The train network in Spain is very extensive with services suited to every budget. Travelling on the AVE is the fastest option, with a money-back guarantee that the train will reach its destination no more than 5 minutes late. They have drastically cut their prices, now making them a very attractive travel choice.

Other long-distance train services, known as *larga distancia*, are divided into *diurnos* (daytime) and *nocturnos* (night-time). *Talgos* trains are slightly more luxurious and expensive, offering both day- and night-time travel. Night trains offer the option of private cabins with beds. *Media distancias* run daytime from city to city within a limited area. *Cercanías* are commuter trains running from large towns to the suburbs.

Bookings and Reservations

Train tickets can be booked online or in travel agencies with the RENFE logo. It is advisable to book long-distance journeys in advance; booking is essential if you travel on public holidays *(días festivos)* or long weekends *(puentes)*. You can book a ticket up to 60 days in advance. Alternatively, use an auto check-in machine at major stations up to 15 minutes before travelling. Auto check-in machines can also be used for making changes to your scheduled itinerary. Discounts are usually given for advance bookings, last-minute bookings and round trips.

More information is available on RENFE's website.

Tickets

Train travel in Spain is fairly reasonably priced. *Larga distancia* and *media distancia* have first and second class *(preferente/turista)*. The tickets on Spanish trains always show a number for your seat (or bed on sleepers). Tickets are sold online, at main line stations, at some *cercanías* stations and in RENFE-authorized travel agencies. *Cercanías* tickets may be bought in the ticket office or by using self-service machines. Credit cards are accepted at all stations.

The ticket counter at Córdoba railway station

Spain's Principal RENFE Network

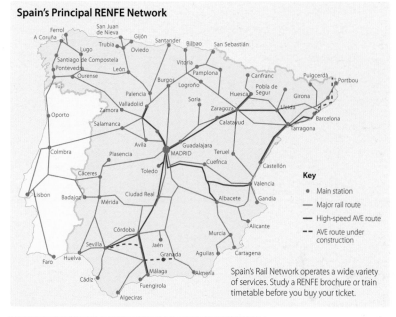

Key

- • Main station
- —— Major rail route
- ━━ High-speed AVE route
- -- AVE route under construction

Spain's Rail Network operates a wide variety of services. Study a RENFE brochure or train timetable before you buy your ticket.

Santa Justa railway station, Seville

Timetables

The punctuality rating of trains in Andalucía is quite high, particularly for the AVE. Brochures with prices and timetables are distributed free and are easy to follow. Information for *laborables* (weekdays) and *sábados, domingos y festivos* (Saturdays, Sundays and public holidays) is at the bottom of the timetable.

Seville

Santa Justa is a modern and user-friendly station, located about 5 minutes by car or bus from the city centre.

Use the self-service ticket machines to buy *cercanías* tickets. The auto check-in machines allow you to print out tickets reserved online.

Numerous amenities include a café, tourist office, car hire agencies, shops, newsstands, ATMs and money-changing facilities. For lost property, ask at the office marked *Atención al Cliente*.

Bus stops and taxi ranks are located in front of the station.

Córdoba

Córdoba has a grand, modern station. Located in the north-west of the city, it is just a few minutes by car or taxi to the city centre. The AVE to Madrid takes just 2 hours; to Seville 45 minutes. The station is well served with cafés, shops, auto check-in machines and a tourist office. Outside, there are bus stops, a taxi rank and car hire agencies. The coach station is adjacent.

Platforms at Córdoba railway station

Platform at Granada railway station

Granada

Small and provincial, the station in Granada is housed in an old building and has few amenities. There is a small café-cum-restaurant and a taxi rank outside. Most trains that pass through are regional or *cercanías* but long-distance trains do run to Madrid, Seville, the Costa Blanca, Barcelona, Almería, Córdoba and Málaga. Storage lockers are available.

Málaga

Málaga's Maria Zambrano station expanded when the AVE line was added, making it the largest in Spain. There is a direct daily train to Barcelona and a connection to Madrid (via Córdoba). There is also a high-speed AVE line direct to central Seville under construction. A *cercanías* train connects to Málaga airport and the

station will soon be linked to major towns through a Metro connection.

Málaga's station has many amenities, including auto check-in machines, luggage storage, car-hire agencies and a tourist office. Outside, there are bus stops and a taxi rank. A four-star hotel and large shopping centre are conveniently attached.

Almería

Almería's *Estación Intermodal* train and coach stations share the same building. Direct trains connect to Granada and Seville; to reach Córdoba you will need to make a connection in Granada; for Málaga, change at Antequera.

The station is small, with limited services such as a café, bank, newsstand, some shops and car hire agencies. Outside are bus stops and a taxi rank.

Scenic Routes

Travel by *cercanías* trains offers some very scenic routes. The most remarkable is a lengthy ride from Bobadilla (50 minutes north of Málaga), which heads south through gorges and mountains, passing through picturesque villages, before arriving in Algeciras. It takes about 3 hours and costs from €11.80.

A shorter ride, from Málaga to Fuengirola (30 minutes from the airport; 45 from Málaga station) provides stunning views of the Mediterranean from the mountains above for just €2.85.

DIRECTORY

Travelling By Train

RENFE Booking Agents
Tel 902 32 03 20.
W renfe.es
W rumbo.es

Handicap Assistance Atendo
Tel 902 24 05 05.
W renfe.com/viajeros/atendo

Almería
Plaza de la Estación s/n.

Córdoba
Glorieta de las Tres Culturas s/n.

Granada
Avenida de Andalucía s/n.

Málaga
Explanada de la Estación s/n.

Seville
Avenida Kansas City.
Map 2 F5 & 4 F1.

Málaga's Maria Zambrano railway station at night

Travelling by Coach

The major coach links between Andalucía and the rest of Europe are with France, Holland, Belgium, Switzerland and Austria. Within the region itself, coach travel is very popular and has improved enormously. Most coaches now run on bio-diesel and most have air conditioning and toilet facilities. Travelling by coach is very economical and thanks to Andalucía's improved roads, it can be quick and enjoyable. However, around the many holidays in the Spanish festive calendar, travelling can be difficult: coach stations tend to be over-crowded, coaches slow to depart and the roads busy.

Arriving by Coach

The major coach stations in Andalucía are in Seville, Córdoba, Granada, Málaga and Almería. Coaches run frequently between major cities and towns, and may provide the only public transport to and from small villages, offering a chance to experience local regions.

The main departure hall of Plaza de Armas coach station in Seville

Tickets and Reservations

Reservations for medium- to long-distance travel can be made at bus stations, online via Movelia (www.movelia.es), or on the websites of individual bus companies. You can buy tickets on board regional buses, but during peak seasons it is wise to purchase them in advance. Discounts are given for round-trip tickets and there may be online reductions.

"Supra" coaches operated by **Alsa** on popular routes are direct and boast leather seats, extra legroom, free Wi-Fi, and on-board refreshments.

Seville

Seville has two coach stations in the centre of town, Plaza de Armas and Prado de San Sebastián. Buses from Prado de San Sebastián head mainly south, with destinations such as Cádiz, Jerez and Algeciras. Both

stations have a café and newsstand. At Plaza de Armas there is Metro and Metro-Centro (see p272) access outside.

Córdoba

The main coach station in Córdoba is run by a regional branch of Alsa, Alsina Graells. It is basic, with a small waiting area, café, newsstand and lockers. Coaches depart regularly for Granada, Cádiz, Almería, Málaga and Seville.

Granada

In Granada, travellers may be confused by the choice of coach companies, each with a variety of destinations. Alsa is the largest coach company, and its station is referred to as the central coach station. This station offers routes all over Murcia and Andalucía. Coaches for Madrid leave from the main train station.

Málaga

Málaga coach station is located in the centre of town, behind the train station. Coaches depart daily to all of Spain, as well as some international destinations. The station has a café, newsstand, shop, Internet café and money exchange. A taxi rank and bus stops are located outside.

Almería

Almería's coach and train stations share a building. It has little in the way of amenities, but does provide transport to destinations across Andalucía and Murcia.

DIRECTORY

Coach Stations

Almería
Estación Intermodal
Plaza de la Estación s/n.
Tel 950 26 20 98.

Córdoba
Terminal Alsina Graells
Glorieta de las Tres Culturas.
Tel 957 40 40 40.

Granada
Terminal Alsina Graells Sur
Carretera de Jaén, Granada.
Tel 902 42 22 42.

Málaga
Estación de Autobuses
Paseo de los Tilos.
Tel 952 35 00 61.

Seville
Estación Plaza de Armas
Plaza de Armas.
Map 1 B5 & 5 A2.
Tel 902 45 05 50.

Prado de San Sebastián Estación
Map 4 D3.
Tel 954 41 71 11.

Coach Companies

Alsa
W alsa.es

Damas
W damas-sa.es

Leda
W leda.es

Socibus
W socibus.es

Transportes Generales Comes
W tgcomes.es

Regional coach operated by the Alsa company

Driving in Andalucía

Many of the main roads and motorways in Andalucía are new and in very good condition. The road network is continually expanding, so always check a recently published map. Fold-out maps can be obtained at airports or tourist offices. You should also bear in mind that the number of accidents on Spanish roads is quite high, due to the confusion in road rules. Always drive with caution, but particularly in July and August when the roads are packed with holiday-makers who do not know the area. When visiting towns and villages, it is best to park your vehicle away from the centre and then walk in.

Typically narrow Andalucían street blocked by a parked car

Arriving by Car

Visitors bringing their own vehicles from other countries will need documentation in Spain. You should always make sure you have your driving licence, vehicle registration document and insurance. Your insurance company should be able to arrange an overseas extension of your car insurance. To hire a car in Spain you need a current driving licence and be over 18 years of age.

If you are travelling from the UK you will need your pink plastic photocard and an International Driving Permit, which can be obtained from the RAC or the AA.

Most Spanish motorways are well equipped with an SOS network of telephones, which provide instant access to the emergency and breakdown services. Ask for *auxilio en carretera*.

Rules of the Road

In Spain people drive on the right, so you must give way to the right. At intersections and roundabouts always proceed with caution.

The speed limits are 50 km/h (30 mph) in built-up areas; 90–100 km/h (55–60 mph) outside them and 120 k/h (75 mph) on motorways. Seat belts are compulsory both in the back and front; motor cyclists must wear crash helmets. Drivers must always carry two warning triangles and a reflective vest, as well as a first-aid kit.

Road Signs

Standard European road signs are used in Andalucía. However, signposting is often confusing and inconsistent, so be especially attentive when navigating in or out of cities. When leaving a town, scan the road for direction signs to other towns. Some are small and easily missed. If you need to change direction, look for signs, which say *Cambio de Sentido*. They generally lead to bridges or underpasses where you can turn around.

Local Drivers

Many drivers in Andalucía ignore road signs and speed up at amber traffic lights. It is common for drivers to come up close to the car in front to signal that they want to overtake. Indicators are not necessarily used by Spanish drivers, so be alert to the movements of nearby vehicles.

Motorways

In Andalucía almost all the motorways *(autovías)* are toll-free; except for the A4 *autopista*

Road Signs in Andalucía

Look out for the following road signs: *Peligro*, indicating danger, *Obras*, meaning roadworks ahead, *Ceda el Paso*, showing that you should give way and *Cuidado*, advising caution.

A road sign showing major routes at a crossroads

Overhead sign indicating the road is a motorway

Be alert to the fact that bulls may be on the road

Warning of the likelihood of snow or ice

(toll motorway) that connects Seville and Cádiz, and the AP7 along the Costa del Sol, which has some sections with tolls.

When driving on the *autopista*, the toll booths are at sporadic intervals. At the booths a sign posts the corresponding fare. Drive into one of the lanes with a green light indicating the method of payment you wish to use.

Driving in the Sierra Nevada along one of the highest roads in Europe

Driving in the Countryside

Only head off the major "N" roads *(rutas nacionales)* if you are not in any hurry. Some of the minor roads in Andalucía wind and climb, and their surfaces will often be in poor condition. In addition, although diversions may be marked, when you take them you may find they are inadequately signposted. Taking a minor road may add hours to a journey.

Buying Petrol

Many petrol stations in and around Andalucía still have attendants. Petrol stations out of town tend to remain open 24 hours a day. At self-service stations you generally have to pay for the petrol before it is dispatched. *Gasoil* (diesel) and *sin plomo* (unleaded) are usually available. Credit cards are widely accepted.

Driving in Town

Driving in the towns and cities of Andalucía can be difficult. The centres of Seville and Córdoba have streets that are narrow, labyrinthine and hard to negotiate in a car. Coupled with the often inconsiderate driving

of the residents, this can make it quite stressful to drive. Also, parking access is time-limited in Seville and completely restricted to city residents in some parts of Granada's centre.

Breakdown Services

If you break down, pull to a safe location at the side of the road. Put on the reflective vest (required to be carried in your car at all times) and place one reflective triangle in front and another approximately 50 m (165 ft) behind the car. If necessary, call for assistance, from breakdown services such as **ADA**, **Europ Assistance** or **RACE**.

Parking

In Seville, on-street parking is extremely difficult to find and is metered for a maximum stay of 1–2 hours. The best option for visitors is a parking garage – a few public garages operate, otherwise some hotels offer parking for guests.

There are few car parks in Córdoba and parking costs €1.50-2.50 per hour in Seville, Granada, Córdoba & Málaga.

Logos for AVIS and Hertz, popular car rental companies

Car Rental

In major cities, car hire agencies are near the airports, with some near train stations. **Avis**, **Hertz** and **Enterprise** provide good bargains, but be wary of anyone asking for a large credit card deposit. Most cars are manual; automatics cost more. The minimum age for renting a car is usually 21. Some firms charge a supplement for under 21s, provided they hold a licence that has been valid for at least a year.

DIRECTORY

Breakdown Services

ADA
Tel 915 19 33 00.
W **ada.es**

Europ Assistance
Tel 902 15 85 85
(outside Spain 34 915 149 900).
W **europ-assistance.com**

RACE
(affiliated to the RAC in the UK)
Tel 902 40 45 45.

Parking

Almería
Garage Belén
Avenida Federico García Lorca 42.
Tel 950 25 30 60.

Córdoba
Aparcamientos Isolux Corsan Córdoba S.L.
Avenida Custodios 2.
Tel 957 29 96 19.

Granada
Parquigran
Plaza de San Agustín s/n.
Tel 958 29 60 33.

Málaga
Parking Las Delicias
Calle Don Rodrigo 3.
Tel 952 21 24 78.

Seville
Aparcamientos Magdalena
Méndez Núñez 1.
Tel 954 22 83 33.

Car Rental

Avis
W **avis.es**
Córdoba
Tel 957 40 14 45.
Granada
Tel 958 44 64 55.
Málaga
Tel 902 09 02 82.
Seville
Tel 902 11 02 83.

Enterprise
W **enterprise.es**
Jerez (Cádiz) Airport
Tel 956 18 68 14.
Málaga
Tel 952 23 18 58.
Seville
Tel 954 51 47 35.

Hertz
W **hertz.es**
Córdoba
Tel 957 40 20 61.
Granada
Tel 958 20 44 54.
Málaga
Tel 952 35 50 40.
Seville
Tel 954 51 47 20.

Getting Around Towns and Cities

Many of Andalucía's cities, towns and villages have small, historic centres, characterized by narrow streets and tiny squares. Walking is an excellent and practical way of getting around the sights, especially as entry by car is restricted to residents in parts of many towns. For the same reason, city buses are generally not much good for travelling between monuments, but they are useful to get to shopping areas or from your hotel into the centre of town. Buses are very cheap, clean and safe, and generally only crowded at rush hours.

Typical *circulares* bus, operating around Seville

Guided tour visiting the Patio de las Doncellas at Seville's Real Alcázar

Walking

In many Andalucían towns, major sights are often only a short walk from where you are likely to be staying – at most just a short bus or taxi ride away. One of the joys of Andalucía's cities is to lose yourself in their narrow streets and to stumble upon the sights as you go.

Drivers in Spain tend not to respect pedestrians, even where pedestrians have the right of way. Crossings with pedestrian signals often have only a flashing amber light showing to oncoming drivers, even when the signal pedestrians see shows a green man; therefore it is advisable to be very cautious.

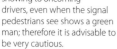
Red signal for wait; green for walk with care

Guided Tours

There is no better way to soak up the ambience of Andalucía's fine cities than from the seat of an old-fashioned, horse-drawn carriage. Drivers wait in line with their carriages near major monuments. They take up to four

people and cost from €35–45 for 40 minutes. For tours on foot, consult local tourist offices about multilingual walking and cultural tours with **El Legado Andalusi**.

In Seville, **Bici 4 City** can rent you a bike that comes complete with an MP3 guided tour. A more relaxing option is a cruise up the Guadalquivir River on a riverboat, with pretty views of the city. Open-topped double-decker **City Sightseeing** buses offer hop-on-hop-off tours with audio guides, available in Seville, Granada, Cádiz and Málaga. **Feel the City Tours** offer free walking tours of Seville and Granada. Tips are appreciated. They also run paid guided tours that include entry to key sights. Tours in Granada need to be booked in advance online on the Feel the City Tours website.

City Buses

City buses are most useful for getting to outlying sights as the historical centres are mostly

pedestrianized. In Seville, the useful lines for visitors are the *circulares*, numbered C1 to C6, which run around the city centre. In Granada, buses are less useful except for Nos. 31, 32 and 34, which run from the centre of the city to Albaicín, Alhambra and Sacromonte.

In Córdoba the Nos. 3 and 16 take passengers from the historic area to the more commercial centre of the city. Málaga's L3 services the town hall area and train station, while in Almería the No. 1 bus operates around the Old Town.

Metro

Seville's Metro system was designed to aid transport between the outer areas of Seville and the city centre. Line 1 is useful for getting from the historical centre (Puerta Jerez) to shopping centers (Nervión or Ciudad Expo's MetroMar). The system will eventually consist of four Metro lines, which will provide easy access to bus and train stations and include a line to the airport (Line 4).

Place your card *(see Tickets section)* over the reader to pass through barriers, and press the green button by the train door to open it. On-board overhead monitors announce the stops.

Metro-Centro

The Metro-Centro tram opened in 2008 in Seville city centre. It provides climate-controlled, rapid transport between San Bernardo station and Plaza Nueva in an otherwise pedestrian-only zone. Other lines are planned over the next few years, extending the network to Puerta Osario and Santa Justa train station.

Pay at the machine at tram stops (or pass your card over

the reader on board); press the green button to open the door. Stops are announced on overhead monitors. Metro-Centro trams pass every 3–5 minutes and stop briefly at all stops.

Tickets

A *billete sencillo* or *univiaje* (single ticket) can be purchased on buses, but be sure to carry small change. In Seville, the *tarjeta multiviaje* (multi-trip pass) and *tarjeta turística* (1–3 day pass) are valid on all TUSSAM means of transport (city bus, airport bus and Metro-Centro).

Cards can be purchased and topped up at newsstands or Tussam information kiosks, and are also rechargeable at Metro and Metro-Centro stops. Metro cards can be purchased in the entrance of stations and are for use exclusively on the Metro.

Tarjeta multiviaje and *tarjeta turística* electronic passes

Taxis

Spanish towns and cities are generously supplied with taxis, so there is not usually a problem

Standard, white Seville taxi, with its logo and official number

finding one, day or night. Taxis are always white and have a logo on the doors, which displays their official number. Drivers rarely speak any English, so learn enough Spanish to explain where you are going. The meter marks up the basic fare; however, supplements are added for *tarifa nocturna* (night-time driving), *maletas* (luggage) or *días festivos* (public holidays). If you are in doubt of the correct price, ask for the *tarifas* (tariff list).

Cycling

There are cycle lanes in most cities. Seville has pedestrianized a main throughfare in the centre, creating a wide promenade, which allows for bikes. Helmets are recommended.

SEVICI is a self-service bike rental programme in Seville, with 2,500 bikes available 24 hours a day. Bikes can be hired free for 30 minutes and are charged per hour after that. A €150 credit card deposit is paid and refunded on return of the bike.

Motorists tend to treat cyclists as a nuisance and city traffic can be dangerous for cyclists. **Andalucian Cycling Experience** offer trails into the country on mountain bikes.

Bicycles lined up ready for hire at SEVICI docking stations, Seville

General Index

Page numbers in **bold** refer to main entries

A

Abd al Rahman I 50
  Alcazaba (Málaga) 183
  Mezquita (Córdoba) 148
Abd al Rahman II 50, 148
Abd al Rahman III 50–51
  Alcazaba (Almería) 206
  Córdoba 146
  Medina Azahara 142–3
Abul Hasan, Sultan 202
Accommodation see Hotels
Acero, Vicente de 204
Acinipo 177
Addresses, Spanish 263
Admission charges 254–5
Aguilar **151**
Air sports 249, 251
Air travel 264–5
Airlines 264, 265
Airports 264–5
Alameda de Hércules (Seville) 13, **92**
Alba, Dukes of 90, 209
Albaicín (Granada)
  Street-by-Street map 196–7
Alcalá de Guadaíra
  hotels 217
Alcalá la Real **154**
Alfonso VIII, King 155
Alfonso X the Wise, King
  Arcos de la Frontera 177
  Cantigas 52
  Iglesia de Santa Ana (Seville) 107
  Iglesia de Santa María de la Oliva (Lebrija) 136
  Medina Sidonia 172
  Reconquest 52
  sign of Seville 79
Alfonso XI, King 146
Alfonso XII, King 57
Alfonso XIII, King 58
  Hotel Alfonso XIII (Seville) 100
Algeciras
  festivals 39
  restaurants 232
Alhama de Granada **192**
Alhambra (Granada) 125, 190, **198–9**
  architecture 27
  Generalife 202
  Patio de los Leones 199
  Puerta de la Justicia 44
Aljaraque
  restaurants 230
Almería 15, 189, **206–7**
  festivals 39, 43
  hotels 219
  map 207

Almería (cont.)
  restaurants 236
Almería (province) see Granada and Almería
Almohads
  architecture 26
  Moorish Conquest 50, 51
  Reconquest 52
Almonte
  restaurants 230
Almoravids 50, 51
Almuñécar **193**
  festivals 41
Álora **180**
Las Alpujarras 15, 54, 189, 200–201
  Las Alpujarras tour **204–5**
Amadeo, King 57
American Legation (Tangier) 187
Al Andalus 50–51
Andújar **155**
  festivals 38
Animals see Wildlife
Añora 143
Antequera 14, **181**
Antiques shops 241
Apéritifs 227
Apes, Gibraltar 175
Aposeosis de Santo Tomás de Aquino (Zurbarán) 71
Aquariums:
  Aquarium (Roquetas de Mar) 208
  Selwo Marina (Benalmádena) 246, 247
Aracena **130**
  hotels 217
Arches, Moorish 27
Archez 185
Archidona **181**
Architecture
  azulejos 26, **80**
  early 20th century 59
  Moorish **26–7**
  Moorish Revival 58
  Patios of Córdoba 150
  Post-Moorish **28–9**
  Sevillian bell towers 94–5
Archivo de Indias (Seville) 12, 76, **84–5**
Arcos de la Frontera 13, 124, 176, **177**
  hotels 218
  restaurants 232
El Arenal (Seville) **67–73**
  area map 67
  hotels 216
  restaurants 228
  Street-by-street map 68–9
Arévalo, Luis de 195
Arts and crafts shops 241
ATMs 260

Autumn in Andalucía 40
AVE (Tren de Alta Velocidad Española) 266, 267
Averroes of Córdoba 51
The Axarquia **183**
Ayamonte **130**
Ayuntamiento (Arcos de la Frontera) 179
Ayuntamiento (Carmona) 136–7
Ayuntamiento (Seville) 29, **78–9**, 110
Azulejos 26, **80**

B

Babaloo Beach 37
Baelo Claudia **173**
Baena **151**
  festivals 38
Baetica 48
Baeza 15, **156–7**
  hotels 217
  restaurants 231
  Street-by-street map 156–7
Bailén
  Battle of (1808) 57
  restaurants 231
Baixeres, Dionisio
  The Court of Abd al Rahman III 50–51
El Balcón de Europa (Nerja) 182
Banderilleros 31
Banking 260–61
Baños del Alcázar Califales (Córdoba) 144, 146
Baños Arabes (Jaén) 152
Baños de la Encina 125, **155**
El Bañuelo (Granada) **195**, 197
Baras, Sara 33
Barbate **172–3**
Baroque architecture 29
Los Barrios
  restaurants 234
Bartolomé de Jaén, Maestro
  Baeza Cathedral screen 157
  Capilla Real (Granada) 194
  Capilla del Salvador (Úbeda) 158
  Capilla de San Andrés (Jaén) 153
Basílica de la Macarena (Seville) 13, **93**
Baza **204–5**
  festivals 40
Beaches **36–7**
Beato de Liébana 50
Bécquer, Gustavo Adolfo 102
Bed and breakfast 214–15
Beer 226
Belalcázar 143
Belalcázar, Sebastián de 143
Bell towers, Seville 94–5
Bélmez 142

Benahavis
restaurants 232
Benalmádena **184**
Benaojan
restaurants 232
Berbers 51, 174
Bernadet, Fernando 107
Bicycles 273
Bienal de Arte Flamenco (Seville)
40, 244, 247
Birds see Wildlife
Bizet, Georges 100
Blood Wedding (Lorca) **209**
Blues Festival (Cazorla) 39
Boabdil, Sultan
Alhambra (Granada) 199
fall of Granada 52–3
imprisonment in Lucena 151
sword 194
Bodegas
Jerez de la Frontera 166, **167**
Montilla 151
El Puerto de Santa María 167
Sanlúcar de Barrameda 166
Bolonia 37
Bolshevik Triennium 59
Bonaparte, Joseph 56, 57
Bormujos
restaurants 230
Bourbon kings **56–7**
Breakdown services 271
Breakfast 220
Brenan, Gerald 203, 205
Bronze figures, Iberian 46–7
Bubión 15, 203
restaurants 236
Buddhist stupa (Benalmádena) 184
Bullfighting 21, **30–31**, **246**, 247
Plaza de Toros de la Maestranza
(Seville) 30, 68, **72**, 246
Ronda 179
Bulls, safety 258
Bureau de change 260
Buses 272, 273
El Buzo (Seville) 69
Byron, Lord 168

C
Cabello, Luis 195
Cable cars
Teleférico Benalmádena 246,
247
Cabo de Trafalgar 172, **173**
Cabopino 37
Cabra 140, **151**
festivals 39
Cadiar 205
festivals 40
Cádiz 13, 14, **168–71**
A 90-Minute Walk Around
Historic Cádiz **170–71**
1812 Constitution **56–7**, 170

Cádiz (cont.)
festivals 40, 41, 43
history 45, 47, 54, 58
hotels 218
restaurants 232–3
Cádiz and Málaga **163–87**
Exploring Cádiz and Málaga
164–5
hotels 218–19
restaurants 232–6
Caesar, Julius 48
La Calahorra 189, **203**
Calle Betis (Seville) 12, 111
Calle de la Feria (Seville) 90
Calle Mateos Gago (Seville) 77
Calle Pelay y Correa (Seville) **107**,
111
Calle Rodrigo de Triana (Seville)
106, 111
Calle Sierpes (Seville) 12, **78**, 110
Calléjon del Agua (Seville) 77
Camarón de La Isla 33
Camera Oscura (Seville) **93**
Camp sites 214, **215**
La Campana (Seville)
hotels 216
Campiña 139
Campo, Juan del 194
Canales, Antonio 33
Cano, Alonso 155, 194
El Cano, monument to 98
Los Caños de Meca 37, 173
hotels 218
Capileira 15, 203
Capilla see Churches
Caravanning 214, 215
Carboneras
restaurants 236
Carlist Wars 56, 57
Carlos I, King see Carlos V,
Emperor
Carlos II, King 55
Carlos III, King **56**, 84
Carlos IV, King 56
Carlos V, Emperor (King Carlos I)
Palacio Carlos V (Granada) 29,
195, 199
Puerto de Jaén y Arco de Villalar
(Baeza) 157
Real Alcázar (Seville) 86
Seville's Golden Age 54
Carmen **100**
Royal Tobacco Factory (Seville)
56, 57
Carmona **136–7**
hotels 217
restaurants 230
Los Carnavales 41, **43**, 168
La Carolina **155**
Cars
driving in Andalucía 270–71
hiring 265, 271

Carthage 46, 47, 48
Carthusians
Monasterio de Santa María de
las Cuevas (Seville) **109**
La Cartuja (Seville) 105, 108
hotels 216
Cartuja '93 (Seville) **108**
Casa de la Condesa Lebrija
(Seville) see Palacio de Lebrija
Casa de Pilatos (Seville) 12, 80, **81**
Casa de los Tiros (Granada) 194–5
Casares
restaurants 233
Casas Viejas 59
Cash machines 260
Castellar de la Frontera 173
hotels 218
Castillo de Colomares
(Benalmádena) 184
Castles and fortresses
Alcazaba (Almería) 51, 206
Alcázar (Jerez de la Frontera)
166
Alcázar de Rey Pedro (Carmona)
137
Baños de la Encina 155
Belalcázar 143
Bélmez 142
La Calahorra 189, 203
Castillo de Almodóvar del Río
142
Castillo Arabe (Álora) 180
Castillo Arabe (Antequera) 181
Castillo Arabe (Salobreña) 193
Castillo de Gibralfaro (Málaga)
183
Castillo de Guzman el Bueno
(Tarifa) 173
Castillo de Niebla (El Condado)
133
Castillo San Marcos (El Puerto
de Santa María) 167
Castillo de San Miguel
(Almuñécar) 193
Castillo de Santa Catalina (Jaén)
152
Castillo de Vélez Blanco 205
Castillo de la Yedra (Cazorla) 160
Cástulo (Jaén) **155**
Fortaleza de la Mota (Alcalá la
Real) 154
La Iruela (Cazorla) 160
Kasbah (Tangier) 186
Melilla La Vieja 175
San Sebastián fort (Cádiz) 171
Segura de la Sierra 160
see also Palaces
Cathedrals
Almería 206
Baeza 157
Cádiz 124, **168**, 171
Córdoba 138, **148–9**

Cathedrals (cont.)
Granada 194
Guadix 29, 204
Jaén 125, 152
Jerez de la Frontera 166
Málaga 182
Seville 12, 76, **82–3**
Catholic Church 23, 255
Catholic Monarchs *see* Fernando
II of Aragón; Isabel of Castilla
Caves
cave paintings 46
Cueva de los Leteros 205
Cueva de los Murciélagos 46
Cuevas de Nerja 182
Cuevas de la Pileta 47, 179
Gruta de la Maravillas 130
St Michael's Cave (Gibraltar) 175
Cayón, Gaspar 204
Cazalla de la Sierra 136
hotels 217
Cazorla 141, **160**
hotels 217
restaurants 231
Cecilio, San 197
Celts 46, 47
Cerámica Santa Ana (Seville) 106,
239, 241
Ceramics
azulejos 80
Triana (Seville) 106
What to Buy in Andalucía 242
Certamen Internacional de
Guitarra Classica Andrés
Segovia (Almuñécar) 41
Cervantes, Miguel de
Archivo de Indias (Seville) 84
Corral de los Olmos 84
Don Quixote 55
imprisonment 78
Ceuta **187**
Charco de la Pava Flea Market
(Seville) **108**, 240
Children
clothes shops 241
entertainment for 246, 247
in restaurants 221
Chipiona **166**
Chocolate, drinking 227
Christians, Reconquest 52–3
Churches
Basílica de la Macarena (Seville)
13, 93
Capilla de los Marineros (Seville)
107
Capilla Real (Granada) 15,
194
Capilla del Salvador (Úbeda)
158
Capilla de San Andrés (Jaén)
152–3
Capillita del Carmen (Seville)
107
Ermita de Nuestra Señora del
Rocío **133**

Churches (cont.)
Iglesia de la Asunción (Palma
del Río) 142
Iglesia de la Asunción (Priego
de Córdoba) 154
Iglesia de la Magdalena (Seville)
72, 95, 111
Iglesia de Nuestra Señora de la
O (Sanlúcar de Barrameda) 28,
166
Iglesia de Nuestra Señora de la
O (Seville) **109**
Iglesia de San Hermenegildo
(Seville) 94
Iglesia de San Ildefonso (Seville)
81, 95
Iglesia de San Marcos (Seville)
28, 91, **94**
Iglesia de San Pablo (Úbeda)
158–9
Iglesia de San Pedro (Seville) 90,
94, **95**
Iglesia de Santa Ana (Granada)
28, **196**
Iglesia de Santa Ana (Seville)
107, **109**, 111
Iglesia de Santa Catalina
(Seville) 91, **95**
Iglesia de Santa María la
Coronada (Medina Sidonia) 172
Iglesia de Santa María de la
Oliva (Labrija) 136
Iglesia del Salvador (Seville) **79**
Iglesia San Ildefonso (Jaén) 153
Iglesia San Jorge (Palos de la
Frontera) 132
Iglesia San Juan Bautista
(Hinojosa del Duque) 142
Oratorio de San Felipe Neri
(Cádiz) **169**, 171
Santa María de los Reales
Alcázares (Úbeda) 158
Santuario Virgen de la Cabeza
155
Templo San Juan (Almería) 206
visiting 255
Churrigueresque architecture 29
Cinemas *see* Film
Civil War 45, **58–9, 155**
Classical music **245**, 247
Claudius, Emperor 173
Climate 39–41
Clothes
in churches 255
in restaurants 220
shops 241
Coach travel 269
Cobos, Francisco de los 158
Coffee 227
Coín
restaurants 233
Coja, Paquita la 209
Columbus, Christopher 101, **131**,
192
Archivo de Indias (Seville) 84

Columbus, Christopher (cont.)
La Cartuja (Seville) 105
Castillo de Colomares
(Benalmádena) 184
Fiestas Colombinas 39
Huelva 131
Monasterio de la Rábida **131**
Monasterio de Santa María de
las Cuevas (Seville) 109
monument to (Seville) 85
Palos de la Frontera 127, 132
sails to America 52, 53
Sanlúcar de Barrameda 166
ships 53
statue of (Punta del Sebo) 131
tomb of 83
Comares 183
Communications 262–3
Cómpeta 183
Concurso Nacional de Flamenco
(Córdoba) 38
El Condado **133**
Constantina 136
Constitution (1812) 56–7, 170
Consulates 254, 257
Convents *see* Monasteries and
convents
Conversion chart 257
Córdoba 14–15, **144–50**
entertainment 244–7
festivals 38, 39, 42–3
hotels 217–18
map 147
Mezquita 14, 124, 138, 145,
148–9
Moorish conquest 50–51
patios **150**
restaurants 231–2
shops 239, 241
Street-by-Street map 144–5
transport 267–9, 272, 273
Córdoba and Jaén **139–61**
Exploring Córdoba and Jaén
140–41
hotels 217–18
restaurants 231–2
Córdoban Caliphate 26
El Cordobés 142
Cornejo, Pedro Duque 109, 149
Coronel, Doña María 95
Corpus Christi 39, 43
Corral del Carbón (Granada) 194
Corrida Goyesca (Ronda) 40, 179
Cortés, Hernán 101
Archivo de Indias (Seville) 84
conquers Mexico 54
Cortés, Captain Santiago 155
Cortes de la Frontera
hotels 218
Costa de Almería 37
Costa de la Luz 36, 163, 173
Costa del Sol 39, **185**
beaches 36, **37**, 163
golf 37, 249, 251
history 60, 61

Costa del Sol (cont.)
  landscape 24
Costa Natura 37
Costa Tropical 36, 193
Coto Doñana *see* National parks
Courier services 262, 263
Credit cards **260**
  in hotels 214
  lost 258
  in restaurants 221
  in shops 238
Crime 258
Cristo de la Expiración (Orgiva) 38
Cuban War 58
Cueva *see* Caves
Culture 22–3
Currency 61, 261
Cycling 248, 251, 273

D

Dalí, Salvador 187
Dance *see* Flamenco
Department stores 238, 241
Desfiladero de Despeñaperros
  139, **155**
Día de la Cruz (Córdoba/Granada)
  38, 42
Día de Reyes 41
Día de la Toma (Granada) 41
Dialling codes 262
Díaz, Daniel Vásquez 131
Disabled travellers **256**, 257
  in hotels 214, **215**
  in restaurants 221
Domes, Moorish 26
Don Carlos (beach) 37
Don Juan **73**
Doñana, Parque Nacional de 25,
  127, **134–5**
Drake, Sir Francis 54, 168
Drinks *see* Food and drink
Driving licences 270
Las Dunas 37

E

Écija **137**
Egas, Enrique de 143, 194
Eisenhower, Dwight D. 60
El Ejido 25
Electrical adaptors 257
Embassies 257
Emergency numbers 258, 259
Entertainment **244–7**
  booking tickets 244, 247
  bullfighting **246**, 247
  for children **246**, 247
  cinema 245, 247
  flamenco **244**, 247
  folk music 245
  football 246, 247
  nightlife **245**, 247
  opera and classical music **245**,
    247
  outdoor activities 248–51
  practical information 244, 247

Entertainment (cont.)
  rock, pop and jazz **245**, 247
  theatre **244**, 247
Equestrian sports 248–9,
  251
Ermita de Nuestra Señora del
  Rocío **133**
Estepa **137**
Estepona **185**
  restaurants 233
Etiquette 255
Expo '92 45, 60, 61, 105, 108, 109

F

Fadrique, Infante Don 92
Falange 58, 59
Falconete, Pedro Sánchez 73
The Fall of Granada (Vigarney)
  52–3
Falla, Manuel de 58, 171
  tomb of 168
Fashion shops 241
Felipe II, King 54, 85
Felipe III, King 55
Felipe IV, King 55
Felipe V, King 56
Felipe el Hermoso 194
Feria de Abril (Seville) 38, 42, 60
Feria de Almería 39, 43
Feria del Caballo (Jerez de la
  Frontera) 38
Feria de Málaga 39, 43
Feria de Mayo (Córdoba) 38
Feria de Pedro Romero (Ronda)
  40
Fernández, Alejo 109
Fernando II de Aragón
  Alcazaba (Almería) 206
  Alcázar de los Reyes Cristianos
    (Córdoba) 146
  and Christopher Columbus 131
  death 54
  festivals 41
  Granada Cathedral 194
  marriage 53
  Real Chancillería (Granada) 196
  Reconquest 52, 192
  Santa Fé 192
  tomb of 15, 194
Fernando III, King
  Castillo de Santa Catalina (Jaén)
    152
  conquers Baeza 156
  Córdoba 146
  Reconquest 52
  statue of (Seville) 78
Fernando VI, King 56
Fernando VII, King 56, 57
Ferries, to North Africa 265
Festival de Cine Iberoamericano
  (Huelva) 40
Festival de la Guitarra (Córdoba)
  39
Festival Iberoamericano de Teatro
  (Cádiz) 40

Festival Internacional de Jazz
  (Granada) 40
Festival Internacional de Música y
  Danza (Granada) 39, 245
Festival Internacional de Teatro y
  Danza (Seville) 38
Festival de Música Antigua
  (Seville) 41
Festival de los Patios (Córdoba)
  38, 42–3, 150
Festivals **38–43**
Fiesta de San Marcos (Ohanes) 38
Fiesta de la Vendemia (La Palma
  del Condado) 40
Fiesta de los Verdiales (Málaga)
  41
Fiesta del Vino (Cadiar) 40
Fiesta de la Virgen del Carmen 39
Fiestas 30, **38–43**
Fiestas Colombinas (Huelva) 39
Fiestas de la Exaltación del Río
  Guadalquivir (Sanlúcar de
  Barrameda) 39
Figueroa, Antonio Matías de 100
Figueroa, Leonardo de
  Hospital de los Venerables
    (Seville) 85
  Iglesia de la Magdalena (Seville)
    72
  Iglesia del Salvador (Seville)
    79
  Iglesia de Santa Catalina
    (Seville) 95
  Museo de Bellas Artes (Seville)
    71
Film 245, 247
  Festival de Cine Iberoamericano
    (Huelva) 40
  spaghetti westerns 208
Finis Gloriae Mundi (Valdés Leal)
  73
Fino 226
First aid 258, 259
First Republic 57
Fishing 248, 251
Flamenco 21, **32–3**, **244**, 247
  Bienal de Arte Flamenco 40,
    244
  Jerez Annual Flamenco Festival
    41
  Museo del Baile Flamenco
    (Seville) 79
  shops 241
Flores, Rosario 245
FOCUS (Fundación Fondo de
  Cultura de Sevilla) 85
Folk music 245
Food and drink
  Andalucían cuisine 220
  Flavours of Andalucía 222–3
  markets 240
  sherry **34–5**
  shops 241
  tapas 222, **224–5**
  What to Buy in Andalucía 243

Food and drink (cont.)
  What to Drink in Andalucía
  226–7
  see also Restaurants
Football 246, 247
Ford, Richard 21, 100, 227
Forestier, Jean-Claude 102
Fortresses *see* Castles and
  fortresses
Franco, General Francisco
  and Cádiz 168
  Civil War 58, 59
  death 45, 60, **61**
  World War II 60
Frigiliana 183
Fuengirola **184**
  restaurants 233
Fuente Agria 204
Fuente Obejuna 142
Fuente de Piedra **180–81**

G
Galleries *see* Museums and
  galleries
García, Esteban 79
Garcilaso de la Vega 151
Gardens *see* Parks and gardens
Garganta del Chorro 163, **180**
Gaucín 13, 14, 176
  restaurants 233
Gay and lesbian travellers **256,
  257**
Generalife (Granada) 202
Gerena
  restaurants 230
Gibraltar **174–5**
  airport 265
  Great Siege of (1779–83) 56
  history 46, 56
  hotels 218
  restaurants 233
  World War II 60
La Giralda (Seville) 12, 54, 76, **82**
Golden Age, Seville **54–5**
Golf 37, 249, 251
González, Anibal 102, 107
González, Felipe 60, **61**
González, Gutiérrez 153
Gothic architecture 28
Goya y Lucientes, Francisco José
  de
  Corrida Goyesca (Ronda) 40
El Gran Capitán 195
Granada 15, **194–7**
  airport 265
  Albaicín Street-by-Street map
  196–7
  Alhambra 190, **198–9**
  entertainment 244–7
  festivals 38–41, 43
  Generalife 202
  hotels 219
  map 195
  Reconquest 52–3
  restaurants 236–7

Granada (cont.)
  shopping 240, 241
  transport 268, 269, 272, 273
Granada and Almería **189–209**
  Exploring Granada and Almería
  190–91
  hotels 219
  restaurants 236–7
Granados, José 79
Grand Socco (Tangier) 187
Grapes, sherry 35
Grazalema 176
  festivals 39
  hotels 218
El Greco 155
Greeks, ancient 46, 47
Green travel **264**
Gruta de la Maravillas 130
Guadalquivir, River 68, 110
  bridges 60–61
Guadix 189, **204**
  Cathedral 29
Guided tours **272**
Guitars, Spanish **32**, 239, 243
Guzmán, Fernando Gómez de
  142
Guzmán el Bueno 110, **173**
Gypsies 32, 197, 258

H
Habsburg dynasty 45
Hadrian, Emperor **48**, 101
  birthplace 136
Al Hakim II 50, 146, 148, 155
Hannibal 152
Health 258–9
Henry II of Trastámara 52, 53
Herbs and spices 243
Hercules 168, 169
Hermenegildo, St 94
Hernández, Rafel Rodríguez 93
La Herradura 37
Herrera, Francisco de 95
Herrera, Juan de 29, 84
Hinojosa del Duque 142
Hiring cars 265, 271
History **45–61**
Holidays, public 41
Holy Roman Empire 54
Homo sapiens 45, 46
Horse-drawn carriages 76, 102,
  272
Hospital de la Caridad (Seville) 69,
  73
Hospital de la Reina (Alhama de
  Granada) 192
Hospital de Santiago (Úbeda)
  159
Hospital de los Venerables
  (Seville) 12, 77, **85**
Hospitals 259
Hotel Alfonso XIII (Seville) 99, **100**
Hotel Balneario (Alhama de
  Granada) 192
Hotel Continental (Tangier) 186

Hotels **212–19**
  booking and checking in 213
  Cádiz and Málaga 218–19
  Córdoba and Jaén 217–18
  disabled travellers 214, **215**
  grading and facilities 212–13
  Granada and Almería 219
  Huelva and Sevilla 217
  paradors 213, 214
  paying in 214
  prices 213
  Seville 216
  where to look 212
Hoyos, Cristina 40
Huelva **131**
  festivals 39, 40, 42
  restaurants 230
Huelva and Sevilla **127–37**
  Exploring Huelva and Sevilla
  128–9
  hotels 217
  restaurants 230–31
Huercal Almería
  restaurants 237
Humeya, Aben 205
Hungry Years 60

I
Ibero-American Exposition (1929)
  59, 97, 98, 100, 101, 102
Iglesia *see* Churches
Immigration 254
Los Infiernos 192
La Inmaculada (Valdés Leal) 70
La Inmaculada Concepción
  (Seville) 41
Inquisition **55**
  Alcázar de los Reyes Cristianos
  (Córdoba) 146
  autos-da-fé 55, 78
  expulsion of Moors 54
  headquarters 109
  Ronda 178
Insurance
  car 270
  health 259
  travel 258, 259
Internet **262**, 263
Interpreters 259
Inurria, Mateo 146
Irving, Washington 77, 197
  Alhambra apartments
  (Granada) 199
  Tales of the Alhambra 57
Isabel II, Queen 56, 57
Isabel of Castilla
  Alcazaba (Almería) 206
  Alcázar de los Reyes Cristianos
  (Córdoba) 146
  and Christopher Columbus 131
  death 54
  festivals 41
  Granada Cathedral 194
  Iglesia de la Encarnación
  (Alhama de Granada) 192

Isabel of Castilla (cont.)
marriage 53
Real Alcázar (Seville) 86
Real Chancillería (Granada)
196
Reconquest 52
Santa Fé 192
tomb of 15, 194
Isabelline architecture 28
Isicio, San 160
Isidoro, San 49
Isla Cristina **130**
festivals 41
hotels 217
restaurants 230
Isla Mágica (Seville) **108**, 246
La Isleta 209
Itálica 124, 127, **136**
Roman remains **48–9**

J
Jabugo 130
restaurants 231
Jaén 15, 125, 139, **152–3**
festivals 42–3
hotels 218
map 153
parador **152**
restaurants 232
Jaén (province) *see* Córdoba
and Jaén
Jamete, Esteban 158
Jamón ibérico (ham) 130
Jardines de Murillo (Seville) 13, **85**
Jazz **245**, 247
Jerez de la Frontera 14, **166**
airport 265
bodegas **167**
equestrian sports 249
festivals 38, 41
restaurants 233
Jews 51
Córdoba 144
Jimena de la Frontera 13, 14, 173,
178
Jiménez, Juan Ramón
Museo de Zenobia y Juan
Ramón Jiménez (Moguer) 132
Juan Carlos I, King 60, 61
Juan de la Cruz, San 159
Juana la Loca 194
Junta de Andalucía 254
Justa, Santa 106

K
Kasbah (Tangier) 186
Ketama 32
Knights Hospitallers 196
Knights Templar 130

L
Lafita, José 76, 84
Landscape **24–5**
Lanjarón 15, 191, **193**
festivals 39

Lawyers 259
Leandro, San 49
Lebrija **136**
Lee, Laurie 163, 185, 193
Legal assistance 259
Leone, Sergio 208
Libraries
Archivo de Indias (Seville) 12,
84–5
La Línea de la Concepción 175
restaurants 234
Loja **192**
hotels 219
restaurants 237
Lopéz, Julian (El Juli) 31
Lorca, Federico García 30
Blood Wedding **209**
death 59
Yerma 59
Lost property 258
Lucena **151**
Lucía, Paco de 32
Lunes de Toro (Grazalema) 39
Lynxes 135

M
La Macarena (Seville) 13, **89–95**
area map 89
hotels 216
restaurants 229
Street-by-Street map 90–91
Machado, Antonio 156
Maeda, Asensio de 93
Maestranza
hotels 216
Maestranza Bullring (Seville) *see*
Plaza de Toros de la
Maestranza
Magazines **263**
listings 244
Magellan, Ferdinand 54, 98
Sanlúcar de Barrameda 166
Maimónides 51
statue of (Córdoba) 146
Málaga 13, 14, **182–3**
airport 265
Alcazaba 182–3
Civil War 58
festivals 38, 39, 41, 43
hotels 218
restaurants 234
transport 268, 269
Málaga (province) *see* Cádiz and
Málaga
Mañara, Miguel de 73
Manilva
restaurants 234
Mano Negra 58
Manolete 31
Al Mansur 51, 148
Maps
A 90-Minute Walk Around
Historic Cádiz 170–71
A 90-Minute Walk in Seville
110–11

Maps (cont.)
Almería 207
Las Alpujarras tour 204–5
Andalucía at a glance 124–5
Baeza 156–7
beaches 36–7
Cádiz and Málaga 164–5
Civil War 58
Córdoba and Jaén 140–41
Discovering Seville 10–11
early Andalucía 46
Granada 195
Granada: Albaicín 196–7
Granada and Almería 190–91
Greater Seville 18
Huelva and Sevilla 128–9
Jaén 153
Jerez de la Frontera 167
Landscape of Andalucía 24–5
Moorish domain (800) 50
Moorish domain (1350) 52
Parque Nacional de Doñana
134–5
present-day Andalucía 60
Pueblos Blancos tour 176–7
Rail network 267
Roman Spain 48
Ronda 178–9
Seville 18–19
Seville: Across the River 105
Seville: El Arenal 67, 68–9
Seville: Around the Universidad
98–9
Seville: at a Glance 64–5
Seville: La Macarena 89, 90–91
Seville: Parque María Luisa 97
Seville: Santa Cruz 75
Seville: Santa Cruz Street-by-
Street 76–7
Seville: Street Finder 112–21
Seville: Triana 106–7
sherry regions 34
Sierra Morena tour 142–3
Spain 16–17
Spain in Europe (1812) 56
Spanish empire (1700) 54
Tangier 186
Úbeda 159
Western Europe 17
Marbella 13, 14, **184–5**
beaches 36
hotels 218
restaurants 234–5
Marbella Golf 37
María Cristina, Queen 58
María Luisa, Princess
Costurero de la Reina (Seville)
98
Parque María Luisa (Seville)
102–3
statue of (Seville) 102
Markets 240
Charco de la Pava Flea Market
(Seville) 108, 240
Martínez, Domingo 71

Martínez, Ginés 157
Matadors 30–31
Matalascañas **133**
  restaurants 231
Mazagón **132**
  hotels 217
Mecina Bombaron
  hotels 219
Medical treatment 259
Medina Azahara 27, 50, 51,
  142–3
Medina Sidonia **172**
Medina Sidonia, Duchess of 60
Medina Sidonia, Dukes of 134, 172
Medinaceli, Dukes of 81
Melilla **187**
Mena, Pedro de 194
Mendoza, Rodrigo de 203
Menus 220–21
Merimée, Prosper 57, 100
Mesa, Juan de 94
Metropol Parasol 60, 95
Mezquita (Córdoba) 14, 124, 138,
  145, **148–9**
Mijas
  hotels 218
  restaurants 235
Millán, Gómez 93
Los Millares 46, 47, 207
Minas de Riotinto **130**
Mirador de San Nicolás (Granada)
  195
Miró, Joan 185
Mobile phones **262**, 263
Moguer **132**
Mojácar 15, **209**
  hotels 219
Molina, Tirso de 73
Monachil
  hotels 219
Monasteries and convents
  Convento de la Merced Calzada
    (Seville) 70
  Convento de Santa Clara
    (Seville) 92
  Convento de Santa Inés (Seville)
    95
  Convento de Santa Paula
    (Seville) 91, **94**
  Monasterio de la Cartuja
    (Granada) 29, **195**
  Monasterio de la Rábida **131**
  Monasterio de San Clemente
    (Seville) **92**
  Monasterio de Santa Clara
    (Moguer) 132
  Monasterio de Santa María de
    las Cuevas (Seville) **109**
  Real Monasterio de Santa Clara
    (Jaén) 153
  Santa Isabel (Seville) 94
Money 260–61
Montañés, Juan Martínes
  Convento de Santa Clara
    (Seville) 92

Montañés, Juan Martínes (cont.)
  Iglesia del Salvador (Seville) **79**
  St John the Baptist 94
  statue of (Seville) 79
Montefrío **192**
Montes de Málaga **183**
Montilla **151**
Montoro **143**
Montpensier, Dukes of 100
Moors 21–2, 45, **50–51**
  Las Alpujarras uprisings 54
  architecture **26–7**
  azulejos 26, 80
  expulsion from Spain 54, 55
  Granada 194
  Reconquest 52–3
Morocco **186–7**
  travel to 265
Moros y Cristianos (Válor) 40
Mosaics
  azulejos 80
  Roman 48
Mosques
  Grand Mosque (Tangier) 186
  Mezquita (Córdoba) 14, 138,
    145, **148–9**
Motorways 270–71
Motril
  hotels 219
  restaurants 237
Moulay Ismail, Sultan 186
Mountain refuges 214, **215**
Movies *see* Film
Mudéjar architecture 26, **28**, 52
  azulejos 80
Muhammad V, Caliph 198, 199
Mulhacén 25, 203
Murallas (Seville) **93**
Murallas de San Carlos (Cádiz) 170
Murillo, Bartolomé Esteban 70,
  110, 146, 168
  baptism 72
  Hospital de la Caridad (Seville)
    69, 73
  Jardines de Murillo (Seville) 85
  Palacio Arzobispal (Seville) 84
  Santa Justa and Santa Rufina
    106
  Seville Cathedral 83
  La Virgen de la Servilleta 71
  Young Beggar 55
Museums and galleries
  admission charges 254–5
  Archivo de Indias (Seville) 12,
    84–5
  La Atalaya Theme Centre (Jerez
    de la Frontera) 166
  Casa Museo de Martín Alonso
    Pinzón (Palos de la Frontera) 132
  Casa Natal de Picasso (Málaga)
    182, 183
  Castillo de la Yedra (Cazorla)
    160
  Centro Andaluz de Arte
    Contemporáneo (Seville) 109

Museums and galleries (cont.)
  Centro de Interpretación
    Cuevas de Guadix (Guadix) 204
  Centro de Recepción e
    Interpretación de la Naturaleza
    (Parque Natural de Cazorla,
    Segura y las Villas) 160
  Centro del Vino Condado de
    Huelva (El Condado) 133
  Convento de Santa Paula
    (Seville) 94
  Dar El Makhzen (Tangier) 186
  Gibraltar Museum (Gibraltar) 175
  Museo de Alfarería (Guadix) 204
  Museo de Almería 207
  Museo Arqueológico (Baza) 205
  Museo Arqueológico (Córdoba)
    147
  Museo Arqueológico (Granada)
    195, 197
  Museo Arqueológico (Málaga)
    183
  Museo Arqueológico (Seville)
    13, **101, 103**
  Museo Arqueológico (Úbeda)
    159
  Museo Arqueológico Cueva de
    Siete Palacíos (Almuñécar) 193
  Museo Automovilístico y de la
    Moda (Málaga)182, 183
  Museo de Artes y Costumbres
    Populares (Seville) 13, **101**, 103
  Museo del Baile Flamenco
    (Seville) **79**
  Museo de Bellas Artes
    (Córdoba) 146
  Museo de Bellas Artes
    (Granada) 195
  Museo de Bellas Artes (Seville)
    12, 66, **70–71**
  Museo de Cádiz (Cádiz) 168–9
  Museo Carmen Thyssen
    (Málaga) 13, 14, 182, **183**
  Museo del Grabado
    Contemporáneo (Marbella) 185
  Museo Hispano-Musulman
    (Granada) 195
  Museo Julio Romero de Torres
    (Córdoba) 146
  Museo de la Legión (Cueta) 187
  Museo Minero (Riotinto) 130
  Museo de Picasso (Málaga) 13,
    14, 182, 183
  Museo Provincial (Huelva) 131
  Museo Provincial (Jaén) 153
  Museo Taurino (Córdoba) 146
  Museo de Zenobia y Juan
    Ramón Jiménez (Moguer) 132
  opening hours 255
  Palacio de Nájera (Antequera)
    181
Music
  festivals 38–43
  flamenco **32–3**, **244**, 247
  folk **245**

Music (cont.)
  opera and classical music 245, 247
  rock, pop and jazz **245**, 247

N
Napoleon I, Emperor
  Alhambra (Granada) 198
  Battle of Bailén 153
  and Cádiz 169
  Napoleonic Wars 56
Naranjas y Limones (Torres) 146
Nasrid dynasty 45, 194
  Alhambra (Granada) 198–9
  architecture 26
  Generalife (Granada) 202
  Reconquest 52
National parks
  Parque Nacional de Doñana 25, 127, **134–5**
  Sierra Nevada 203
Nature reserves
  Bahia de Cádiz Nature Reserve 169
  Parque Natural de Cabo de Gata 15, 125, **208**
  Parque Natural de Cazorla, Segura y Las Villas **160, 161**
  Parque Natural de Los Alcornocales 13, 14, **173**
  Parque Natural de Montes de Málaga 183
  Parque Natural Sierra de las Nieves **180**
  Parque Natural del Torcal 181
  Yesos de Sorbas 209
Naturism 250, 251
Las Navas de Tolosa, Battle of (1227) 52
Neanderthals 46
Necrópolis Romana (Carmona) 137
Nelson, Admiral Horatio 57, 173
Neolithic period 46
Nerja **182**
  beach 165
  hotels 218
  restaurants 235
New World 54
Newspapers 263
Niebla 133
Nightlife **245**, 247
Níjar **209**
"NO8DO" **79**
Noche de San Juan 39

O
Ocampo, Andrés de 94
Ohanes
  festivals 38
Ojén
  hotels 218
Olavide, Pablo de 155
Olives 25, 49
  olive oil **152**

Opening hours 255
  banks 260
  shops 238
Opera **245**, 247
Order of Calatrava 154
Ordóñez, Bartolomé 194
Orea, Juan de 206
Orgiva 203, **204**
  festivals 38
  hotels 219
  restaurants 237
Osuna 137
  restaurants 231
Osuna, Dukes of 137
Outdoor activities 248–51
Oviedo, Juan de
  Casa de Pilatos (Seville) 81
  Convento de la Merced Calzada (Seville) 70
  Convento de Santa Clara (Seville) 92

P
Pacheco, Francisco de 81
Palaces
  Alcázar de los Reyes Cristianos (Córdoba) 14, 144, **146**
  Alhambra (Granada) 27, 125, **198–9**
  Casa de Pilatos (Seville) 12, 80, **81**
  Casa de los Tiros (Granada) 194–5
  Medina Azahara 142–3
  Palacio Arzobispal (Seville) 84
  Palacio de las Cadenas (Úbeda) 158
  Palacio de las Dueñas (Seville) **94**
  Palacio Carlos V (Granada) 29, **195**, 199
  Palacio de Jabalquinto (Baeza) 28, 156
  Palacio de Lebrija (Seville) 13, **78**
  Palacio de la Madraza (Granada) 194
  Palacio del Marqués de la Gomera (Osuna) 29, **137**
  Palacio del Marqués de Salvatierra (Ronda) 179
  Palacio del Mayorazgo (Arcos de la Frontera) 177
  Palacio Mondragón (Ronda) 178
  Palacio Pedro I (Seville) 53
  Palacio de Pemartín (Jerez de la Frontera) 166
  Palacio de Peñaflor (Écija) 137
  Palacio de San Telmo (Seville) 96, 99, **100**
  Palacio de Viana (Córdoba) 23, 147
  Real Alcázar (Seville) 12–13, 77, **86–7**
  see also Castles and fortresses
La Palma del Condado 133
  festivals 40
Palma del Río **142**
  hotels 218

Palma del Río (cont.)
  restaurants 232
Palomares incident (1966) 60
Palomino, Antonio 195
Palos de la Frontera 127, **132**
  restaurants 231
Pampaneira 15, 203
Paquirri 143
Paradors **213**, 214
Parking 271
Parks and gardens
  Alcázar de los Reyes Cristianos (Córdoba) 144
  Generalife (Granada) 202
  Jardines de Murillo (Seville) 13, **85**
  Moorish gardens 26
  Parque Genovés (Cádiz) 170
  Parque María Luisa (Seville) 12, 13, 97, **102–3**
  Parque Ornitológico (Almuñécar) 193
  Real Alcázar (Seville) 86
Parlamento de Andalucía (Seville) **93**
Parque María Luisa (Seville) 12, **97–103**
  area map 97
  restaurants 228–9
  Street-by-Street: Around the Universidad 98–9
Parque Nacional *see* National parks
Parque Natural *see* Nature reserves
Passports 254, 258
Patio de las Doncellas (Seville) 80, 86
Patios of Córdoba **150**
Pechina
  hotels 219
Pedrajas, Francisco Javier 154
Pedro I (the Cruel), King
  Alcázar del Rey Pedro (Carmona) 137
  death 53
  Real Alcázar (Seville) 86
  Reconquest 52
Pedroche 143
Pemán, José Maria 168
Peñarroya-Pueblonuevo 142
Peninsular War 56, 57
People of Andalucía 22–3
Pérez, Juan 131
Perfume shops 241
Personal security 258–9
Petrol 271
Pharmacies 259
Phoenicians 46, 47, 168
Picadores 30
Picasso, Pablo 58, 187
  Casa Natal de Picasso (Málaga) 182, 183
  Museo de Picasso (Málaga) 13, 14, 182, 183
  Self-portrait 58
Pickman, Charles 109

Pickpockets 258
Pico Veleta 203
Pinzón, Martín 132
Pinzón, Vincente 132
Pisano, Nicola 94
Pizzaro, Francisco 54
Plateresque architecture 29
Playa Agua Amarga 37
Playa de los Genoveses 37, 209
Plaza de la Corredera (Córdoba) 146–7
Plaza de España (Seville) **101**
Plaza del Pópulo (Baeza) 157
Plaza de San Juan de Dios (Cádiz) 170
Plaza Santa Cruz (Seville) **77**, 110
Plaza de Toros (Antequera) 181
Plaza de Toros (El Puerto de Santa María) 167
Plaza de Toros de la Maestranza (Seville) 12, 68, **72**, 246
Plaza del Triunfo (Seville) 76, **84**
Plaza Vieja (Almería) 206
Plaza Virgen de los Reyes (Seville) 12, 76, **84**
Police 258, 259
Pop music **245**
Poqueira Valley **203**, 204
Post-Moorish architecture **28–9**
Postal services 262, 263
El Postigo (Seville) **69**
Pottery *see* Ceramics
Pozo, Aurelio del 73
Pozoblanco 143
Priego de Córdoba **154**
PSOE (political party) 61
Public holidays 41
Public toilets 255
Pueblos Blancos tour 14, **176–7**
Puente de Isabel II (Seville) 57, 107, 111
Puente Nuevo (Ronda) 178
Puente Romano (Córdoba) 145, **147**
Puerta de Purchena (Almería) 206–7
Puerto Banús **185**
Puerto de la Ragua 205
El Puerto de Santa María **167**, 169
  hotels 219
  restaurants 235
Punta Umbría **131**

Q
Queipo de Llano, General 59
Quesada, Diego de 95

R
Radio 263
Rail travel 266–8
Rainfall 40
Raphael, St 145
Real Alcázar (Seville) 12–13, 77, **86–7**
  azulejos 80

Real Chancillería (Granada) 196
Real Escuela Andaluza de Arte Ecuestre (Jerez de la Frontera) **166**, 246
Reccared, King 49
Reconquest **52–3**
  architecture 28
Religious objects shops 241
Renaissance architecture 29
RENFE 266, 267
Republican army, Civil War 58–9
Responsible travel **256–7**
Restaurants **220–37**
  Andalucían cuisine 220
  Cádiz and Málaga 232–6
  children in 221
  Córdoba and Jaén 231–2
  disabled travellers 221
  Flavours of Andalucía 222–3
  how to dress 220
  Granada and Almería 236–7
  Huelva and Sevilla 230–31
  meal times 22, 220
  reading the menu 220–21
  Seville 228–9
  smoking 221
  tipping 255
  what it costs 221
  wine choices 221
Riaño, Diego de 79, 110
Ribera, Catalina de 93
Ribera, José de 137
Rincón de la Victoria **37**, 183
  hotels 219
La Rinconada
  restaurants 231
El Rinconcillo (Seville) 91
Riofrío 192
Riotinto Company 128, 130, 131
Rivas, Felipe de 92
Rivera, General Primo de 58, 59
Roads
  crossing 272
  driving in Andalucía **270–71**
  road signs 270
El Rocío 127, **133**
  hotels 217
  restaurants 230
Rock music **245**
Rodalquilar 209
Rodríguez, García
  Andalusian Patio 150
Rodríguez, Ventura 153, 192
Roldán, José 153
Roldán, Luisa 93
Roldán, Pedro
  Hospital de los Venerables (Seville) 85
  Iglesia de Nuestra Señora de la O (Seville) 109
  Iglesia San Ildefonso (Jaén) 153
  Iglesia de San Ildefonso (Seville) 81

Roldán, Pedro (cont.)
  Iglesia de Santa Catalina (Seville) 91, 95
Romans 45, **48–9**
  Acinipo 177
  Baelo Claudia 173
  Itálica **136**
  Necrópolis Romana (Carmona) 137
Romería de los Gitanos (Cabra) 39
Romería de Nuestra Señora de la Cabeza (Andújar) 38, 43, 155
Romería del Rocío (Huelva) 38, 42, 133
Romería de San Isidro 38
Romería de San Miguel (Torremolinos) 40
Romerías 42
Romero, Pedro 40, 181
Ronda 13, 14, 163, 179, **178–9**
  bullfighting 179
  festivals 40
  hotels 219
  restaurants 235
  Street-by-Street map 178–9
Ronda la Vieja **177**
Roquetas de Mar **208**
  restaurants 237
Royal Tobacco Factory (Seville) 56, 57, 80, 99, **100–101**
Rue es Siaghin (Tangier) 187
Rueda, Jerónimo Sánchez de 154
Rufina, Santa 106
Ruiz, Hernán
  Córdoba Cathedral 149
  La Giralda (Seville) 82
  Puente Romano (Córdoba) 147
Ruiz, Hernán the Younger 93

S
Sacromonte (Granada) 197
Saint Bruno in Ecstasy (Zurbarán) 168
St John the Baptist (Montañés) 94
Salares 185
Sales tax 238, 255
Salido, Fernando Ortega 158
Salobreña **193**
  restaurants 237
San *see also* Churches
San Fernando
  restaurants 235
San Hugo en el Refectorio (Zurbarán) 70
San Jerónimo (Torrigiano) 70
San José **208–9**
  hotels 219
San Pedro de Alcántara 187
Sánchez Coello, Alonso 54–5
Sanlúcar de Barrameda **166**
  festivals 39
  hotels 219
  restaurants 235
Santa Cruz (Seville) 12, **75–87**

Santa Cruz (Seville) (cont.)
A 90-Minute Walk in Seville
110–11
area map 75
hotels 216
restaurants 228–9
Street-by-Street map 76–7
Santa Fé **192**
Santa Justa station (Seville) 267
Santiponce 136
Santuario see Churches
Scenic routes **268**
Scipio Africanus
founds Itálica 48, 127, 136
Punic Wars 155
Security, personal 258–9
Segovia, Andrés 58, 194
Certamen Internacional de
Guitarra Classica Andrés
Segovia (Almuñécar) 41
Segura de la Sierra **160**
Self-catering accommodation 214
Semana Santa 23, **38**
in Seville 42
Virgen de la Macarena 93
Seneca the Elder 48
Seneca the Younger 48, 146
Senior travellers **256, 257**
Setenil 177
Sevilla (province) see Huelva and
Sevilla
Sevilla en Otoño (Seville) 40
Seville **63–121**
A 90-Minute Walk in Seville
110–11
Across the River **105–9**
airport 264
El Arenal 67–73
Cathedral and La Giralda 76,
82–3
entertainment 244–7
festivals and fiestas 38–42
Golden Age **54–5**
hotels 216
La Macarena 89–95
maps 18–19, 64–5
maps: Street Finder 112–21
Museo de Bellas Artes 70–71
Parque María Luisa 12, 97–103
Real Alcázar 12–13, **86–7**
restaurants 228–9
Santa Cruz 12, **75–87**
shopping 239, 241
Three Days in Seville 12–13
transport 266–9, 272–3
Triana **106–7**
Two Days in Seville 12
Seville School 70
Sherry **34–5**, 226
Jerez de la Frontera 166–7
El Puerto de Santa María 167
Sanlúcar de Barrameda 166
Shoe shops 241
Shopping **238–43**
how to pay 238

Shopping (cont.)
markets 240
VAT exemption 238, 255
What to Buy in Andalucía
242–3
when to shop 238
Sierra de Aracena 126, 127, 128,
129, **130**
Sierra de Cabo de Gata 208
Sierra de Cazorla 25, 139, 161
Sierra de Grazalema 13, 24
Sierra Morena 136, 139
Sierra Morena tour **142–3**
Sierra Nevada 25, 189, **203**
skiing 249, 251
Sierra Norte **136**
Siestas 39
Siloé, Diego de 158
Almería Cathedral 206
Granada Cathedral 194
Guadix Cathedral 204
Iglesia de la Encarnación
(Alhama de Granada) 192
Iglesia de la Villa (Montefrío) 192
Málaga Cathedral 182
Real Chancillería 196
Templo de San Gabriel (Loja)
192
Skiing 249, 251
Smoking 221, 255
Soraya, Sultana 202
Sorbas **209**
Sotogrande **175**
Soult, Marshal 73, 84
Spaghetti westerns 208
Spanish Foreign Legion 187
Spas and Arab baths 250, 251
Alhama de Granada 192
Baños del Alcázar Califales
(Córdoba) 144, 146
Baños Arabes (Jaén) 152
El Bañuelo (Granada) **195**, 197
Fuente Agria 204
Lanjarón 193
Special needs, travellers with see
Disabled travellers
Specialist holidays 250, 251, 256,
257
Speed limits 270
Sports 246, **248–9**, 251
Spring in Andalucía 38
Stamps, postage 262
Stations 267–9
Steinacher, Gustavo 107
Student travellers **256**, 257
Suárez, Adolfo 60
Summer in Andalucía 39
Sunshine 39
Susillo, Antonio 100
Synagogues
Córdoba 144, 146

T
Tabernas **208**
Tangier **186–7**

Tapas 222, **224–5**
Tapas bars 225
Tarifa 13, 14, **173**
beach 37
hotels 219
restaurants 235
Tarifa, 1st Marquess of 81
Tariq ben Ziyad 50
Tarraconensis 49
Tartessus 46, 47
Taxes, VAT exemption 238, 255
Taxis 273
safety 258
Teatro see Theatres
Tejero, Antonio 61
Telephone services 262, 263
Television 263
Telmo, St 100
Temperatures 41
Tena, Lucero 33
Tennis 249, 251
Tenorio, Don Juan 73
Terán, Luis Marín de 73
Theatres **244**, 247
Gran Teatro (Córdoba) 244, 247
Teatro Lope de Vega (Seville) 99,
101, 244, 245
Teatro de la Maestranza (Seville)
68, **72–3**, 244, 245
Theme parks
Isla Mágica (Seville) **108**, 246
Mini Hollywood (Tabernas) 246,
247
Tivoli World (Benalmádena) 246,
247
Theodosius, Emperor 49
Tickets
buses 273
coaches 269
entertainment 244, 247
trains 266
Tiles 26, **80**, 106
Time zones 257
Timetables, train 267
Tipping 255
in hotels 214
Toilets, public 255
Toledo
fall of (1085) 51
Third Council of (589) 49
El Torcal 14, **181**
Torcuato, San **204**
Torre de la Calahorra (Córdoba)
147
Torre de Don Fadrique (Seville) **92**
Torre del Oro (Seville) 12, 69, **73**
Torre Sevilla (Seville) 61, **109**
Torre Tavira (Cádiz) 13, **169**, 171
Torremolinos **184**
festivals 40
restaurants 235–6
Torres, Julio Romero de
Museo Julio Romero de Torres
(Córdoba) 146
Naranjas y Limones 146

Torrigiano, Pietro
  San Jerónimo 70
Tortello, Benvenuto 81
Tourist information **254**, 257
Tours by car
  Las Alpujarras **204–5**
  Pueblos Blancos **176–7**
  Sierra Morena **142–3**
Trafalgar, Battle of (1805) 56, **57**,
  173
Trains 266–8
Trajan, Emperor 48, 101
  birthplace 136
  statue of (Baelo Claudia) 173
  Triana (Seville) 105, 106
Trams **272–3**
Translation services 259
Travel **264–73**
  air 264–5
  bus 272, 273
  Cádiz and Málaga 165
  car 270–71
  coach 269
  Córdoba and Jaén 141
  cycling 273
  Granada and Almería 191
  Huelva and Seville 129
  insurance 258, 259
  rail 266–8
  taxis 273
  walking 272
Traveller's cheques **260**
Trevélez 15, 204
Triana (Seville) 12, 105
  A 90-Minute Walk in Seville
  110–11
  hotels 216
  Street-by-Street map 106–7
Triana, Rodrigo de 106

U

Úbeda 15, **158–9**
  hotels 218
  map 159
  parador **158**
  restaurants 232
Ubrique 177
UNESCO World Heritage Sites 15,
  156–9
Universidad (Seville) 98–9, **100–
101**
Utrecht, Treaty of (1713) 56, 174

V

Valdés, Lucas
  Hospital de los Venerables
  (Seville) 85
  Iglesia de la Magdalena (Seville)
  72
  Monasterio de San Clemente 92
Valdés Leal, Juan de 69, 146
  Ayuntamiento (Seville) 79
  Finis Gloriae Mundi 73
  Hospital de los Venerables
  (Seville) 85

Valdés Leal, Juan de (cont.)
  La Inmaculada 70
Valencina de la Concepción
  hotels 217
Valera, Lorenzo Coullaut
  Glorieta de Bécquer 102
Válor 205
  festivals 40
Vandals 49
Vandelvira, Andrés de 156
  Baeza Cathedral 157
  Capilla del Salvador (Úbeda) 158
  Cathedral (Jaén) 152
  Hospital de Santiago (Úbeda) 159
  Iglesia de San Pablo (Úbeda) 159
  Palacio de las Cadenas (Úbeda)
  158
El Vapor Boat (Cádiz) 169
VAT exemption 238, 255
Vázquez de Molina, Juan 158
Vega, Garcilaso de la 151
Vega, Lope de
  Fuente Obejuna 142
  Teatro Lope de Vega (Seville) 101
Vejer de la Frontera 14, **172**
  hotels 219
  restaurants 236
Velázquez, Diego **55**
  Ayuntamiento (Seville) 79
  baptism 90, 95
Los Vélez, Marqués de 205
Vélez Blanco **205**
Vélez Málaga 183
Vera
  restaurants 237
Veronica, St 152
Vespasian, Emperor 48
Victor's Beach 37
Vigarney, Felipe de 194
  The Fall of Granada 52–3
Virgen de la Macarena 88, **93**
La Virgen de la Servilleta (Murillo) 71
Virgin Mary 23
Visas 254
Visigoths 45, **48**, 49
  architecture 27
  Moorish Conquest 50

W

Walking
  in towns 272
  walking and trekking holidays
  248, 251
War of the Spanish Succession
  56, 174
Washington, George 84
Water, drinking 227
Water sports 249, 251
Weather 39–41
Welles, Orson 187
Wheelchair access *see* Disabled
  travellers
"White Villages" *see* Pueblos
  Blancos
Whitney, Gertrude Vanderbilt 131

Wildlife **25**
  Aquarium (Roquetas de Mar)
  208
  Bahia de Cádiz Nature Reserve
  169
  Centro Rescate de la Fauna
  Sahariana (Almería) 207
  Fuente de Piedra 180–81
  Parque Nacional de Doñana 25,
  134–5
  Parque Natural de Cabo de
  Gata 208
  Parque Natural de Cazorla,
  Segura and Las Villas
  25, **161**
  Parque Natural de Los
  Alcornocales 173
  Parque Natural de Montes de
  Málaga 183
  Parque Natural de Torcal 183
  Selwo Aventura (Estepona) 246,
  247
  Selwo Marina (Benalmádena)
  246, 247
  Sierra Nevada 203
  wildlife and birdwatching
  holidays 248, 251
  Yesos de Sorbas 209
  Zoobotánico (Jerez de la
  Frontera) 246, 247
Windfarms 173
Wine 133, **226**
  in restaurants 221
Winter in Andalusia 41
Wiring money **260**
Women 22–3
World War II 60

Y

Yegen 205
Yerbabuena, Eva 33
Yesos de Sorbas 209
Youth hostels 214, **215**

Z

Zahara de los Atunes 14, 172
  restaurants 236
Zahara de la Sierra 176
Zamora, Niceto Alcalá 154
Zoobotánico (Jerez de la
  Frontera) 246, 247
Zuheros
  hotels 218
Zurbarán, Francisco de 55, 146,
  168
  *Apoteosis de Santo Tomás de
  Aquino* 71
  Ayuntamiento (Seville) 79
  Iglesia de la Magdalena 72
  Palacio Arzobispal (Seville) 84
  St Bruno in Ecstasy 168
  San Hugo en el Refectorio 70
  The Sleeping Girl 166

Acknowledgments

Dorling Kindersley would like to thank the following people whose contributions and assistance have made this book possible.

Main Contributors

David Baird, resident in Andalucía from 1971 to 1995, has written many articles and books on Spain, including *Inside Andalusia*.

Martin Symington is a travel journalist and author who has written extensively on Spain. He is a regular contributor to *The Daily Telegraph* and also worked on the *Eyewitness Travel Guide to Great Britain*.

Nigel Tisdall, contributor to the *Eyewitness Travel Guide to France*, is the author of many travel publications, including the *Insight Pocket Guide to Seville*.

Additional Contributors

Louise Cook, Josefina Fernández, Adam Hopkins, Nick Inman, Janet Mendel, Steve Miller, Javier Gómez Morata, Clara Villanueva, John Gill, Mari Nicholson.

Additional Illustrations: Richard Bonson, Louise Boulton, Brian Cracker, Roy Flooks, Jared Gilbey, Paul Guest, Christian Hook, Mike Lake, Maltings Partnership, John Woodcock.

Additional Cartography: James Anderson, DK Cartography, Uma Bhattacharya, Mohammed Hassan, Jasneet Kaur.

Revisions and Relaunch Team

Asad Ali, Ashwin Raju Adimari, Emma Anacootee, Hansa Babra, Lynnette McCurdy Bastida, Claire Baranowski, Marta Bescos, Francisco Bastida Cabaña, Hilary Bird, Subhadeep Biswas, Eugenia Blandino, Greta Britton, Maggie Crowley, Cathy Day, Niki Foreman, Vinod Harish, Kaberi Hazarika, Tim Hollis, Claire Jones, Rahul Kumar, Vincent Kurien, Jude Ledger, Colin Loughrey, Francesca Machiavelli, Nicola Malone, Susan Mennell, Michael Osborne, Rakesh Kumar Pal, Sachida Nand Pradhan, Rada Radojicic, Ellen Root, Alice Saggers, Olivia Shepherd, Azeem Siddiqui, Beverly Smart, Anna Streiffert Limerick, Sylvia Tombesi-Walton, Priyansha Tuli, Catherine Waring, Conrad van Dyk, Nikhil Verma, Word on Spain.

Index

Helen Peters.

Additional Photography

Lynnette McCurdy Bastida, Rolando Naranjo Campos, Patrick Llewelyn-Davies, David Murray, Martin Norris, Ian O'Leary, Rough Guides/ Demetrio Carasco, Clive Streeter, Peter Wilson.

Photographic and Artwork Reference

Concha Moreno at Aeropuerto Málaga; Fanny de Carranza at the Area de Cultura del Ayuntamiento, Málaga; Tere González at Oficina de Turismo, Ayuntamiento, Cádiz; and staff at Castillo San Marcos, El Puerto de Santa María, Itálica, Seville cathedral and the Museo Bellas Artes, Seville.

Special Assistance

Dorling Kindersley would like to thank all the regional and local tourist offices, *ayuntamientos* and *diputaciones* in Andalucía for their valuable help, and especially the Oficina de Turismo de Sevilla de Junta de Andalucía and other departments of the Junta de Andalucía. Particular thanks also to: Javier Morata, Jose Luis de Andrés de Colsa and Isidoro González-Adalid Cabezas at Acanto Arquitectura y Urbanismo, Madrid; Juan Fernández at Aguilar for his helpful comments; Robert op de Beek at Alvear, Montilla; Francisco Benavent at Fundación Andaluza de Flamenco, Jerez de la Frontera; staff at the Locutorio, Granada; Paul Montegrifo; Amanda Corbett at Patronato Provincial de Turismo de Sevilla; José Pérez de Ayala at the Parque Nacional de Doñana; Gabinete de Prensa, RENFE, Sevilla; Graham Hines and Rachel Taylor at the Sherry Institute of Spain, London; Dr David Stone; Joaquín Sendra at Turismo Andaluz SA; *6 Toros 6* magazine, Madrid.

Photography Permissions

The publisher would like to thank all those who gave permission to photograph at various *ayuntamientos*, cathedrals, churches, galleries, hotels, museums, restaurants, shops, transport services and other establishments too numerous to thank individually.

Picture Credits

a = above; b = below; c = centre; f = far; l = left; r = right; t = top.

Works of art have been reproduced with the permission of the following copyright holders: (c) Suceesion Picasso/ DACS, London 2006 56clb; DACS, London 2011 58cb.

Photos taken with the assistance of **Al-andalus, Casa-museo Fg Lorca**, Fuentevaqueros, Granada: 199b; **Teatro de la Maestranza**, Seville: 244cla; **Canal Sur**, Sevilla: 263cb.

The publisher would like to thank the following individuals, companies and picture libraries for permission to reproduce their photographs:

123RF.com: jarp5 30-31c; joserpizarro 61cra; nuttaphong kanchanachaya 65bc; **Adif:** 226br, 267cl, 267br, 268tl, 268bl; **Aena:** 264br, 265tl; **Aisa Archivo Iconográfico**, Barcelona: 4tr, 47cr, 48ca; Universidad de Barcelona, *La Corte de Abderramán*, Dionisio Baixeres (1885) 50cr– 51cl; 51tc, 51bl, 52bc, 52br, 53bl, 54bl; Bloomberg-Rissman 173tl; Museo Naval Madrid, *Retrato de Magallanes*, 54br; Cason del Buen Retiro, *La Rendición de Bailén*, J Casado del Alisal (1864) 57tl; Greenwich Museum, *Battle of Trafalgar*, G Chamberg 57ca (d); 56cr–57cl, 59br, Algar 48bc; Servicio Histórico Nacional, *Alfonso XII*, R de Madrazo 57br (d); M Ángeles Sánchez 42t; **Alamy images:** age fotostock 27br, 47crb, 59cb, 169br; Jerónimo Alba 210-11; Antiqua Print Gallery 31bl, 32cl; Pierre Bonbon 220bl; Jon Arnold Images/ Jon Arnold 110cla; dbimages/ Allen Brown 272cla, blickwinkel 249br; Luis Dafos 200-1; Danita Delimont/ Alan Klehr 175tr; Kathy deWitt 111cr; Mark Eveleigh 170tr; fine art 262cb; Peter Forsberg 273tc; Granger Historical Picture Archive 51crb; Robert Harding Picture Library Ltd/ Michael Jenner 223cl HelloWorld Images Premium 11br; Hemis 213br; Heritage Image Partnership Ltd 47tl; Rolf Hicker Photography 104; Peter Horee 197br; imageBROKER 42cl; Jose Antonio Jimenez 173br; G. Aunion Juan 46bc; John Kellerman 2-3; Chris Knapton 248bl; Christ Lawrence 111tl; Lightworks Media 249tr; Melvyn Longhurst 171tc; Jose Lucas 46c, 47cl; Perry Van Munster 60–61c; Photographyto 94t; Stefano Politi Markovina 12c; Barry Mason 250br; Rod McLean 68; Geoffrey Morgan 246br; PRISMA ARCHIVO 47tc; Prisma by Dukas Presseagentur GmbH 25crb; David Sanger Photography/ Sam Pascal Saez 260bl; SAS 182tc; Carmen Sedano 249cl; Alex Segre 225tr; Gordon Sinclair 170bl; 170cla;

Peter Howard Smith 256tr; image broker/Karl Heinz Spremberg 263tl, Trigger Image 108tr; Lucas Vallecillos 74; Renaud Visage 222cla; Ben Welsh 248cra; Ken Welsh 144cl; Peter M. Wilson 171br, 172bl; **Alsa Groups S.L.L.C:** 269bl; **Arenas Fotografía Artística**, Seville: 53cr, 120cl, Monasterio de la Rábida, Huelva, *Partida de Colón*, Manuel Cabral Bejarano 131br (d); **Avis Budget Group:** 271c; **AWL Images:** Neil Farrin 213tr; **La Bobadilla:** 219tr; **Casa Grande:** 218tc; **Casa Juan:** 236b; **Casa Juanito:** 231tr; **Casa Museo F. Garcia Lorca:** 209br; **Casa Numero Siete:** 216br; **Casa Paco:** 233t; **Casa Robles:** 228bl; **Cephas:** Mick Rock 24tr, 34tr, 34cl, 35cr, 35br, 163; **Cerámica Santa Ana:** 239c; **El Churrasco:** 232br; **Colegas:** 256bl; **Dee Conway:** 33cr; **Corbis:** Owen Franken 223tl; The Gallery Collection 8-9; Sylvain Sonnet 66; **Giancarlo Costa, Milan:** 31bc (d), 45b; **JD Dallet, Málaga:** 22bl, 36clb, 36br, 39br, 40cla, 150cr; **Dreamstime.com:** Alfonsodetomas 27bl; Arenaphotouk 13tl, 21b; Delstudio 111bl; Sergey Dzyuba 139b; Iakov Filimonov 197clb; Fotomicar 15b; Freesurf69 5cr; Gerth Hochmuth 172cra; Infomods 81t; Javarman 122–3; Javlindy 250tl; Joserpizarro 43tr, 43cl, 54cl; García Juan 50clb, 53c; Kirsten Karius 161crb; Kasto80 125bl; Vichaya Kiatying-angsulee 138; Kmiragaya 48c; Lunamarina 37ca, 61tl; Carlos Soler Martinez 76bl; Juan Moyano 184tl, 206cl; Neirfy 12br; Nevenm 5cl; Antonio Ribeiro 87bl; Alvaro Trabazo Rivas 30cl; Sidqi 14tr; Nikolai Sorokin 10tl; Jose I. Soto 4cr, 49cra; Taiga 61ca; Asier Villafranca 14bl; **Agencia EFE, Madrid:** 60clb, 60b, 61bl, 61cr; **Egaña Oriza:** 229tl; **Empresa Pública de Emergencias Sanitarias:** 259ca; **Equipo 28 Seville:** 33tl; **Mary Evans Picture Library:** 100br, 181br (d); **El Faro de el Puerto:** 235bl; **La Finca:** 237bc; **Fotolia:** Artur Bogacki 20; citylights 96; **La Fructuosa:** 233bc. **Garum:** 234t; **Getty images:** AFP 31cr; Charles Phelps Cushing / ClassicStock 58crb; Christophel Fine Art 54-55c; Culture Club 59ca; DEA / A. DAGLI ORTI 56clb; DEA / C. SAPPA 168tr; DEA / G. DAGLI ORTI 31br, 52cla, 52c; DEA / G. NIMATALLAH 46br; Florilegius 30bc; Werner Forman 51ca; JORGE GUERRERO 40br; Heritage Images 56cl; Historical Picture Archive 30br; Keystone 187bc; Juan Carlos Muñoz 46clb; Print Collector 54clb; Chris Sattiberger 62–3; Universal History Archive 59crb Andrés Valdaliso Martinez 15tc; Visions Of Our Land 13br; **The Roland Grant Archive:** *"For a Few Dollars More"*, United Artists 208tl; **Giraudon, Paris:** 46cr; Flammarion-Giraudon 47c; **Robert Harding Picture Library:** Sheila Terry 53crb; **Hemispheres images:** Hervé Hughes 111crb; Stefano Torrione 172cra; **Hertz:** 271cb; **Hospes Palacio de Bailio:** 217tr; **Hulton Deutsch:** 58cr–59cb, 175bc; **Incafo Archivo Fotográfico, Madrid:** 161ca; A Camoyán 161cb; JL Glez Grande 161cla; Candy Lopesino/Juan Hidalgo 161cb; JL Muñoz 161bl; **Index, Barcelona:** 47cb, 48br, 50cla, 50bl, 50br, 51cb, 56br, 57crb, 57clb (d), 57cb; Image/Index Private Collection, *Sucesos de Casaviejas*, Saenz Tejada 59tl; Iranzo 48clb; **The Image Bank:** Stockphotos inc © Terry Williams 188; **Images:** 4b, 24b, 25tl, 25bl, 36tr, 38br; AGE Fotostock 30tr, 31c, 32br, 35cl, 41cla, 41br, 141tr,

161c, 226tr, 246tl; courtesy **Isla Magica:** 108tl, 108bl; **iStockphoto.com:** IPGGutenbergUKLtd 262ca, Juanmonino 23c; **JCDecaux Spain:** 273bl; **Pablo Juliá, Seville:** 245br; **Anthony King:** 25tr; **Life File Photographic Library:** 152bl; **José Lucas, Seville:** 86br, 169tc, 246c, 258clb, 272tr; **Neil Lukas:** 134clb, 134bc; **Arxiu Mas, Barcelona:** 49tc, 52cr–53cl; Museo América, Madrid, *View of Seville*, Sánchez Coello 54cr–55cl; © Patrimonio Nacional Madrid 49br, 52cl; **Magnum**/Jean Gaumy 61cb; **El Molino de la Romera:** 230tr. **NHPA:** Vicente Garcia Canseco 135ca; **Naturpress, Madrid:** Jose Luis G Grande 135bc; Francisco Márquez 25br; **Network Photographers:** 35tl; Rapho/Hans Silvester 38cl; **Oronoz Archivo Fotográfico, Madrid:** 30ca; Private Collection *Reyes Presidiendo a una Corrida de Toros* (1862), Anonymous 47ca, 47br, 47tl; María Novella Church, Florence, *Detail of Averroes*, Andrea Bonainti 51tl; 51bc, Diputación de Granada, *Salida de Boabdil de la Alhambra*, Manuel Gómez Moreno; 54cla; Museo del Prado, *Cristo Crucificado*, Diego Velázquez 55ca (d); Museo del Prado, *Expulsión de los Moriscos*, Vicent Carducho 55c (d); Musée du Louvre, Paris, *Joven Mendigo*, Bartolomé Murillo 55bc (d); © Patrimonio Nacional Madrid, Palacio Real, Riofrio, Segovia, *Carlos III Vestido de Cazador*, F Liani 56bl; © DACS London 1996, Sternberg Palace, Prague, *Self-Portrait*, Pablo Picasso 58clb; Private Collection, Madrid, *Soldados del Ejército Español en la Guerra de Cuba* 58br; 59bl, 61tc, 147tr; Private Collection, Madrid, *Patio Andaluz*, Garcia Rodríguez 150cl; Museo de Bellas Artes, Cádiz, *San Bruno en Éxtasis*, Zurbarán; 197bl; **Eduardo Paez, Granada:** *Porte de la Justice*, Baron de Taylor 44; **Paisajes Españoles, Madrid:** 93tc; **Parador Gibralfaro:** 234bl; **Jose M Perez de Ayala, Doñana:** 134tr, 134cla; **Pictures:** 43br; **Prisma, Barcelona:** 55tl; *Vista desde el Puerto* Nicolás Chapny (1884) 183t; 245tl; Hans Lohr 165br; Anna N 178ca; Sonsoles Prada 47crb; **Robert Harding Picture Library:** Quadriga Images 215t; **Ruta del Veleta:** 237tr; **M Ángeles Sánchez, Madrid:** 242tr, 242tc; **STA Travel Group:** 256c; **Tony Stone Images:** Robert Everts 86cla; **Visions of Andalucía Slide Library, Málaga:** M Almarza 25cr; Michelle Chaplow 23br; 32cr–33cls, 166br; A Navarro 40clb; **SOL.com:** 110bl; **Superstock:** age fotostock 88, 162, 214tl, 215br; The Art Archive 227br; Jacobo Hernández 126; Iberfoto 49tl, 49crb, 50-51c, 56-57c; José Lucas / age fotostock 140bl; Oronoz / Album 51tl, 52cb, 53tl, 53ca, 53clb, 55cb, 146br; Ken Welsh / Design Pics 212b; Felipe Rodríguez 252–3; Greg Stechishin 188; **Taberna del Alabardero:** 229br; **El Tamborilero:** 230bl; Tragabuches 235tr; **Tussam:** 264cla, 273cl, 273clb; Peter Wilson 39cla, 65crb, 178tr, 178bl, 183tr.

Front Endpaper: **Alamy Images:** Manfred Gottschalk Rtr; **Corbis:** Sylvain Sonnet Rcla; **Dreamstime.com:** Vichaya Kiatying-angsulee Ltr; **Fotolia:** citylights Rcra; **Superstock:** age fotostock Lbl ,Rtl; Jacobo Hernández Ltl; Greg Stechishin Rbr.

Cover Images: Front and spine – **Alamy Images:** Manfred Gottschalk; back – **Dreamstime.com:** Sean Pavone.

Map Images: **Alamy Images:** Manfred Gottschalk.

Phrase Book

In Emergency

Help!	¡Socorro!	soh-**koh**-roh
Stop!	¡Pare!	**pah**-reh
Call a doctor!	¡Llame a un médico!	yah-meh ah **oon** **meh**-dee-koh
Call an ambulance!	¡Llame a una ambulancia!	yah-meh ah **oonah** ahm-boo-**lahn**-thee-ah
Call the police!	¡Llame a la policía!	**yah**-meh ah lah poh-lee-**thee**-ah
Call the fire brigade!	¡Llame a los bomberos!	**yah**-meh ah lohs bohm-**beh**-rohs
Where is the nearest telephone?	Dónde está el teléfono más próximo?	dohn-deh ehs-**tah** ehl teh-**leh**-foh-noh mahs prohx-ee-moh
Where is the nearest hospital?	Dónde está el hospital más próximo?	dohn-deh ehs-**tah** ehl ohs-pee-**tahl** mahs prohx-ee-moh

Communication Essentials

Yes	Sí	see
No	No	noh
Please	Por favor	pohr fah-**vohr**
Thank you	Gracias	**grah**-thee-ahs
Excuse me	Perdone	pehr-**doh**-neh
Hello	Hola	**oh**-lah
Goodbye	Adiós	ah-dee-ohs
Good night	Buenas noches	bweh-nahs noh-chehs
Morning	La mañana	lah mah-**nyah**-nah
Afternoon	La tarde	lah **tahr**-deh
Evening	La tarde	lah **tahr**-deh
Yesterday	Ayer	ah-**yehr**
Today	Hoy	oy
Tomorrow	Mañana	mah-**nya**-nah
Here	Aquí	ah-**kee**
There	Allí	ah-**yee**
What?	¿Qué?	keh
When?	¿Cuándo?	**kwahn**-doh
Why?	¿Por qué?	pohr-**keh**
Where?	¿Dónde?	**dohn**-deh

Useful Phrases

How are you?	¿Cómo está usted?	**koh**-moh ehs-**tah** oos-**tehd**
Very well, thank you.	Muy bien, gracias.	mwee bee-**yehn** **grah**-thee-ahs
Pleased to meet you.	Encantado de conocerle.	ehn-kahn-**tah**-doh deh koh-noh-**thehr**-leh
See you soon.	Hasta pronto.	ahs-tah **prohn**-toh
That's fine.	Está bien.	ehs-**tah** bee-**yehn**
Where is/are …?	¿Dónde está/están …?	dohn-deh ehs-**tah**/ehs-**tahn**
How far is it to …?	Cuántos metros/ kilómetros hay de aquí a …?	**kwahn**-tohs **meh**-trohs/kee-**loh**-meh-trohs **eye** deh ah-**kee** ah
Which way to …?	¿Por dónde se va a …?	pohr **dohn**-deh seh **vah** ah
Do you speak English?	¿Habla inglés?	**ah**-blah een-**glehs**
I don't understand	No comprendo	noh kohm-**prehn**-doh
Could you speak slowly please?	¿Puede hablar más despacio por favor?	pweh-deh ah-**blahr** mahs dehs-pah-thee-oh pohr fah-**vohr**
I'm sorry.	Lo siento.	loh see-**ehn**-toh

Useful Words

big	grande	**grahn**-deh
small	pequeño	peh-**keh**-nyoh
hot	caliente	kah-lee-**ehn**-teh
cold	frío	**free**-oh
good	bueno	**bweh**-noh
bad	malo	**mah**-loh
enough	bastante	bahs-**tahn**-teh
well	bien	bee-**yehn**
open	abierto	ah-bee-**ehr**-toh
closed	cerrado	thehr-**rah**-doh
left	izquierda	eeth-key-**ehr**-dah
right	derecha	deh-**reh**-chah
straight on	todo recto	toh-doh **rehk**-toh
near	cerca	**thehr**-kah
far	lejos	**leh**-hohs
up	arriba	ah-**ree**-bah
down	abajo	ah-**bah**-hoh
early	temprano	tehm-**prah**-noh
late	tarde	**tahr**-deh
entrance	entrada	ehn-**trah**-dah
exit	salida	sah-**lee**-dah
toilet	lavabos, servicios	lah-**vah**-bohs sehr-**vee**-thee-ohs

more	más	mahs
less	menos	**meh**-nohs

Shopping

How much does this cost?	¿Cuánto cuesta esto?	**kwahn**-toh kwehs-tah ehs-toh
I would like …	Me gustaría …	meh goos-tah-**ree**-ah
Do you have?	¿Tienen?	tee-yeh-nehn
I'm just looking.	Sólo estoy mirando, gracias.	soh-loh ehs-**toy** mee-**rahn**-doh **grah**-thee-ahs
Do you take credit cards?	¿Aceptan tarjetas de crédito?	ah-**thehp**-tahn tahr-**heh**-tahs deh **kreh**-dee-toh
What time do you open?	¿A qué hora abren?	ah **keh** oh-rah **ah**-brehn
What time do you close?	¿A qué hora cierran?	ah keh oh-rah thee-**yehr**-rahn
This one.	Este	**ehs**-teh
That one.	Ese	eh-seh
expensive	caro	**kahr**-oh
cheap	barato	bah-**rah**-toh
size, clothes	talla	**tah**-yah
size, shoes	número	noo-**mehr**-oh
white	blanco	**blahn**-koh
black	negro	**neh**-groh
red	rojo	**roh**-hoh
yellow	amarillo	ah-mah-**ree**-yoh
green	verde	**vehr**-deh
blue	azul	ah-**thool**
antique shop	la tienda de antigüedades	lah tee-**yehn**-dah deh ahn-tee-gweh-**dah**-dehs
bakery	la panadería	lah pah-nah-deh-**ree**-ah
bank	el banco	ehl **bahn**-koh
book shop	la librería	lah lee-breh-**ree**-ah
butcher	la carnicería	lah kahr-nee-theh-**ree**-ah
cake shop	la pastelería	lah pahs-teh-leh-**ree**-ah
chemist	la farmacia	lah fahr-**mah**-thee-ah
fishmonger	la pescadería	lah pehs-kah-deh-**ree**-ah
greengrocer	la frutería	lah froo-teh-**ree**-ah
grocery	la tienda de comestibles	lah tee-**yehn**-dah deh koh-mehs-**tee**-blehs
hairdresser	la peluquería	lah peh-loo-keh-**ree**-ah
market	el mercado	ehl mehr-**kah**-doh
newsagent	el kiosko de prensa	ehl kee-**yohs**-koh deh **prehn**-sah
post office	la oficina de correos	lah oh-fee-**thee**-nah deh kohr-**reh**-ohs
shoe shop	la zapatería	lah thah-pah-teh-**ree**-ah
supermarket	el supermercado	ehl soo-pehr-mehr-**kah**-doh
tobacconist	el estanco	ehl ehs-**tahn**-koh
travel agent	la agencia de viajes	lah ah-**hehn**-thee-ah deh vee-**ah**-hehs

Sightseeing

art gallery	el museo de arte	ehl moo-**seh**-oh deh **ahr**-teh
cathedral	la catedral	lah kah-teh-**drahl**
church	la iglesia la basílica	lah ee-**gleh**-see-ah lah bah-**see**-lee-kah
garden	el jardín	ehl hahr-**deen**
library	la biblioteca	lah bee-blee-yoh-**teh**-kah
museum	el museo	ehl moo-**seh**-oh
tourist information office	la oficina de información turística	lah oh-fee-**thee**-nah deh een-fohr-mah-thee-**yohn** too-**rees**-tee-kah
town hall	el ayuntamiento	ehl ah-yoon-tah-mee-**yehn**-toh
closed for holiday	cerrado por vacaciones	thehr-**rah**-doh pohr vah-kah-thee-**yoh**-nehs
bus station	la estación de autobuses	lah ehs-tah-thee-**yohn** deh owtoh-**boo**-sehs
railway station	la estación de trenes	lah ehs-tah-thee-**yohn** deh **treh**-nehs

Staying in a Hotel

Do you have a vacant room?	¿Tiene una habitación libre?	tee-**yeh**-neh **oo**-nah ah-bee-tah-thee-**yohn** lee-breh
double room	habitación doble	ah-bee-tah-thee-**yohn** doh-bleh
with double bed	con cama de matrimonio	kohn **kah**-mah deh mah-tree-**moh**-nee-oh

twin room	**habitación con dos camas**	ah-bee-tah-thee-**yohn** kohn dohs **kah**-mahs
single room	**habitación individual**	ah-bee-tah-thee-**yohn** een-dee-vee-doo-**ahl**
room with a bath	**habitación con baño,**	ah-bee-tah-thee-**yohn** kohn bah-nyoh
shower	**ducha**	**doo**-chah
porter	**el botones**	ehl boh-**toh**-nehs
key	**la llave**	lah **yah**-veh
I have a reservation.	**Tengo una habitación reservada.**	tehn-goh oo-na ah-bee-tah-thee-**yohn** reh-sehr-**vah**-dah

Eating Out

Have you got a table for …?	**¿Tienen mesa para …?**	tee-**yeh**-nehn meh-sah pah-**rah**
I want to reserve a table.	**Quiero reservar una mesa.**	kee-yeh-roh reh-sehr-**vahr** oo-nah **meh**-sah
The bill please.	**La cuenta por favor.**	lah **kwehn**-tah pohr fah-**vohr**
I am a vegetarian	**Soy vegetariano/a**	soy beh-heh-tah-ree-**yah**-no/na
Waitress/ waiter	**Camarera/ camarero**	kah-mah-**reh**-rah kah-mah-**reh**-roh
menu	**la carta**	lah **kahr**-tah
fixed-price menu	**menú del día**	meh-**noo** dehl **dee**-ah
wine list	**la carta de vinos**	lah **kahr**-tah deh **bee**-nohs
glass	**un vaso**	oon **vah**-soh
bottle	**una botella**	oo-nah boh-**teh**-yah
knife	**un cuchillo**	oon koo-**chee**-yoh
fork	**un tenedor**	oon teh-neh-**dohr**
spoon	**una cuchara**	oo-nah koo-**chah**-rah
breakfast	**el desayuno**	ehl deh-sah-**yoo**-noh
lunch	**la comida el almuerzo**	lah kah-**mee**-dah ehl ahl-**mwehr**-thoh
dinner	**la cena**	lah **theh**-nah
main course	**el primer plato**	ehl pree-**mehr plah**-toh
starters	**los entremeses**	lohs ehn-treh-**meh**-sehs
dish of the day	**el plato del día**	ehl plah-toh dehl **dee**-ah
coffee	**el café**	ehl kah-**feh**
rare	**poco hecho**	**poh**-koh eh-choh
medium	**medio hecho**	**meh**-dee-yoh **eh**-choh
well done	**muy hecho**	mwee **eh**-choh

Menu Decoder

al horno	ahl **ohr**-noh	baked
asado	ah-**sah**-doh	roast
el aceite	ah-**theh**-ee-teh	oil
las aceitunas	ah-theh-**toon**-ahs	olives
el agua mineral	**ah**-gwa mee-neh-**rahl**	mineral water
el ajo	**ah**-hoh	garlic
el arroz	ahr-**rohth**	rice
el azúcar	ah-**thoo**-kahr	sugar
la carne	**kahr**-neh	meat
la cebolla	theh-**boh**-yah	onion
la cerveza	thehr-**veh**-thah	beer
el cerdo	**therh**-doh	pork
el chocolate	choh-koh-**lah**-teh	chocolate
el chorizo	choh-**ree**-thoh	red sausage
el cordero	kohr-**deh**-roh	lamb
el fiambre	fee-**ahm**-breh	cold meat
frito	**free**-toh	fried
la fruta	**froo**-tah	fruit
los frutos secos	**froo**-tohs **seh**-kohs	nuts
las gambas	**gahm**-bahs	prawns
el helado	eh-**lah**-doh	ice cream
el huevo	oo-**eh**-voh	egg
el jamón serrano	hah-**mohn** sehr-**rah**-noh	cured ham
el jerez	heh-**rehz**	sherry
la langosta	lahn-**gohs**-tah	lobster
la leche	**leh**-cheh	milk
el limón	lee-**mohn**	lemon
la limonada	lee-moh-**nah**-dah	lemonade
la mantequilla	mahn-teh-**kee**-yah	butter
la manzana	mahn-**thah**-nah	apple
los mariscos	mah-**rees**-kohs	seafood
la menestra	meh-**nehs**-trah	vegetable stew
la naranja	nah-**rahn**-hah	orange
el pan	pahn	bread
el pastel	pahs-**tehl**	cake
las patatas	pah-**tah**-tahs	potatoes
el pescado	pehs-**kah**-doh	fish

la pimienta	pee-mee-**yehn**-tah	pepper
el plátano	**plah**-tah-noh	banana
el pollo	**poh**-yoh	chicken
el postre	**pohs**-treh	dessert
el queso	**keh**-soh	cheese
la sal	sahl	salt
las salchichas	sahl-**chee**-chahs	sausages
la salsa	**sahl**-sah	sauce
seco	**seh**-koh	dry
el solomillo	soh-loh-**mee**-yoh	sirloin
la sopa	**soh**-pah	soup
la tarta	**tahr**-tah	pie/cake
el té	teh	tea
la ternera	tehr-**neh**-rah	beef
las tostadas	tohs-**tah**-dahs	toast
el vinagre	bee-**nah**-greh	vinegar
el vino blanco	**bee**-noh **blahn**-koh	white wine
el vino rosado	**bee**-noh roh-**sah**-doh	rosé wine
el vino tinto	**bee**-noh **teen**-toh	red wine

Numbers

0	**cero**	**theh**-roh
1	**uno**	**oo**-noh
2	**dos**	dohs
3	**tres**	trehs
4	**cuatro**	**kwa**-troh
5	**cinco**	**theen**-koh
6	**seis**	says
7	**siete**	see-**yeh**-teh
8	**ocho**	**oh**-choh
9	**nueve**	**nweh**-veh
10	**diez**	dee-**yehz**
11	**once**	**ohn**-theh
12	**doce**	**doh**-theh
13	**trece**	**treh**-theh
14	**catorce**	kah-**tohr**-theh
15	**quince**	**keen**-theh
16	**dieciséis**	dee-eh-thee-**seh**-ees
17	**diecisiete**	dee-eh-thee-see-**yeh**-teh
18	**dieciocho**	dee-eh-thee-**oh**-choh
19	**diecinueve**	dee-eh-thee-**nweh**-veh
20	**veinte**	**beh**-yeen-teh
21	**veintiuno**	beh-yeen-tee-**oo**-noh
22	**veintidós**	beh-yeen-tee-**dohs**
30	**treinta**	**treh**-yeen-tah
31	**treinta y uno**	treh-yeen-tah ee **oo**-noh
40	**cuarenta**	kwah-**rehn**-tah
50	**cincuenta**	theen-**kwehn**-tah
60	**sesenta**	seh-**sehn**-tah
70	**setenta**	seh-**tehn**-tah
80	**ochenta**	oh-**chehn**-tah
90	**noventa**	noh-**behn**-tah
100	**cien**	thee-**yehn**
101	**ciento uno**	thee-**yehn**-toh oo-noh
102	**ciento dos**	thee-**yehn**-toh dohs
200	**doscientos**	dohs-thee-**yehn**-tohs
500	**quinientos**	khee-nee-**yehn**-tohs
700	**setecientos**	seh-teh-thee-**yehn**-tohs
900	**novecientos**	noh-veh-thee-**yehn**-tohs
1,000	**mil**	meel
1,001	**mil uno**	meel oo-noh

Time

one minute	**un minuto**	oon mee-**noo**-toh
one hour	**una hora**	**oo**-na oh-rah
half an hour	**media hora**	**meh**-dee-a **oh**-rah
Monday	**lunes**	**loo**-nehs
Tuesday	**martes**	**mahr**-tehs
Wednesday	**miércoles**	mee-**ehr**-koh-lehs
Thursday	**jueves**	**hweh**-vehs
Friday	**viernes**	bee-**yehr**-nehs
Saturday	**sábado**	**sah**-bah-doh
Sunday	**domingo**	doh-**meen**-goh